Reading Diagnosis
for Teachers

Reading Diagnosis for Teachers

An Instructional Approach

Third Edition

Rebecca Barr
National-Louis University

Camille L. Z. Blachowicz
National-Louis University

Marilyn Wogman-Sadow
Late of Chicago State University

 Longman *Publishers USA*

Reading Diagnosis for Teachers: An Instructional Approach, Third Edition

Longman, 10 Bank Street, White Plains, N.Y. 10606

Associated companies:
Longman Group Ltd., London
Longman Cheshire Pty., Melbourne
Longman Paul Pty., Auckland
Copp Clark Longman Ltd., Toronto

Senior acquisitions editor: Laura McKenna
Development editor: Virginia L. Blanford
Production editor: Linda W. Witzling
Editorial assistant: Matthew Baker
Cover design and illustration: SILVERSdesign
Production supervisor: Richard Bretan

Library of Congress Cataloging-in-Publication Data

Barr, Rebecca.
    Reading diagnosis for teachers / Rebecca Barr, Camille L. Z.
Blachowicz, Marilyn Sadow. — 3rd ed.
        p.   cm.
    Includes bibliographical references (p.) and index.
    ISBN 0-8013-0842-9
    1. Reading—Ability testing.   I. Blachowicz, Camille L. Z.,
II. Sadow, Marilyn W.   III. Title.
LB1050.46.B37   1995
372.4'076—dc20   94-27768
                                              CIP

6 7 8 9 10-MA-99

To our families

Contents

CHAPTER 5   READING COMPREHENSION: ITS NATURE AND DEVELOPMENT   131

CHAPTER 6   READING COMPREHENSION: ASSESSMENT AND INSTRUCTIONAL SUPPORT   161

Preface

OUR PURPOSE IN WRITING THIS TEXT

Our goal for this book is to help you, as classroom teachers, to acquire the knowledge and skill you will need to assess the reading and writing of your students and to plan appropriate instruction. In planning a text to accomplish this purpose, we have been influenced by many considerations. Most important among these are our views on the nature of learning and the role of assessment in classroom instruction.

Reading and writing are active processes in which students interact with text to construct the messages of authors and their own messages. Research in recent years emphasizes the extent to which literacy depends on the knowledge that students have already developed. Printed symbols are signs that lead an active mind to reflect on alternatives during the process of constructing knowledge.

Children learn to read and write as they, with the support of their teachers and peers, explore alternative ways to make sense of text. Some of your students may have difficulty with this process because of confusions they experience with printed words or because they have limited understanding of some concepts that are central to the message of an author. Still others, even with adequate knowledge of print and underlying concepts, may construe messages that depart radically from what an author intends.

Your role in this process is extremely complicated. For students who are unable to make use of the signs provided by authors because they lack adequate knowledge of print, you must find ways to develop this knowledge. Similarly, for students who lack basic concepts, this knowledge must be developed through experience, discussion, and explanation. Finally, some students with good knowledge of print and underlying concepts profit from the experience of comparing their interpretations with those of other students and exploring their basis; others benefit from more direct help in weaving the meaning of authors from sentence to sentence and across paragraphs.

To assist you in assessing the literacy development of your students and planning appropriate instruction, the text helps you to develop your knowledge and skill in the following areas:

- understanding the nature of literacy development—how students develop knowledge of print, vocabulary concepts, and reading comprehension strategies
- becoming good observers of students' reading and writing and learning to make sense of what you see and hear—in other words, becoming able to understand the nature of student problems and strengths
- becoming familiar with alternative teaching strategies to help your students solve their problems with reading and writing

UNIQUE FEATURES OF THE BOOK

Just as we believe that learning is an active process for your students, we also believe that it should be an active process for you. Thus, we have planned a series of activities to promote thinking and problem solving. The text is unique in the following ways:

- We present a general model in the first chapter that will help you to think about assessment and to organize your observations. Each chapter provides opportunities for you to refine your observational skill; tasks of increasing complexity provide practice with previously acquired understandings.
- Your learning is grounded in more than 25 case studies exemplifying various problems that developing readers and writers may encounter. Each case provides the material from which to derive general principles as well as shows how the specifics of each situation shape assessment and instruction.
- We view reading and writing as reciprocal processes that are mutually supportive in their development. Throughout the text, we treat children's writing as a window into their thinking, and in a separate chapter we focus directly on the integration of writing and reading.
- We encourage your active problem solving through the following features:
  Chapter Goals for the Reader at the beginning of each chapter to focus your learning
  Classroom Vignettes that tie the focus of each chapter to the classroom
  Pause and Reflect activities in which problems are posed for your reflection

Try It Out activities at the end of each chapter through which you are encouraged to apply the understandings developed in the chapter and to build

Student Portfolios

A Teaching Portfolio

For Further Reading suggestions to enable you to explore selected ideas on your own in greater depth

HOW THE BOOK IS ORGANIZED

Unlike most texts that are topically organized, this one is developmental in design. The first chapter of the book develops a general way to think about reading assessment and instructional planning. The next six chapters develop understandings related to the assessment and instructional planning of print (Chapters 2 and 3), prior knowledge and vocabulary (Chapter 4), reading comprehension (Chapters 5 and 6), and writing (Chapter 7). The following two chapters require application and integration of previously learned concepts to classroom readings (Chapter 8) and informal reading inventories (Chapter 9). In the final chapter, we focus on the decision making that occurs as you organize, use, and communicate information gained through assessment.

ACKNOWLEDGMENTS

Like all projects that involve the development of ideas over an extended period of time, this one has depended on the support and critical insight of many people. We owe a great debt to a number of students from the National College of Education of National-Louis University. These students provided important insights into the diagnostic process and helped us evaluate the manuscript in its many stages. Some students provided us with case materials and helped us refine the text; we are especially indebted to Jesse Blachowicz, Pam Pifer, Katherine Morsbach, Jennifer Gross, and Gary Rith. We also gratefully acknowledge the help of Laura McKenna from Longman and the editorial work of Anita Portugal.

Our efforts were encouraged by our colleagues at the National College of Education and those from the literacy education community. In particular, Darrell Morris, Laurie Nelson, and Diane Sullivan have contributed to our thinking about literacy assessment and instructional planning. In addition we benefited from the clinical experiences and insights that Judith Daskal shared with us, as well as from the many comments and suggestions of:

Peter Afflerbach, University of Maryland

Peg Ballard, Mankato State University

Susan M. Blair-Larsen, Trenton State College

Cathy Collins Block, Texas Christian University
Renee M. Casbergue, University of New Orleans
Patricia N. Chrosniak, Western Illinois University
Baron D. Conaway, Arkansas State University
Nancy Cooley, Central Michigan University
Mary Ann Doyle, University of Connecticut
Jane Meeks Hager, Old Dominion University
Timothy L. Keaton, Cedarville College
Sandra Imdieke, Northern Michigan University
Mary S. Kelly, Western Connecticut State University
Priscilla Manarino-Leggett, Fayetteville State University
Darrell Morris, Appalachian State University
Deborah L. Norland, Luther College
Nancy H. Phillips, Lynchburg College
Leo Schell, Kansas State University
Lynn C. Smith, Southern Illinois University
Deborah L. Tidwell, University of Northern Iowa
Mary Jane Urbanowicz, Shippensburg University
Renee K. Weisberg, Beaver College

chapter 1

Model for Reading Diagnosis and Instructional Planning

CHAPTER GOALS FOR THE READER

To become familiar with the theoretical, historical, and research bases of reading diagnosis

To understand reading diagnosis as an integral part of ongoing classroom instruction

To learn to apply a model of reading diagnosis that identifies major decision points and areas of reading difficulty

To appreciate the importance of responsive instructional planning

CLASSROOM VIGNETTE: TESSA AND HER STUDENT, JOHN

We believe that one way to achieve our goal of increasing your understanding of children's knowledge of print is to have you consider the cases of elementary school teachers and their students who are learning to read. From these case studies, you will learn the questions teachers ask and how they pursue answers to them through careful observation and questioning.

Tessa has been teaching sixth grade for four years. Each year four or five of her students encounter difficulty reading some of the materials she assigns, particularly those for social studies and science. While she has taken several courses and workshops in teaching reading and writing, she is still unable to assess her students' specific areas of strength and difficulty. Thus, Tessa has decided to take a course in reading diagnosis. She hopes to acquire sufficient skill in assessment to understand her students' reading as she meets with them daily and to learn how she can provide them appropriate instructional support.

John, one of the students you will read about later in this chapter, is a member of Tessa's class. As you read his case study, think about the instructional support you would want to provide if you were Tessa. She is searching for answers to the following questions:

What are John's strengths on which I can build?

How can I help John feel that he is a part of the classroom group and encourage him to continue to develop his reading strategies?

CHAPTER OVERVIEW

In this chapter we first describe our view of reading and consider the goals we had in mind as we wrote this book. We hope that our sequence of case studies will provide the opportunities you need to develop your observational and interpretive skills. In the second section we describe the long and distinguished history of reading diagnosis, mainly in clinical settings, and the more recent research literature. Although we build on this tradition, in the third section of the chapter we argue that most diagnostic assessment of students' reading should be undertaken in the classroom by classroom teachers.

In the fourth section of the chapter we describe a model for reading diagnosis and its major decision points. We believe this model will be particularly useful because it will help you to organize the multitude of observations you will make about your students' reading during the rapid give-and-take of classroom activities. The model will not only guide your observations but also aid you in making sense of what you observe. We show the usefulness of this diagnostic model not only for beginning readers but also for much older students with greater reading proficiency.

In the final section of the chapter, we consider reading instruction. We discuss current trends in the field of reading and the importance of developing instruction that provides appropriate support for student growth and permits students to share their ideas about what they are reading.

CHAPTER OUTLINE

Our View of Reading

What Are Our Goals for Reading Instruction?

History of Reading Diagnosis

Reading Diagnosis as Part of Classroom Instruction

OUR VIEW OF READING

What do we do when we read? Some literacy experts believe that the process of reading involves translating printed symbols into speech; they assume that comprehension then occurs easily and automatically for the reader. This view ignores the active role of the reader in constructing meaning. It also neglects the ways written language differs from spoken language. In fact, readers must actively assign one meaning to text from a variety of possible meanings, based on their prior experiences and the context of the selection. Beginning readers also must become familiar with the conventions of written text, the more formal structure of written sentences as opposed to spoken ones, and the organization of larger units of text. Some history texts, for example, organize information chronologically; others structure it by cause–effect relationships.

Another view of the reading process is that knowledge is in the mind of the reader, who relies on print only to test his or her ideas. This view fails to acknowledge print as a vehicle for information. Through print, readers are led to construct not only familiar ideas but also innovative thoughts and lines of argument.

Our view of the reading process lies between these two extremes. We see reading as an interactive activity. Recent research suggests that proficient readers process print in a thorough and efficient manner (Adams, 1990). However, they do not automatically assign meaning to what they read. Readers construct meaning from the print they perceive using context and prior experiences as the materials with which they interpret what they read.

Until recently, researchers have focused on aspects of reading pertaining to thinking and knowledge (cognitive dimensions); but affective dimensions related to the interests and feeling of students may be even more important. Some children, usually those who learn to read easily, find joy in reading exciting stories and in the challenge posed by new information and arguments. Other students, usually those who encounter difficulty learning to read or those for whom reading has become a chore, experience reading negatively. When their first encounters with reading are difficult or boring, they develop an aversion toward reading, and those students who avoid reading never discover its pleasures.

Research on reading programs shows that when children's first experiences are with good children's literature, they develop more positive attitudes and interest toward reading than when instruction focuses on reading skills. Interacting with books they enjoy and find interesting leads children to a positive motivational cycle, allowing them to develop increased interest in and pleasure through reading.

For these reasons, we view reading as an interactive process. It is supported by children's knowledge of print, informed by their prior experiences and knowledge of word meanings, facilitated by their comprehension strategies, and fueled by their love for reading. What then are the implications of this perspective on reading for reading instruction?

WHAT ARE OUR GOALS FOR READING INSTRUCTION?

Reading enriches our lives. All of us know the thrill of reading a good story and the satisfaction of locating needed information. As teachers we are committed to helping our students use and appreciate the experiences reading affords. Our goals must be to support children as they develop reading skill and to instill in them a love for reading.

Achieving these goals is easy with some children. They learn to read easily, and the satisfaction they experience leads them to read often and with pleasure. Unfortunately, there are other children who experience considerable difficulty in reading, viewing it as an unpleasant and undesirable activity. These are the children we worry about. The purpose of this book is to help you as their teachers develop the understanding you need to help these children. As your students acquire greater proficiency in reading and read material that interests them, they will begin to appreciate the power reading gives them to enrich their own lives.

What do you need to know to diagnose children's reading strengths and difficulties? What do you need to know to provide students with appropriate instructional support? These questions are not easy to answer. Research on reading diagnosis and instruction has provided much information that would be useful to you in meeting the needs of your students, but you must be able to access it in such a way that you can use it during the active give-and-take of everyday instruction. The challenge to us as authors of this book is to organize and sequence the fundamentals of diagnosis and instructional planning in a form that will be most useful to you. In this book, we present principles for you to follow and descriptions of development that provide an overview of the changes children undergo. But we also use these in the context of many case studies to convey the rich details of children's lives.

Educators have long been concerned with the difficulties children encounter as they learn to read. By the early years of this century some important insights were being developed. In order to place the work of reading diagnosis in context, we discuss what we mean by "reading diagnosis" and briefly describe its history.

HISTORY OF READING DIAGNOSIS

Reading diagnosis as we use it in this book refers to "an astute analysis of the process by which [a student] gains meaning, significance, enjoyment, and value from printed sources" (Harris & Hodges, 1981, p. 86). We view diagnosis as an ongoing process.

Assessment is similar but refers to the "process of gathering data in order to better understand some topic or area of knowledge, as through observation, testing, interviews, etc." (p. 22). Diagnosis depends then on careful assessment, but goes beyond it by involving judgments about the data.

Physicians were among the earliest specialists to undertake a form of reading diagnosis (e.g., Morgan, 1896). Early in the 20th century, two developments in the field of education converged to support the scientific study of reading difficulty. First, Huey (1898, 1968) and others (Dearborn, 1906; Dodge, 1905, 1907) set the conceptual and empirical basis for understanding the psychology of reading. Second, advancements in psychometric theory laid the foundation for developing test instruments to measure human traits.

Before the 1920s tests had been developed to assess school learning, and the results were used to identify the special needs of individuals (Uhl, 1916; Zirbes, 1918). The earliest diagnostic work was conducted in the school setting by teachers and other school personnel. The first professional book on reading diagnosis, *Deficiencies in Reading Ability: Their Diagnosis and Remedies,* written by Clarence T. Gray in 1922, relied in large part on what researchers had learned from school-based studies of reading difficulty.

At the same time, educators realized that more detailed study of students who were experiencing reading difficulty would provide insight into how the reading process operates. They began doing detailed case studies to develop more refined testing procedures and effective remedial instruction. Special educational laboratories and reading clinics were established in university settings for this purpose (see, for example, Fernald & Keller, 1926; Gray, Kibbe, Lucas, & Miller, 1922).

Other research in the 1920s and 1930s expanded and developed the knowledge gained through clinical case studies. Pelosi (1977) noted several developments during this period that contributed to the refinement of reading diagnosis. First, case study investigation, which continued to be the dominant method of research, became more elaborate and sophisticated. Then, precise diagnostic instruments and procedures were developed. Finally, there was an ever-increasing interest in the nature of reading processes and the causes of reading disability (Robinson, 1937).

During this period researchers in such related fields as medicine and psychology popularized the term *dyslexia* when referring to children with reading difficulties. Literally translated, it means a dysfunction with words (the Latin prefix *dys* means "difficult" or "faulty" and the Greek root *lexia* refers to "words"). Thus the term is simply descriptive; it does not address the underlying nature of the difficulty. We believe that such labeling is not particularly useful, especially since it often carries the connotation that the child has a central functioning impairment. Similarly, we believe that other forms of labeling such as "visual learner," "left-brain dominant," and "perceptually handicapped" are of little help to teachers in planning appropriate instruction, and they may be misleading in that they imply simplistic remedies. As we show in the following sections of this chapter, we prefer to identify the nature of the reading difficulty and strength in a way that anticipates appropriate instruction.

Three main developments have influenced our thinking about reading diagnosis. First is the extensive research undertaken during the 1970s and 1980s on the nature of reading processes. In contrast to the behavioristic perspectives of earlier studies, this research showed that the characteristics of readers, in particular their knowledge and expectations, influence their comprehension—that is, readers actively construct their understandings on the basis of the knowledge they bring with them and the context of what they read.

Second, during this same period several reading researchers turned their attention to classroom instruction. Their work showed that some of the problems children experience result from the way they are taught. How teachers organize children for instruction, what materials they have children read, how much time they provide for reading, and what level of instructional support they provide all have a direct bearing on how well children learn (Allington, 1983).

More recent research has documented the important influence that students' writing has on their reading development. Writing enhances both children's awareness of sounds in words and their skill as readers (Clarke, 1989). Writing in response to reading encourages students to reflect and deepens their understanding. Later we discuss the importance of student writing, an activity you need to consider both for assessment and in planning instruction.

Motivation is also essential in learning. Studies of literature-based classes show the important motivational consequences of having children read books they enjoy (Dahl & Freppon, 1991; Morrow, 1992). Helping children select good quality books that are of interest to them not only has the immediate benefits of making instruction more enjoyable but also serves our goal of creating lifelong readers.

READING DIAGNOSIS AS PART OF CLASSROOM INSTRUCTION

The approach to reading diagnosis presented in this book is based not only on clinical case studies and the research literature but also on our understanding of the goals of classroom teachers in contrast to those of teachers in the clinic setting. Classroom teachers want to help their students acquire the skill necessary to be part of the mainstream of classroom reading instruction. In contrast, clinical teachers are more concerned about whether students are reading up to their potential levels of achievement. The comparison of actual and potential reading level, used in clinical settings, may occasionally be a useful approach for teachers; but generally in the classroom, teachers prefer an approach to diagnosis that identifies students as needing special support when they are unable to read the materials used for class discussion.

This is the path we follow in this book. While it is consistent with the goals of most classroom teachers, it does have several consequences. One result will be that some children with limited knowledge will be identified to receive special attention. The focus of this attention will be to develop their word knowledge and general understanding so they will be able to participate in class discussion. Use of this approach also means that some students (with a discrepancy between potential and actual reading) may receive no special support since they are able to read the class materials.

Another difference between classroom and clinical teachers has to do with test materials and the number of students taught. Teachers and specialists who work with groups of students in classrooms do not find it easy to undertake extensive testing with individual students. We suggest that standardized tests are unnecessary for classroom teachers because they have access to a wealth of evidence about the reading, writing, and language development of their students on a daily basis. They listen to children read orally, note their answers to comprehension questions, and observe how they think, write, and talk about a variety of topics. Thus, they do not need special test instruments to assess their students' needs. They must, however, become good observers and interpreters.

Teachers' observations tend to be haphazard, partly because they must manage the class as well as instruct their students, but also because they have had little training in how to observe and interpret students' responses. Most teachers have not been taught to develop informal questions or oral reading tasks designed to clarify the nature of a student's misunderstanding. Typically, teachers learn to assess reading difficulties by interpreting scores and reading behavior on standardized and informal reading tests. They must generalize from the results of these tests to the student's performance on classroom materials. We believe a more sensible approach is to help teachers acquire the observational and interpretive skills that will enable them to use the wealth of evidence that is available and ongoing in the classroom.

In this book we introduce observational and interpretive strategies in a gradual manner. You will learn to analyze and interpret reading responses through detailed case studies. We *do not* expect you to undertake such extensive case studies in the classroom, *nor* do we expect you to follow in a step-by-step fashion the procedures we have developed. We do hope that once you have done the detailed analyses outlined here you will have gained the understanding that will support your more informal and ongoing observation in your classroom.

As a classroom teacher, you will usually see your students over an entire school year. With this time advantage, you should strive to develop working hypotheses about how children learn, revising them as you continue to observe a student's reading and writing. Because you can collect evidence over time, it will not be necessary for you to attempt the detailed diagnosis that clinical teachers undertake or even the sort of case studies that we have used to introduce concepts in the remainder of the book.

Finally, you have an advantage in planning supportive instruction because you possess information about your students' interests and family support. This information, along with your ongoing observations, will let you plan instruction that is both conceptually and motivationally appropriate. It will also let you make informed decisions about how best to proceed if external support is needed.

MODEL FOR READING DIAGNOSIS

Our view of reading diagnosis and instructional planning assumes that students are active problem solvers. Therefore, the manner in which they develop reading skill is influenced by the instructional tasks they confront from grade to grade. For example, if students are instructed with a systematic phonics program, they learn to solve a set of problems somewhat different from the ones they encounter if they are instructed with a literature-based program that emphasizes comprehension and writing. Similarly, if students are given considerable experience reading and answering questions on expository materials, they develop comprehension skills different from those they develop if they read mainly narrative materials.

Two implications follow from this view. First, diagnostic assessment must consider how students currently approach the task of reading in relation to the reading tasks they have encountered in the past. Second, subsequent instruction must build on this foundation. Thus, diagnosis by a teacher who is familiar with the instructional history of students and who tests their response to current instructional materials provides an optimal basis for instructional planning.

What must you know in order to diagnose the nature of your students' reading difficulty? A diagnostician is much more than someone who knows how to administer tests. The diagnostician is like an active explorer whose search is guided by a carefully developed conceptual scheme. This scheme identifies the major decision points in the diagnostic process and then, once a particular decision is made, certain subsidiary decision points. Through this sequential decision-making procedure, you can progressively evaluate plausible explanations for the difficulty.

Major Diagnostic Decisions

In the basic model of reading diagnosis shown in Figure 1.1, the central and most important process in reading is **comprehension,** the ability to reconstruct meaning from printed text. Within the classroom setting, the goal of reading is to accomplish the normal reading tasks that are part of instruction. Certain underlying processes such as print skill and vocabulary knowledge are viewed as supporting effective comprehension. These underlying areas become important if a student is experiencing difficulty with comprehension. Within our thinking in this book, the main goal of reading diagnosis and reading instruction is to help all students develop effective strategies for comprehension.

FIGURE 1.1 Basic model of reading diagnosis

Comprehending Text.   A first decision that you need to make is to determine whether your students comprehend the textual materials that are part of instruction; if they don't, you can conclude that they are experiencing problems in reading. We believe that a student's expected reading level—and whether he or she has a reading problem—should be established in terms of the level of materials used by the class or the student's subgroup. If a student is able to read and comprehend classroom material, we conclude that he or she has no reading problem. The student can be assigned the appropriate materials and given suitable instruction during the daily reading lesson. However, when there is evidence that a student cannot adequately understand the materials used for regular class instruction, we consider that student to have a reading problem warranting further diagnosis.

When there is evidence that a student has a reading problem, the second decision point requires you to identify the general nature of the problem. The goal of reading is comprehension of text. A student can have difficulties in three general areas that may interfere with comprehension: (1) inadequately developed print skill; (2) inadequate vocabulary knowledge pertaining to the ideas described in a passage; and (3) inadequately developed strategies for understanding text (see Figure 1.1).

Print skill refers to the ability of readers to translate printed symbols efficiently into spoken language or meaning. This area includes not only skill with phonics, structural analysis, and syllabication, which permit a student to identify previously unknown words, but also the acquisition of a set of words that are recognized instantaneously. It includes the proficient integration of word recognition and word identification with contextual information as a student responds to prose to develop fluency.

Most children acquire basic print skill during their early reading instruction, and this skill becomes integrated and automatic through a variety of home and school reading experiences. Note that the emphasis of early instruction can have a profound influence on the particular print concepts that students learn. Further, students who have difficulty acquiring print concepts that are taught explicitly also have difficulty inferring those that are not explicitly taught. For example, some reading programs emphasize the development of phonic concepts but do not teach the process of blending and the application of phonic knowledge in context. For students who do not spontaneously infer how to blend phonic values, a good knowledge of phonics may be of little value in identifying unknown words. Print skill is more fully described in the next two chapters.

Vocabulary knowledge refers to knowledge of the key words contained in particular reading selections as well as the encompassing concepts being conveyed and the ways word meaning is revealed by context—prior knowledge, in general. For example, to understand a passage about the discoveries of Copernicus and Galileo, students must be familiar with the meanings of such words as *planet* and *telescope;* but beyond these, the encompassing concept of "movement" is central to an understanding of how the solar system works. Students differ in the extent to which they can comprehend a passage without adequate knowledge of the concepts they are presumed to know. Vocabulary knowledge includes both general language concepts and specific literacy concepts concerning the functions of print, writing, and communication as well as a knowledge of genre and grammar.

For students who speak English as a second language, assessment of prior knowledge is particularly important. Assessment needs to distinguish between a student's knowledge of underlying concepts (in any language) and his or her knowledge of the specific English vocabulary associated with the concepts. The diagnostic model is useful for understanding the literacy development of bilingual students, but you may need to do a more extensive assessment and interpretation in the area of prior knowledge than will be needed for English-speaking students. Prior knowledge is more fully considered in Chapter 4.

In addition to experiencing problems in print skill and/or vocabulary knowledge, students may have problems in their *comprehension strategies.* That is, a student may have no difficulty with print translation and may be familiar with the meanings of the words and concepts that are central to understanding a passage but may still fail to comprehend. This failure may indicate that the student is having difficulty integrating information across a text. Whereas a writer begins with a conception of the message to be conveyed in a passage and then confronts the problem of how to write this in words, sentences, and paragraphs, the reader must reconstruct the author's message by processing these units and recombining them into one or several arguments or descriptions. Some readers experience difficulty with this integration process as well as with the monitoring and fix-up strategies necessary to recognize and address these problems. For example, readers often encounter pronouns, nouns, or phrases that refer to a previously identified person or topic, and they must realize that a new topic is not being introduced but that more information is being provided about the same topic or person. Then they must understand what to look for and how to reread and connect the information they missed on first reading. Comprehension strategies are considered in Chapters 5 and 6.

Identifying the Nature of the Difficulty.   The second step in diagnosis then is to determine whether a student is experiencing difficulty with print skill, vocabulary knowledge, and/or comprehension strategies. While these three areas are part of an integrated process, it is useful to consider them separately for several reasons. Different sorts of information and assessment procedures are required to determine the status of each one. Print skill is typically assessed by having students read passages, words, or word parts aloud, whereas discourse processing is typically assessed by having the reader "retell" the passage content, think aloud during reading, or respond to comprehension questions based on a selection that has been read. Vocabulary knowledge assessment does not necessarily involve reading; rather, it uses questions to elicit a student's understanding of selected terms. The three areas are also different in the sorts of instructional procedures that enhance their development. The instruction that is useful for helping a student develop word identification strategies is quite different from that which is effective in facilitating discourse comprehension.

The model for diagnosis shown in Figure 1.1 assumes not only that these three areas can be considered separately but also that two of them—print skill and vocabulary knowledge—represent conditions that facilitate the effective employment of the third—comprehension strategies. Accordingly, if a student fails to comprehend a passage, it is important to examine the student's print strategies and vocabulary knowledge for problems. Problems in either of these areas could account for the observed difficulty in comprehension. Thus, it is difficult in such cases to ascertain whether the student is experiencing problems in comprehension over and above those that stem from deficiencies in print skill or vocabulary knowledge. Comprehension strategies constitute a central category within the model: Problems are assumed to occur in this area when comprehension is weak *and* both vocabulary concepts and print skill are adequately developed.

In order to begin thinking in terms of the diagnostic scheme, let us consider the strengths and difficulties of four students (Cases 1.1–1.4) who have encountered problems reading classroom materials. You are encouraged to consider the evidence and determine each student's relative strength in the areas specified by the diagnostic model. On this basis, you should be able to specify the area(s) in need of further diagnosis.

CASE 1.1: JOHN

John is 11 years and 2 months old and is in the sixth grade. His teacher, Tessa, has found that he has considerable difficulty understanding not only his social studies and science textbooks but also the stories in the fifth-grade-level reading book used by her slowest-paced group. His oral reading, however, is flawless and he even reads the social studies and science passages with considerable fluency. Tessa first noticed that he has extremely vague concepts pertaining to biological terms and then pursued his understanding of more common terms. She found that he knows only superficially or not at all words from his reading book such as *revenge, comrade, foundation,* and *craftsmen.*

PAUSE AND REFLECT.   Pause for a moment to consider John's case. In terms of the diagnostic scheme, which are the areas of John's difficulty? As we learned at the beginning of this chapter, Tessa is seeking a better understanding of John's reading. From this brief description of his reading, what are his areas of strength on which she could build? What are your ideas about how Tessa might provide support so that John would feel that he is a part of the classroom group and be encouraged to continue to develop his reading strategies?

Diagnosis

The oral reading evidence indicates that John has strength in the area of print skill. John's inability to answer the questions posed by Tessa therefore seems attributable to inadequate vocabulary knowledge and/or poor comprehension strategies. The possibility that he is deficient in vocabulary knowledge is suggested by his lack of knowledge about terms known by his classmates. Thus, we tentatively conclude that vocabulary knowledge is John's major problem area. It is possible that he also has comprehension difficulties, but this remains to be determined by having him read a passage for which his vocabulary knowledge is sufficient. Vocabulary knowledge, then, should be the first area of focus.

CASE 1.2: MARY

Mary is 7½ years old and in the second grade. She is currently in the middle reading group, which uses second-grade-level materials. When she reads aloud during reading instruction, she does so fluently, making few errors. However, many of her answers to postreading questions show that she has not understood major events within the story. Her answers to questions about important terms within the story reveal that she has a good command of English and is more knowledgeable than other students in the group.

PAUSE AND REFLECT.   Consider the following questions: Does Mary have any problems in reading and, if so, in what area(s)? What evidence supports these conclusions?

Diagnosis

Obviously, Mary's reading difficulty is not associated with inadequately developed print skill or vocabulary knowledge. Her inability to comprehend what she reads may therefore derive from sentence and paragraph level inadequacies. Accordingly, we should consider further exploration of comprehension strategies.

CASE 1.3: LARRY

Larry is 10 years old and in fourth grade. He is in the slowest-paced group in the class, which reads from third-grade materials. Larry's teacher had almost immediately noted his difficulty in reading aloud. Although Larry had developed familiarity with some common words, he would wait for the teacher to assist him on many other words, particularly those that were multisyllabic. His comprehension of stories that he read silently was extremely low; however, he comprehended well when the others in his group read aloud. He also demonstrated good understanding of key words in the reading selections; indeed, he was one of the most knowledgeable class members when it came to science activities and social studies discussions.

PAUSE AND REFLECT.   Consider the nature of Larry's reading. What do you consider to be his reading strengths and difficulties?

Diagnosis

Larry experiences difficulty in the area of print skill but also in comprehension of materials that he has read. He is strong in vocabulary knowledge. Therefore, we conclude that his comprehension difficulty reflects his poorly developed print skill. There is evidence to support this conclusion, namely, his good comprehension when he listens to others read. Once he acquires skill with print, he should become a proficient reader, given his well-developed vocabulary knowledge. Our task is to diagnose his print skill further in order to learn how to facilitate his development in this area.

CASE 1.4: TOM

Tom is 7 years and 9 months old and in the third grade. In second grade he was with the middle reading group, and his third-grade teacher has continued that placement. His answers to comprehension questions indicate excellent understanding of what he reads, whether silently or aloud. Further, informal questioning about key vocabulary words indicates a breadth of vocabulary knowledge and fluency of expression. However, his oral reading is characterized by frequent substitutions of words. He seems to have developed extremely careless reading procedures.

PAUSE AND REFLECT.   Consider how we might make sense of these reading characteristics. Does Tom have a reading problem and, if so, what is its nature?

Diagnosis

It is clear that Tom's strengths are his good vocabulary knowledge and his adequate comprehension. Nevertheless, his print skill appears to be inadequately developed and should be explored further. Note that in terms of the model, Tom's pattern of reading strengths and weaknesses is one that is unlikely to occur. The model suggests that adequately developed print skill is a prerequisite for adequate comprehension, and typically this is true. Exceptions occur, however, among students with extremely well-developed vocabulary knowledge. Such students, on the basis of this knowledge and minimal information from print, are able to make sense of a story or passage. While we may conclude that Tom has no reading problem at the present time, his print skill may become inadequate to the demands of reading as the materials become more technical and precise in their informational content. Therefore, it is appropriate to treat Tom as having a reading problem in the area of print skill and to diagnose further the nature of his difficulty.

DIAGNOSTIC PATTERNS

These cases show how the diagnostic model may be used to determine whether a student has a reading problem and to identify the areas in need of further diagnostic exploration. In a more systematic fashion, Table 1.1 shows the number of different patterns of reading skill that are possible when comprehension, print skill, and vocabulary knowledge are considered. For example, John, the first case we considered with poor comprehension and vocabulary knowledge but good print skill, conforms to Pattern 3. The second case, Mary, with adequate print skill and vocabulary knowledge but inadequate comprehension, conforms to Pattern 2. The third case, Larry, represents Pattern 5, with poor print skill and comprehension but good vocabulary knowledge. Finally, Tom conforms to the relatively uncommon Pattern 6, with good comprehension and vocabulary knowledge but inadequate print skill.

In Pattern 1, reading comprehension and underlying print skill and vocabulary knowledge are all sufficient for the student to cope with his or her reading tasks. Because there appears to be no reading difficulty, further diagnosis is unnecessary.

Pattern 2 consists of adequate print skill and vocabulary knowledge but inadequate reading comprehension. Clearly, the potential for adequate comprehension is strong, but the student has not yet acquired some skills or organizing concepts for processing text. Further diagnosis in the area of comprehension is needed for you to determine the nature of the problem.

Pattern 3 is that of the student often identified as a "word caller"—the student who possesses adequate print skill but inadequate vocabulary knowledge and reading comprehension. Where you see this pattern, you assume that limited vocabulary and concepts interfere with reading comprehension: The student's limited experiences set a ceiling on what he or she can comprehend through print. Further exploration of the student's language functioning is appropriate. For example, a student may have experienced certain situations or events but failed to acquire the pertinent verbal labels. The instruction recommended for this student would be very different from that recommended for a student who also lacked the experiential base.

In Pattern 4, reading comprehension and both sets of underlying skills are inadequately developed. Further exploration of the student's vocabulary knowledge and print skill is appropriate.

Pattern 5 characterizes the student who has difficulty translating print into familiar language. Here you may assume that poor print skill accounts for poor reading comprehension. The student has the strength of good language development, as indicated by strong vocabulary knowledge. Further diagnosis should focus on how he or she identifies and recognizes words.

Because reading comprehension typically depends on the development of print skill and vocabulary knowledge, the remaining three patterns, in which comprehension is good while print skill and/or vocabulary knowledge are poor, occur infrequently. Pattern 8, in fact, occurs rarely, and if observed, probably reflects invalid measurement in one of the three areas. Pattern 6, as we have seen, occurs mainly for extremely able students with well-developed verbal skills. These students are able to

TABLE 1.1 Diagnostic patterns of print skill, vocabulary knowledge, and reading comprehension strategies

Skill Area	Common Patterns					Uncommon Patterns		
	1	2	3	4	5	6	7	8
Reading comprehension	+	0	0	0	0	+	+	+
Print skill	+	+	+	0	0	0	+	0
Vocabulary knowledge	+	+	0	0	+	+	0	0
Further diagnostic exploration[a]	Discontinue diagnosis	Explore comprehension strategies	Explore vocabulary knowledge		Explore print skill			

[a]In Patterns 3, 4, and 5, comprehension strategies might also be an area of weakness. However, this area is directly explored only when vocabulary knowledge and print skill have been eliminated as major factors in reading difficulty.

compensate for rather poorly developed print skill by using a combination of contextual cues, minimal print cues, and past experience; as a result, they score at an adequate level in reading comprehension. For this pattern, further examination of print skill is recommended. Although the student will often tolerate the frustration of the reading task when working with you on an individual basis, he or she may avoid reading tasks when left to work alone. Although such students may be able to compensate for skill deficiencies at this stage, later they may be unable to comprehend more difficult reading material.

Finally, Pattern 7 rarely occurs. If it is observed, it probably reflects a kind of "production deficiency." That is, a student, although able to summarize a passage or respond to questions based on it, may have difficulty generating definitions of terms or demonstrating their use.

The purpose of diagnosis is to examine each of the three reading skill areas shown in Table 1.1 and to determine its relative status. This procedure ensures that major problem areas will not be overlooked and that areas for more intensive exploration are identified.

DEVELOPMENTAL FLEXIBILITY OF THE MODEL

The diagnostic model is applicable to all levels of skill, from initial reading acquisition to mature reading proficiency. That is, it is useful in helping you understand the strengths and difficulties of a beginning reader as well as of a college student. The flexibility of this diagnostic approach derives from its conceptualization of reading as having the three component areas: reading comprehension, print skill, and vocabulary knowledge. Each area represents a different pattern of development, in accordance with the different problems posed by the reading materials that students are expected to understand at successive levels. (See Chall, 1983, for a more comprehensive but somewhat different treatment of developmental stages in reading.) These changing demands of reading materials, considered here briefly, are treated more comprehensively in subsequent chapters.

The first two years of reading instruction usually emphasize the development of skill for translating print to speech or meaning. Some reading programs focus on the development of phonic concepts, others on the development of a sight vocabulary, and still others on the orchestration of strategies. Most current programs develop print concepts through direct instruction and extensive reading of contextual materials. These contextual materials are generally narrative in form, with the characters (people or animals) performing acts and speaking thoughts that are familiar to young children. Accordingly, most children already possess the relevant vocabulary knowledge and have acquired the necessary comprehension strategies through listening to stories read to them. However, when students lack this knowledge or listening experience, these aspects of reading must become areas of instructional focus for them, along with print skill.

Students refine and integrate their print skill during subsequent years in several ways. They become able to tackle longer and more complex words, some of which they have never heard before. They become so familiar with the characteristics of print that processing becomes almost automatic for "easy" materials. As a consequence, their reading rates improve dramatically.

As their print skill is refined, however, new problems arise. Beginning with third or fourth grade, students typically encounter new forms of printed materials. They are expected to read texts other than narratives—texts that are often characterized by a markedly different paragraph structure. In subject areas such as science and social studies, paragraphs are often organized around a major topic with examples of supporting information, or structured in terms of temporal, spatial, logical, or cause-and-effect relationships. Such a structure differs not only from that of narrative materials but also, of course, from the oral language forms with which students are familiar. Once students encounter expository materials, they must acquire many new skills for processing information.

Along with these new discourse-processing problems, students encounter new demands on their vocabulary knowledge. In sharp contrast to the primary materials, science, social studies, math, and more advanced forms of literature introduce vocabulary and underlying concepts and text structures that go beyond the students' prior experiences and vocabulary knowledge. Thus, students must learn how to obtain new knowledge from text.

The problems posed in elementary school continue throughout high school and college because students are assigned reading materials that make increasingly difficult conceptual and organizational demands. Further, students must become independent readers in order to accomplish homework assignments. The increasing amount of required reading demands that students become increasingly efficient in print processing. And they must evaluate, compare, and integrate information from a variety of sources in ever more sophisticated reports and projects. This brief discussion indicates some of the ways in which reading demands change over time. The point to which we return is that despite the changing nature of reading acquisition, the diagnostic model is able to account for reading difficulties at all levels.

INSTRUCTIONAL PLANNING

In Chapters 2, 4, and 5, we describe the ways in which the knowledge of children develops as they learn about print, word meanings, and comprehension strategies. This focus on development and learning processes may seem unusual in a book on diagnosis; however, we have emphasized these areas because we believe that you will not be able to plan appropriate instruction unless you have internalized an understanding of the ways children develop knowledge as they learn to read.

There was a time, not so long ago, when teachers of reading proceeded mainly by following the suggestions in the manual that accompanied the basal reading series. Children entering kindergarten or first grade were typically assumed to know little about reading. They were thought of as "empty vessels" or "blank slates" to be filled with sight words, phonics skills, and other skills. Learning to read was defined in terms of acquiring a variety of skills. In other words, a **behaviorist** philosophy informed instruction.

In contrast to this view, studies of emergent literacy (see Chapter 2) have shown that children enter school knowing a great deal about literacy. They have observed their parents reading, they enjoy being read to, they examine the labels on a variety of products, they attempt to write. They do not simply memorize information, but they make sense of their new experiences in terms of their previous experiences. This active response to new experiences has been referred to as the **construction of events.** Children do not passively receive knowledge as is assumed by a behavioristic perspective; rather, they make or construct their unique interpretations of events. This activity includes events about which they read. This view of learning represents a **constructivist** perspective.

Teachers who accept this perspective on how children learn know the importance of ensuring that the selections children read "make sense," that they relate directly to the experiences of children. This attitude accounts for the increased use of children's literature in many classrooms, whether in the form of trade books or basal reading series that include children's literature.

To facilitate the reading development of children you should follow three related activities: (1) Identify the knowledge that children have already acquired about print, word meanings, and comprehension strategies; (2) consider this knowledge in terms of a developmental view of literacy; (3) identify the interests of students and how you can build on these. Appropriate instructional support will enable students to progress to the next stage of development. Central to instructional planning is the view that instructional support should be geared just beyond what children are able to accomplish independently in order to help them progress to the next level of proficiency (Rogoff, 1990; Vygotsky, 1978).

In the case studies in the following chapters we describe instruction that is responsive to students' developmental stages. We accept the position that learning develops in a social/cultural environment (Vygotsky, 1978). In other words, we believe that learning in the classroom occurs interpersonally through social interaction before individuals should be expected to use strategies on their own. Accordingly, we recommend that new concepts and ideas be introduced and discussed with your support. Concepts and strategies developed in this manner will later be applied independently by individuals. We also recommend that you select instructional materials with students to reflect their areas of interest.

SUMMARY

Reading diagnosis entails analyzing the process by which students gain meaning from text. Building on the insights and methods that have developed historically, we describe a model to guide the observations and judgments you will make about your students' reading in the classroom.

The model draws your attention to three major decisions. The first decision concerns whether a student comprehends the materials being read in your classroom. If not, your diagnosis continues to the second decision point where you consider whether difficulties in (1) print skill, (2) vocabulary knowledge, and/or (3) reading comprehension strategies are interfering with comprehension. The pattern of strengths and difficulties that students show in the three areas will inform your third decision concerning instruction. Your understanding gained through diagnosis and your observations concerning the interests and feelings of your students will help you to identify instructional materials that are appropriate for them in difficulty and interest and will assist you to provide them with needed instructional support.

TRY IT OUT

1. Look at Table 1.1 (p. 15) and think about children you know and have observed reading. Can you see reading patterns that describe their reading? Think about the data you used—what you observed—in drawing your conclusion. Given your tentative conclusions about their reading and your knowledge of their interests, what sort of instructional materials and support would be appropriate?

2. **Student Portfolio Ideas:** Ask students from your class to collect materials that reflect the three areas of the model in Figure 1.1. That is, have them reflect on their skill with print, their knowledge of word meanings, and their comprehension strategies. What from their work reflects their skill in each of these areas? As a class, discuss, compare, and evaluate what they choose to represent each area.

3. **For Your Teaching Portfolio:** Consider the assessment you already do in your classroom. Do you collect data reflecting all the relevant areas of Figure 1.1? Do you collect data on the interests and feelings of your students? Are there areas that you would like to make more explicit in the model by adding subheadings or new headings? File this as your model of diagnosis. Revisit it as you complete the book.

FOR FURTHER READING

Au, K. H. (1993). *Literacy instruction in multicultural settings.* Orlando, FL: Harcourt Brace.
    For excellent suggestions on appropriate literacy instruction that is responsive to multicultural characteristics.

Salinger, T. (1993). *Models of literacy instruction.* New York: Macmillan.
    Further elaboration of alternative models for considering literacy instruction.

Wixson, K. K., & Lipson, M. Y. (1991). Perspectives on reading disability research. In R. Barr, M. Kamil, P. Mosenthal, & P. D. Pearson (Eds.), *Handbook of reading research* (Vol. 2, pp. 539–570). White Plains, NY: Longman.
    For a comprehensive summary of perspectives on reading disability that have been used to guide research.

chapter 2

Knowledge of Print: Its Development, Assessment, and Instructional Support

CHAPTER GOALS FOR THE READER

To understand how children become aware of reading and writing and their
  purposes

To understand how children learn about print

To understand how childen consolidate their strategies to become fluent readers

To develop skill in assessing and interpreting the reading and writing of emergent
  readers

To develop skill in planning instruction for emergent readers

CLASSROOM VIGNETTE: RACHEL AND HER STUDENTS, JESSE AND JODY

In this chapter, we consider the case of Rachel, a kindergarten teacher, and
two of her students, Jesse and Jody. Jesse, an active and enthusiastic student,
has "always liked to read and write." In the chapter, you will examine a letter
that she wrote to her aunt.

Jody is alert but quiet. Rachel is concerned about her because she has
shown little interest in reading and writing (literacy) activities. As you read the
section on emergent literacy, think about how this description may be useful
in helping Rachel to understand Jody's literacy development.

Later, we will describe what Rachel does to gain insight into Jody's
understanding of how print works. First, she has Jody read a familiar

storybook. Rachel also considers Jody's writing, her knowledge of letter names, and her visual and auditory acuity.

Children like Jody are common in American schools. When they encounter problems learning to read and become frustrated, we, their teachers, need to be able to understand how they approach reading and help them to develop their reading strategies further. The discussion and activities in this chapter and the chapters that follow should help you to understand how children acquire knowledge about print, how to assess this knowledge, and how to provide instruction to support their continued development.

CHAPTER OVERVIEW

This chapter has three main parts. The first section explores *how children learn about print* and the relationship of print to speech and meaning. We consider some of the following questions:

How do very young children make sense of printed language?

What are the different sorts of problems they solve as they learn to read?

How does their knowledge become consolidated so that they read fluently?

The second section focuses on *the strategies you can use* to assess the knowledge that children have about print. Here you learn how to assess Jody's understanding through storybook reading and how to obtain additional information about her knowledge of print. In the final section, you learn *how to plan appropriate instruction*.

CHAPTER OUTLINE

How Children Develop Knowledge of Print
    Stages of Understanding Print
    Development of Print Awareness
    Development of Print Knowledge
    Case 2.1: Jesse's Writing
    Development of Integration and Fluency

Assessing Children's Emergent Literacy
    Storybook Reading Procedures
    Case 2.2: Jody's Storybook Reading
    Writing Assessment Procedures
    Case 2.3: Jody's Writing

Planning Appropriate Instruction
    Encouraging Story Reading
    Encouraging Writing

Try It Out

HOW CHILDREN DEVELOP KNOWLEDGE OF PRINT

Learning to read is a complex process in which children solve many different problems. Both this and the next chapter focus on the problems that children must solve and the stages they pass through in learning how print relates to speech and meaning.

Stages of Understanding Print

While we agree that meaning and function of reading and writing should be clear to children in the beginning stages of reading as well as later, we also believe that teachers need to understand changes that occur in the awareness and knowledge that children possess about printed text. Accordingly, we have delineated three major stages through which they progress as they learn about the nature and functions of print. We refer to the first as the development of *print awareness*. During this stage, children begin to notice print and to speculate about its meaning; some even begin to understand that print is related to speech and meaning in complicated ways.

During the second stage, the development of *knowledge of print,* children acquire systematic knowledge about the nature of words and letters. When children first try to remember words, they may do so on the basis of one or a combination of characteristics. These may include the initial letter, word length, an unusual letter, or a smudge on a card bearing the printed word. As they learn more about words, they attend to word features in a more systematic fashion, such as noting initial and final consonants, letter sound cues, medial letters, and a greater number of features in combination. This learning is often referred to as the dual development of a sight vocabulary and phonics knowledge. During this stage, children are also solving the problem of how speech, in particular, and meaning, in general, relate to print.

During this stage children struggle to integrate their reading strategies. **Integration** refers to putting together information from a variety of sources including prior knowledge, prior story and sentence context, and print. Some children, often influenced by instructional method, tend to rely too much on a single source of information while others easily solve the problem of coordinating information from several sources.

The third stage is the development of *reading fluency,* in which children consolidate knowledge of print and recognize words rapidly and automatically, permitting them to give their undivided attention toward comprehending the meaning. Reading fluency depends on well-developed knowledge about print as well as the integration of print knowledge with information derived from context.

In this chapter, we discuss these three stages to help you build an understanding of the knowledge children develop about print. Then, to help you learn to assess this knowledge, we demonstrate the procedure of storybook reading as a window into Jody's emergent literacy. We also consider other procedures for obtaining additional information about her knowledge and discuss appropriate instructional strategies.

Development of Print Awareness

Printed words are a common part of our culture. Walking down streets, we notice street signs, advertisements, T-shirt slogans, and printed directions. Inside our homes we see magazines, letters, labels, and trademarks. Even when we watch television, we frequently see printed words. Because of the number of printed messages in our environment, almost all children encounter printed words and see people reading and writing. Some become aware of print at a very early age (Taylor, 1983). In this sense, learning to "read" print begins long before children engage in formal reading instruction.

Emerging Concepts of Print.   Many children come to understand why people read and write by actually participating in acts of reading and writing. If they are read stories, they see that reading provides entertainment. If they participate in reading recipes, they see that reading provides information. If they help in writing lists, they see the value of writing as an aid to memory. Some children, however, do not participate directly in reading and writing. They observe adults doing so but develop only vague notions of why people read and write. Actively participating in and observing literacy activities is important because once children view these activities as pleasurable, useful, and informative, this experience forms the basis for their wanting to learn to read.

More difficult than inferring the reasons for reading and writing is understanding what people actually do when they read. It is not outwardly apparent what goes on in the minds of adults and older children when they look at print as they read or write. Children must guess about what is read or written and how the process works. Studies of young children inform us bout some of the ideas children have about reading and writing and how these change over time (Harste, Woodward, & Burke, 1984).

From being familiar with stories, children learn about the conventions for writing English and other languages. Learning about the arrangement of text involves knowing where a book begins, where to begin reading on a page, in what direction to move, what to do at the end of a line, and what to do at the end of a page. Further, it involves learning that printed words—and not just pictures—are reliable cues to speech and meaning.

For some children, learning about books and print begins long before school instruction. At home and in preschool, they have been read to from books, and they examine books themselves, sometimes with the help of a friend or older sibling. They ask questions about reading, try to mimic reading, and sometimes ask a reader to demonstrate reading by pointing to words as the story progresses. Knowledge about the arrangement of print develops through a variety of experiences extended over time. Some children, however, come to school without the advantage of these experiences, and, accordingly, lack much of the knowledge about print that their more fortunate peers have acquired. Studies reveal that children differ considerably in their knowledge about print (Clay, 1975, 1979). Thus, you must know how to examine these differences so as to be able to provide appropriate instruction.

Young children also grow in their understanding about the nature of story reading. Sulzby (1985), for example, had preschool and kindergarten children read their favorite stories to her. Predictably, she found that children could be divided into two main groups: those who depended mainly on such cues as pictures and their memory of a story as the basis for their storytelling, and those who relied on the print as the basis for reading. Further, she found that children in the first group differed in the extent to which (1) their stories were well formed and (2) they reflected oral versus written language patterns. Some children mainly labeled or commented on the pictures while others retold the actions in the story. Some told stories in a fashion similar to the way they talked while others sounded as if they were reading (although their story showed little conformity to the story as printed in the book).

There were also differences among children who were aware that print in storybooks serves as the basis for reading. Such awareness was demonstrated by some children in their refusal to read because of not knowing the "words"; others focused on a limited number of known letters or words; and still others demonstrated varying degrees of reading proficiency. Studies such as this show that children vary in their understanding of the nature of stories and what it means to read.

One of the earliest problems to be solved by children concerns the nature of print. Children must come to realize that print is more than a series of marks. Failure to appreciate the representational nature of writing is common for very young children (Ferreiro & Teberosky, 1982). For example, Ferreiro (1984) reported that when asked, "What could be read here?" (pointing to the text), a 3-year-old responded, "Letters." When asked further, "What does it say in the letters?" he responded, "Letters." This and other evidence suggested that the child was not yet aware that letters were more than letters; he had not discerned the symbolic function of writing. In other words, print was seen as being no different from other marks or designs. Thus a major development toward literacy is achieved when children understand that writing represents meaning.

Young children must learn what it is that is read and written. They frequently believe that pictures as well as print are read. For example, Hiebert (1981) found that many 3-year-olds and some older preschoolers pointed to pictures when they were asked what readers should look at in books containing both pictures and print. Later, even when children distinguished pictures from print, they continued to identify numbers as letters. Gradually, they formed a concept of what people do when they read and write.

As part of this process, children must determine where writing goes in relation to pictures. On the basis of responses of preschoolers, Ferreiro (1984) speculated that children believe that writing must be inserted into drawings or abutted next to them to have meaning. Only later do they learn that the position of writing on a page can change in relation to the picture without changing the meaning of the text.

Somewhat later, children experiment with the number of letters that should be used to represent words. For example, Ferreiro (1984) reported that Fernando at 4 years, 11 months, represented "one corncob" with a single letter and "three corncobs" with three. Four months later he represented both "one child" and "five children" with three letters. He had progressed from believing that each letter corresponded to each object to the concept of words as composed of a fixed number of letters. Ferreiro also found that some children at a later stage represented longer spoken words with more letters than shorter words, one for each syllable. Her research also showed that different children approach the problem in different ways and develop somewhat different hypotheses.

During this period of early print awareness children also learn to "read" words in context. That is, they can recognize labels and other signs that regularly occur in the same contexts, such as "stop" on an octagonal red sign at the street corner or "PEPSI" within a red-white-and-blue design. Careful studies show, however, that when the words are taken out of context, children do not always recognize them; further, when the writing itself is altered ("XEPSI" instead of "PEPSI"), they don't always detect the change (Masonheimer, Drum, & Ehri, 1984; see also Mason, 1980). This means that children identifying words in this manner have not yet entered the stage of word learning when they depend solely on the letters and other print-related features to recognize printed words.

Increased Language Awareness.   Each of these studies helps us to gain insight into the problems that young children must solve as they grow in their understanding of printed messages. To gain even greater appreciation of the complexity of the task, consider the ways in which children's knowledge about their language must be related to the printed words they see. When they first become aware of print, they already possess a well-formed language system. Nevertheless, they have not learned to think about their language in an objective fashion. For linguists, language is a complex, hierarchical system in which smaller units of language are nested within larger ones. For example, large units of discourse can be divided into sentences, and sentences into words, or morphemes. Words are themselves composed of smaller units—syllables—which in turn are composed of sounds—phonemes. Although students do not need to acquire the sophisticated perspective of a linguist to learn to read, they must become more aware of the nature of their language to understand the various ways spoken language corresponds to writing.

The correspondence between speech and writing is complicated because relationships occur on a number of levels and are by no means always obvious. At the most general level, the message of written exposition relates to a spoken counterpart. At a lower level, a printed sentence will also correspond to a spoken sentence. But whereas a capital letter and a period indicate the boundaries of the printed sentence, inflectional characteristics may indicate the boundaries of the spoken sentence. Spoken words also relate to printed words; but whereas printed words are marked by spaces, spoken words are not delineated from each other. Indeed, children may begin reading with little awareness of how speech becomes partitioned into word units. As children learn to read and spell, they acquire a visual representational system that allows them to see what they say and hear. Thus, word learning as a part of reading instruction involves learning about the nature of printed words as well as discovering how language may be segmented into units that correspond to printed words.

Below the level of meaningful words, spoken phonemes and syllables correspond to letters (graphemes) and series of letters. Establishing the relations between sounds and letters is complicated for several reasons. First, just as children are not aware of word units in their spoken language, so they are not aware of the sounds that compose spoken words. In fact, some researchers have argued that it is experience with letters that sensitizes childrens to the phonemes of words (Ehri, 1983, 1991). Second, although there are only 26 letters, some are easily confused because they are mirror images (*b* and *d*) or rotations (*n* and *u*) of each other. Finally, in English, more than one letter is sometimes needed to represent one phoneme. For example, the pairs *sh, th,* and *ch* each represent a single phoneme. Further, particularly for vowels, a letter may stand for several different phonemes, and a phoneme may be represented by several different letters and/or combinations.

In sum, children learn to understand language in an objective fashion on four main levels. At the level of stories and other textual messages, they develop **pragmatic awareness,** or the ability to relate sentences and messages to each other within the larger context in which they occur. This form of metacognitive strategy is discussed in Chapter 5 with regard to comprehension. At the level of sentences, they develop **syntactic awareness** about how the words in sentences relate to each other. For example, children reading a sentence often anticipate the part of speech that should occur next in the sentence. At the level of words, they develop **word awareness,** or the understanding of how language is segmented into printed word units. Finally, at the level of word elements, children develop **phonemic awareness,** or the ability to hear and manipulate subunits of words.

Recent research supports the importance of children's being able to develop their ability to hear and objectify subunits of language. In particular, phonemic awareness has been identified as critical in the development of reading skill (Bradley & Bryant, 1983; Ehri, 1979; Goswami & Bryant, 1990). While there is some evidence that this awareness can occur through instructional tasks that help children hear the sound units in words without seeing how words are written (Lundberg, Frost, & Petersen, 1988), we believe that this ability is most naturally developed in classrooms in the context of reading and writing tasks.

We have selected diagnostic and instructional approaches that can be used easily with groups of children in classrooms. However, we believe it is important for teachers to understand how to identify the stages where children are in their development of word and phonemic awareness. For example, children give evidence of word awareness when their storybook reading closely conforms to the text. The methods for developing "concept of word" in the section on instruction later in this chapter represent ways in which teachers can help their students develop word awareness.

We believe that writing tasks represent a natural way for teachers to examine their students' phonemic awareness. Further, as we suggest in the chapter on writing instruction, teachers can help students hear sounds in words as they help class groups to write language experience stories and as they help students with their individual writing.

During their early years, children become aware of the nature of print and its relation to speech and meaning in many ways. Children differ greatly in the understanding they have achieved at the time they enter school. Some, in spite of extensive story reading and exposure to print, fail to make connections about the nature of storybook reading and writing. Others experience a less rich print environment and many are read stories infrequently. Often these children have not had the opportunities or encouragement to begin exploring the nature of print. Teachers must be able to assess their students' awareness of print and language if they are to plan appropriate instructional activities for them.

PAUSE AND REFLECT. Imagine for a moment that you are Rachel and that Jody is one of your students. What would you want to learn about Jody's growing awareness of literacy? What are three things that you would do with Jody in order to learn more about her knowledge of reading and writing?

Development of Print Knowledge

Instructional Influences. Teachers in preschools and often those in kindergartens view their role as supporting the emergence of print awareness through informal activities such as story reading, language experience stories, and writing tasks. Traditionally, more direct reading instruction occurs in first grade. In thinking about the development of print knowledge, it is important for you to consider the instruction that children have received because their learning, and to some extent their confusions, may reflect the nature of their past reading instructional program.

Many children learn to read from basal programs that include opportunities to read stories and informational selections, write, and develop skills and strategies (Chall & Squire, 1991). Typically, the skill instruction in word elements (compound words, word endings, letter–sound associations, etc.) proceeds in an orderly fashion, with a new concept introduced in each lesson. The stories and other selections children read are sequenced to increase in difficulty. For example, stories they read read at the beginning of first grade may be composed of sentences that are predictable in pattern. Stories they read later in first grade are typically more complex in sentence pattern and in the number of different printed words included. The materials are sequenced in terms of difficulty so that children will not become frustrated by having to deal with too many new concepts (sentence patterns or words). Words such as "in," "the," "but," and "are" tend to recur in stories, and this repetition helps children develop a set of quickly recognized words. Some teachers refer to these words as "sight words" because readers recognize them instantly without resorting to letter–sound identification.

Not more than a decade ago, many American children read from basal programs in which the difficulty of reading selections was controlled in an artificial fashion. The number of new words, letters, or spelling patterns introduced and repeated in successive stories was carefully measured. This systematic introduction and repetition of words or letters was done to simplify the complexities of early reading and to help children learn printed words and letter–sound associations. At the same time, many of the sentences that resulted were stilted and unlike those children were accustomed to hearing, either in conversation or in stories read aloud to them. Consequently, children had difficulty using their prior knowledge and their understanding of story and sentence context to help them with word recognition.

Research has shown that children who had been taught with beginning reading materials controlled in these ways made distinctive reading errors. Learning from materials in which letters were controlled, children frequently produced either nonwords or words that violated the sense of a passage. Those reading from word-controlled materials tended to make the error of using real words that made sense in terms of sentence context, but which were not the words printed on the page (Barr, 1974; Cohen, 1974–75; Juel & Roper/Schneider, 1985).

Generally in education there has been a shift away from behaviorist views to those that emphasize the constructive nature of learning. While earlier behaviorist theory was centered more on item learning (words, letters), the focus has shifted now toward integrated strategies that children use to make sense of text. **Integrated strategies** entail the coordination of information from prior knowledge, story and sentence context, and print.

This shift in the way we view learning has led to a modification of basal programs as well as adoption of *whole language* programs in which children learn to read from trade books (stories or informational texts written by children's authors) and from being encouraged to write. To make the books accessible, teachers in whole language classrooms ensure that the stories are familiar to children, either by previewing the book with them or reading it aloud. As children read from trade books, by themselves or with a friend, they are encouraged to construct meaning from a variety of sources: their memories of the story, clues that the pictures provide, story and sentence context, and associations from print.

Word Awareness and Learning Words by Sight.   The discussion on emergent literacy shows how children develop a growing understanding of print and its relation to speech and meaning through their participation in reading and writing activities. Through story reading, they learn how stories are arranged in books and come to understand that printed words are meaningful. When children write, they explore the nature of writing and how it relates to spoken words. At some point in their development, they realize that printed words are individual nameable objects. Once children become aware of this concept, they are able to learn words and to explore the relationships within words, between letters and sounds.

At the same time, some knowledge of letter names or sounds helps children to develop a stable concept of word (Ehri, 1980; Morris, 1988). As Ehri (1980) argues, knowledge of letter–sound associations constitutes the "glue" that holds word images in memory. The development would seem to be reciprocal in that some knowledge of letter sounds makes new words more familiar. At the same time, a sense of printed word boundaries in relation to speech allows children to infer additional knowledge about letter–sound correspondences.

Ehri (1980) describes this process of word learning in the following way:

> Since beginners already know how words are pronounced, their task is to assimilate the word's printed form to its phonological (speech sound) structure. They do this by matching at least some of the letters to phonetic or phonemic segments detected in the word. These segments serve as "slots" in lexical memory which are filled by images of letters seen in the word's spelling. (p. 313)

In other words, children form mental images of printed words that are stored in memory with the spoken (phonological) identity of the word and its meaning. The image when first stored may be fragmentary, but as children repeatedly read the words and increase their ability to segment words phonemically, they build a more complete image.

Within this development view, the ability to learn words is closely interwoven with the ability to learn the sound components of words. Research suggests that the development of phoneme awareness is a critical achievement in the process of learning to read (Bradley & Bryant, 1983; Goswami & Bryant, 1990; Lundberg, Frost, & Petersen, 1988; Tunmer, Herriman, & Nesdale, 1988).

One of a child's most important achievements in reading is learning to recognize printed words instantaneously. In word learning, beginning readers must confront two problems. The first is learning to segment oral language into parts that correspond to printed words (word awareness). The second is learning to discriminate among the printed words. In the following sections we consider the nature of word awareness and learning first, and then the development of phoneme awareness and word identification strategies. While we treat these two aspects of learning to read separately, remember that the two develop concurrently and are interconnected.

Word Awareness.   Literate adults have difficulty imagining that young children may listen to sentences without being aware of the specific words that compose them, yet evidence from research indicates that this is true. Perhaps the study that has most influenced our thinking about the development of word awareness was conducted by Karpova (1955, as described in Slobin, 1966). Karpova found that the word consciousness of children develops in three stages. In the first, at 3–4 years of age, children understand sentences as semantic units, without distinguishing individual words. For example, they report that a sentence such as *Galyla and Vova went walking* contains two words: *Galyla-went-walking* and *Vova-went-walking*. During the next stage, prereaders become able to separate sentences into subject and predicate. Finally, during the third stage, children learn to identify the words that compose sentences, although they experience difficulty with compound and multi-syllabic words and fail to distinguish some function words as separate units. They must also learn the conventions of English that pertain to wordness—for example, that *not happy* and *full spoon* are represented by two words in English, whereas *unhappy* and *spoonful* are represented by one.

Failure to develop word awareness during the initial stages of reading is manifested in oral reading that bears little or no correspondence to the printed words being read. The development of such awareness is evident in Clay's (1967) description of the stages through which beginning readers progressed while being instructed in a sentence method:

> As [the children] developed skill in matching behavior, fingers were used to point to those parts of the text that were supposed to correspond to the vocal responses. Fluency gave way to word by word reading. At this point the child's reading became staccato as he over-emphasized the breaks between words. He could be thought of as "reading the spaces" or "voice pointing" at the words. (p. 16)

Thus, pointing to words during the initial stages of reading indicates the development of awareness of words and of the correspondence between spoken and written language. Voice pointing and, subsequently, natural phrasing reflect increasing familiarity with and control over print. Both finger and voice pointing should be interpreted as signs of progress, and as Clay notes, they are not behaviors to be "hurriedly trained out." Nevertheless, continued use of finger pointing may also indicate difficulty in visual coordination or acuity.

Most children do not encounter difficulty in becoming aware of words and learning them. However, some require explicit instruction before they attend carefully to printed words and understand the nature of the correspondence between print and language. The instructional methods developed by Morris (1986), described later in this chapter, show how teachers can help children develop concept of word and the word awareness that underlies it.

Sight Word Learning.   **Sight word learning** involves comparing new words with previously learned words to identify features that are useful for distinguishing among them (Goswami & Bryant, 1990; Goswami & Mead, 1992). For example, in learning the words *red, blue, yellow, green,* and *orange,* children need only attend to the initial letter of each word to discriminate among them and give a correct response. If, however, the word *brown* is added to the set, the children will need to consider more than the initial consonant to discriminate correctly, since *blue* and *brown* begin with the same letter.

Thus, a problem with the discrimination learning of printed words is that as the set of words learned becomes larger, features that were initially useful in discriminating among words are no longer sufficient and students must attend to other features. Primary teachers observe this problem most often in the failure of students to distinguish among words with similar beginning and ending letters but different medial vowels (e.g., *but, bat,* and *bit*). Most children eventually learn to attend to enough word features that they rarely confuse words. In addition, they learn to use other sources of information, such as phonics and contextual cues, to facilitate rapid word recognition. Discrimination among printed words is also reinforced when children write sentences based on what they have read. By writing words, children become conscious of all letters in a word.

Beyond word discrimination, the ease with which children learn words is associated with the meaning the words carry. Abstract words, such as *in, the,* and *very* are more difficult for children to remember and identify quickly than more concrete and meaningful words such as *baby, ball,* and *dinosaur.* Repeated exposure to words makes it more likely that children will remember and identify them quickly. The basal program authors who controlled the repetition of words were attempting to help children learn words through concentrated practice. When children read from books with limited amounts of print and predictably patterned sentences, they are more likely, in the initial stages of learning words, to remember the set of words being stressed. Thereafter, children should be encouraged to read and reread stories in order to get the experience necessary for sight word learning.

Practice with isolated words is quite different from practice in context. It is through contextual reading that children begin to associate the visual form of a word with its meaning as well as its spoken identity. Isolated word drill may help children associate the printed forms of words with their spoken identities, but without context, they do not have to specify the meaning of words in terms of story context and prior experience. As a result, the concepts of words stored in memory are less semantically rich and less easily recalled.

Most children who learn words through basal instruction are simultaneously taught phonics concepts. Children in whole language classrooms tend to learn these concepts through writing. In either case, becoming aware of the elements of words and how they represent phonemes is critical to word learning and the ability to decode words. In the next section, we consider how students learn word elements.

Knowledge of Word Elements.   Knowledge about words and their elements develops over time as words are learned. *Word element* means the knowledge that children have of English spelling (orthography) that enables them to identify words they have not seen before. Knowledge of word elements pertains to letter–sound associations and the structural components of words, such as root words and affixes (e.g., *-ing, -ed, re-, un-*), as well as procedural knowledge about word elements. The latter includes knowing how to blend word elements to form a word as well as how to analogize from a known to an unknown word, as in using the ending of *sat* to help in identifying *mat* (Goswami & Bryant, 1990; Goswami & Mead, 1992). Underlying the development of knowledge of word elements is phoneme awareness.

Phoneme Awareness.   Children first learning to speak discern differences at the phonemic level within words; that is, they are able to distinguish between words that differ in only one sound (e.g., *cat* and *bat*). At the same time, they have little conscious awareness over phonemes as distinctive units; they are unable to treat them in an objective fashion. Various research strategies suggest that children become aware of phonemes only gradually. For example, children below the age of 7 experience considerable difficulty reporting the word that remains when a phoneme is deleted (e.g., when /h/ is deleted from *hill* or /d/ from *card;* Bruce, 1964; Rosner & Simon, 1971). Liberman, Shankweiler, Fischer, and Carter (1974) report that none of a preschool group and only 17 percent of a kindergarten group were able to segment words into their phonemic components, whereas 70 percent of a first-grade group were successful.

Research has established convincingly a correlation between the development of phoneme awareness and reading, but there is debate over whether phonemic awareness is a prerequisite or a facilitator of reading development, whether it develops concurrently with reading, or whether reading leads to phoneme awareness (Ehri, 1979). Although we know that instruction to develop phoneme awareness enhances later reading achievement (Bradley & Bryant, 1983; Lundberg, Frost, & Petersen, 1988), we also have seen that reading influences the way children perceive phonemes (Ehri, 1983). For our purposes here, you need as a teacher to be conscious that many children profit from instruction that encourages them to hear phonemes in words. Rather than providing intensive instruction in phoneme awareness followed by instruction in letter–sound associations, we believe that the two should occur together as part of reading and writing activities.

The problem of distinguishing phonemes within words is complicated by the fact that each phoneme has several sound variants, and these are treated as equivalent in the writing system. This situation makes it difficult to explain and illustrate the concept of phonemes.

How do children learn to hear phonemes in words? One natural approach is through word families. By hearing and seeing rhyming words, children become aware of how the beginning consonants or consonant blends (*onsets*) change while the word endings (*rimes*) stay the same. Treiman (1985) has shown that children discern the linguistic units of onsets and rimes more easily than they do phonemes. Moreover, rimes relate in a more predictable fashion to phonemes than do the same letters taken individually (Adams, 1990).

Children also learn sounds when they are encouraged to invent spelling. By saying words in an elongated fashion as they attempt to spell them, children become able to hear the sounds, first at the beginning and ending of the word and then in the middle (Clay, 1979; Elkonin, 1963). Hearing sounds within words enables children to relate sounds to letters, leading to improved word recognition (Ball & Blachman, 1991; Bradley & Bryant, 1983; Clarke, 1989).

Word Identification.   The phonemes of English correspond (more or less well) to graphemes, and these correspondences are referred to as *phonic concepts.* Almost all beginning reading programs now in common use introduce phonic concepts. Where programs with a heavy emphasis on phonics are used, students' reading progress is heavily dependent on their mastery of phonic concepts. However, in many of the phonic programs, phonemes are introduced in isolated form and students miss the important learning that words can be segmented into phonemes. Accordingly, students learn phonic correspondences on an item-by-item basis and fail to acquire a general procedure by which to relate word forms and phonemes.

Many children learn to read from programs that include instruction in phonics and other word elements. Others learn word elements inductively: They discover spelling patterns through writing. This is particularly true for children in whole language classrooms. There is evidence that those children who learn to read easily also develop knowledge about word elements easily, beyond what has been taught to them through direct instruction. The knowledge of average and less-proficient learners, by contrast, tends to reflect the concepts they have been taught directly through their writing and reading programs (Barr & Dreeben, 1983). Therefore, you need to be able to assess children's knowledge of word elements. If children are not making progress, they may need supportive instruction to help them to hear sounds in words and learn spelling–sound relationships.

Further, while some children may demonstrate knowledge of word elements, unless they can organize this knowledge systematically to support word identification and spelling, it is of little functional value. Children's early writing, which demonstrates spelling that differs in systematic ways from standard spelling, can provide a window into their knowledge (Bissex, 1980; Read, 1971). The early spelling responses of children can be classified developmentally according to stages (Henderson, 1981, 1985). In the first stage, as shown in Figure 2.1, children represent words by letters and numbers but the spellings bear no resemblance to correct spellings. Such responses indicate that children understand that words are represented by a series of letters, but they have not yet solved the problem of how to represent the elements within spoken words.

In the second stage, children begin to use alphabetic writing representing some sounds of words in a systematic way, particularly those at the beginning of words (see Figure 2.1). This stage can be divided into two substages: the first, or "initial consonant" stage, in which only initial consonants are represented, and the second, or "consonant frame," in which both initial and final consonants are represented. In the third stage, children represent within-word patterns more completely; in particular, they include letters representing vowels and those that mark the pronunciation of

FIGURE 2.1 Spelling strategy classifications for five children

SOURCE: From *Teaching Spelling* (Fig. 2.5, p. 47) by Edmund Henderson. Copyright © 1985 by Houghton Mifflin. Used with permission.

Tim Kindergarten Stage 1	Anne Kindergarten Stage 2	Jonathan 1st Grade Stage 2	Silvia 2d Grade Stage 3	Jane 2d Grade Correct
AMINƆ	J	CHIRP	CHIRP	CHIRP
EM3321	SB	SAP	STAMP	STAMP
SEMAᕈS	AT	EDE	EIGHTEEY	EIGHTY
19ИHM	J	GAGIN	DRAGUN	DRAGON
SAMH	P	PRD	PURD	PURRED
MENENA	TP	TIP	TIPE	TYPE
ENIMM	T	CHUBRL	TRUBAL	TROUBLE

vowels (e.g., final-*e* pattern). Nevertheless, as is shown in Figure 2.1, the spellings still depart in systematic ways from standard spelling for some words. Finally, children learn to spell words in standard form (Henderson & Beers, 1980).

This development in spelling reflects growth in the underlying knowledge that children have about words and the elements that compose them. To think of this development in terms described earlier by Ehri (1980), the images of words that children store in memory become more complete. Her research shows that children spell words not simply on the basis of letter–sound knowledge but also on the basis of their stored images of words, because silent as well as voiced letters are represented in their spellings.

Children progress through similar stages in their ability to identify unknown words. Reading aloud, children reveal their knowledge of sight words and also their skill in identifying unknown words. By analyzing the match between the printed words and a child's miscues, you can develop some hypotheses about the nature of his or her knowledge of word elements. These procedures are demonstrated in Chapter 3 when we consider children's oral reading.

CASE 2.1: JESSE'S WRITING

Children in a kindergarten class differ greatly in their skill in reading and writing. Rachel's class is no exception. Figure 2.2 shows a message written by Jesse to her aunt.

PAUSE AND REFLECT.   Examine the message in Figure 2.2 that Jesse wrote. Is there some evidence that she understands that sounds are represented by letters? What do you conclude about her knowledge of word elements? What sounds does she represent in spelling? How would your characterize Jesse's spelling in terms of the Henderson stages?

You may have noticed that Jesse accurately represents consonant sounds in her writing. Even for longer words, such as "birthday" and "Marshall," she writes all the sounds that she is able to hear. "Wednesday" is a particularly telling example because the only consonant Jesse does not write is the "d," which is not pronounced. Two consonants occurring together in a word may still pose problems for Jesse; for example, the "n" in "aunt" and the "t" in "went" were omitted.

Vowels are also represented in most of the words she wrote. She is able to write most short vowel sounds, particularly when they occur in short words. She seems to be working on the problem of how to represent digraphs ("how," "mouse," "soon," "dear"). It is not possible from this sample to assess her knowledge of long vowel markers. On the basis of this evidence, we can conclude that Jesse is able to write words phonetically, and that she has not yet reached the stage of spelling conventionally.

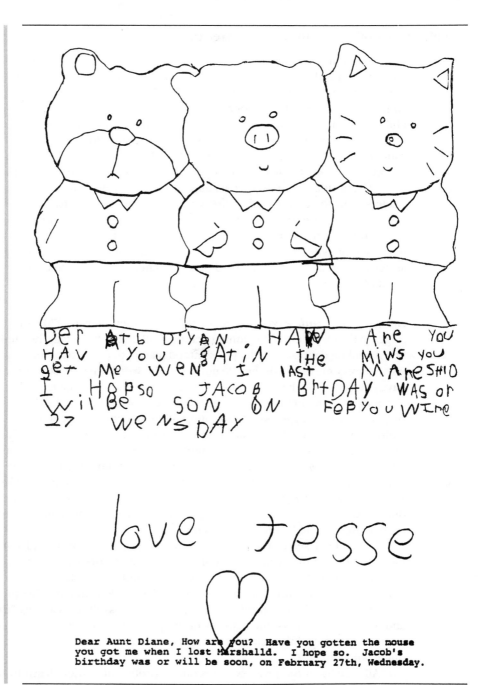

FIGURE 2.2 Jesse's message

Development of Integration and Fluency

In this section we focus on the integration of reading strategies and reading fluency. **Integration** is the ability to use prior knowledge, contextual information, and print cues simultaneously in a coordinated fashion. **Fluency** is reading unfamiliar as well as familiar selections with appropriate intonation, phrasing, and rate. It is possible for children to demonstrate fluent reading with familiar stories they have read many times, but unless this same fluency is demonstrated with unfamiliar selections, we cannot conclude that they are fluent readers. The capability to read fluently depends on two conditions: (1) instantaneous recognition of an extensive set of printed words, and (2) considerable practice reading contextual selections. Some skillful young readers achieve fluency in their first year of reading. Many, however, require several years of reading experience before they acquire sufficient word knowledge and contextual practice to read unfamiliar material fluently. The focus of this section is on determining whether children have achieved fluency when reading unfamiliar selections and delineating the reading experiences they need to further the development of fluency.

Integration and Reading Strategies.   Biemiller (1970) describes three stages of development in beginning reading skill. In the first stage, beginning readers, when reading contextual selections, attend mainly to contextual information; that is, when they come to words they do not know, the words they substitute are words they have guessed on the basis of context. For example, the sentence *The red wagon rolled down the hill,* might be read as "The red wagon *sped* down the hill." The substitution of *sped* for *rolled* suggests that the child, failing to recognize the word *rolled,* used the contextual meaning of the sentence to determine an appropriate substitute.

In the second stage, children appear to focus much more on the print: When they encounter an unknown word, their substitutions tend to match some part of the unknown word. For example, a child at this stage reading the sentence *The red wagon rolled down the hill* might substitute the nonsense word *railed* for *rolled* if he or she did not know the word *rolled.* Children at this stage are beginning to attend much more closely to the features of printed words.

In the final stage, they integrate information from print and context when identifying unknown words. Biemiller found that errors they made tended to be appropriate both to the context of the sentence and the graphic features of the word. For example, in reading the same sentence the student might substitute the word *raced* for *rolled.* The substitution makes sense in terms of the meaning of the sentence and it matches some of the features of the printed word. During this stage readers learn to integrate information from context and print to aid them in identifying unknown words.

All readers in the process of becoming proficient readers learn to incorporate information from a variety of sources while reading. This integration of information can be seen most clearly in beginning readers. In the early stages, they seem able to consider only one source of information (context or print) at a time. Later when they confront unknown words, their substitutions indicate use of information from several sources (Biemiller, 1970; Weber, 1968).

Fluent Reading.   An issue of considerable importance is whether the ability to integrate information from a variety of sources underlies fluent reading, or whether fluent reading comes about in some other way. In essence, the debate focuses on whether fluent reading is achieved through coordination of print and contextual information, with decreased attention to print in favor of meaning, or whether knowledge of words and word identification proficiency are solely or mainly responsible for fluent reading (Stanovich, 1986).

On one side, many reading experts argue that fluent reading arises from the complex coordination of information sources (Bussis, Chittenden, Amarel, & Klausner, 1985; Clay, 1979). Goodman (1976) asserts, "Skill in reading involves not greater precision, but more accurate first guesses based on better sampling techniques, greater control over language structure, broadened experiences and increased conceptual development" (p. 504). Some adherents to this position even argue that heavy dependence on print causes poor reading. Smith (1971) claims that "the more difficulty a reader has with reading, the more he relies on visual information; this statement applies to both the fluent reader and the beginner" (p. 221).

Others have articulated an opposing position. Among the first to focus on the development of fluency or automaticity, LaBerge and Samuels (1974) proposed that instantaneous processing of print evolves as component skills of word identification become automatic through practice. They suggest that practice facilitates two different developments. First, it helps the reader consolidate separate processes. At a basic level, for example, he or she consolidates phonic associations and blending within word identification. That is, children learn to blend letter–sound associations to identify previously unknown words. At a more advanced level, visual recognition leads immediately to awareness of meaning with or without consciousness of the sound of the letter or word. Readers are no longer aware of the visual forms or sound of words they read—only their meaning. This consolidation is revealed when children no longer hesitate in recognizing words. Second, practice permits the reader to grasp larger units, allowing him or her to go from reading word by word to reading word groups or phrases. This reorganization is sometimes manifested in an increase in reading rate.

In the initial version of the formulation, fluency was seen as developing through automaticity of word knowledge; the role of context was not considered (see Samuels, 1979, for later versions that consider the role of contextual facilitation in the development of fluency). Later researchers have attempted to clarify the role of context in fluent reading. Perfetti (1985) has shown that there is a linear relation between isolated word recognition time and contextual facilitation: The more difficult a word is to recognize (because a reader lacks word knowledge or because a word is printed unclearly), the more important context becomes in contributing information.

Stanovich (1980, 1986) develops this position further by distinguishing between two forms of contextual support: an automatic contextual facilitation that occurs outside of conscious control, and a consciously controlled process. The automatic process is viewed as operating in memory without reader awareness; the topic under consideration triggers or activates related concepts, thereby making them easier for a reader to retrieve. The conscious process is directed by the purpose of the reader, with his or her full attention. Stanovich argues that this conscious use of context occurs when readers encounter problems recognizing words; one negative consequence, however, is that the resulting focus of attention on word recognition detracts from comprehension. Good readers, who have developed automaticity in word knowledge, encounter few problems with word identification when they read and therefore can direct all their attention toward meaning. Poor readers who encounter many problems with print are forced to use context to help them identify words, and this division of attention between print and meaning leads not only to poorer comprehension but also to less adequate contextual information to support word identification.

In this book we suggest that the goal of reading is comprehension, and that adequate comprehension depends on the integration of knowledge from different sources, including the reader's background knowledge on a topic, his or her developing understanding of an author's message, knowledge of language structures, and knowledge of print. At the same time, we believe that fluent processing of print depends on automaticity of word knowledge, when the reader quickly recognizes words without having to devote effort to their analysis. We agree with Stanovich that when readers encounter few problems in word identification, they are able to focus more completely on reconstructing the messages of authors. Remember, however, that there is a stage before fluent reading when most readers profit from learning to integrate information from print and context to aid their word identification.

ASSESSING CHILDREN'S EMERGENT LITERACY

One of the easiest ways for you to gain insight into the knowledge your students have about print is to listen to them as they read aloud. For children who are in the initial stages of becoming aware of reading and writing, the storybook reading that Rachel, Jody's teacher, used with her provides insight into how Jody thinks about reading. Before we describe Jody's reading, however, we should look at the procedures you may wish to follow when you try this approach. Then, as you read about Jody, note the procedures Rachel used to support Jody's reading and to interpret her reading strategies.

Jody's storybook reading raised certain questions in Rachel's mind. In order to understand more clearly, she asked Jody to write about an experience. As you read this portion of the case, consider what Jody's writing reveals about her knowledge of print. Rachel then had Jody name the letters of the alphabet to assess her knowledge in this area. Finally, because of concerns about her visual and auditory acuity, she referred Jody to the school nurse for screening tests.

Storybook Reading Procedures

One effective way to explore children's understanding of reading and writing is to use the **storybook reading procedures** developed by Sulzby (1985) in which a child reads a "favorite" storybook. To begin this informal diagnostic process, ask the child to select a favorite book from the class library, then take the child to a quiet corner of the room and place the book sideways, cover down on the table. You then say, "Read me your book." If the child hesitates or refuses, encourage her by saying, "Well, pretend you can. Pretend-read it to me."

While the child reads or pretends to read the story, you need to draw conclusions about how well she understands the conventions of writing and whether her reading is based on pictures in the book or on the text. The form shown in Figure 2.3 can be used to summarize your observations during the assessment of a child's storybook reading.

FIGURE 2.3   Form for summarizing results from storybook reading

---

SUMMARY FORM—STORYBOOK READING CHECKLIST

Date

Conventions of Writing

   Little knowledge_____

   Some knowledge_____

   Complete knowledge_____

Picture-Based Reading

   Labeling and commenting_____

   Well-formed story in the form of oral language_____

   Well-formed story in the form of written language_____

Text-Based Reading

   Refusal—doesn't know the words_____

   Identifies a limited number of words/letters_____

   Reads known words with substitutions for unknown words_____

   Reads word by word_____

   Reads fluently_____

Comments:

With respect to the conventions of writing, you should note whether the child

- knows how to hold the book right side up
- begins at the beginning of the story
- begins reading at the top of the left-hand page
- reads across the page from left to right

While the child reads, you need to judge whether the reading is based on pictures or text. If what she reads does not match the text, you need to determine whether the "story" is a series of comments or a well-formed narrative. If the story is well formed, listen to the intonation: Is it similar to the way the child speaks, or is it in the form of written language?

If the reading corresponds to the text, you need to determine whether the child watches the print or is "reading" from memory. When a child responds to the print, you can then determine the extent of her knowledge: Can she identify some letters or words, read some words substituting responses for unknown words, read word by word, or read fluently?

Sometimes there will be a mixture of reading and storytelling. Other times the child may refuse to read because she doesn't know the words. This refusal shows that the child knows what she reads must be text based.

CASE 2.2: JODY'S STORYBOOK READING

Rachel wanted to learn more about Jody's understanding of storybook reading. She asked Jody to bring her favorite storybook to school. After placing the storybook sideways, cover down on the table, Rachel began the storybook reading in the following way:

R: What's the name of your book?

J: *Baby Come Out* (by Fran Manushkin)

R: And your Mom's having a baby so you must really like to read that!

J: Yeah.

R: Okay. Please read me your book.

J: I don't know how to read it.

R: That's fine; pretend you can. Pretend-read it to me.

J: If I make a mistake, it's okay?

R: Sure, it's okay.

J: This mother was having a baby and every day she felt her tummy and she said, "Baby do you like your breakfast?" And the baby said "Ahhhhh." (Aside to teacher: 'cause she couldn't say 'Ummmm' yet.)

R: Not yet . . .

J: So she said, "Ahhhh." (giggle)

R: The next morning she went into the painting room to paint a picture and she said to her baby, "Baby, do you like the picture that I'm making for you?" And she said, "Ahhhh." (giggle)

Jody continued reading the storybook in this fashion. Rachel observed that she began reading at the beginning of the book and turned the pages one by one as she reenacted the story. She looked at the right-hand page first as she read and often did not even look at the left-hand page. She reconstructed the story through the pictures, often pointing at them for her own benefit or to show Rachel something. At no time did she point at the words or attend to the print.

The intonations and inflections she used reflected the use of both oral and written language. Although she began the story in an oral language mode ("This mother was having a baby and every day she feeled her tummy"), she quickly shifted into dialogue-characteristic intonational patterns of written language ("She said, 'Baby do you like your breakfast? And the baby said, 'Ahhhhh.' ") This mixture of oral and written language styles continued during the remainder of the story.

PAUSE AND REFLECT.   Think about Jody's responses. According to this evidence, at what stage of development is Jody in terms of her storybook reading? What does she know about the conventions of writing? What is the basis for her reading? Given the evidence provided, is Jody's reading based on pictures or on the text? How should the form in Figure 2.3 be completed?

Rachel noted that Jody started at the beginning of the book and continued in a page-by-page fashion. Jody clearly has some knowledge of the conventions of writing. At the same time, she did not attend to the print and she focused first and sometimes only on the right-hand page. This indicates that she does not yet have complete understanding of the conventions of print. Thus, in completing the Print Awareness Summary Form, Rachel recorded the date next to "Some knowledge" to show that on October 15, Jody had some knowledge of the conventions of reading.

Rachel further observed that Jody was reading the pictures and that she did not attend to the printed words. Indeed, there was little correspondence between the text as printed in the storybook and Jody's reconstruction of the story. Thus it is appropriate to classify her reading as picture-based. But she certainly went beyond labeling and commenting on pictures, to retell the action of the story in a well-formed fashion. What kind of language did she use to tell the story? Did it approximate oral language or written language? Since both forms were represented, it is appropriate to record the date in both places. The fact that some of the story was related in the form of written language shows that Jody is developing awareness of the nature of written language. She has not yet developed an understanding that spoken words must correspond to the text, or the awareness of how language can be segmented into word units so as to match printed words.

Later in the winter or spring Rachel may have her read another favorite storybook to observe her growth in awareness about the nature of stories. At this later time, Rachel will use the same summary form to record new dates to show Jody's progress during the year.

Writing Assessment Procedures

On the basis of Jody's storybook reading, Rachel learned that she has not yet started to see relations between print and speech at the word and letter level. To gain more information about Jody's knowledge of print, Rachel decided to obtain a sample of her writing. In the following section, we show how Rachel supported Jody's writing and what she learned from it, and we describe procedures that you may use to encourage a child to write. We also discuss some of the criteria you may use in interpreting the writing.

Assessment of print awareness through writing occurs most easily in classrooms where print is being used for a variety of purposes. Printed messages embedded in situational contexts and accompanied by oral language enable children to "read" before they have acquired control of mechanical skills. For example, labels are placed on the block bin, the snack closet, and the bathroom door. When children are making decisions about where to go on a field trip or what to name a class pet, the suggestions are written in list form and reviewed. Notes to parents or children reminding them of important events and deadlines are posted in conspicuous places. When children have drawn pictures, they are helped to label them. Moreover, when you write language experience stories, children have the opportunity to model writing.

To obtain a sample of a child's writing, simply ask that child to write. Help her think through what she wants to write by talking with her about it. Perhaps she will want to draw a picture first and then label it or describe it in some way. If a child responds that she cannot write, encourage her to "do it your own way" or "pretend-write"; assure her that it does not have to look like "grown-up" writing.

After the child has finished writing, you need to ask her what she has written in order to interpret it accurately. After she has read her writing to you once, ask her to point to the writing as she reads it and notice the degree of correspondence between what is written and what is read.

Assessment occurs in two stages:

1. Examine the symbols the child uses.
   a. Are they scribbles, or numbers, or letters?
   b. If there is a picture on the page, where is the writing placed in relation to the picture?
   c. If letters are used, are they grouped to form wordlike images?
   d. Does the writing proceed from left to right, and from top to bottom?

SUMMARY FORM—WRITING CHECKLIST

Date

Scribbles not related to meaning_____

Scribbles related to meaning_____

Letterlike sequences related to meaning_____

Letters related to words_____

Letter sequences related to words_____

Letter–sound correspondence_____

Comments:

FIGURE 2.4   Form for summarizing results from writing task

2. Consider the nature of the correspondence between what was written and how it is read by the child.
   a. How many symbols are used to represent each spoken word?
   b. Is there a direct correspondence between the number of symbol groupings and the number of spoken words? If so, what is the correspondence? Are words typically represented with one or more symbols? Are some words represented by letters that relate systematically to the word?

The form in Figure 2.4 can be used to summarize the observations that you can make while assessing a child's writing. The results can be updated periodically on the same form.

CASE 2.3: JODY'S WRITING

This was not the first writing done by Jody. Rachel had previously asked her to write stories. Rachel had recorded her stories and she had participated with the rest of the class in writing a story. In addition, when Rachel invited her to write on her pictures, she frequently did. Jody and Rachel began the activity in the following way:

RACHEL: Do you have something you'd like to write about?

JODY: Yeah, at day camp we played outside.

R: You did?

J: We played kickball and . . . and kickball and (long pause).

R: Were there other kids there?

J: Yeah.

R: Did you play something else besides kickball?

J: Yeah, I'm thinking of what we played . . . of what it's called. Some kind of ball . . . it was when you kick the ball and, um, you have to roll the ball and you have to try to catch someone. Was it . . . (long pause)

R: Dodgeball?

J: Oh, yeah. We had fun playing dodgeball.

R: All right, that sounds like a good idea for a story. Here's a pencil and here's some paper. Okay, now take a few minutes to write.

J: How do you spell "we"? (This was the first word Jody was attempting to write.)

R: Do it your way—it doesn't have to be like "grown-up."

While Jody wrote, her concentration was intense. Although she wrote her name from left to right, she started the story on the right side of the page and proceeded across the line to the left. Unlike many young writers, she did not say the words softly to herself in elongated fashion as she wrote them. Although she labored over some parts of her writing, whe executed other parts more rapidly. Jody worked intensely for about four minutes and then announced that she was done with her story. Her writing is shown in Figure 2.5.

When Jody was finished, Rachel continued the activity as follows:

R: Okay, now I'd like you to read it to me.

J: "We played kickball and . . . dodgeball at camp."

R: Okay. That's a good story. Do you want to add more?

J: No.

R: Okay. Now what I'd like you to do is read it back to me and point to what you're reading as you read it.

J: "We played kickball and . . . dodgeball at camp."

R: Okay. That's it! Thank you very much. It's a terrific story.

When asked to read what she had written, Jody did so with "written language" intonation. On both readings, she seemed to have difficulty remembering the word "dodgeball." On the second reading, when asked to point to what she was reading, she began on the right side of the page; she pointed several times to some sequences and skipped over others.

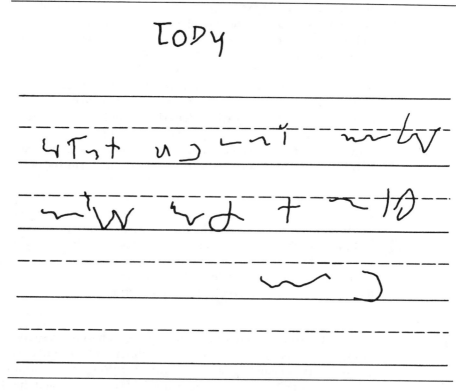

FIGURE 2.5   Sample of Jody's writing

PAUSE AND REFLECT.   Stop for a moment and consider the evidence. Given Jody's writing and her reading of it, what have you learned about her awareness of print? Look closely at the nature of her symbols. Are they scribbles, letters, or numbers? What is the nature of the correspondence between what she wrote and how she read it? How would you complete the form shown in Figure 2.4?

Rachel observed that some of Jody's writing looked very letterlike, while some must be classified as scribbles. The forms, however, seem to be grouped into clusters that resemble words. The writing did not proceed from left to right, although the second line of writing indicates a top to bottom progression.

With respect to the nature of the correspondence between what she wrote and how it was read, Rachel concluded that Jody is aware that writing represents meaning, as indicated by her intent to write a story and her ability to read what she had written. However, spoken words are not yet paired in any systematic way with print, as indicated by her failure to point to what she had written to represent the words she was "reading." Though the initial "W" is suggestive and may be used to represent "We," and the "C" may represent "camp," there are no other examples of words being represented by letters that relate systematically to the word. Jody is at the stage in writing in which letterlike sequences relate in a general way to meaning. Thus Rachel, in completing the "writing checklist," recorded the date next to "Letterlike sequences related to meaning" to show that on October 15, Jody had some knowledge of the nature of writing and its relation to meaning (see Figure 2.4).

As was true for the storybook reading, you need to work with individual children to acquire diagnostic skill in assessing children's writing. This includes learning to record children's reading of their writing and interpreting the nature of the relationship to infer their awareness of print. Through observing the writing of several children in a systematic fashion, you can develop the observational and interpretive skills that enable you to monitor the progress of your students in a more informal way during classroom instruction.

Further Assessment: Jody's Letter Naming. Given Jody's response to the reading and writing tasks, Rachel became curious about her knowledge of letter names. To assess her understanding, Rachel began by writing letters from Jody's name in mixed-up order. Jody was able to name the "D," the "O," and the "J," but not the "Y." Then Rachel wrote several upper case letters (S, N, T, B) but Jody was not able to name any of these. Finally, she wrote several letters in lower case form (r, d, m, c); Jody was also unable to name these letters.

Rachel was pleased that Jody had learned to name most of the letters in her name. She may have learned them while she had learned to write her name. Generally, however, Jody was in the initial stages of learning the names of letters. This was an area that Rachel would work on with Jody. While Rachel does not provide direct instruction in letter names, she teaches them informally through "mini-lessons" offered during reading and writing activities.

Further Assessment: Visual and Auditory Acuity. During both the reading and writing tasks, Rachel noted that Jody frequently rubbed her eyes and held the book in a funny position, closer to her eyes than usual. She also noted that Jody asked her to repeat what she had said several times. Because of these signs, she decided to have Jody see the school nurse for assessment of her vision and hearing. Table 2.1 lists some of the symptoms that may indicate sight or hearing problems. Particularly when children are just learning to read, you need to watch for vision or hearing problems that may explain the difficulties some children encounter with reading and writing.

TABLE 2.1. Symptoms that may indicate sight or hearing problems

Visual Acuity

1. Does the student experience frequent eye infections or pain?
2. Does the student rub his or her eyes or evidence other signs of visual discomfort, particularly when reading?
3. Does the student finger-point or use a marker while reading long after other students have discontinued such practices?
4. Does the student hold books in atypical positions or at unusual distances from his or her eyes?
5. Does the student frequently skip words or lines when reading?

Auditory Acuity

1. Does the student experience frequent ear infections or pain?
2. Is the student's speech unusual in any way (slurred, monotonic, inarticulate, or loud)?
3. Is the student frequently inattentive?
4. Does the student often either fail to follow directions or ask to have them repeated?
5. Does the student fail to pronounce new words and names correctly?

In the remainder of this chapter, we describe some instructional procedures that would be appropriate for children similar to Jody who are becoming aware of the nature and functions of reading and writing. Given your understanding of Jody's literacy development, as you read, think about whether the suggested procedures would be appropriate ways in which Rachel could help Jody develop her knowledge of reading and writing.

PLANNING APPROPRIATE INSTRUCTION

Assessment is of little value unless it helps you to identify the activities and instructional support that will help children further develop their reading and writing skill. Although assessment necessarily focuses on the needs of children one at a time, teachers typically organize instruction for groups of children. Thus it is necessary for you to consider the special needs of *all* children in a group and to provide a composite form of instruction that will meet all their needs. For example, Jody may be a member of a small group of children in kindergarten. When planning instruction, Rachel must consider not only Jody's special needs but also those of the other children in the group.

Instructional planning consists of three main steps: (1) identifying the needs and appropriate instruction for individual children; (2) considering the range of needs and instructional possibilities for a group of children; and (3) selecting those instructional approaches that will further the development of all children.

The instructional approaches that we describe in this section are broad gauged in that they permit children to engage in them on a variety of levels. Children who are less mature, such as Jody, will profit from the instructional experience in a somewhat different way from those with more advanced understanding of reading. Generally, young children who show few signs of print awareness need to be provided with experiences that provide such knowledge. The two types of experiences that we recommend here, story reading and writing, are particularly useful in classrooms because they allow children at different stages of development to participate at the level of their existing knowledge. They can be used with the whole class or with small heterogeneous groups.

Encouraging Story Reading

Story reading in classrooms can occur in a variety of ways. Certainly you should read good children's literature to your classes and encourage students to discuss the stories. The form of story reading most effective in developing print awareness is shared reading of stories. Children need to see the print as it is being written or read in order to understand how print is arranged and related to speech.

One form of story reading involves large-sized **"big" books** that let students see the print and participate in the reading (Holdaway, 1979). You should talk about where the story begins and demonstrate with a hand motion the portion of the text that is currently being read. Similarly, concepts pertaining to positions ("top," "end"), print ("word," "letter"), and punctuation can be explained and demonstrated. In this form of supported reading, you may read the story aloud several times on different occasions. Once children are familiar with the story, they may wish to engage in choral reading or take turns reading sentences with your support.

A second approach, the **Language Experience Activity (LEA)** (Stauffer, 1970), encourages children, with the support of the teacher, to write a story about a shared experience. The story must be written large enough on a big sheet of paper or the blackboard that all the children can see it as it is being composed and reread. The steps to follow in undertaking a LEA are the following:

1. You can encourage children to discuss an experience or a topic. Usually, topics based on common experiences (field trips, a storybook reading, raising pets in class) are more effective because they are familiar to all the children and all can contribute.
2. Following a period of initial discussion, children dictate the story while you record it. As part of the authoring, there may be revisions, additions, and deletions. You guide the process by asking questions such as, "And then what happened?" and "Is this what you want to say?" You record the story in the natural language of the students.
3. You and your students reread the story in unison, making any needed changes (clarifying ambiguous sentences, adding or omitting sentences).
4. The story should be read and reread in a variety of ways. Although use of word or phrase cards to develop a sight vocabulary and cloze activities to encourage guessing on the basis of context are typically prescribed as part of the method, we recommend a somewhat modified presentation of these procedures as described below.

The procedure for demonstrating and assessing "concept of word" developed by Morris (1980) can be used as an effective instructional procedure with language experience stories, big books, and familiar poems and songs. The activities include:

1. You read the first line of the selection aloud to students, pointing to words as you read. You continue modeling the "finger-point reading" procedures while reading the remainder of the selection.
2. Next, you encourage the children to participate in choral reading of the entire selection while you read and point to the words.
3. You then mark off the first line and ask if there is a child who would be willing to read it while pointing to the words. Other children are given the opportunity to finger-point read the remaining lines.
4. You then ask if any child can point to a word you name in the sentence. You continue by asking other children if they can locate other words in the first and remaining sentences.

This set of procedures can be used flexibly. You may begin with the choral reading and repeat this step until the children are familiar with the selection. The final step may be omitted altogether. The procedure is extremely useful because it models the relationship between printed and spoken words for children who are in the beginning stages of print awareness, and it lets more advanced children demonstrate their knowledge of print. Their accuracy in finger-point reading and locating words shows how well they understand the relationship of printed and spoken words, or the extent to which they have formed a "concept of word." One interesting observation made by Morris was the tendency of children to point more than once for words of several syllables. On the second syllable of a longer spoken word they would point to the next printed word on the line. This indicated that they had not yet completely solved the problem of how spoken words relate to print.

These instructional procedures have been incorporated into a three-day cycle of activities (Morris, 1986) as follows:

Day 1: The teacher leads the children in a discussion of a shared experience: for example, making popcorn, making valentine cards, watching snowflakes fall, visiting the school library or cafeteria, planting a seed, retelling the story of Columbus's voyage, and so on. Following the oral discussion, the children dictate two or three sentences describing the experience, and the teacher records these few sentences in manuscript print on a large sheet of chart paper.

Making Popcorn

We made popcorn.
We made it in a popcorn popper.
We put butter and salt on the popcorn.

Next, the teacher models a reading of the completed experience story, pointing to each word as she reads. Finally, the children join in choral-reading the story several times, with the teacher continuing to point to the words on the chart paper as the group reads.

Day 2: The Day 1 story is brought out and choral-read several times, with the teacher again modeling finger-point reading. Next, some informal questions can be asked and games played with the now familiar story. For example:

- Who can come up to the chart and show me where we start reading? Where we end? Where do we go when we reach the end of a line?
- These little dots in our story are called "periods." What do they tell us?
- Who knows this word (teacher points to "popcorn")? Good! Can someone else find the same word at another place in the story?
- What is the first letter in this word (teacher points to the *p* in *put*)? Can you find another word in our story that begins with *p*?

Day 3: On Day 3 the teacher works at a table with groups of seven to eight children at a time. The "popcorn" story has been transferred from the large chart paper to the bottom of an 8½ × 11 piece of paper, and each child at the table has a copy. The teacher reads the story several times and the children attempt to follow along on their own copy. Next, the teacher instructs the children to illustrate the popcorn story on the top half of the paper. As the children begin drawing, the teacher moves around to each child and asks him or her to finger-point read the three-line story. (Note: Early in the year the teacher may have to use an echo-reading strategy. That is, the teacher reads one or two lines and then the child attempts to echo-read these lines while pointing to the words on the page.) If the child is successful in finger-point reading the story—that is, matching spoken words to written words in an appropriate manner—the teacher can afterwards point randomly to individual words in the text and see if the child can identify them, immediately or by using context.[1]

Kindergarten children will differ considerably in their ability to finger-point read a short, familiar text like "Making Popcorn." Therefore, the Day 3 procedure described above, aside from its instructional value, is important diagnostically. It allows the teacher to observe carefully the reading development of individual children at a low cost in time, one to two minutes spent with each child (Morris, 1986, pp. 5–6).

Encouraging Writing

The best way to encourage young children to write is to create an environment in which reading and writing are clearly functional (Calkins, 1986; Sulzby & Teale, 1987;

---

[1]From *Teaching reading in kindergarten: A language-experience approach* (Occasional Paper No. 13, pp. 4–6) by D. Morris (1986). Evanston, IL: The Reading Center, National College of Education. Reprinted by permission.

Temple, Nathan, Burris, & Temple, 1988). Cochran-Smith (1984) describes a preschool class in which a variety of literacy activities are routinely interwoven as part of everyday situations. Printed notes are sometimes used as substitutes for oral conversation; for example, notes to parents are posted on the front door to remind them of special trips or of tuition due; parents include notes to children in their lunches. Print is used as a source of information; for example, in the classroom, labels mark the snack cupboard; outside the classroom, street signs, posters, and advertisements are noted. Printed words clarify the status of objects and pictures: who owns them (child's name on an object), and what they are about (a picture labeled "my dog"). Writing is also used to help the class solve problems such as naming the guinea pig; listing names helps children remember and select an appropriate name. More traditional literacy activities also occur, such as writing stories to recall trips and other experiences. The purpose of such writing activities in naturally occurring contexts is not to develop knowledge of the formal characteristics of print but rather to develop awareness of the functions that print serves in our society.

You can also help children develop knowledge about print through more traditional writing activities. For example, while writing a language experience after a field trip or some other experience, you pronounce longer words syllable by syllable as you write them to model the division of words into parts. At a later time, you can solicit help from the class in dividing words into syllables. When you write words on the chalkboard, you can ask students to listen for the sound at the beginning of the word. Later during the year you can say words slowly to see whether children hear their phonemic components. These experiences, which develop phoneme awareness, can also be undertaken with individual students as you assist children during seatwork. Such experiences help children to develop an awareness of print that later helps them as they learn to read and write in less contextually supported situations (Griffith & Olson, 1992; Yopp, 1992).

SUMMARY

In this chapter we considered the complex knowledge involved in learning about print and becoming fluent readers. We identified three phases of learning. Young children become aware of the nature of reading by being read to, by observing print at home and in the neighborhood, by "pretend-reading" storybooks, and by observing others read. Similarly, they become aware of writing by seeing their parents and others write and by writing themselves. Through these experiences and more formal instruction, they gradually develop knowledge of print. They begin to understand how words are composed of sounds and how these sounds relate to letters. Through practice reading stories and informational text, they develop as fluent readers.

We described two assessment procedures that reveal the nature of young children's developing understanding of reading and writing. The first, storybook reading, lets you judge the extent to which children are familiar with the conventions of writing and explore their conceptions of reading—whether "reading" consists of memorizing stories and interpreting pictures or responding to the text. The second procedure, in which you have children write, lets you infer their conception of writing and their knowledge of consonant and vowel letter—sound associations. As we learned through the cases of Jesse and Jody, their spelling provides a useful window into their knowledge.

We discussed broad-gauged instructional procedures for developing print awareness in the final section of the chapter. Some children come to school with a well-developed awareness of print; many, however, need supportive instruction with stories and writing to help them develop greater familiarity and security with printed messages. These experiences prepare children to learn printed words and the relationships between letters and sounds within words.

TRY IT OUT

1. The next time you are with a young child who has shown an interest in storybook reading, use the same approach Rachel used. If you have a tape recorder, record the interaction so that you can listen to it again later. After the child has finished "reading" the book to you, try to determine his or her knowledge of the conventions of writing and whether the reading is picture or text based.

2. **Student Portfolio Ideas:** Extensive reading constitutes one of the best ways for children to expand their sight vocabularies, apply their developing word identification strategies, and become fluent readers. Thus, having students keep a record of the books they are reading each week represents an essential component of their portfolios. Beyond this, depending on the stage of your students, you might like to have them keep track of the new words they are learning or keep a list of the new strategies they have learned for word identification.

3. **For Your Teaching Portfolio:** Use what you have learned from this chapter to add to your teaching portfolio. You might include
   • your responses to "Pause and Reflect" on Jody and Jesse
   • your response to the "Try It Out" suggested in #1
   • a sample instructional lesson on storybook reading or beginning writing that you tried and evaluated
   • your reflections on one of the "For Further Reading" selections for this chapter

FOR FURTHER READING

Bissex, G. L. (1980). *GYNS AT WRK: A child learns to write and read.* Cambridge, MA: Harvard University Press.
A detailed chronicle of a young child learning to write and read.

Clay, M. M. (1991). Introducing a new storybook to young readers. *The Reading Teacher,* 45(4), 264–273.

Excellent strategies for introducing storybooks to children learning to read.

Rhodes, L. K., & Nathensen-Mejia, S. (1992). Anecdotal records: A powerful tool for ongoing literacy assessment. *The Reader Teacher,* 45(7), 502–509.

Discusses how teachers can make descriptive and interpretive notes about the reading and writing of their students.

Teale, W. H., & Sulzby, E. (1986). *Emergent literacy: Writing and reading.* Norwood, NJ: Ablex.

Theoretical and practical chapters written by various authors on the development of young readers and programs to enhance their development.

Yopp, H. K. (1992). Developing phonemic awareness in young children. *The Reading Teacher,* 45(9), 696–703.

Describes practical techniques for helping children become aware of the sounds in words.

chapter 3

Knowledge of Print: Oral Reading Analysis and Instructional Support

CHAPTER GOALS FOR THE READER

To understand how students' oral reading can be used to learn about their knowledge of print

To develop skill in taking running records and interpreting the oral reading of children

To develop skill in recording and interpreting the oral reading of more advanced students

To develop skill in using informal techniques to explore students' print knowledge

To understand how to plan appropriate instructional support for students based on your analysis of their oral reading

CLASSROOM VIGNETTE: TWO STUDENTS AND THEIR TEACHERS

In this chapter, we consider how two teachers observe and make sense of the oral reading of their students. Eileen, a first-grade teacher, was contacted by one of her students' parents in the spring of the year. They were concerned about their son Ken's slow progress learning to read and requested a meeting with her. They asked if she thought he would need to be tutored during the summer following first grade. Eileen wondered if they were worried about his being retained in first grade.

Before the conference, Eileen listened to him read orally to assess his word learning, knowledge of word elements, and reading fluency. This assessment raised certain questions in her mind about his sight vocabulary and knowledge of word elements; she pursued these more informally. Finally, based on this information, along with her experience with him during the year, she considered several ways to support the development of his reading strategies.

The second teacher, Martha, has been teaching at Hyde School, an inner- city school, for the past four years. Early in the school year, she became concerned about the failure of one of her students, Eva, to complete her homework assignments. Martha had Eva read aloud a story from her reader in order for Martha to learn about her strategies with print. From the oral reading analysis and interpretation, Martha learned about Eva's strengths and identified the problems she has yet to solve.

We include these case studies later in the chapter so that you can learn how two teachers used oral reading analysis to understand better the reading of their students and to plan appropriate instruction. As you read the cases, consider what you might do if you were the teachers.

CHAPTER OVERVIEW

This chapter has three main parts. In a brief first section, we describe how you can explore your students' knowledge of print by having them read aloud. In the second section we provide an overview of the procedures you will follow while recording the oral reading of students. In the case study sections, we first consider the case of Ken and describe the procedures Eileen followed in making and interpreting a *running record* for him. A running record, developed in New Zealand, is a way to record oral reading (Clay, 1985). All a teacher needs to make this record is a blank piece of paper. It is a particularly useful approach for beginning readers. In the next case study, we consider a procedure that is more useful with more advanced readers. These records are overlaid on a copy of the text. To demonstrate these procedures, we consider the case of Eva and describe the procedures Martha followed in recording and interpreting Eva's oral reading. In the final section, we describe procedures you can use to help children develop their knowledge of sight words, their understanding of word elements, and their reading fluency.

CHAPTER OUTLINE

Oral Reading Analysis: Areas of Reading Assessed
    Knowledge of Print: Sight Words and Word Identification
    Integration of Reading Strategies
    Reading Fluency
Procedures for Recording Oral Reading
    Preparation

ORAL READING ANALYSIS: AREAS OF READING ASSESSED

By listening to students read contextual selections, you can identify problems that exist in three areas: (1) knowledge of print, (2) integration of knowledge sources, and (3) reading fluency. In this section we describe the areas of reading that are assessed through oral reading of contextual selections. Following this we describe the specific procedures that you may follow to learn how to assess oral reading competently.

Knowledge of Print: Sight Words and Word Identification

As children become familiar with print, they become able to identify an increasing number of words instantaneously without analysis. We refer to these words as **sight words**. Sight words occur frequently, accounting for about 70 percent of running text. Children learning to read learn those words that recur frequently in print as sight words. Sight words usually include some common nouns, verbs, and adjectives; in addition, many words that form the structure of sentences such as *the*, *his*, *here*, and *but* may be recognized easily on "sight." Edward Dolch (1936) was among the first to describe the set of commonly occurring words that children tend to learn first as sight words. (Dolch's sight word list is shown in Appendix A.) Most children learn these as sight words because they recur frequently in text. In addition, each child will develop a sight vocabulary that uniquely reflects the stories and other selections he or she has been reading. Proficient readers develop a large sight vocabulary; the words they see repeatedly become familiar and are recognized on sight.

Some children learning to read have a difficult time learning and remembering sight words. Thus, it is useful for you, as their teacher, to note whether they are quickly (without analysis) identifying this set of words. Fluent reading requires the recognition of sight words. Thus, when you assess the oral reading of students, it is important to ask how quickly and accurately they recognize these basic sight words. It is also instructive to observe how their oral responses differ from the printed words.

Children learning to read develop strategies for identifying words they do not yet know. These strategies may take a variety of forms: letter-by-letter synthesis of the sounds associated with letters, analogizing the pronunciation of unknown words from known words, guessing on the basis of context. Content words that children mispronounce during contextual reading provide a window into their word identification strategies. While you listen to children read aloud, note whether they read portions of words correctly and whether they can deal with multisyllabic words. It is also useful to consider how their oral responses differ from the printed words.

Methods for examining sight word knowledge and word identification based on oral reading are described in the second section of the chapter. There we observe Eileen and Martha as they learn about the sight word knowledge and word identification of their students, Ken and Eva.

Integration of Reading Strategies

Listening to students' oral reading of contextual selections allows you to assess their word knowledge and also to examine how well they can combine their knowledge of print with information from other sources to identify unknown words. Picture cues, story themes, prior sentence context, knowledge of syntax, and experience with a topic are all useful sources of information that may aid a student in identifying unknown words. Students who have not developed balanced strategies for word identification need to be shown how to use information from a variety of sources to identify words more efficiently and effectively.

Students' oral reading responses can be analyzed in terms of *how* as well as *whether* they match responses that are expected on the basis of the text (Goodman, 1965, 1967, 1969). Some incorrect responses, or *miscues*, as Goodman prefers to call them, may reflect use of information about print; others may be influenced by prior sentence context. That is, they may make sense in terms of contextual meaning derived from the story topic, pictures, or the previously read portion of the sentence. Some responses may reflect both these factors, whereas others may show the influence of neither. Some children in the beginning stages of reading rely on context or picture cues to the neglect of print cues; others produce nonwords that are cued by print but show no influence of context. Analyzing how oral reading responses match expected responses permits you to learn about the strategies students use when they encounter unfamiliar words. If most miscues show the influence of contextual information, you can conclude that the student used context to try to make sense of what he or she read.

The number and types of miscues that readers attempt to correct also give you information on their ability to integrate contextual and print information and to monitor their reading. Researchers have identified several categories of correction behavior in oral reading (Page & Barr, 1975). When a reader corrects a response, he shows that he is dissatisfied with the original response. Conversely, when he fails to attempt a correction, he indicates a lack of dissatisfaction or insufficient knowledge on which to base a correction. Consider an oral reading response that is semantically and syntactically acceptable but differs in letter–sound correspondence from the expected response, as in *Tim ran down the* **road** for *Tim ran down the lane.* If the reader does not attempt to correct the miscue, you can assume that semantic and grammatical cues from the context permitted her to verify the response and feel satisfied with it. We can also assume that, to some degree, the phonic discrepancy did not cause her to feel dissatisfied.

If no pauses or other miscues immediately precede or follow the response, your assumption concerning a lack of influence from phonics cues is strengthened. If the reader uses *road* and *lane* interchangeably in a semantically acceptable way throughout the passage, your assumption is further strengthened. If, on the other hand, she attempts to correct her substitution of *road* for *lane*, you may assume that the phonics cues are operating at this point, because her original response caused her some dissatisfaction. This attempt to correct may be successful or unsuccessful. If it is successful, you may assume that phonics cues are influencing the reader's processing.

The production of a semantically and grammatically unacceptable response, such as *Tim ran down the* **lone**, would lead to a similar interpretation in terms of corrections. If the reader did not attempt a correction, you could assume that she was not processing adequately the available semantic, grammatical, and phonics information. If she corrects with a vowel change such as *lean* for *lane*, the phonics cues are probably generating her correction attempt. On the other hand, if she inserts *line* for *lane*, she may be using all sources of information. At any event, if you look carefully at why she makes the correction changes she does and what miscues she fails to correct, you can learn a great deal about the student's reading process.

It is also important to ask students how they were able to identify unfamiliar words. Often students are able to describe their methods in ways that may provide you with ideas for further instruction.

Reading Fluency

Fluency or lack of fluency is evident when you listen to the oral reading of students. For children who have not yet mastered the component skills of print processing, their reading shows substitution errors, long pauses, frequent repetitions, and inappropriate phrasing. In other words, their problems with word knowledge are hindering their development of fluent reading.

Oral reading analysis sometimes reveals no major problems—few substitutions, pauses, and repetitions—but phrasing that is inappropriate to the syntax and meaning of the selection. The child reads word by word or in clusters of words with brief pauses between them. It is as if his print knowledge is not sufficiently automatic to permit him to pay attention to phrasing during oral reading or recoding of the message.

Sometimes a student's difficulty with reading fluency is caused by other problems, such as sight word knowledge and word identification; but this is not always the case. You can distinguish a primary fluency problem from one that is secondary to other reading problems by having the student read text that is extremely easy for him. If the characteristics of nonfluent reading—poor intonation, inappropriate phrasing, long pauses, and word-by-word reading—persist, then you can conclude that the problem is primarily one of fluency. Some readers become extremely anxious when asked to read aloud, and their oral reading is disrupted, not necessarily because they lack fluency but because of their anxiety. In such cases, it is not possible to assess reading fluency accurately by having the students read aloud. However, you can gain some understanding of their fluency by noting their rate of silent reading.

From about third-grade level and beyond, a reading rate in the average range can be used to determine adequate fluency. When this information is combined with oral reading evidence, you can draw useful conclusions about the development of print knowledge and reading fluency. Once students no longer have problems with word identification, you may appropriately help them develop their reading rate.

As is illustrated in Table 3.1, students' reading rates on unfamiliar selections improve dramatically from first to second grade and thereafter show steady but more moderate increases. Although a comparison of the average reading rates of students on a number of reading tests shows wide variation (Harris & Sipay, 1980, p. 556), this variability in part reflects differences in the difficulty of the test material. Some tests consist of extremely easy passages while others include more technical material. The rates shown in Table 3.1 are based on passages that are appropriate in difficulty to the grade of the students tested; these ranges provide a useful standard against which to compare the reading of students at different grade levels. Generally, however, the rates of first graders on familiar materials will be somewhat higher than those shown in Table 3.1. Silent reading rates are somewhat higher than the ranges shown for oral reading, particularly for the intermediate grades and beyond (Carver, 1983; Taylor, 1965). Reading rates below the ranges shown in Table 3.1 indicate lack of fluency.

To conclude, listening to students read a selection orally enables you to judge their fluency in terms of both phrasing and intonation and reading rate. Your conclusions about their fluency and word knowledge will help you plan appropriate instruction. The goal of the diagnosis is to determine the fluency of the student's reading as well as the level of material where he or she encounters few problems with print. If the reading is not fluent, it is important for you to provide instruction that will

TABLE 3.1. Average reading rates

Grade Level	Average Range[a] Words per Minute
1.8	30–54
2.8	66–104
3.8	86–124
4.8	95–130
5.8	108–140
6.8	112–145
7.8	122–155
8.8	136–167

[a]The average range includes approximately 54% of students, those in stanines 4, 5, and 6 and in the 23–76 percentile band.

SOURCE: After Table 3, *Manual of Directions.* Gilmore Oral Reading Test. Copyright © 1968 by Harcourt Brace Jovanovich, Inc. Reproduced by permission. All rights reserved.

help the student build knowledge about print and to encourage him or her to practice extensively on problem-free materials in order to develop reading fluency.

PROCEDURES FOR RECORDING ORAL READING

To learn how to listen to students as they read aloud, it is important for you to practice oral reading assessment following systematic procedures. Many complex decisions are involved in selecting an appropriate story or expository passage, learning to record oral reading responses, analyzing the responses, gaining further needed information, and finally, interpreting the results. It is necessary for you to practice oral reading assessment with children individually before you become sufficiently proficient to undertake such assessment informally during the rapid give-and-take of classroom instruction.

The procedures for oral reading response analysis are described here in considerable detail. If oral reading analysis is new to you, you should follow each recommended step. As always in learning a new skill, your first attempts to use these procedures will be difficult and time-consuming. However, with practice, the appropriate skills and knowledge will become automatic so that you can accomplish oral reading response analysis easily. Indeed, after you have developed listening and interpretive skills, you can perform a useful diagnosis by simply listening to students' oral reading. The procedures involve four main steps. First, some *preparation* is necessary before you listen to a student read. Following this preparation, you *administer* the passage and record the student's oral reading. Then you *analyze* the response patterns.

Once this phase of the assessment is completed, you may formulate additional questions that you wish to pursue. The final step is to *develop an appropriate plan* for instructional support, based on all the information you have about the student's reading. Next we consider the preparation you must make before you have a student read aloud.

Preparation

Normally you will select a passage from instructional materials being used in the classroom. You should make a judgment about the level at which the student is able to read. A trial run with several short selections may be necessary. Oral reading may be from any appropriate book including the student's basal reader. The portion used for analysis should be 50–100 words in length for beginning readers and 100–200 words or more for more advanced readers. The total length should approximate the amount students typically read at any one time in the classroom.

The oral reading responses of any student can be recorded and analyzed to determine how he or she translates print into spoken language. In this chapter, we describe two methods of recording oral reading. The first, running records (Clay, 1985), is particularly useful when you are working with children in the beginning stages of learning to read. The second is one traditionally used to record responses.

Running Records.   All you need to make a record of a child's oral reading is a pencil and a blank sheet of paper—and, of course, a child willing to read aloud for you. For each word, the child reads correctly, you make a check mark (✔). When he substitutes a different word for a printed word, you write the printed word, draw a line above it, and then write the word spoken by the child. When he omits a word, you write the printed word with a line above it and then a period (.) to indicate the omission. When he repeats a word or phrase, draw a line with an arrow over the repeated portion, with an "R" to indicate a repetition. When the child self-corrects a miscalled word, write "SC." When he pauses, write "P."

The record for a child reading the nursery rhyme "Jack and Jill" might be recorded as follows:

From the record, we know the child read correctly all the words recorded as a "✔." In the first sentence, he substituted the word "a" for "the." The word "get" was substituted for "fetch" but then he self-corrected (SC) the substitution. He repeated the first phrase of the second sentence and corrected the substitution of "head" for "crown." Finally, the child paused in the final phrase, likely to examine the word "tumbling" more carefully.

In the Case Study section, you will see Eileen's record of Ken's oral reading and her interpretation of its meaning. For a more detailed description of running record procedures, see Clay (1985).

Traditional Method of Recording Oral Reading.   The symbols used for recording oral reading responses using traditional procedures are similar. Figure 3.1 shows one method of recording the ways a student's oral reading departs from the responses expected on the basis of the text. However, if you have already learned a somewhat different system, you should continue to use that system. As shown in Figure 3.1, substituted words are recorded by crossing out the mispronounced word and writing the student's pronunciation over the miscued word. Similarly, pauses (breaks in phrasing) are recorded with a (P). You should be familiar with this or some similar scheme. We recommend that the student's oral reading be tape-recorded as well, so that you can check the accuracy of your recording. The reason for the assessment should be discussed with the student.

Omissions. Circle the word, group of words, or part of a word omitted.

Insertions. Write in the word or word part inserted. Indicate its position with a caret.

Substitutions or mispronunciations. Identify the mispronounced word(s) by drawing a line over it (them). Write in the substituted word(s).

Repetitions. Underline or overline repeated words using a line and arrow.

Corrections. Indicate corrected responses by "SC" or "C" for self-correct.

Pauses. Indicate pauses by a "P."

Punctuation. Indicate failure to pause for a comma or period by circling.

FIGURE 3.1   Symbols for recording oral reading responses

Administration

Make sure your student is comfortable and sufficiently relaxed. If the oral reading is to be tape-recorded, you should obtain the student's permission. It is important for you to make a brief statement to help orient the student to the content and theme of the selection (see Beck, Omanson, & McKeown, 1982, for procedural suggestions). It is also important to explain to the student what he or she should do. For example, you may say the following:

> This is a story in which . . . [theme-related preparatory statement]. Please read this story aloud for me. If you come to a word you don't know, try to figure it out, guess at it, or skip it. I will not be able to help you, so do the best you can.

You should record the student's responses on a photocopy or typed version of the story. You should record responses even if the oral reading is tape-recorded. The time that the student begins and finishes reading the passage should also be noted.

If the student becomes frustrated at some point, you should reassure him that it is all right to guess at a word or skip it. If he continues to pause and becomes upset, you should tell him the word causing difficulty. If the reading passage proves generally too frustrating, discontinue the assessment and try it at a later time with an easier passage.

Analysis

Examine the oral reading record to determine whether the passage is of appropriate difficulty and adequate to assess the student's sight word recognition, word identification strategies, and reading integration and fluency.

Passage Difficulty. This analysis pertains to the level of material that would be appropriate for various purposes (such as for reading instruction as opposed to independent reading) and is based on the student's overall accuracy and fluency of word recognition. The criteria for judging whether a passage is appropriate, summarized in Table 3.2, derive from those originally recommended by Betts (1954). Betts suggests that more than 1 error for every 10 words read indicates that the material is too difficult for the student. That is, when the student reads less than 90 percent of a passage correctly, the material is at the student's frustration level. Betts claims that students should make no more than 1 error per 20 words on materials they read as part of instruction. That is, when instructional support is provided, students should be able to read passages with 95 percent accuracy or greater. There is, thus, a borderline range of 90 to 94 percent accuracy. What should you do when students perform in this region? Typically, students are asked to read diagnostic passages with little or no instructional support. Therefore, when students perform in the borderline range, you should study the kinds of problems they encounter to determine whether instructional support might be developed to bring their oral reading accuracy into the acceptable instructional range (95 percent accuracy or greater).

Betts states that materials intended for independent reading should pose very few problems for students. Specifically, he recommends that there be no more than 1 problem per 100 words read. However, this standard is based on testing wherein students read a passage silently before they read it aloud. Thus, we recommend a slightly lower standard for oral reading on sight: no more than 2 errors per 100 words. Perhaps more important than the number of errors is evidence of the student's fluency. The material that a student reads independently should be sufficiently easy that he or she reads with good intonation and phrasing.

Powell's research (Powell, 1970; Powell & Dunkeld, 1971) suggests more lenient oral reading standards for primary grade readers than those noted above. However, subsequent research (Ekwall, 1976; Pikulski, 1974) shows some inconsistency with Powell's findings. Given this inconsistency and our own clinical experience, we suggest standards that are generally in line with those originally suggested by Betts. We caution you, however, that these standards should not be used mindlessly. In addition to counting the number of errors, it is also extremely important to consider the quality of the errors (Biemiller, 1979; Kibby, 1979; Whaley & Kibby, 1981). Some, for example, may indicate serious problems with print while others may suggest carelessness.

TABLE 3.2. Criteria for determining reading levels

Level	Oral Reading Accuracy (%)
Independent	98–100
Instructional	95–97
Borderline	90–94
Frustration	Below 90

These criteria pertain to oral reading accuracy. Obviously, in judging the appropriateness of materials, you must consider comprehension as well. In Chapter 8, criteria for evaluating comprehension are discussed.

In determining whether a passage is of appropriate difficulty, you should study the entire passage for dialect influence and for repeated errors (i.e., where a character name or word is mispronounced more than twice). Note whether the student ever solves the identification of the word, especially when it is a key word. All but the first instance of any repeated error and all dialect-influenced responses should be disregarded in further analysis.

You should note the proportion of omissions, insertions, and substitutions (including mispronunciations, but not responses that the student later corrected) in relation to the total number of words in the passage. The total number of miscues should be divided by the total number of words to get a percentage figure. For example, if a student makes 7 miscues on a passage of 140 words, the proportion of miscues is 5 percent. If you subtract the proportion of miscues from 100, you determine the proportion of the passage that was error free—in this case, 95 percent. The criterion scores shown in Table 3.2 should be used for judging oral reading performance. The results from this assessment of passage difficulty should be recorded on the oral reading summary form shown in Figure 3.2 in the space provided under A.

Sight Word Recognition.   You should separate the sight word errors from the miscues made in response to unfamiliar content words. For miscues in response to sight words, the following questions should be considered:

1. What is the proportion of sight word errors in relation to the total number of words in the passage?
2. Is the reading fluent and do these miscues distort the author's meaning?
3. Are these miscues corrected by the reader?

On the basis of this evidence, you should determine whether sight word errors pose a problem and decide whether word recognition should be checked further. Sight word errors should be recorded under B, on the left side of the form. If further exploration is necessary, the Evaluation section on the right side of the form should not be completed until this is accomplished.

Word Identification.   To study the student's word identification strategies, you should record unfamiliar word miscues in section C of the form in the following way. Single-syllable words should be separated from multiple-syllable words. Classifying miscues in this fashion makes it easier to identify patterns in a student's approach to word identification and hence facilitates further exploration of word identification skills.

ORAL READING ANALYSIS

Name _____ Grade _____ Date _____

Book/Page _____ Level _____

A. Difficulty

_____ /_____   _____% Correct

Level: Independent   Instructional
       Borderline   Frustration

B. Word Learning: Sight Word Errors

Printed Word	Oral Response	Further Exploration	Evaluation
_____	_____	_____	
_____	_____	_____	
_____	_____	_____	
_____	_____	_____	
_____	_____	_____	
_____	_____	_____	
_____	_____	_____	
_____	_____	_____	

C. Word Identification: Content Word Errors

Printed Word	Oral Response	Further Exploration	Evaluation
_____	_____	_____	
_____	_____	_____	
_____	_____	_____	
_____	_____	_____	
_____	_____	_____	
_____	_____	_____	
_____	_____	_____	
_____	_____	_____	
_____	_____	_____	
_____	_____	_____	
_____	_____	_____	
_____	_____	_____	
_____	_____	_____	
_____	_____	_____	
_____	_____	_____	
_____	_____	_____	

D. Integration–Fluency

Integration: _____

_____

Fluency: Rate _____ /_____ = _____ wpm Evaluation _____

Phrasing _____

FIGURE 3.2 Oral reading response analysis form

After the printed words and miscues are recorded, you should examine them to identify patterns. The following questions should be considered:

1. To what extent do the errors resemble the expected response graphically? Is the reader in command of the following phonics associations: consonants, consonant blends and digraphs, vowels, and vowel digraphs? Is the function of markers understood?
2. Are miscues corrected by the reader and, if so, on what basis?
3. What does the evidence reveal about the reader's ability to identify affixes and syllables?

On the basis of this evidence, you should decide whether the student has difficulty in any area of word identification and whether skill in selected areas should be explored further. When additional exploration is indicated, the Evaluation section should not be completed until this has been done.

Integration and Fluency.   You should determine whether the student's miscues show use of contextual information. For example, are more than half the errors contextually appropriate and does the student have and use contextually based correction strategies? You should also describe the student's reading fluency and calculate his or her reading rate. To calculate the rate, divide the number of seconds that the student took to read the passage by 60 to get the number of minutes involved; then divide the number of words in the passage by the number of minutes to get a words-per-minute rate. This information should be recorded in section D of the form.

Summary.   In summarizing the results, the following questions should be addressed:

A. Does the passage represent an appropriate level of difficulty in terms of the reader's print skill?
B. Is the reader developing a sight vocabulary or are there problems in this area?
C. Has the reader evolved a successful strategy for identifying unknown words or is further development needed?
D. Has the reader evolved a strategy that is based on the integrated processing of graphic and contextual information?
   [When few print processing problems exist, it is appropriate to pursue the final question.] Is the reader's rate of reading in accord with that of his or her classmates or are there problems of reading fluency that need correction?

Sometimes it will be unnecessary for you to analyze results systematically in the ways described in this section. This will be especially true once you have gained skill in more systematic analysis. If you are developing your skill in oral reading analysis, however, we recommend that you follow these more systematic procedures.

In the cases described next, Eileen uses systematic procedures in analyzing the running record of Ken's reading; but she does not use the form shown in Figure 3.2 to organize her results. Typically, the form is more useful as an organizational device when you are studying the oral reading patterns of more proficient readers. Martha, in trying to understand Eva's oral reading, does use the form to organize and extend her observations. In any analysis, whether you use the form or not, you should address the questions summarized above. To answer these questions, you may need to gather evidence beyond that gained through the oral reading analysis. In the two cases described next, we present such exploratory procedures.

CASE 3.1: KEN—RUNNING RECORDS

Ken had transferred into the school in the fall of the year, and compared with other children in the class, his prior experiences with reading and writing had been limited. Ken's teacher, Eileen, was developing a whole language program for her class. She believed that language experience stories and reading from predictably patterned books were appropriate experiences, particularly for her children who were having some difficulty learning to read.

Prior to the conference she had arranged with Ken's parents, she obtained one more sample of his oral reading. In addition, she had one sample from December and one from February, as well as many samples of his writing. She had Ken read aloud a book that he had not read before: *The Carrot Seed* by Ruth Krauss—one that she judged to be of appropriate difficulty for him. During reading instruction with her class, she always introduced stories by "talking" with the children as they paged through the story prior to their reading it.

She followed the same procedure with Ken. She paged through the story, first providing an overview of the story ("In this story, the author tells us about a little boy who planted a carrot seed"), a sense of the characters ("His mother and father and big brother are afraid the seed won't grow"), and the work the little boy undertook ("What's he doing here? Yes, he's pulling the weeds and sprinkling the ground with water"). She then asked Ken, "Do you think the seed will come up?" After his response, she turned to the end of the book and asked, "What happened?" She then turned back to the beginning of the story saying, "Now I'd like you to read the story about the little boy and his carrot seed to me."

Eileen's Running Record of Ken's Reading

While he read, Eileen observed his reading and made notes using a running record format described on page 61. Eileen's running record is shown on the right half of the page in Figure 3.3, and we've included the text Ken read on the left, although this would not ordinarily be part of the record. In other words, as described previously, the running record consists of check marks (✔) for correctly read words, mispronounced words written above printed words, "SC" for corrections, "P" for pauses, and "R" plus a line and arrow for reread portions of the story. Eileen also made a tape recording so she would be able to share and discuss Ken's reading with his parents.

Eileen noted that Ken pointed to each word as he read. Only twice, once while

(Text)

A little boy planted a carrot seed.

His mother said, "I'm afraid it
    won't come up."

His father said, "I'm afraid it
    won't come up."

And his big brother said, "It won't
    come up."

Every day the little boy pulled up
    the weeds around

the seed and sprinkled the ground
    with water.

But nothing came up.

And nothing came up.

Everyone kept saying it wouldn't
    come up.

But he still pulled up the weeds
    around it every day

and sprinkled the ground with
    water.

And then one day,

a carrot came up.

Just as the little boy had known it
    would.

FIGURE 3.3   Text from *The Carrot Seed* and the running record of Ken's oral
reading

SOURCE: Text only from *The Carrot Seed* by Ruth Krauss, illustrated by Crockett Johnson. Text
copyright © 1945 by Ruth Krauss. Illustrations © 1945 by Crockett Johnson. Reprinted by
permission of Harper & Row Publishers, Inc.

reading the fourth sentence and then again in the final sentence, did he lose the
match between his spoken word and the printed word to which he was pointing.
She also noted that this reading seemed to be a valid one. That is, Ken seemed to
"be having a good day" and his reading was typical of his daily reading. These
observations made by Eileen add to the knowledge that she has about his reading.

Eileen's Analysis of Ken's Running Record

Once an oral reading sample has been obtained, only through analysis and
reflection will we gain insight into the ways Ken's understanding of print is
developing. It is important to reflect on how the prereading preparation may have
influenced his reading. The book overview seemed to prepare him for some new
words that would have been unfamiliar to him such as "planted," "carrot," "seed,"

and "afraid," and it seemed to provide him with a sense of the story. In general, Ken's oral reading indicates that he has learned a lot about print.

PAUSE AND REFLECT.   Think about Ken's responses. One useful way to gain insight into his reading is for you to read aloud the story in the way he read it. That is, using the running record, reconstruct his reading. What are three things that you notice about his reading?

There is no simple, linear way to undertake an analysis, although the questions discussed in the prior section offer guidance. For running records, you may not choose to use the systematic form shown in Figure 3.2. Instead, you may prefer to follow the more informal procedures used by Eileen. Because of the brevity of most running records, the formal approach may be unnecessary. Even so, you will address the same basic questions.

One question that you need to consider is whether the story is too difficult. Was this story too difficult for Ken? He was able to read many of the words in the story correctly (90 of 101 words for 90 percent accuracy if one counts self-corrections as correct). What sense do we make of this? Is this story too hard for him? As we learned earlier, an accuracy level between 90 percent and 94 percent is usually considered to be in the borderline range for children. But we believe, in the early stages of reading, that such standards may be too stringent. It may be more useful to consider the sense-making strategies that a child is using and his growing knowledge of sight words and word elements. From this perspective, we would consider this story to be appropriate for Ken, particularly with instructional support and rereading.

In understanding a child's reading strategies, it is particularly useful to examine pauses and repetitions. We learn that Ken pauses while he is thinking of some unfamiliar words. For example, he paused before correctly identifying "planted" and "sprinkled." He also paused before the sight word "And," which he first misidentified as "Said," and then correctly identified as "And." He also uses repetitions (rereading a portion of a sentence) sometimes to reinforce the meaning of a sentence (sentences 1, 8, and 10), sometimes to fill in omitted words ("up" and "around" of sentence 5), and perhaps to aid subsequent word identification ("sprinkled" in sentence 5). These strategies indicate that he is actively making sense of text. His omissions (sentences 8 and 10) are not corrected when they make sense, but are when they do not make sense (sentence 5). If you read sentences 8 and 10 aloud as they were read by Ken, you will see that they make sense.

At the same time that we are pleased with Ken's awareness that reading should make sense, we need to be concerned about the development of his sight vocabulary. Sometimes it is useful to examine the words omitted and miscued by listing them. In the lists that follow, we include words that were self-corrected (SC) as well as those that were not.

Omitted Words	*Miscued Words*	
	Printed Word	*Oral Response*
around (SC)	His	The (2)
kept	said	did (SC)
still	And	Said (SC)
just	big	brother (SC)
as	every	each
had	wouldn't	won't
	came	come
	known	knew

This form of listing makes it easier to see the types of words that Ken is choosing to omit. All are basic sight words, and most are words that Eileen thought were in his sight vocabulary. Thus, she will explore whether he actually knows these words in isolated form; he may have had difficulty with them in context because of the other problems he was trying to solve.

Ken's reading miscues indicate several areas of stength. First, he was able to correct three of the nine substitutions. This suggests that the words may well be known by him. Second, his difficulties (as indicated by substitutions as well as omissions) tend to occur at the beginnings of sentences where there is less available context. This type of error again suggests his reliance on meaning as part of his reading strategy.

The nature of his substitutions suggests his awareness of graphic cues. Seven of the nine substitutions show a match at the beginning of the word in initial letter (2), at the end (2), or both (3). Only the repeated substitution of "The" for "His" shows little correspondence in terms of print; but the miscue does make sense in terms of sentence context. Thus, we see that Ken is aware of letter cues and makes use of this knowledge. Most of his miscues not only match the print in some way, but also make sense in context. Eileen may have questions about the nature of his knowledge of print. Is he making use of a visual match or has he learned letter–sound associations and using these as a cuing system?

Eileen's Further Exploration of Ken's Reading

Sight Words. Eileen explored Ken's knowledge of sight words in two ways. First, she wanted to see whether he knew the words he miscued when he read *The Carrot Seed*. She wrote the words on a paper and had him read them aloud. As she had thought, he had no difficulty recognizing each of the words to which she pointed.

In order to check his sight word development more systematically, she had him respond to a subset of the list of "basic" sight words developed by Dolch (1936). If she had been using a basal reading program with Ken, she might have tested him on the set of words that tended to recur in the basal stories. She wanted to see how he might respond to the reading selections he would encounter in second grade; thus, she decided that the Dolch list would provide some evidence of his knowledge in this area. The sight word list (shown in Appendix A) and other similar lists (Harris & Jacobson, 1982) include words that frequently occur in early reading materials. Because they account for about 70 percent of running text, they are an important set of words for children to learn. These words should be written on cards or in list form and presented one at a time.

Eileen had written the Dolch words on cards. When she presented them to Ken, she observed whether he was able to recognize them immediately or after a delay. She found that he was able to recognize about half the words immediately. This is appropriate for children nearing the end of first grade. He did not, however, seem to have any strategies for identifying those he did not know by sight. In interpreting the results, she considered whether Ken had had the opportunity to learn the words he did not know. There were a few that he had encountered earlier in the year that he no longer knew, but generally he was able to recognize most words that he had previously read and reread in stories.

Word Elements. Eileen wanted to know more about Ken's knowledge of word elements. She knew from the running record that his substitutions tended to match in the beginning and final consonants. She had learned from the sight word task that he was not able to identify unknown words when they were printed in isolation. Thus, she further explored his knowledge in two ways. The first involved additional exploration of the sight words he did not know. The exploration of unknown words takes the form of assisting students in their attempts to pronounce the words correctly. When children have difficulty, the task is simplified by having them respond to only part of the word, first the initial consonant or consonant blend and then the word ending.

Eileen listed four words for Ken to identify and wrote them (*his, kept, still,* and *just*) on a piece of paper. She then had him look at *his* and asked him if he knew it. He said no. She then covered all but the initial consonant (*h*). He was able to give the sound corresponding to *h*. She then covered the initial consonant and asked him to pronounce the portion remaining. He did this successfully. She then asked him if he knew the word. He said he couldn't get it. She next said the consonant sound followed by the word ending. On the other three words, he identified *k* and *j* and the word ending *ill*, but had difficulty with the word elements that included consonant blends. She tentatively concluded that Ken might profit from instructional support in writing and recognizing consonant blends and from instruction in blending word parts.

The second approach Eileen used to gain information about Ken's knowledge of word elements involved a spelling task in which she had him write 10 words. His performance on this task is described in Chapter 7. The knowledge he displayed was consistent with that revealed when Eileen asked him to respond to word parts. She confirmed that Ken has good command of consonants in the beginnings and endings of words but that he is not yet able to blend consonants and vowels.

Eileen's Plans for Providing Instructional Support
The results from these analyses show that Ken is developing his sight vocabulary, but that he sometimes does not recognize words he knows when they appear in context. He has fairly good knowledge of initial and final consonants, but is not yet

able to undertake more systematic forms of decoding. The nature of his corrections and repetitions shows that he views reading as a meaning-making process.

Eileen believes that he would benefit from the rereading of familiar stories to consolidate his sight vocabulary. She also believes he would profit from instruction that focuses on the representation of consonant blends in his writing and the blending of word parts. In general, she believes that his classroom program is appropriate, but she will provide more specialized support in writing and blending word elements, either individually or as part of class instruction.

Because Ken entered first grade with less reading and writing background than most of the other children in the class, special tutorial support during the summer may be appropriate. After sharing samples of Ken's work with his parents, Eileen will discuss this possibility with them.

The running record procedure Eileen used with Ken is particularly valuable for children during their first year of reading. Thereafter, we prefer to make a record of the oral reading on a duplicate copy of the text being read: Older readers typically read longer segments, and it is easier to compare their responses with the text when the record is marked directly on the text. In the following section where we consider the case of Eva, the procedures for oral reading analysis are described in detail.

PAUSE AND REFLECT.   Think over what you have learned about Ken. What special instructional support do you believe a tutor should offer? List two things you would want a tutor to do. Then, as you read the description of instructional strategies in the final section of this chapter, identify other approaches that may be useful with Ken.

CASE 3.2: EVA—ORAL READING ANALYSIS

As we discussed earlier, Martha was concerned about Eva's lack of interest in classwork and homework. She suspected that Eva might be having difficulty with reading and wanted to know how she could help her. Martha decided to analyze Eva's oral reading. Eva was 10 years, 5 months old at the time and in the second month of fifth grade. She had changed schools four times in the previous four years and there was little in her record to help Martha understand her achievement problems. It should be noted that although Eva is fluent in English, Spanish is sometimes spoken in her home.

Martha's Record of Eva's Oral Reading

Martha selected a story from the third-grade reader that was being read by her group of students who were experiencing some difficulty with reading and writing. Eva met regularly with this group. The story selected was "The Picnic Mystery." Although Eva read the entire story, only a representative portion is analyzed here. Eva was told that the story was about a boy and his uncle who happened upon a picnic. Martha asked her to read the story to see whether she was able to figure out what happened to the people. The record of Eva's oral reading, which was also tape-recorded, is shown in Figure 3.4.

PAUSE AND REFLECT.   Think about Eva's oral reading. What strategies does she have for making sense of text? On what evidence are you basing your ideas? How would you characterize her knowledge of print? Does she possess a well-developed sight vocabulary? What does she know about word elements? Would you characterize her reading as fluent?

Martha's Analysis of Eva's Oral Reading

Immediately following the oral reading, Martha considered whether she could trust its results. Was Eva comfortable? Was she involved? Was the reading typical for her? Martha felt that Eva had been comfortable during the reading and that this oral reading sample was representative of her reading. Some of her substitutions, however, should not be counted as substitutions since they reflect her dialect. She

FIGURE 3.4   Record of oral reading: Eva

SOURCE: Passage from *Discovering Treasure*, pp. 46–50, in *The New Open Highways*, published by Scott, Foresman, 1973. Story entitled "The Abandoned Picnic," from *The Second Baffle Book* by Lassiter Wren and Randle McKay. Copyright 1929 by Doubleday & Company, Inc. Copyright 1929 by Clues, Inc. Reprinted by permission of Doubleday & Company, Inc.

The Picnic Mystery

Lee's uncle was a famous detective. During the ride Lee asked him dozens of questions about his work. At last the detective laughed, "You ask more questions than I do during a police case,"

he said. "Let's stop and rest for a while."

He drove until he came to a group of shade trees in a field. As he parked the car, he saw something strange.

Spread under one of the trees was a white paper tablecloth. Picnic food was set out on the cloth. But there was no one in sight.

"Where is everyone?" asked Lee. "I don't see a place where anyone could hide. Why would

people go off and leave their picnic?"

Dialect-based and corrected miscues were not counted.

tends to drop the final "s" during conversation, and here has mispronounced *Lee's* as *Lee*. This was therefore not counted as a miscue.

The numbers at the right of each line in Figure 3.4 indicate the number of miscues per line. Note that miscues that are subsequently corrected are not counted as errors, even though they may be indications of difficulty. That they were subsequently corrected is noted by a © on the oral reading analysis sheet, and these corrections are considered a sign of strength.

Difficulty. With respect to difficulty, Eva committed 9 miscues while reading this portion of the story. The length of the selection is 115 words. If we divide 9 by 115 (and multiply by 100), we find the percentage of miscues, which is 8 percent. Accordingly, she read 92 percent of the passage correctly. When we compare this level of accuracy with the criteria levels in Table 3.2 we find that it falls below an acceptable instructional level, in the borderline range. Martha can now complete section A of Eva's oral reading analysis form (the section pertaining to passage difficulty), as shown in Figure 3.5.

Word Learning. The next step is for Martha to record the miscues in response to sight words in the first two columns of section B of the form. As shown in Figure 3.5, three of the miscues are in response to high-frequency words. (The Dolch Basic Sight Vocabulary, contained in Appendix A, may be used as an aid in identifying sight words.) Eva had corrected all three miscues, apparently on the basis of subsequent contextual information. The fact that they were corrected is indicated by a © in the second column under B.

Although Eva read most of the sight words in the passage correctly, the three errors represent about 2 percent of the total passage (3/115). Because the sight word errors are few in number and because they were corrected spontaneously during contextual reading, Martha concludes that Eva has no major problem in this area. However, that such errors were made at all suggests that Eva has not consolidated her sight vocabulary.

Word Identification. The next step is for Martha to record in section C miscues Eva made in response to unfamiliar content words. She begins with miscues first in response to single-syllable then to multisyllable printed words. Errors of omission are listed following the substitution errors, as shown in Figure 3.5. In contrast to sight word recognition, Eva makes no successful corrections of unfamiliar context words.

Three of the seven miscues deviate from the printed word in more than one element and involve substitution of multisyllable for single-syllable words. The next two miscues, which show a close correspondence, are also in response to single-syllable words. Finally, Eva omits rather than attempts two words that are two syllables in length. This pattern of response suggests that Eva has serious difficulty in word identification.

Although almost all of Eva's miscues show an initial consonant match, she erred on four of five initial consonant blends and digraphs. Vowels in miscued words are mispronounced more often than not, and she seems to have no knowledge of

ORAL READING ANALYSIS

Name *Eva. W.* Grade *5* Date *April*

Book/Page *Discovering Treasure* Level *gr. 3*

A. Difficulty

10 / *115*   *91* % Correct

Level: Independent   Instructional
    (Borderline)   Frustration

B. Word Learning: Sight Word Errors

Printed Word	Oral Response	Further Exploration
where	when Ⓒ	✓
everyone	anyone Ⓒ	✓
would	was Ⓒ	✓

Evaluation

Sight word errors are few in number and were corrected during contextual reading. Thus, no major problem exists. However, Eva needs to consolidate her sight word knowledge.

C. Word Identification: Content Word Errors

Printed Word	Oral Response	Further Exploration
shade	several	should
field	forest	fill
strange	sparkling	NR*
case	care	care
group	grape	grape
spread	setting	NR
white	wide	wide
famous	[omitted]	NR
dozens	[omitted]	NR

Evaluation

On one syllable words, she uses initial consonants – but word middles and endings do not always correspond. Her knowledge of initial consonants is limited. On a probe of word elements, she produced a word rather than a sound in response to initial consonants. She seems to recognize words on the basis of visual cues and context. She does not attempt unknown multisyllabic words.

* NR = no response

D. Integration–Fluency

Integration: Overreliance on prior context; most miscues violate author meaning. Effective use of repetitions and pauses to correct errors.

Fluency: Rate *115* / *1.8* = *64* wpm Evaluation Slow even for a second grader.

Phrasing Rapid reading interspersed with long pauses for word recognition.

FIGURE 3.5 Analysis of oral reading responses: Eva

vowel digraphs and markers. Affixed words were, however, an area of strength; Eva correctly pronounced *laughed*, *during*, *asked*, and *parked*. Overall, the evidence suggests that Eva has little skill in word identification. This possibility will be explored further.

Integration and Fluency. Eva does not integrate well, relying heavily on context in identifying unknown words. With few exceptions, her substitutions in response to content words are plausible with respect to prior sentence context, but they show low correspondence with print. Although Eva uses repetition effectively to correct sight word errors, she is unable to correct her content word miscues.

Her reading is not fluent, as it is characterized by many pauses before unfamiliar words. She read this portion of the story in 108 seconds. By dividing the number of seconds by 60, Martha gets a time of 1.8 minutes, as shown in Figure 3.5. By then dividing the number of words in the passage—namely, 115—by 1.8, Martha determines Eva's reading rate: 64 words per minute.

This rate is extremely slow; it is below even the average range for second graders shown in Table 3.1. Martha expects, however, that Eva's rate would be faster on easier materials that posed fewer word identification problems for her. Because word identification difficulties are seriously interfering with her reading fluency, Martha will not make further exploration of this aspect of Eva's reading at this time. Rather, further exploration will focus on the development of her sight vocabulary and her word identification skills.

Martha's Further Exploration of Eva's Reading

Sight Words. Eva's response to the three sight words that she missed during contextual reading was rapid. Further, she pronounced all of them correctly (indicated by a check in the third column of B).

The results from the exploration suggest that Eva knows most basic sight words, even if she at times confuses certain similar words. These results support the hypothesis that Eva's main problem in word learning is not in knowing the words but rather in being able to recognize them quickly when under the pressure of difficult contextual reading. Eva needs to consolidate her existing set of sight words through contextual reading of easy materials as summarized under Evaluation in B.

Word Identification. Further exploration focused on Eva's ability to deal with unfamiliar content words. As shown in Figure 3.5, when words that were miscued during contextual reading were presented in isolation, Eva was still unable to recognize them.

During the further exploration that followed, Martha first asked Eva to respond to initial consonants, in order to confirm their apparent effectiveness as a cue system. Surprisingly, Eva experienced extreme difficulty producing the sounds that correspond to the initial consonant letters identified. This finding suggests that she uses initial consonants as effective visual cues to search for known words in her memory but not as elements that cue an appropriate initial sound.

Because of Eva's extreme difficulty with initial consonants, Martha undertook further exploration at this time to assess her knowledge of other letter–sound associations. That will come later, once initial consonants become an explicit part of her knowledge about print. Further exploration did reveal that with support, Eva is able to segment off the initial phoneme of a known word. This is probably the point from which instruction should begin.

Assessment of Eva's knowledge of the structural characteristics of words revealed that she is familiar with most common word endings (e.g., *-ing, -ed, -er, -est*). She has no knowledge about how to segment multisyllabic words into pronounceable units. However, when some of the words were divided for her, she was able to pronounce a few syllables correctly because they resembled known words. This facility suggests that Eva may be able to use her relatively well-developed sight vocabulary to help her identify syllables through an analogizing procedure.

Martha's Plans for Providing Instructional Support

The instruction you develop must follow from the understanding you gain through ongoing diagnosis. In Eva's case, Martha must determine whether she can profit from the instruction appropriate for Martha's low group members and/or whether Eva should receive individualized instruction. Because Eva lacks knowledge in the area of word identification, instruction must be designed to develop her underlying knowledge of word elements. Martha's initial plan (to be modified with new evidence) was as follows:

Reading Materials. Eva should be reading from materials at two levels of difficulty. First, in order for her to consolidate her sight vocabulary, material should be at a level that poses few word identification problems for her. Whether second-grade-level materials would be appropriate for this purpose needs to be established. Second, Martha should experiment with instructional support prior to and during the reading of basal stories to determine whether the current (third-grade) materials can be used. It is important to keep Eva involved in ongoing class activities if at all possible. However, if the third-grade basal materials are still too difficult with instructional support, Martha will need to establish an individual reading program for Eva with somewhat easier materials.

Sight Words. Eva's sight vocabulary is quite well developed, as indicated by the large number of sight words she recognized during contextual reading and her ability to pronounce all miscued sight words correctly when they were presented in isolation. However, the fact that she miscued on sight words during contextual reading means that she has not yet learned them to the level of immediate and automatic recognition. In order to consolidate her sight vocabulary, Eva should be encouraged to read and reread easy, highly interesting materials. Martha should keep charts to let Eva see her reading progress.

Word Identification. Martha would like to help Eva develop strategies for independent word identification. Building on Eva's strengths, she will help her to become more aware of her implicit knowledge of sounds at the beginnings of words (initial consonant associations). She will do this through writing and spelling activities. As Eva writes words, Martha will help her to pronounce each word slowly and to think how the initial sound might be represented.

Second, she will introduce a method for identifying multisyllabic words. Again building on Eva's strength with sight words, Martha will help her chunk words into syllabic units and to analogize from known words to identify the syllables of unknown words.

Teaching syllabication and syllable pronunciation can easily be incorporated into small-group reading instruction. After introducing a new story but before reading it, Martha should present any unfamiliar content words. Using some of these words, Martha can conduct the following two-part exercise. She writes the words on the board, one at a time. After a word is written, students should speculate how it might be divided into "chunks" that can be pronounced. A line should be drawn after each chunk and Martha should proceed to the right until the word has been completely divided. Even when the final product does not conform exactly to what is specified by rules for syllabication, Martha should proceed with the lesson. If students wish to revise their prior decisions, they should be allowed to do so.

In the second part of this exercise, students learn analogizing. After examining the first chunk, students are asked if it looks like any word they know. Martha should then write the word the students suggest above the syllable to see if they can use it to identify the syllable. If they are unable to think of a word, Martha should supply one or provide the phonogram with which the syllable ends as an alternative. The students should then use a consonant substitution (word family) approach to identify the syllable. Correct and incorrect attempts should be presented to the group for their evaluation.

You can use this procedure for three, four or more of the multisyllabic words appearing in the story, as long as the attention of the group is sustained. You should simply pronounce other unfamiliar words as part of a discussion of the meaning of all unfamiliar words and how they pertain to the theme of the story.

Integration. Eva's overreliance on contextual information indicates that integration is a problem for her. Her difficulty reflects the lack of a proper balance between the use of contextual information and attention to graphic information. Therefore, her integration should be reexamined after she develops greater proficiency with word identification. Her learning more about print should lead automatically to a more balanced use of cues from print and context.

Fluency. As part of her program, it is important for Eva to experience "problem-free" reading, that is, reading selections that pose few word identification problems for her. This easy reading and rereading will help to consolidate her sight vocabulary and give her the opportunity to focus on meaning free from word identification distractions. It is on material at this level that Martha may wish to incorporate some of the instructional approaches designed to promote integration and fluency that are described in the following section.

INSTRUCTION TO ENHANCE FACILITY WITH PRINT

Some children develop knowledge of print and reading fluency simply by reading many stories and informational selections. Others need more direct forms of instruction to help them solve problems related to print. In this section of the chapter, we review several approaches that you may use to help children learn sight words. We also describe instructional support designed to help students develop their knowledge of word elements. The heart of your instruction will focus, however, on helping students to develop an integrated set of reading strategies and fluency through contextual reading. Thus, we also describe instruction that you may use to promote integration and fluency.

Instruction to Develop Knowledge of Sight Words

It is not our intention in this section to describe procedures that are introduced in most reading methods courses. We will, however, describe supplementary procedures that you can use with your reading groups to reinforce learning. You should draw new sight words to be taught to the student from contextual materials. Instruction should never involve only words in isolation. Contextual reading should be a part of every instructional session so that it reinforces the learning of sight words. The number of new sight words you introduce each day should depend on the students' mastery. For example, if you introduce five new words but students master only two, reduce the number to two or three at the next session.

You can adjust the degree of instructional reinforcement to what students need for retention. Word-sort activities, writing, and spelling can all be used to reinforce students' initial learning of sight words.

Word Banks. The use of word banks is an outgrowth of the language experience approach in which various reinforcement activities help students learn and remember words (Stauffer, 1970). The **word bank** consists of words a student is learning through contextual reading (basal materials or language experience materials) and other words of interest. When a new word is encountered or identified, it is printed on a 3 × 5 card for each student. Since some beginning readers have limited ability to write evenly and accurately, it is sometimes better for you to print the words in a form similar to print in books. The student can use the back of the card to draw a picture or write a sentence that will cue him or her to the identity of the word. As students learn new words, the cards accumulate. Give students a box and rubber bands to help them keep and organize their word cards.

The cards may be used for a variety of reinforcement activities. Children may review them working individually or in pairs. They may use them to form sentences as a small-group or individual activity.

Word Sorts. One of the most productive activities involves sorting the words into various classes on the basis of specified features (see Gillet & Temple, 1982, for a more detailed description of procedures to be followed during **word sorts**). During small-group instruction you may ask children to go through their cards to find words that have a certain characteristic. For example, ask them to select words that begin or end like the word *balloon*, that name an animal, or that are three syllables in length. Alternatively, invite students to identify words that conform to a criterion of their choosing. Once they have identified and displayed a group of four to six words to their classmates, they can see whether the other students can determine the characteristic the selected words share.

Writing and Spelling.   Beginning readers who have difficulty learning words are often helped to remember them by being encouraged to spell and write words you introduce in their reading materials. These activities seem to prompt children to scrutinize words carefully, particularly the medial portions, and to become more aware of the words' phonemic correlates. Further, once they have learned to write basic sight words, students often draw on these high-frequency words during their other writing activities. Thus, writing is made easier and basic sight words are reinforced.

Contextual Reading Practice.   One of the best ways to consolidate sight vocabulary is through extensive contextual reading. Many basal programs are designed to provide practice on words that have been introduced by including them in subsequent stories. However, such practice may be insufficient for students who have great difficulty remembering words. Thus, it is important for you to devise ways to give students more practice on the words they are learning. Easy-to-read books such as the "Frog and Toad" series by Arnold Lobel are appropriate. Also, some basal series provide supplementary materials for this purpose. Alternatively, students may reread stories they have previously read. For example, once a book is completed, you may ask students to identify their favorite stories from the book and then let them take turns reading the stories. You may pose a new question about a previously read story and have children read the story silently to find the answer. Sometimes a prior edition of a basal series provides a different set of stories that include many of the words introduced in the newer edition. These texts may be useful as supplementary reading for students having difficulty learning words.

One reason teachers fail to provide supplementary reading is that students in the slowest paced group do not read very fast at best. To take time for more contextual practice would seem to place an additional burden on these already slow readers. However, they cannot increase their reading skill without practice. Thus, in order to provide additional practice, you may have to plan extra small-group instructional time. For example, you may want to meet with children progressing most slowly twice daily (morning and afternoon) rather than once a day.

Instruction to Develop Knowledge of Word Elements

In considering instruction in the area of word identification, you may need to distinguish between students who have difficulty identifying single-syllable words and those who have difficulty mainly with words of two or more syllables. The first group of students need to become aware of letter–sound associations and/or how to apply such knowledge when identifying single-syllable words. The second group needs to learn how to divide words into pronounceable "chunks" so as to be able to identify these units with the knowledge they possess.

Single-Syllable Words.   Some students have acquired extensive knowledge of word elements (consonants, consonant blends, vowels, vowel markers, word endings) but fail to apply this knowledge when identifying unknown words, particularly during contextual reading. Other students lack basic knowledge of word elements and must be taught these (Stahl, 1992).

Word Elements.   In teaching phonic associations, you should examine the instructional materials used in the class to determine the sequence in which the word elements unknown by the student are introduced. For example, some programs introduce long vowels before short, others short before long. Learning to hear the phonemes (sounds) in a word is the first step in learning phonics associations (Griffith & Olson, 1992; Yopp, 1992). Some students may need to develop phoneme awareness by listening to words of two or three phonemes to identify the number of different sounds they hear. During this process, children should be encouraged to say the words in segmented fashion, as they do when attempting to spell the word. Sometimes drawing a series of connected boxes corresponding to the number of phonemes in a word helps children to hear the sounds (Elkonin, 1963). You can write the letters corresponding to phonemes as the children say them and then supply any unknown elements.

Each phonics association to be taught should be introduced through a series of words in which the phoneme occurs in initial position. If students have difficulty remembering the phoneme, you can introduce a key word (which contains the phoneme at the beginning) in printed form. Whenever students encounter words beginning with the newly learned phonics association, they should be encouraged to pronounce that portion of the word. This activity teaches them that phonics associations provide valuable cues for word identification. Finally, students should be encouraged to use phonics knowledge in conjunction with contextual information during contextual reading.

In teaching phonics associations, it may be useful to introduce the concept of *markers* (see Venezky, 1970, for discussion of this concept). In certain contexts, vowel letters generally and some consonant letters as well "mark" the pronunciation of another letter in that context (e.g., the *e* or *i* following a *c* marks the pronunciation of *c* as /s/). However, the concept of markers should not be taught as a rule but rather by presenting examples from which students can infer the generalization. You should begin with the final *e* concept (*can–cane, mat–mate, tap–tape*) and then move to vowel combinations (*pad–paid, ran–rain, bat–bait, man–main*). Though most students pick up this concept rather easily, they sometimes have problems applying it during contextual reading.

Some students who have acquired a large sight vocabulary encounter difficulty reading multisyllabic words in the intermediate grades because of their limited knowledge of word elements. Some of them experience extreme difficulty learning phonics associations. Often, however, they can learn to pronounce syllables using an alternative strategy.

Once words are divided into syllables, these students need instruction in analogizing in order to see how known words and word parts can be used to identify unknown syllables. Students are encouraged to think of a word that ends the same as the first syllable of the unknown multisyllabic word and then to use a consonant-substitution method to identify the syllable. For example, in identifying the word *barter*, students are first encouraged to split the word into two units *(bar–ter)*. Then you can ask them to think of a word that ends the same as *bar*, such as *car*. If the students have difficulty thinking of an appropriate word, you should supply one. Finally, the cue word is written on top of the first syllable and students are encouraged to identify the syllable by substituting initial consonants. The procedure continues for the remaining syllable. To begin, only multisyllabic words with obvious sight word analogies should be selected. Once the procedure is mastered, words without obvious analogies should be attempted under your guidance. Often the step of dividing multisyllabic words into units is sufficient to permit their identification.

For students who have considerable difficulty thinking of appropriate cue words, the systematic training procedure described by Cunningham (1978; see also 1975–76, 1979) may be effective. In this approach, students are made aware that they are familiar with a large number of sight words that can be used to identify unknown words. In the first step, ask students to write the words *he*, *went*, *her*, *can*, and *car* on index cards. Then ask them to select two of the cards that match parts of such unknown words as *banter*, *ferment*, *meter*, *barber*, *percent*, and *garment*. Add additional sight words during the second and third steps and provide further matching practice. In the fourth step, encourage students to use "the whole store of words in their heads as words to match to unfamiliar [two-syllable] words" (pp. 610–611). In the fifth and final step, apply the procedures to words of three or more syllables.

Application and Blending.   Many students with knowledge of word elements fail to attempt blending because they have developed a habit of hastily guessing at words, particularly those in context, on the basis of partial information. They need to be taught a new procedure for dealing with unknown single-syllable words. This procedure consists of five steps:

1. Pause (instead of guess).
2. Look at the initial part of the word and pronounce it.
3. Look at the remainder of the word and pronounce it.
4. Blend the word parts together into a word.
5. Check to see if the word makes sense in context.

After applying this procedure slowly and systematically, students will become able to scan words more rapidly and pronounce them accurately using their print knowledge.

Some students, however, have difficulty with the fourth step of the procedure: blending word elements together. To teach blending skill, you can use the following procedures, either with individual students or with groups. Instruction should begin with the blending of syllables (*but–ter, wag–on, ti–ger*). If this is difficult for the students, compound words such as *football, doghouse,* and *cowboy* should be presented along with pictures corresponding to the component words. The students should identify the picture that corresponds to the "word-syllable" being pronounced. When students can blend compound words, they can attempt other two-syllable words. Next, phoneme blending should be developed. First a vowel unit should be blended into a final consonant (*ca–t, bo–x, de–sk*), then a consonant into an ending (*f–oot, h–and, p–en*), and finally, three units should be blended (*r–a–t, f–a–ce, p–a–ge*). Many students are helped by seeing the sequence of letters while they hear you pronounce the sounds and by imitating the way you separate and blend sounds within words. Blending should be practiced for short periods every day for several weeks.

Multisyllabic Words.   Students who experience difficulty mainly with longer words and relatively little difficulty with single-syllable words need to be taught how to "chunk" or divide multisyllable words into pronounceable units. To learn the concept of syllable, students should listen to you pronounce two-, three-, and even four-syllable words and tap the number of syllables they hear. Next, they should examine the syllables of two-syllable words that are regular in pattern (*butter, rabbit, window, pencil, apron, table, open,* and *paper)* to see whether they can figure out what constitutes a syllable (that it contains at least one vowel) and determine typical syllable patterns.

You can advise students to pronounce vowels in multisyllabic words as they would in one-syllable words and then to blend the syllables into a word that makes sense. The concept of an "open" syllable (e.g., *be*) suggesting a long vowel pronunciation and a "closed" syllable (e.g., *bet*) indicating a short vowel pronunciation is difficult for some students to learn. The most effective procedure for developing the concept involves word comparisons or word sorts (for further discussion, see Henderson, 1985). To begin, select two-syllable words familiar to the students. The first set should include words such as *hopped* and *hoped, dinner* and *diner.* The students should focus on the first syllable, and you can guide them to see that the nature of the syllable (open or closed) influences vowel pronunciation. Then words within the same initial vowel can be compared: *hopped, potter, hoped, hotel, cotton.* Students should be able to give a reason for sorting certain words together. Finally, the words compared or sorted can include several different vowels: *butter, paper, rabbit, window, favor.*

Some students have extreme difficulty with syllable pronunciation because syllables are *nonsense.* One way to help students deal with this problem is to use a word family approach: Students should identify several known words first, then related syllables (*bat, cat–lat, tat*), next a real word followed by a syllable (*bed–med, rod–fod, cab–pab*), and finally a list of nonsense syllables.

Once students understand how to divide longer words into syllables and to identify the syllables, it is important that you provide them with regular practice doing this as part of their reading instruction. When you assign stories or expository selections, you should identify approximately three to five multisyllabic words that may pose a problem for the students and write these words on the blackboard. You should ask the students how the first word can be divided into syllables. Sometimes there will be disagreement among group members. Students should then be encouraged to pronounce the syllables, identify the word, and draw a conclusion about the best way to divide the word. Once the words are identified, you should check to see that the meanings are familiar to all students in the group. The concepts underlying any unfamiliar words should be discussed using procedures described in Chapter 4.

Instruction to Promote Integration

Students frequently encounter words that they do not know. Those who have not developed balanced strategies for word identification need to be shown how using information from a variety of sources leads to more efficient and effective word identification.

Cloze Tasks.   If few of a student's oral reading miscues are contextually appropriate, you should explore further, through tasks such as the **cloze test,** to determine whether the student is able to use context to anticipate words (see, e.g., Blachowicz, 1977; Bortnick & Lopardo, 1973). In a modified cloze approach, words that students were unable to pronounce during contextual oral reading are identified and students are instructed to read the sentences in which the words occurred, saying "blank" for the unknown words. After they have read the sentence with the "blank," they are encouraged to think of words that might make sense in the blank. If they are able to produce words that are semantically acceptable within the sentence, we conclude that they are able to make use of context for word identification. It should be noted, however, that some sentence contexts provide little relevant information to aid word identification. Such sentences should not be used for this activity.

Application.   If students are able to complete a cloze blank correctly but show little use of contextual information during oral reading, we can conclude that the problem is one of application. The students know how to use contextual information but have developed a reading strategy that usually does not draw on context as a source of information for anticipating responses and for correction. This type of strategy development is not unusual for some students who have been instructed with a synthetic phonics approach. Students who are able to complete cloze blanks, once alerted to context as a source of information and encouraged to use it, usually learn quite easily to use contextual information during passage reading.

Finally, during activities when students read aloud, it is appropriate for you to ask students who pronounce difficult words correctly how they identified the word. It is also appropriate after cloze procedures have been introduced to ask students whether a response "makes sense." Once students have received instruction focusing on the division of words into syllables and syllable identification, you may ask them to identify the first syllable of an unknown word and then attempt to identify the word on the basis of context and the first syllable.

Instruction to Develop Fluency

Reading Practice. Contextual reading practice is the most effective means for developing fluency (Morrow & Weinstein, 1986). Many disabled readers fail to achieve fluency because they are continually asked to read materials that are too difficult. They have little opportunity to experience the pleasure of problem-free reading and to develop reading fluency (Allington, 1983). Thus, if they are to improve fluency through practice, they *must* have material that is easy for them to read. It should pose almost no word identification problems and no comprehension problems.

Having students reread selections can often eliminate many problems posed by a selection. After a first reading, the student is familiar with the context and can recognize most difficult words. Thus, he or she is more able to focus directly on meaning and to read at a faster rate. The method of repeated readings can also be used more formally (Chomsky, 1976; Lopardo & Sadow, 1982; Nelson & Morris, 1988; Samuels, 1979). First you identify a segment to be read orally and have the student read it aloud, noting the errors and the reading speed. The student then rereads the same selection and you compare the number of errors and reading speed for the second reading with those of the first. The procedure can be continued one or two more times.

Typically, reluctant readers need tangible forms of reinforcement to encourage them to practice reading. Charts showing the number of pages read per day or week within a certain period of time (e.g., 15 to 30 minutes) provide a tangible record allowing students to see the amount they have read and any increase in the number of pages read within the time period (reading rate). Similarly, records of repeated reading can be used to show student improvement in reading accuracy and speed over a period of weeks.

Modeling Fluent Reading. It is sometimes useful for either you or an older student who is a proficient reader to read to a student to demonstrate the nature of fluent reading. One method effective for disfluent readers is to *model phrase reading* (Walker, 1988). First you would tape the student reading a short selection that is of appropriate difficulty (instructional level). Then you read a sentence with brief pauses between phrases of the sentence. The student reads the same sentence with similar phrasing. Once the student demonstrates adequate phrasing, you read more than one sentence, with the student repeating what you have read. Finally, the student reads the remainder of the selection independently or along with you. You then tape the student reading the entire selection and compare the phrasing and general fluency on the final reading with that of the first reading.

An alternative method consists of having a student read with a fluent reader or slightly after the proficient reader. The model reads slightly ahead and somewhat louder than the student, finger-pointing to the line of print as it is read. Once the student reads fluently, the model can relinquish control to the student by reading more softly and somewhat behind the student. In general, the purpose of providing a model of fluent reading is to show clearly the nature of fluent reading and to get the student to compare his or her earlier reading with reading that is fluent.

Reading Rate Improvement.   Teachers are well aware of differences in reading speeds among their students. Although little emphasis has been placed on increasing the reading rates of students, it is appropriate to encourage them to improve their rates once they have developed a sight vocabulary, word identification strategies, and reading fluency. To read material at a faster rate, they must often change old habits of word-by-word reading and focus instead on silent reading of phrases.

Two types of reading selections should be used: easy, independent-level materials that the student is interested in reading (a novel, biography, science fiction, etc.), and expository selections followed by comprehension questions (it is also useful if a word count is included). The student first reads the easy materials for a specified time period (approximately 15 minutes) and counts the number of pages read or, alternatively, reads a specified number of pages and records the time taken. He or she then reads the expository selection and responds to the comprehension questions. Finally, the student determines his or her reading speed on the easy material (the average number of words per page times the number of pages read divided by the number of minutes), the reading speed on the expository selection, and the percentage of comprehension questions correctly answered.

This information is recorded on a chart and compared with that from the prior reading session. The student should be encouraged to increase reading speed on the easy material while maintaining adequate comprehension on the expository material. As reading rate on the easy material increases, a corresponding speed increase on the study-type materials is typically observed. If no check is made of the comprehension of study-type materials, the student may develop skimming procedures that sacrifice comprehension.

SUMMARY

Oral reading analysis provides a window into the knowledge that your students have about sight words and word identification. Even more important, it reveals how students integrate and make sense of information from various sources—context, sight words, phonic cues, pictures—as they read. It permits you to hear the reading rate, pauses, and intonational patterns of children in order to draw conclusions about their fluency.

In order to learn to use diagnostic strategies such as oral reading analysis, you must study them and then use them with children on an individual basis. Later, once you are familiar with the procedures, you can use them more informally in the classroom while children work on reading and writing activities independently or during small group instruction. Your knowledge about what particular children know about words and word elements will become more precise over time. Eileen's running record of Ken's oral reading and Martha's analysis of Eva's oral reading show the steps that are useful in recording oral reading and the types of information being used by children.

Such analyses are useful only when they lead to instruction to help students further develop their reading strategies. We described word banks, word sorts, writing and spelling activities, and extensive easy reading as ways to help children who have difficulty remembering sight words. We reviewed instruction strategies for developing knowledge of word elements and for enhancing integration. Finally, we encouraged reading practice, modeling fluent reading, and reading rate improvement activities as ways to support the development of reading fluency.

TRY IT OUT

1. Working with first graders and other children in the beginning stages of reading demands expertise both in appropriately structuring the oral reading task for them and in analyzing the results. Repeated practice is essential. Find a child who is in the beginning stages of learning to read. Select a storybook with predictable text. Introduce the story and use the running record format to record the child's reading. Examine the record to see what it reveals about the child's reading strategies and his knowledge of print.

2. Find an older student for whom reading is challenging. Ask him about the selections he is currently reading and those he prefers. Explain that you are learning how to record oral reading and ask the student if he would be willing to read aloud for you. Make a photocopy of the text you have selected. Preview the selection with the student. If possible, tape-record as you mark his oral reading on the photocopy of the text. Later, replay the oral reading and check the accuracy of your record. Then examine the record to see what it reveals about the student's reading strategies and knowledge of print.

3. **Student Portfolio Ideas:** For any of your students who are developing either their knowledge of print or their fluency, set up a recording booth so they can record their oral reading several times during the year. Have them select a section of their oral reading from the beginning of the school year to compare with more recent recordings. Ask them to identify the changes they notice.

4. **For Your Teaching Portfolio:** Use what you have learned from this chapter to add to your teaching portfolio. You might include
   - your responses to "Pause and Reflect" on Ken and Eva
   - your response to the "Try It Out" suggested in #1 or #2
   - a sample instructional lesson related to the development of sight words, knowledge of word elements, or fluency that you tried and evaluated
   - your reflections on one of the "For Further Reading" selections for this chapter

FOR FURTHER READING

Clay, M. M. (1991). *Becoming literate: The construction of inner control.* Portsmouth, NH: Heinemann.
Detailed description of the methods for making running records, interpreting results, and planning Reading Recovery instructional support.

Lyons, C. A., Pinnell, G. S., & DeFord, D. E. (1993). *Partners in learning: Teachers and children in Reading Recovery.* New York: Teachers College Press.
Comprehensive description of the Reading Recovery program and its implementation in the United States.

chapter 4

Prior Knowledge and Vocabulary: Development, Assessment, and Instructional Support

CHAPTER GOALS FOR THE READER

To understand the connection between knowledge, words, and meaning and how these develop in children

To develop skill in assessing and interpreting background and vocabulary knowledge through the reading of an extended passage

To build a portfolio of ideas for vocabulary instruction

CLASSROOM VIGNETTE: TWO STUDENTS

Raymond and Tanya are two seventh-grade classmates who may be like students you've encountered. Raymond is a lively student who usually does well in class activities when getting the general idea of a selection is required. However, he sometimes has difficulty when important ideas depend on specific vocabulary. Tanya is a student for whom English is a second language (an ESL student), and sometimes her intelligence doesn't show through in discussions following reading. She often appears lost or is silent. In both cases, their teacher, Paul, wants to take a deeper look at these students' vocabulary knowledge and find ways to help them in their class work and participation.

This chapter presents an overview that can help you understand how vocabularies grow and how instruction can affect that process. Then detailed cases for Raymond and Tanya are presented to give you examples of how vocabulary knowledge can be investigated and developed.

CHAPTER OVERVIEW

This chapter has three parts. The first section introduces some of the issues essential to understanding the development of prior knowledge and vocabulary. Here are some questions to consider:

> What do we mean when we talk about knowledge, words, meanings, and concepts?
>
> How do students learn words?
>
> How can instruction influence word learning?

The second section focuses on assessment and presents a procedure and the cases of Raymond and Tanya. Although these students both have problems with new vocabulary, they have different profiles. Tanya, as a student whose first language is not English, exemplifies the difference between background and vocabulary difficulties. The third section focuses on instructional techniques including learning from context; relating new words to what students already know; and extending, elaborating, and recalling word meaning.

CHAPTER OUTLINE

Understanding Vocabulary knowledge and Development
    Knowledge, Words, and Meanings
    Meanings and Concepts
    How Words Are Learned
    The Influence of Instruction
Assessing Prior Knowledge and Vocabulary Difficulty
    Assessment Procedures
    Standardized Vocabulary Tests
    Case 4.1: Raymond
    Case 4.2: Tanya
Instruction to Support Vocabulary Development
    Learning Word Meanings from Context
    Building Conceptual Neworks
    Extending and Elaborating Word Meaning
Try It Out

Unifying the three parts of this chapter is the assumption that words are basic units of meaning in language. When we examine the relationship between vocabulary knowledge and reading comprehension, we typically find a very high correlation (Davis, 1968; Thorndike, 1973). Yet recent attempts to demonstrate a simple causal relation between knowledge of specific words and the comprehension of texts containing those words have not been uniformly successful. Markedly increasing the number of difficult words in a text leads to poorer comprehension, just as decreasing the number of difficult words leads to better comprehension (Wittrock, Marks, & Doctorow, 1975), but teaching students the difficult words before reading does not necessarily result in comprehension gains (Jenkins, Pany, & Schreck, 1978; Tuinman & Brady, 1974).

One explanation of this latter result is that knowing words well enough to select appropriate synonyms on a multiple-choice vocabulary test is not necessarily sufficient for comprehension. The reader must also be somewhat familiar with the **cultural context** or **domain of knowledge** in which the words occur. A high school student may know that a geologist studies the history of the earth through its rock formations, but this student will have difficulty comprehending the function of a geologist on a deep-sea expedition unless she is also aware of recent technological advances that make it possible to study the earth beneath the ocean floor. Thus we need to recognize a distinction between word knowledge as traditionally conceived (and measured) and the cultural or general knowledge that may be necessary for understanding a given text. This distinction is somewhat analogous to the difference between a dictionary and an encyclopedia, between a definition and a full-fledged concept. Nevertheless, it is through words that readers gain access to their relevant stores of knowledge—their mental encyclopedias as well as their mental dictionaries—and through them that we assess that knowledge in diagnosing comprehension difficulties.

When a student fails to show good comprehension, and print skill is not the primary source of difficulty, the problem can often be traced to lack of familiarity with a particular word or words. In this chapter we discuss and illustrate some procedures for investigating this possibility.

UNDERSTANDING VOCABULARY KNOWLEDGE AND DEVELOPMENT

The words of a language make up its **lexicon.** Different languages have different lexicons in the sense that they use different sequences of *sounds* (phonemes) to express the same *meanings*. But languages also differ in the meanings or concepts, the aspects of experience, and have words that reflect the different concerns and interests of the communities that speak them. For this reason, the lexicon of a language is never static. Words are constantly being added to express new thoughts and conditions; and some words fall into disuse while others undergo changes in primary meaning or intent. In a very real sense, the lexicon is an inventory of the concepts available to a language community, a map of the categories into which reality has been segmented and organized. Although words are the names we give to objects and actions, events and experiences, and so on, this naming activity involves, in the first place, the construction of concepts that determine the way in which the environment is subdivided into parts and the parts grouped into categories. For example, in English we divide the color spectrum in such a way that the colors blue and green are placed into separate categories designated by the words *blue* and *green.* Some languages, however, do not have different words for the colors blue and green but use a single word to designate this portion of the color spectrum. To take another example, some languages have words for individual kinds of trees but lack a general term for the entire class analogous to the English term *tree.* These differences are not just linguistic curiosities. They reflect differences in the categorization of experience and illustrate the important principle that the categories of objects, actions, and properties labeled by words are not "given" by the nature of things but rather reflect our desire to organize our experiences.

Knowledge, Words, and Meanings

What does it mean to know a word in the lexicon? It means, first of all, knowing how the word sounds when it is spoken and, in the case of literate speakers, how it looks in printed or written form. Proficient readers occasionally have print knowledge but not spoken knowledge. We have all had the experience of discovering, upon hearing a word for the first time after years of encountering it in print, that it is pronounced quite differently from what we had thought. This is most evident when we first encounter "loan words," which come into English from another language. If someone pronounces *détente* to rhyme with *repent-y,* it is a fair inference that the speaker learned the word from print, not from hearing it used in everyday speech. Both the spoken and printed forms of a word can provide direct access to the listener's/reader's stored knowledge of its meaning; that is, either can provide a virtually instantaneous pairing of word with meaning.

In addition, knowing a word means knowing the aspect of reality to which it refers—which entities in the universe of entities it labels. In the case of a noun, this means knowing the objects or ideas, persons, and places to which it refers. In the case of a verb, it means knowing the actions it denotes. And in the case of adjectives and adverbs, it means knowing the qualities of objects and actions these words designate. When you tell students that a *snare* is a trap or that a *squabble* is a quarrel, you are identifying the real-world referents of these words, the known objects or ideas they name (on the assumption that traps and quarrels are familiar as real-world entities).

Yet, it should be clear that words are not simply verbal labels for particular experiences or individual segments of reality. They are labels for *categories* of things. The child who believes that the word *dog* refers only to the family pet does not know the meaning of the word, for that entails understanding that the word applies to all other animals of a similar kind.

To be sure, we use words to refer to specific things—the *car* we drive, the *meal* we ate, the *anger* we feel. That is their central function, enabling us to talk of things in their absence, of events in the past or future, of thoughts and feelings that cannot be seen. But the meaning of a word is not so much embodied in its referents as in the attributes of its referents that are criterial in distinguishing them from the referents of other words. That is, it consists of the properties that determine whether something is or is not an instance of a category. The meaning of the word *story,* for example, does not begin and end with any particular story, or type of story, or even all the stories in the world. It consists, rather, of what a thing must be like in order to be considered a story, as distinguished, for example, from a poem or essay.

The meaning of a word may be seen as closely akin to what dictionaries attempt to record. The typical dictionary definition gives the essential properties of a category of objects, actions, or qualities, which may be used to identify word referents, or instances of that category. And it does this in a most economical way, by naming the extensive, or superordinate, category to which the word referents belong and then setting forth the special characteristics that distinguish them within this more extensive category. This system eliminates the need for specifying for each word the properties of the extensive category to which it belongs.

That word meanings and (dictionary-type) definitions are more or less equivalent at least in common parlance, is nowhere more evident than in the responses people make to questions about meaning. When adults are asked "What does _____ mean?" or "What is (a) _____?" they most commonly use the dictionary format—that is, they name the superordinate and the differentiating features, or give a word with similar meaning (a synonym). Students aged 9 or 10 also use this definitional form more often than any other (and this tendency increases with age). Younger children, on the other hand, are most likely to define words in terms of function or salient physical characteristics. Thus, an adult will say that *straw* is "dried grass," *gown* is a "long dress," and *orange* is "a fruit," whereas a young child will say of *straw,* "It's yellow"; of a *gown,* "You wear it, what you sleep in"; and of an *orange,* "You eat it." Similarly, a young child will say that *puddle* is "what you step in," while an older child will say that it is a "small pool of water" or "water that gathers after a rain." An explanation type of response (e.g., *skill* is "being able to do something"; *priceless* means "worth a lot of money") is infrequent among younger children but occurs at age 11 or 12 as the second most frequent response, though still considerably less frequent than the superordinate or synonym response (Feifel & Lorge, 1950).

Researchers have long believed that these age-related differences in definitional form reflect the developmental changes in conceptual processes. Accordingly, "functional" definitions, which seem to be more personal and less generalized than explanations, superordinates, and synonyms, are considered less mature. However, Anglin (1977) points out that adults and older children often include use, or function, in their definitions, "the difference being that children mention only use whereas adults mention a superordinate category as well" (p. 21). Nelson (1974) has also argued that function is an important aspect of word meaning for adults as well as children. Moreover, all types of definitions are found at all ages, and the shift from predominantly functional to categorical meaning is a gradual one (Wolman & Barker, 1965). If the form in which children defined words were primarily a manifestation of the children's stage of cognitive development, each stage being qualitatively different from the preceding one, we would expect the transition from one form to another to be more sudden. It may be that children's definitions gradually become more like those of adults mainly as reflections of their gradually increasing knowledge about the nature, origin, and categorization of things. In other words, as children gain in knowledge of where things come from, how they are made, used, and classified, their definitions are likely to include such information. After all, one must know that straw *is* dried grass in order to define it that way. Another knowledge-related explanation suggests that children sometimes may not use superordinate terms because they are not familiar with them. When asked to define a word such as *robin,* a majority of children may give a "mature" definition because they almost all know the superordinate term, *bird.* In contrast, when defining a word with a low-frequency superordinate (e.g., *pencil*), students may use a "semantically empty" superordinate, such as *something* (e.g., "A pencil is something to write with."). This suggests they know that a superordinate is required, but don't have the correct term available (Blachowicz & Fisher, 1989).

Meanings and Concepts

We tend to think of concepts as precisely formulated ideas concerning the essential attributes of classes of things. This tendency stems in part from the close association between concepts and scientific thought and also from a long tradition in psychological research. In this tradition, concepts are generally considered to involve a limited set of stable features (e.g., red geometric figures that have four sides and are surrounded by dots). However, it is mainly scientific concepts that are so well defined. Most "natural" concepts—the ones we use in everyday thought and action—do not have clear-cut boundaries. Is a wooden shoe "clothing"? Is coffee "food"?

A further complication is that the various members of a category are not necessarily considered equivalent: Some members seem to be much more central or dominant than others. For instance, people are much more likely to name a sparrow or a robin as an example of a bird than they are to name a penguin or a duck. Similarly, it is easier to verify statements of category membership for central instances or "good examples" of a category than for peripheral instances. It takes less time to verify that a doll or a ball is a toy than to verify that a swing or a skate is one. These phenomena are not merely artifacts of word frequency or familiarity—*doll* and *swing* occur with equal frequency in the language. They appear, rather, to reflect a general awareness of differences in the extent to which individual members of a category exemplify that category. Thus, when college students in an experiment were asked to rank the degree to which various objects were "good examples" of a category, they not only found the task meaningful (i.e., they could respond to it without confusion or wonder) but tended to agree with one another as to the "best" and "worst" examples of the various categories used. For instance, almost 100 percent of the 117 subjects gave chemistry, football, and carrot the highest rating as examples of a science, a sport, and a vegetable, respectively, while history, weight lifting, and pickle, respectively, were given low ratings in these same three categories by a majority of subjects (Rosch, 1973).

It appears that children also develop knowledge of categories from the central to the peripheral. When 9–11-year-old children were asked to verify category membership by answering yes or no to statements like "A chicken is a bird," they made no errors on the items that were rated as "central" by adults, whereas 25 percent of their responses were incorrect on the items rated peripheral (Rosch, 1973). In a similar study, Anglin (1977), found that even preschoolers tended to include the "good examples" as members of a category and exclude the less exemplary ones. What is particularly interesting about Anglin's results is that the good examples did not have to be familiar to the children in order to be classified correctly: pictures of a wombat, an aardvark, and an anteater were identified as animals just as frequently as pictures of a cow, a horse, and a cat. Anglin interprets this as evidence of the "inferential or generative nature of the child's concepts, for they will consistently include in concepts various kinds of instances which they have never seen before, provided they are central instances" (p. 156). On the other hand, familiar items were sometimes misclassified (though not by the majority of children) if they were peripheral. For example, an ant, a butterfly, and a starfish were not considered animals by a few children. This tendency seemed to be related to the fact that the children had another name for familiar objects such as these—they would say, "That's a tree, not a plant"; "That's a butterfly, not an animal."

What these studies suggest is that concepts are much more than definitional. They include (at least when reasonably well developed) not only the attributes necessary for category membership (i.e., the criteria for determining what is or is not a category member) but also what is *characteristic* of most members—information about the people and places, objects and actions with which they are commonly associated as well as information about origins, internal constituents, and functions of category members. Thus, an adult's concept of flowers is not limited to the idea that they are the part of a plant in which seeds are formed. Rather, it includes the knowledge that flowers wilt, are considered pretty, are likely to be seen at funerals as well as weddings and parties, and much more.

To conclude, words are the names we give to categories of objects, actions, and the qualities of objects and actions, and their meanings lie in the properties that distinguish one category from another. A statement of these properties constitutes a definition, and the things to which a word applies by virtue of having these properties are its word referents. Thus, words are terms of reference for specific objects as well as units of the language with intrinsic meaning. But, as we have seen, the properties that define a category are only part of what an individual knows about that category, only part of his or her word knowledge. Underlying each word in an individual's lexicon is a concept, and this may be thought of as comprising all the significant knowledge an individual possesses in association with that word (including its definition). *Vocabulary knowledge, then, involves the meaning of words in the strict sense and in the broader sense of the concepts underlying words.* It is the sum total of knowledge associated with words. We can also refer to this as "verbal knowledge."

Finally, it is conceptual or vocabulary knowledge, and not definitional knowledge alone, that is important for comprehension. We do not use words merely to refer to things or identify their category of membership. We use words in sentences to describe situations—that is, the relations between objects and actions and the qualities of objects and actions. Even a simple sentence such as *John pulled Mary's hair* involves a series of relationships, between *John* and *pull*, between *hair* and *pull*, and between *Mary* and *hair*. More important, sentences are used in discourse, so that the situations they describe become part of a larger complex. We cannot understand the following vignette:

> John pulled Mary's hair. She ran home crying, and he was sent to the principal's office.

unless our concept of hair includes the knowledge that having it pulled is painful. Concepts, meanings, and the words that express them must be interpreted in the wider framework of what we know about the world, human action, and motivation.

Multiple Meanings.   Many words in the English language have more than one meaning. In fact, there are relatively few words that do not. This situation normally causes little difficulty in communication, however, since the reader or listener can usually tell which meaning is intended from the immediate context or the topic of discourse. For example, the word *cell* is almost sure to refer to the cells of the human body in a biology text and to a small room or apartment in a treatise on monasteries. In a book on reading, the word *passage* will generally refer to a portion of printed text rather than to a hallway. However, words with several meanings pose no special problem *only* if we know the intended meaning and it is readily accessible in memory. If we have never before encountered the word *passage* in reference to written material, we might interpret a "reading passage" as a "hallway in which to read." A word with several meanings is especially likely to confuse. If the reader knows one of its meanings, but not the intended one, she will be more bewildered than if she were completely unfamiliar with the word. When she knows one meaning, not realizing that there are others, she will be drawn into an erroneous interpretation. If, on the other hand, she does not know the word at all, she will approach it simply as an unknown.

Figurative Language.   The several meanings of a word sometimes have little in common. *Bat* is an example. It seems to be purely coincidental that two entirely different entities—a small flying mammal and an item of equipment used in baseball—have the same verbal label. The word *fair* in the sense of "just," and *fair* in the sense of "light-colored, blonde" is another example.

On the other hand, the several meanings of a word can often be closely related. Think of the word *sharp*. In *sharp mind,* it means "quick, intelligent"; in *sharp picture,* it means "not blurry"; a *sharp outfit* is "stylish"; and a *sharp knife* is one that "cuts well." Yet all of these senses seem to share a common core of meaning.

> On purely intuitive grounds, one could maintain that *sharp* in the sense of "having an edge that cuts well" is somehow basic and that the other versions of *sharp* are secondary, being derived from it as essentially metaphorical creations. A mind is sharp in that it cuts with ease through difficult problems; a picture is in sharp focus when the lines are thin and well defined, like the blade of a keen knife; a sharp outfit is one that stands out in sharp focus against the background of mediocrity. (Langacker, 1973, p. 86)

Such extensions of meaning are extremely frequent in English. They are closely related to metaphor as they involve attribution of a quality commonly associated with one kind of thing to another, completely different kind of thing. That is, comparisons are drawn across different realms of experience. If it is common to speak of *pure* water, *pure* food, *pure* air, and so forth, then we can also, by extension, speak of a *pure* heart or mind. And we can have *strong* evidence as well as *strong* muscles. The difference is that in extension the quality we wish to impute is specified, whereas in true metaphor we merely liken one thing to another and the reader must infer which property (or properties) of the one is shared by the other. When Romeo says Juliet is "the sun," we must understand that he is referring to the sun's warmth, brilliance, and life-sustaining qualities (and not to its shape or color).

Research on how we comprehend metaphors is not extensive, but a few interesting observations have been made. For example, many adjectives describing physical sensations are also used to describe psychological characteristics (e.g., *sweet, warm, cold, rough, hard,* and *loud*). In one study, children ranging in age from 3 to 12 were first asked about the literal meanings of several such dual-function words (to verify mastery at this level), and then they were asked about the words' figurative meanings (e.g., "Are people cold? What do they say or do when they are cold?"). Not until children were 7 or 8 did they show some understanding of the psychological meaning of these terms. Even then they were unaware of the connection between psychological and physical meanings, believing the meanings to be entirely unrelated. By 9 and 10, children were more sensitive to this connection; and 11- and 12-year-olds were often actually able to explain the connection (e.g., "hard things and hard people are both unmanageable"; Asch & Nerlove, 1960, cited in Gardner, Winner, Bechhofer, & Wolf, 1978, p. 8). To summarize, children in preschool generally understand the physical or concrete meanings of dual-function adjectives; during the early years of schooling they master the psychological meanings; and during preadolescence, they begin to recognize the metaphoric connection (Gardner et al., 1978).

This pattern of development holds true for metaphoric comprehension in general. Children of 8 or 9 can understand the meaning conveyed by a metaphor, but only on an intuitive basis: They can match a picture to the statement "He has a very heavy heart" but cannot easily paraphrase the statement. This limitation may reflect the avoidance of figurative usage in their own speech by children of this age; perhaps because of their concern with dictionary definitions, they tend to prefer ordinary, established meanings and comparisons, occasionally protesting that figurative expressions are "silly": "A tie can't be loud"; "A person can't be a rock." This may be a necessary stage of development; children must understand what words usually (and literally) mean before they can appreciate the departures and extensions of metaphoric comparisons (Gardner et al., 1978).

This point was recently demonstrated, to some extent, in a study of instruction in the comprehension of metaphors and similes (Readence, Baldwin, & Rickelman, 1983). The investigators hypothesized that the key to comprehension of these expressions is vocabulary knowledge. More specifically, they pointed out that a person must be sufficiently familiar with the "vehicle" term to know which of its features is being attributed to the "topic," the thing being described. For example, in *his hands were sandpaper, hands* is the topic and *sandpaper* the vehicle; that is, *sandpaper* is the means for conveying the idea that his hands were rough. To understand this metaphor, you must be familiar enough with sandpaper to know that roughness is its most significant characteristic. To cite another example, *The smoke from the forest was pea soup* can be understood only if you know that pea soup is thick; knowing that it is green or edible provides no help. The investigators found that when fifth- and sixth-grade students misinterpreted metaphors and similes, usually they did not associate the necessary attribute with the vehicle term. For example, they might not think of pea soup as thick. However, when these students were given lists of attributes (including the one being ascribed to the topic) for the vehicle terms of the metaphorical statements they had misinterpreted, they were able to correct 77 percent of their misinterpretations (Baldwin, Luce, & Readence, 1982).

Similar results were obtained in a related study of similes (cited in Readence et al., 1983). In this study, one control group simply practiced interpreting similes; a second control group studied paragraphs that described the vehicle terms in the experimental materials but did *not* include the specific attributes necessary for their interpretation. The experimental group read descriptions of the vehicle term that included the necessary attribute. As expected, subsequent performance on the test of simile interpretation was considerably superior for the experimental group.

These studies suggest that students' failure to understand metaphorical language is not primarily due to their lack of the necessary reasoning powers or inability to recognize the type of comparison involved. Consequently, "drill exercises in discriminating between literal and metaphorical statements or matching interpretations with metaphors and similes may have little effect" (Readence et al., 1983, p. 111). Rather, direct instruction in the critical attributes of word referents seems more appropriate.

Nevertheless, the difficulty of understanding figurative language must not be underestimated. Familiarity with the terms used is certainly essential, but it is not sufficient. In order to determine which of the possible attributes of a metaphoric vehicle is the intended one, the reader must understand the situational context. We understand what Romeo means when he says Juliet is "the sun" because we know from what has gone before how he feels about her.

By the time students reach the age of 10 or 11, they can paraphrase as well as understand metaphors. Evidently, their conceptual and lexical knowledge is sufficiently consolidated that they do not resist or protest against comparisons between animate and inanimate objects, physical and psychological properties, and so on. However, it is not until adolescence that students are likely to fully appreciate the nature of metaphor; to recognize the links between sensory, physical, and psychological realms; and to perceive the significance of comparisons drawn across them (Gardner et al., 1978).

How Words Are Learned

An eminent psycholinguist, George Miller (1977), observed that young children seem to learn the words that name colors before they learn to match those words to specific color stimuli. That is, they will answer "red," "blue," "green" (or some other color word) in response to the question, "What color is this?" even though the color they name is not the correct one. And when asked to point to all the blue things in any array of objects, they may point to all the tan ones, showing that they can distinguish between colors without knowing which color-name to apply. The same phenomenon has been observed with respect to time words: Children will give time units in response to questions about time, but the numbers they give are often quite bizarre in relation to the questions (e.g., in answer to the question, "When was your daddy little?" a 3-year-old will respond, "Last week").

These observations led Miller to reflect on his own vocabulary knowledge, and he recognized that he, too, knew many words whose specific referents he could not identify or did not understand. For example, he knew that the words *camellia, nasturtium,* and *marigold* were the names of flowers but he did not know what these flowers looked like. Many adults are probably in a similar position with regard to tree names like *sassafras* and *cottonwood* or animal names like *wombat* and *aardvark.*

These observations suggest that both children and adults often learn the general domain of knowledge or experience to which a word belongs before they understand its precise meaning. We should not be surprised, therefore, when students can give only the most general information about certain words—that *anxiety* means "feeling"; *soliloquy* is "a statement"; *penance* means "punishment" (Drum, 1983). This probably represents a first stage in the process of learning words. With further experiences in a variety of contexts, they will be able to differentiate word meanings more precisely.

The phenomenon of overgeneralization of word meaning is well documented among very young children (Clark, 1973). They commonly use the term *dog* as a label for other animals (horses, cows, sheep), *baby* for young children, *tick-tock* for instruments with round dials (gas meter, bathroom scale), *ball* for spherical objects (marbles, balloons), *Christmas tree* for all evergreens, and so on. One child used *open* for both untying of shoes and the peeling of fruit! We can understand these overextensions as stemming from the perceptual similarity of "correct" and "incorrect" word referents. And, to some extent, the child may be aware of the difference between babies and children, a clock and other dialed instruments, and so on, but may not yet have acquired the appropriate verbal labels. This would also explain the child's use of the terms *big* and *little* to cover all dimensions of size—long and short, wide and narrow, thick and thin, high and low. In other words, some overgeneralizations undoubtedly emerge because children must use the terms that are available to them to refer to new objects and ideas.

More difficult to explain is the common confusion between antonym pairs such as *more* and *less, before* and *after, same* and *different.* One theory (the **Semantic Feature Hypothesis**) is that the meanings of words can be broken down into smaller units or elementary components of meaning (semantic features) and words that share many features are likely to be confused. More specifically, the meaning of one word in an antonym pair is likely, at first, to be extended to cover the meaning of the other as well because the contrastive feature of the second word has not yet entered the child's "mental dictionary." In other words, the child may not have differentiated the meanings of *less, after,* or *different* from the meanings of *more, before,* or *same;* the lexical entry for these words is incomplete (Clark, 1973). Perhaps this same notion of incomplete entry accounts for the confusion, found even among adults, between *affect* and *effect, imply* and *infer.*

The Semantic Feature Hypothesis represents just one attempt to understand the development of word meaning, and much can be said about its limitations (cf. Anglin, 1977; Nelson, 1974). From our point of view, one serious limitation is that it is based on observations of preschool children. Nevertheless, it is sometimes useful to think of words as "bundles" of semantic features and to understand students' partial or vague knowledge of words in these terms.

Possibly more frequent than overgeneralizations of word meanings are undergeneralizations. These tend to go unnoticed in spontaneous speech (upon which much of the research on child language is based) because they do not result in erroneous verbal labels—the child merely applies a word to a more restricted range of objects than is necessary. Consequently, undergeneralizations have been relatively neglected in the study of word meaning. They are, however, much in evidence when observations are based on comprehension tasks (Anglin, 1977). Whether a word is overgeneralized or undergeneralized appears to depend somewhat on its level of generality. The reason for this is that perceptual similarity plays an important role in children's categorizing behavior. General terms tend to refer to an assortment of dissimilar items and therefore to be undergeneralized. Thus, Anglin found that with the general terms *food, plant,* and *animal,* atypical instances such as ketchup, trees, and insects, respectively, were excluded. Rarely were these terms overgeneralized. Specific terms, on the other hand, were often overgeneralized to perceptually similar items—*apple* to tomato, *flower* to other plants (cacti, philodendron). In general, then, children's acquisition of word labels cannot be said to progress either from specific to general or from general to specific. Rather, "vocabulary development is characterized by the complementary trends of differentiation and of hierarchic integration" (Anglin, 1977, p. 237).

In conclusion, we believe that underlying the meaning a student attaches to a word is a concept. This includes, even for young children, knowledge of what instances of the concept look like, smell like, taste like, and so on, where they are found, the uses to which they can be put, and what they can do. With development, a child expands a concept to include knowledge of the relations of instances to other things, their internal constituents, and their origins (Anglin, 1977). But it should be clear that there can be concepts without words just as there can be words without conceptual underpinnings. The distinction between words and concepts is an important one for vocabulary instruction; it implies that teaching definitions is not the same as teaching concepts. The teaching of definitions (or synonyms) makes sense when words pertain to well-developed concepts. Even then, new words must be practiced in a variety of verbal contexts if they are to be useful in comprehending discourse. But when the concepts underlying words are somewhat unfamiliar, definitions will be inadequate; instruction must also provide the verbal and nonverbal experiences necessary for concept development.

The Influence of Instruction

We noted earlier that the high correlation between vocabulary and comprehension is not well understood. There is currently some controversy over whether word knowledge is directly "instrumental" in a person's understanding text or is itself a reflection of "deeper and broader knowledge of the culture" (Anderson & Freebody, 1981, p. 81). On the one hand, students who score high on a vocabulary test may simply "know more of the words in most texts they encounter"; on the other hand, it may be that "possessing a certain word meaning is only a sign that the individual may possess the knowledge needed to understand a text" (p. 81). The second position assumes that students who select the right responses on a multiple-choice test know more about words than their definitions (though that is all that is demonstrated on the test). This position is consistent with the view of verbal knowledge we have proposed.

Unfortunately, as Anderson and Freebody (1981) point out, there is little besides logic and intuition to support the view that vocabulary scores reflect primarily conceptual or background knowledge. The tendency among reading researchers has been to study background knowledge as separate and distinct from vocabulary. However, there is a kind of support for the vocabulary-as-background-knowledge view, by default, in the finding that simply teaching definitions does *not* tend to improve comprehension. Out of eight studies reviewed by Mezynski (1983), four resulted in comprehension gains due to vocabulary instruction and four did not. In each of the four that proved unsuccessful, students were taught simple definitions or synonyms, accompanied in some cases by illustrative sentences. By contrast, in each of the successful studies, instruction went beyond this narrow type of drill, a conclusion supported by other metanalyses of research (Stahl & Fairbanks, 1986.)

In one of the successful studies, the additional instruction amounted to little more than answering two questions about each word. For example, in addition to learning that *altercations* are "fights," students answered these questions: "Do you have altercations with your teacher? Do you have altercations with a tree?" (Kameenui, Carnine, & Freschi, 1982). One wonders why this should make the difference between success and failure. Perhaps the questions helped students associate the new word with an underlying concept—meaningful experiences or knowledge—rather than with a rote definition. Some researchers have suggested that the conceptually rich discussion generated by the questions is the real source of word learning (Stahl & Vancil, 1986).

Whereas Kameenui et al. (1982) taught a small number of words (six) and used a short experimental passage incorporating these words to assess the effect of instruction on comprehension, the other successful studies involved large numbers of words taught over a period of many months and assessed the effects of instruction through standardized comprehension tests. Thus, there is evidence in favor of instruction that is geared toward improving students' *general* vocabulary as well as support for direct instruction in difficult passage words. More significantly, in the general vocabulary studies, words not only were taught (i.e., defined, illustrated, explained, and discussed), but also were presented in rich contexts. The Draper and

Moeller (1971) study constituted a veritable "barrage" of new words—1,800 in all—presented in the context of fables, folktales, and Greek and Roman myths. The Lieberman study (cited in Mezynski, 1983) used social studies and English curriculum materials as the context for new words. A slightly different approach was taken by Beck, Perfetti, and McKeown (1982). Instead of providing narrative or expository contexts for newly learned words, they designed activities in which students explored and refined the meanings of words. For example, students completed sentences or answered multiple-choice questions about the situations, behaviors, or events in which word referents might be involved. To illustrate, for the word *accomplice,* students were asked, "Would an accomplice be more likely to (a) squeal to the police in return for not having to go to jail? (b) rob a bank by himself? (c) enjoy babysitting?" (p. 510). Also, the words taught in the Beck, Perfetti, and McKeown study were grouped into semantically related sets, eight to nine words per set, and some questions were designed to probe the overlap among words in a set. For example, *accomplice, novice,* and *hermit* were in the "people" set of words, and the students were asked: "Could an accomplice be a novice? Would a hermit likely be an accomplice?" (p. 510).

This body of research seems to show that instruction in definitions alone does not adequately prepare students for the task of comprehending discourse. Also, contextual learning is a powerful force in the vocabulary development of the school-age child (Nagy & Herman, 1987; Sternberg, 1987). Though the exact size and growth rate of children's vocabularies are arguable, it is clear that instruction cannot account for a major part of our word learning. In their metanalysis of vocabulary research, Stahl and Fairbanks (1986) concluded that a combination of definitional and contextual learning is more effective than either alternative alone. A broad, rich range of experiences seem to be necessary before newly learned words can be understood in novel contexts. Such experiences can evidently be provided through exploratory questions as well as through contextual exercises which engage the learner in discussing, using, analyzing, and playing with new words. These experiences make definitions "come alive": They enable students to connect words with real-world events, situations, and behaviors—with existing conceptual knowledge.

Many suggested guidelines have been given for vocabulary programs in the classroom (Blachowicz, 1985; Carr & Wixson, 1986) and some can also be drawn from meta-analyses of instructional programs mentioned above. The process of word learning should be an active one for learners with the goal of connecting the new words to what they already know.

The goal should be to augment both the breadth and depth of existing word knowledge and to build independent word learning habits (Nagy, 1988). For maximum effect, this development takes place within the context of content learning or, at a minimum, in concert with textual reading instruction and should incorporate the following, though not necessarily in this order:

1. *Assessing what students already know.* Briefly worded explanations, synonyms, associations, or hypotheses about the word's meaning should be elicited from the student, if possible, and elaborated on by the

teacher. When the word is connected to a well-established concept, the dictionary can be consulted (Parker, 1984). For variation, you might present sentences from which target words have been omitted but which contain clear clues to the words' meaning. Students can then supply synonyms to match a new word's meaning (Blachowicz, 1977). If defining is the first instructional step, whatever defining characteristics are proposed should be viewed as tentative and reevaluated after students gain more experience with the word.

2. *Rich active discussion.* The concepts underlying words should be developed through discussion of illustrative situations; meanings should be expanded and clarified through associations with familiar people, places, objects, and actions. Students' own experiences are of course elicited wherever possible. However, when students' experiences are limited, you should invent appropriate scenarios and provide information.

3. *Application.* Students should reinforce and refine concepts through further interaction with illustrative contexts. This activity can take the form of exploratory questions similar to those used by Kameenui, Carnine, and Freschi (1982) and by Beck, Perfetti, and McKeown (1982), or it can involve instructional materials regularly used in reading or content area instruction. In addition, when time permits, you may give students writing assignments in which they generate sentences and paragraphs around the newly learned words.

4. *Use and practice.* Wide reading in context is essential for vocabulary development (Nagy & Herman, 1987) as is hearing the new words used in oral language, storytelling, and story reading (Eller, Pappas, & Brown, 1988). Also, using it in writing is an excellent, and traditional, way to cement a new meaning. Word games and word play provide both practice and motivation for word learning which is so essential for growth.

One final issue should be mentioned before we conclude this discussion of instructional research. It concerns the special importance of vocabulary instruction for less able readers who generally exhibit poor performance on vocabulary assessment measures. Though research continues to emphasize contextual reading as essential for growth in word knowledge, it may not be sufficient for these readers who begin school knowing fewer school-type words than their more able counterparts (Becker, Dixon, & Inman-Anderson, 1980). These are the readers who are frequently unmotivated or unable to do the amount of contextual reading that would close the gap with their age mates. Further, McKeown (1985) found that disabled readers lagged behind able readers in the use of strategies that allow readers to gain new word meaning from context: knowing that one needs to use context; generating possible meanings for an unknown word; using the prior and subsequent context to choose among generated alternatives.

Roser and Juel (1982) looked at readers' performance on word learning tasks in regular reading classrooms. They selected children in first through fifth grades who were either average or poor readers (i.e., who were reading either at or one year below grade level). Each group read stories from their classroom reader, one with vocabulary instruction and one without. The words taught were those identified in the teacher's manual as "new words," and the instructional method emphasized the relationship of each new word to the children's lives. Specifically, new words were presented along with sentences in which blanks were substituted for the new words; the teacher guided the group in selecting the appropriate word for each sentence, centering the discussion on students' knowledge and previous experiences. The results showed a marked increase in passage comprehension after vocabulary instruction only for the poorer readers in third, fourth, and fifth grades. The average readers in all grades performed just about as well without instruction as with it. In first and second grades, not only did instruction have no effect, but the poorer readers performed as well as the average readers. These results are not unexpected, given the fact that beginning reading materials make fewer demands on students' vocabulary knowledge. A noteworthy feature of this experiment was the use of instructional level materials in regular reading lessons conducted by the classroom teacher. Therefore, an appropriate instructional program for disabled readers with poor vocabularies would include motivation and time for wide reading but would also provide instruction of key concept vocabulary and strategy development for effective context use.

ASSESSING PRIOR KNOWLEDGE AND VOCABULARY DIFFICULTY

We have seen from the review of experimental research above that knowing the definitions of words in a passage does not always lead to increased comprehension for students. By the same token, *not* knowing word meanings does not necessarily interfere with their comprehension. Why should this be so? Clearly, much depends on how many unknown words there are and on how important they are to the central content (Freebody & Anderson, 1983a). The influence of these factors on comprehension will depend, in turn, on students' familiarity with the content (cf. Freebody & Anderson, 1983b). A large number of unknown words may present no obstacle to their comprehension in a highly predictable context. For example, a simple 100-word fairy-tale-style story was readily understood by a group of average readers in fifth grade, even though 10 of the words were taken from an eighth-grade list and, moreover, an average of 7 of those words were marked incorrectly by the experimental group on a multiple-choice test given after instruction (Stahl, 1983). On the other hand, even a few unknown words can severely disrupt comprehension if they represent key concepts in an expository passage on an unfamiliar topic.

In the usual case, however, unknown words usually cause losses or misinterpretations of information that are more limited in scope. By way of illustration, a child who did not know the meaning of *snare* and *clipped* read a story that began as follows: "A miller laid a snare, and a baby eagle flew into it. The miller tied him to a pole and clipped his wings" (Hughes, Bernier, & Gurren, 1979, p. 19). The unknown words prevented her from answering questions about the *causes* of the bird's predicament; but the *facts* of its predicament—captivity and inability to fly—were clearly understood from ensuing events. In general, students appear to tolerate unknown words as long as other, compensatory sources of information are available to them, either from the passage itself, in the form of redundant information, or from their own store of knowledge.

In the following section we present two case studies illustrating how word knowledge and topic familiarity influence comprehension. The first case represents the moderate loss in comprehension likely to be observed when passages are not overly demanding relative to the reader's conceptual knowledge. The second shows a more severe loss, as it makes greater demands on the reader. The presentation of these cases, in addition, demonstrates the diagnostic procedures useful in assessing word knowledge and evaluating its effect on comprehension.

Assessment Procedures

The general procedure for reading assessment involves the preparation of materials, administration, preliminary analysis of results, further assessment (Step 4), interpretation, and finally development of an instructional plan. It is during the preparation stage that you select words from the passage for assessing the student's word knowledge. You should also construct comprehension questions at this time. Specific procedures are discussed in the next chapter. Then, after a preliminary analysis of the results, you may select and present additional words during further assessment. The purpose is to determine whether vocabulary knowledge is a major source of difficulty in reading for the student—more specifically, whether uncommon words could have interfered with his or her comprehension and whether unknown words represent unknown concepts as well.

Step 1: Preparation: Selection of Words. Select three to eight words (depending on passage length) for an initial appraisal of vocabulary knowledge. The words should be important to the passage that is chosen from instructional material—that is, they should convey information pertaining to the main ideas and essential details. Figurative expressions and phrases of a technical nature should also be selected, since they too represent possible obstacles to comprehension. Basic to this step, then, is a careful reading of the passage to identify its central content. You must also be alert to the occurrence of common words used in uncommon or metaphorical senses. In selecting words for presentation try to distinguish between those explained by the context of the passage and those without such illuminating contexts. The former can be used to probe for context use strategies whereas the latter words are more appropriate for estimating the difficulty of a particular material for student use.

Step 2: Administration: Presentation of Words. After you have selected the words, present each one to the student separately after asking the comprehension questions. Ask "What does _____ mean?" or "What is a _____?" For words with multiple meanings, you may also provide the context in which the word occurred. If the student cannot formulate a definition, or leaves some doubt as to the accuracy or fullness of his or her vocabulary knowledge, seek additional information, asking for an exemplary object or situation to which the word would apply or requesting that the student use the word in a sentence. Examples as well as sentences often have to be explored still further. For example, Raymond (see Case 4.1) suggested that the word *sophisticated* could be applied to a truck. Although this usage is potentially correct, further questioning indicated that he thought it was motion (rather than modern design or engineering) that made a truck sophisticated.

Step 3: Preliminary Analysis of Results.   In this step note the degree of success the student achieves in defining the words presented in Step 2. If he or she does not know as many as half the words presented, you should consider vocabulary knowledge an area of general weakness. The diagnosis does not end there, however. You must also determine the extent to which the unknown words impede comprehension. To do this you must examine the student's incorrect responses to comprehension questions. In particular, you must determine, for each question that was answered incorrectly, whether the information needed to answer it was unavailable to the student because of an unknown word. If this is true for a majority of incorrect responses, then the student's reading difficulty can be attributed to inadequate vocabulary knowledge.

Obviously, you cannot always anticipate the words and ideas that will cause confusion and misunderstanding for a student during your initial selection of words; often the student's responses to questions reveal difficulties that were entirely unexpected. In Case 4.1, for example, the teacher did not recognize the word *crude* as a possible source of difficulty in her first analysis of the passage; therefore, she did not include it in the initial set of words presented. In such cases, you should select the additional words for presentation to the student during the next step.

You should examine the student's performance on the comprehension questions at this point for evidence that he or she lacked the conceptual knowledge or specific information necessary for general comprehension of the passage. If you find such evidence, formulate questions to explore this possibility and present them during Step 4. This procedure is particularly important when a student's overall comprehension is poor—say 50 percent or less—and specific words do not seem to be directly implicated.

Step 4: Further Assessment.   The additional words identified in Step 3 as potential obstacles to comprehension are presented to the student as in Step 2. The results will enable you to complete the determination, begun in Step 3, of whether the student answered particular questions incorrectly because he or she did not know the meanings of certain words. The questions devised to explore conceptual knowledge and information are also administered in this step. Further, discussing the words explained by context and letting the student refer to the text can provide a window from which you can evaluate the student's context use strategy. These results can give you further insight into the source of his or her comprehension difficulty.

Steps 5 and 6: Interpretation and Instructional Plan. The results of Steps 3 and 4 combined serve as the basis for your final evaluation of the role of vocabulary knowledge in the student's reading difficulties. If the student cannot answer questions about the passage because he or she lacks vocabulary knowledge, then vocabulary knowledge represents an area of weakness in reading for the student and warrants instructional emphasis. For instructional purposes, the passage may be too difficult for this student because of a vocabulary knowledge deficit. You can determine this by assessing the severity of his or her comprehension loss. If the loss is limited in scope, as in Case Study 4.1, then passages of equivalent difficulty will probably be suitable for instruction as long as the student learns important words before reading. On the other hand, if the loss in comprehension is widespread, extending to information not specifically related to unknown words, as in Case Study 4.2, then the student should be assigned an easier level of materials.

Standardized Vocabulary Tests

Though most general reading survey tests contain some measure of vocabulary, they are not typically designed for use in individual diagnoses. However, teachers should be aware of issues related to standardized vocabulary assessment and the choice of tools to use for broad scale assessment. Formats for assessment vary, including words presented in isolation or in context with response formats ranging from matching synonyms to choice of phrases using the words. In a review of these options, Farr and Carey (1986) suggested that teachers choose tests presenting words in context with a word content reflecting their instructional program. They also suggested that these tests be administered in an untimed format so as to have a measure of "power" rather than of speed. In using any vocabulary test, you must be clear as to whether vocabulary knowledge or decoding is being assessed. An effective practice for making this determination is first to administer a test to the student in writing and then to assess further by administering the same test orally.

Several standardized tests assess vocabulary in context using a modified cloze format. You may wish to investigate the following: Degrees of Reading Power (DRP); Diagnostic Reading Scales; Woodcock Reading Mastery Tests. Other standardized assessments may offer insights into analysis (Stanford Diagnostic Reading Test; Metropolitan Reading Diagnostic Tests); receptive vocabulary (Peabody Picture Vocabulary Test); content area vocabulary (Tests of Reading Comprehension); or analogical reasoning with vocabulary (Woodcock Reading Mastery Tests).

Let's look now at our first case. As we progress through the analysis, stop at the "Pause and Reflect" points to develop your own assessment ideas for Raymond. If you are working with a group, develop your own interpretation, then share and compare.

CASE 4.1: RAYMOND

Raymond is a seventh grader whose work in school is generally above average. But he is ambitious and expresses some concern about his reading ability. His teacher did an assessment to identify areas of his performance that might be strengthened through specific instruction.

Preparation

An expository passage from his seventh-grade text, entitled "Kinds of Housing" (275 words in length), was selected for Raymond to read. It is shown in Figure 4.1.

PAUSE AND REFLECT.   Which words would you choose as central content words for Raymond's assessment?

Raymond's teacher, Paul, selected six words. The first, *environment*, is important for understanding the thesis of the passage. The second word, *determines*, is central in understanding the main idea of the passage, that environmental conditions influence the nature of housing. The third, *available*, is a general vocabulary word that is important for understanding why kinds of housing vary according to the locale. The fourth, fifth, and sixth words—*temporary, perma-*

FIGURE 4.1   Diagnostic reading passage: Raymond

SOURCE: "Kinds of Housing" from HBJ Bookmark Reading Program, Eagle edition, *Taking Flight*, Level 13, Reading Skills Workbook, copyright 1983 by Harcourt Brace & Company, reprinted by permission of publisher.

Kinds of Housing

With a few exceptions, environment determines the kinds of shelter people choose. So, houses are usually built from materials that are most readily available in the surrounding areas.

The temporary dwelling, as its name suggests, is not built to last. Nomads, people who are always on the move, build temporary dwellings. For example, Native Americans of the plains developed the tepee made of buffalo hides When buffalo were plentiful, they were an important food source. To avoid waste, Native Americans found a practical use for the hides of the animals. When the tribe moved on, the tepees were left behind.

The grass lean-to is favored by the Bush people of the Kalahari Desert. It is made from grasses and sticks found in the area in which they live.

There are two kinds of permanent housing: crude and sophisticated. Igloos, log cabins, and adobe huts are crude permanent housing. They are built to last. The surfaces, however, are rough and unfinished.

The igloo is a dome made of blocks of hard-packed snow. The snow acts as an insulator. It makes the igloo surprisingly warm.

Log cabins were common during America's westward expansion. As settlers headed west, the thick forests provided timber for housing.

Adobe is sun-dried mud. Adobe huts are found in warm, dry areas, such as parts of Mexico and the American Southwest.

Sophisticated permanent housing can be made from many materials. Homes with concrete foundations are built to last from owner to owner. Very often, these houses have a framework of wood, iron, or steel. The location of steel mills and ironworks often determines the areas where this housing is found.

nent, and *sophisticated*—represent major concepts that distinguish major types of housing. Paul did not include the word *insulator* because the insulating property of snow was deemed incidental to the main point of the passage and because the meaning of *insulator* was explained in the sentence following the one in which it was introduced. This is an example of the type of word that can be used to explore contextual strategies. As with *adobe, igloo,* and *nomads,* also well explained by the context of the selection, Paul can ask Raymond to locate clues to the word's meaning in the passage during the comprehension probe if vocabulary knowledge appears to be a problem.

The preparation stage involved selection of key vocabulary items as well as development of comprehension questions (to be discussed in the next two chapters). These are shown, together with the vocabulary items, in Figure 4.2; the expected answers are in parentheses. The first nine questions can be answered from information either stated or implied in the text; the remaining three require interpretation or application of text information.

Administration

Raymond read the passage aloud while Paul recorded his errors and noted the amount of time he took to read it. The comprehension and vocabulary knowledge questions were administered immediately thereafter. Raymond's responses are shown in Figures 4.3 and 4.4. You should study his answers in order to make a tentative judgment about the adequacy of his comprehension and vocabulary knowledge.

Preliminary Analysis

Print Skill. Raymond had difficulty with only three words, or fewer than 1 percent of the words in the passage. Two miscues involved inserted and omitted sight words that did not alter the meaning of the passage. The third was potentially more serious; it involved the mispronunciation of the word *determines,* with the third syllable pronounced like the word *mines.* Raymond read the passage in 2 minutes and 12 seconds, at a rate of 125 words per minute. This is within the average range for seventh graders. On the basis of this evidence, Raymond's print-processing strategies seem to represent an area of strength.

PAUSE AND REFLECT.   Look at Raymond's responses to the comprehension questions in Figure 4.3 and to the vocabulary knowledge questions in Figure 4.4. How would you evaluate his overall comprehension? Is lack of vocabulary knowledge affecting his comprehension?

Comprehension. Of the nine questions that pertained to text information, Raymond answered five correctly and two incorrectly (items 6 and 8). His answers were only partially correct on the remaining two questions (items 1 and

Comprehension

  1. a. What determines the kind of shelter people choose? (environment; available materials)
       b. Where do we usually get the materials we build houses from? (environment; surrounding area)

  2. What is a temporary dwelling? (one that is not built to last)

  3. What are the people called who build temporary dwellings? (nomads)

  4. Why do some people build temporary dwellings? (they are always on the move)

  5. What are the two types of permanent housing? (crude and sophisticated)

  6. What is the difference between crude and sophisticated permanent housing? (crude are rough and unfinished; sophisticated are made from modern materials)

  7. Name some types of crude permanent housing. (igloo, adobe, log cabin)

  8. What are some materials sophisticated permanent housing is made of? (wood, iron, steel)

  9. What determines where sophisticated permanent houses are built? (location of materials)

 *10. If you had the choice between living in an igloo, a log cabin, or an adobe hut, which would you choose and why? (discuss climate and comfort)

 *11. Of all the types of housing mentioned in the passage—temporary and permanent, crude permanent, and sophisticated permanent—which type do you live in? (permanent sophisticated)

 *12. Do climate and environment still govern what materials we use to build houses today? (discuss role of climate and environment and today's construction)
       *Beyond-text question

Vocabulary Knowledge
Key Concept Words
  1. environment
  2. determines
  3. available
  4. temporary
  5. permanent
  6. sophisticated

Contextually Explained
  7. insulator
  8. adobe
  9. igloo
 10. nomads

FIGURE 4.2   Comprehension and vocabulary knowledge questions: Raymond

9). The partially correct answers involved use of examples rather than the more general formulations called for by the questions. Thus, Raymond's comprehension score (6 out of 9) was below 75 percent. Is there a possibility that his incorrect (or incomplete) answers were due to unknown words? We believe it will be useful for you to consider this issue before reading on; in particular, it is important to examine the way in which information pertinent to the questions Raymond missed was presented in the passage.

½ 1. a. ½ What determines the kind of shelter people choose? (environment; available materials)
    RESPONSE: It can be the grounds, maybe grass or sand; and like if it's cold or sunny.
  b. ½ Where do we usually get the materials we build houses from? (environment; surrounding area)
    RESPONSE: Sometimes we can make it. Like the log cabins, you could get it from the trees around you. The igloos, you could pack the snow yourself.

✓ 2. What is a temporary dwelling? (one that is not built to last)
    RESPONSE: It's not built to stay long.

✓ 3. What are the people called who build temporary dwellings? (nomads)
    RESPONSE: Nomads.

✓ 4. Why do some people build temporary dwellings? (they are always on the move)
    RESPONSE: They are always moving around.

✓ 5. What are the two types of permanent housing? (crude and sophisticated)
    RESPONSE: Crude and sophisticated.

✗ 6. What is the difference between crude and sophisticated permanent housing? (crude are rough and unfinished; sophisticated are made from modern materials)
    RESPONSE: Not sure—crude are built to stay longer and sophisticated is not that long.

✓ 7. Name some types of crude permanent housing. (igloo, adobe, log cabin)
    RESPONSE: Log cabin, adobe hut, igloo.

✗ 8. What are some materials sophisticated permanent housing is made of? (wood, iron, steel)
    RESPONSE: I think one of the houses are igloos made out of snow—or I think wood. [Anything else?] Steel.

½ 9. What determines where sophisticated permanent houses are built? (location of materials)
    RESPONSE: Well, if they were wood, they would be by a forest.

½ *10. If you had the choice between living in an igloo, a log cabin, or an adobe hut, which would you choose and why? (discuss climate and comfort)
    RESPONSE: Igloo, or log cabin . . . . Well, I would choose an igloo because it keeps you warm. Maybe a log cabin; it was built like a house—and that's what we mostly live in, like in cabins in the woods. [So, which would you choose?] Log cabin 'cause it's built like a house.

✓ *11. Of all the types of housing mentioned in the passage—temporary and permanent, crude permanent and sophisticated permanent—which type do you live in? (permanent sophisticated)
    RESPONSE: I think sophisticated. [Is it permanent or temporary?] Permanent.

✗ *12. Do climate and environment still govern what materials we use to build houses today? (discuss climate, environment, today's construction)
    RESPONSE: Not sure. [Do you think people can build any kind of house no matter what the climate is?] Well, not exactly—don't know how to explain it.

*Beyond-text question

FIGURE 4.3   Responses to comprehension questions: Raymond

✓ **1.** *environment*
RESPONSE: The things around you.

✗ **2.** *determines*
RESPONSE: They . . . say it, they predict.
TEACHER: Can you use the word *determines* in a sentence?
RESPONSE: He determined that the number was gonna be five.

✓ **3.** *available*
RESPONSE: That it's . . . I can't explain it.
TEACHER: Then use it in a sentence.
RESPONSE: This pen is available for anybody that wants to use it.

✓ **4.** *temporary*
RESPONSE: It's not built to stay long.

✓ **5.** *permanent*
RESPONSE: That it stays there . . . the house stays up longer.

✗ **6.** *sophisticated*
RESPONSE: I don't know the meaning of that word from the other thing, but I think I know another meaning.
TEACHER: O.K. Tell me the meaning you know.
RESPONSE: Well, I don't know how to explain it.
TEACHER: Could you put it in a sentence?
RESPONSE: This is a sophisticated truck.
TEACHER: What does that mean about the truck?
RESPONSE: That it's in a kind of motion or something. A kind of way.

FIGURE 4.4   Responses to vocabulary knowledge questions: Raymond

Raymond's incorrect responses to the comprehension questions suggest that he might be confused over the terms *crude* and *sophisticated.* In response to the question of the difference between these two types of housing (item 6), he replied that "crude is built to stay longer and sophisticated is not that long." In addition, he could not remember the kinds of materials used in sophisticated housing (item 8), a plausible consequence of unfamiliarity with this term. Again, to gain experience with the diagnostic process, examine Raymond's responses on the vocabulary knowledge assessment at this point. Is there corroborating evidence that vocabulary knowledge interfered with his comprehension?

Vocabulary Knowledge. Of the six words selected for assessment, there were only two that Raymond could not define: *sophisticated* and *determines.* For *sophisticated,* he thought that he knew "another meaning" for it—other than the one intended in the passage—but the meaning he gave ("a kind of motion") was incorrect. Note that the passage characterizes *crude* permanent housing (as in igloos, log cabins, and adobe huts) as "rough and unfinished" and later states that *sophisticated* houses have concrete foundations and frameworks made of wood, iron, or steel. Thus, the meaning of *sophisticated* in the sense of smooth, finished, and involving advanced technology is not given; this must be inferred from the contrast with *crude*. Raymond was evidently unable to make this inference; possibly he did not know what *crude* meant.

Because Raymond's difficulties on the comprehension questions seemed to be caused by his limited understanding of such words as *determines, crude*, and *sophisticated*, Paul decided to focus the further assessment on his vocabulary knowledge. In addition to assessing Raymond's understanding of *crude* and further specifying his knowledge of *determines*, Paul planned to explore his understanding of the words *plentiful, readily*, and *insulator*.

PAUSE AND REFLECT.   How would you use the same passage to further assess Raymond's vocabulary knowledge? Can you think of any way to explore his ability to use context? Compare your choices with those of Paul.

Further Assessment. The next day, after having Raymond reread the passage, Paul asked what *crude* meant. Raymond replied that *crude* "was a kind of housing" (as stated in the text) and he recalled the three examples that were given in the passage. Further questioning revealed that he had never before heard the word used nor could he use it in a sentence himself. It now seemed reasonable to consider Raymond's difficulty with item 6 on the comprehension test as stemming primarily from the unfamiliarity of *crude* and *sophisticated*. Without prior knowledge of these two words, Raymond could only assume that the difference in the materials used in these two types of housing made for a difference in degree of permanence. Although the terms *rough* and *unfinished* were used in the passage to describe crude housing, he evidently failed to relate these words to the meaning of *crude*. Consequently, he could not, in turn, grasp the idea that *sophisticated* was the opposite of rough and unfinished.

In the case of *determines*, Raymond seemed to know what it would mean in the context of people making decisions or predicting outcomes, but he seemed unable to grasp the idea that existing conditions could (so to speak) do the same:

PAUL: The passage states the environment determines the kinds of housing people choose. What does *determines* mean?

RAYMOND: If they lived in a cold place, that would show that they lived in an igloo. If it was hot, that would say that they would live in a hut maybe.

P: Okay. Then what would *determine* the kind of shelter people choose?

R: Well, like the people who run the city, they can choose if they wanted brick or wood.

P: Yes. But what does *determine* mean?

R: They . . . say it, predict.

P: Can you use the word *determines* in a sentence?

R: He determined that the house was gonna be wood.

Thus, it was not so much the meaning of the word itself that gave Raymond difficulty; it was rather the underlying concept, that environmental conditions could set limits on people's choices, that escaped him. His failure to grasp this concept could explain his inability to give generalized answers to the questions, "What determines the kind of shelter people choose?" and "Where do we usually get the materials we build houses from?"

To explore further the possibility that vocabulary knowledge was a limiting factor in Raymond's comprehension, Paul asked him to define several other words. Raymond knew that *plentiful* meant "there is a lot." However, for *readily,* he said, "that it's done, finished, used . . . I'm not sure." And for *insulator,* he understood that it was related to keeping warm but thought it was "a type of machine, a heater." Further, he could not pick out any clue sentences in the selection (such as, "The snow acts as an insulator") to suggest whether his idea of a machine made sense. Paul continued to probe context use. Raymond knew the word *igloo* but couldn't define *nomad* or *adobe.* When he reinspected the passage, he was able to locate their meanings, which were explicitly cued by the context. Although his unfamiliarity with these words did not interfere directly with his overall passage comprehension, the words provided additional evidence that his vocabulary knowledge was somewhat inadequate. With respect to context use strategies, when Raymond was allowed to look back, he could locate and use contextual information that was quite explicit, but he had a harder time picking up contextual clues that were given less explicitly and located across the selection.

PAUSE AND REFLECT.   How would you pull together your information on Raymond to explain your analysis to Paul? What instructional suggestions would you give?

Interpretation

Raymond's responses to the vocabulary knowledge and comprehension questions are summarized in Figure 4.5. The summary indicates that Raymond's comprehension (67 percent) is somewhat below the instructional range (75–89 percent comprehension) but not at his frustration level (less than 50 percent; see Table 8.1, p. 224). When comprehension falls within the borderline range between instructional and frustration levels, it is appropriate to consider whether additional instructional support, directly in the major area of reading difficulty, may

COMPREHENSION–VOCABULARY
KNOWLEDGE SUMMARY

Name _Raymond_ Grade _7_ Date _Feb._

Book/Page _Exploring Paths_ Level _13_
_82–83_

COMPREHENSION

_6_ / _9_   _67_ % Correct

Level: Independent   Instructional
        (Borderline)   Frustration

A. Retelling: Complete   Main Idea   Partial   (Inadequate)

  Comments: _Missed main idea_

B. Text-Related Comprehension

Item #	Response	Further Assessment (Comments)	Item #	Response	Further Assessment (Comments)
1	½	Examples rather than main idea	6	✗	
2	✓		7	✓	
3	✓		8	✗	
4	✓		9	½	
5	✓				

C. Beyond-Text Generalization

Item #	Response	Further Assessment (Comments)	Item #	Response	Further Assessment (Comments)
10	½		12	✗	
11	✓				

VOCABULARY KNOWLEDGE

_5_ / _10_   _50_ % Correct

Item Tested	Response	Comments	Item Tested	Response	Comments
environment	✓		crude (P)*	✗	never heard word before
determines	✗		plentiful (P)	✓	"a lot"
available	✓		readily (P)	✗	defined "ready"
temporary	✓		insulator (P)	✗	knew relation to warmth
permanent	✓		adobe (P)	✓	} could use
sophisticated	✗		nomads (P)	✓	} context to find

* Prefers to probe items

EVALUATION

A. Comprehension: _Remembered examples and details but did not grasp the main idea of the passage; problems are directly related to unknown words._

B. Vocabulary Knowledge _Deficiencies in word knowledge currently interfere with comprehension; prereading activities focused on vocabulary development should improve comprehension._

FIGURE 4.5 Summary of responses to comprehension and vocabulary knowledge questions: Raymond enable Raymond to read passages similar to this one with adequate comprehension.

Raymond's performance on the initial administration of the questions and during further assessment indicates that his major difficulty is in the area of vocabulary knowledge. Generally, he is able to process text with good understanding. However, when the text and/or the questions used to assess comprehension involve terms that are unfamiliar to him, his comprehension is not entirely adequate. For example, he misconstrued the difference between "crude" and "sophisticated" housing. Similarly, although he understood the use of available materials in the specific instances cited in the passage, he did not grasp the general principle or concept that these instances exemplified. In both these failures of comprehension, unknown words were directly implicated. This evidence suggests that Raymond should be able to cope with passages similar to this one in difficulty if special instruction focuses on developing his knowledge of the words they contain.

Instructional Plan

In conclusion, the passage represents an appropriate level of difficulty for instructional purposes as long as important word meanings are discussed before the material is read. Raymond's instruction should focus on two major areas. First, using procedures discussed earlier in this chapter, the development of word meanings should be emphasized during prereading. Second, systematic instruction should be developed in the area of using text information to infer word meanings by analyzing the words in context (Blachowicz & Zabroske, 1990).

CASE 4.2: TANYA

Tanya is a seventh grader who has been in the United States for four years and whose home language is not English. In class, where seventh-grade materials are used, her performance is erratic. Sometimes she is an active participant; at other times she is silent and withdrawn. Paul decides to use a seventh-grade text to determine whether the level of the material is appropriate for Tanya as well as to explore the nature of her difficulty.

Preparation

Paul selected a passage entitled "And Then There Were None" from the Bookmark Reading Program, which was being used for class instruction. The passage, 342

PAUSE AND REFLECT.   Which words would you choose for assessment from Figure 4.6?

And Then There Were None

In 1534, a French sea captain reported that his men had killed more than a thousand "northern penguins" in a single day. But the bird to which the captain referred was not a penguin at all. It was the great auk, which at one time nested safely by the millions from Newfoundland to Scandinavia. Today the only specimens are in museums.

Like the penguin, the great auk could not fly but was a powerful swimmer. Each season, a female laid only one enormous egg, measuring about five inches long. Fully grown, a great auk stood three feet tall.

Originally, the great auk's largest nesting ground was an island off the eastern coast of Newfoundland. But by the early 1800's, fishermen had completely destroyed them. They used the birds' bodies for food or rendered them into cooking oil.

While the Napoleonic wars were raging across Europe, ships were sailing from Reykjavik, Iceland, to nearby Penguin Island, the second largest great-auk nesting colony, to kill the birds for food. There, using only large sticks, sailors slaughtered the proud birds by the thousands. Then, in the spring of 1830, another terrible blow struck the few great auks still at Penguin Island. The island just disappeared beneath the frigid ocean waters. Most of the surviving great auks took refuge on the small island of Eldey. This island was not far from where their home had been.

But Eldey was not to remain their home for long. The birds had become famous in Europe. Collectors paid immense sums for great auk skins throughout the 1830's. In 1884, Carl Siemson of Reykjavik, an agent for prospective buyers, offered a large cash reward in hopes of getting just a few more skins of the almost extinct bird. A daring Icelandic fisherman answered the challenge and went to Eldey with a small crew. There, he looked for and finally discovered two great auks. He promptly killed them both. Soon after, he returned to Reykjavik to collect his reward; 100 crowns ($60) for the last two great auks on earth.

FIGURE 4.6 Diagnostic reading passage: Tanya

SOURCE: From *Exploring Paths: Skills Reader*, HBJ Handbook Reading Program, by Margaret Early, Donald Gallo, and Gwendolyn Kerr, published by Harcourt Brace Jovanovich, Inc., 1979. Passage by Mark Wexler, copyright 1974 by the National Wildlife Federation. Reprinted from the April–May issue of *National Wildlife Magazine*.

words in length, is shown in Figure 4.6. Paul prepared both word meaning and comprehension questions to be administered after Tanya read the passage. Before proceeding, compare the words you selected with those Paul chose: *specimens, slaughtered, surviving, refuge, prospective, immense,* and *extinct.*

Administration

Tanya read the passage in 3½ minutes, a rate of 98 words per minute. The record of her oral reading is given in Figure 4.7. Examine the evidence in order to decide whether print translation represents an area of reading difficulty for her.

Her comprehension and word knowledge responses are shown in Figure 4.8. Examine this evidence to formulate tentative answers to the following three questions. First, is Tanya experiencing difficulty with reading comprehension? Second, is her knowledge of word meanings limited? Third, if she is experiencing

In 1534, a French sea captain reported that his men had killed more than a thousand "northern penguins" in a single day. But the bird to which the captain referred was not a penguin at all. It was the great̂ auk *[est]*, which at one time nested safely by the millions from *[1]* Newfoundland to Scandinavia. Today the only specimens are in museums.

Like the penguin, the great auk could not fly but was a powerful swimmer. Each season, a female laid only one enormous egg, measuring about five inches long. Fully grown, a great auk stood̂ three feet tall. *[at]* *[1]*

Originally, the great auk's largest nesting ground was an island off the eastern coast of Newfoundland. But by the early 1800's, fishermen had completely destroyed them. They used the birds' bodies for food or ~~rendered~~ *[reneered]* them into cooking oil. *[1]*

While ⟨the⟩ ~~Napoleonic~~ *[Napolentic]* wars ⟨were⟩ raging across Europe, ships were sailing from ~~Reykjavik~~ *[Reja]* *[4]*, Iceland, to nearby Penguin Island, the second largest great-auk nesting colony, to kill the birds for food. There, using only large sticks, sailors slaughtered the proud birds by the thousands. Then, in the spring of 1830, another terrible blow struck the few great auks still at Penguin Island. The island just disappeared beneath the frigid ocean waters. Most of the surviving great auks took ~~refuge~~ *[rē-uge]* on the small island ~~of Eldey~~ *[at Italy]*. This island was not far from *[3]* where their home had been.

But ~~Eldey~~ *[Italy]* was not to remain their home for long. The birds had become famous in Europe. *[1]*

Collectors paid immense sums for great auk skins through⟨out⟩ the 1830's. In 1884, Carl ~~Siemson~~ *[Simmons]* of ~~Reykjavik~~ *[Reja]*, an agent for prospect⟨ive⟩ buyers, offered a large cash reward in hopes *[3]* of getting just a few more skins of the almost ~~extinct~~ bird. A daring Icelandic fisherman *[1]* answered the challenge and went to Eldey with a small crew. There, he looked for and ~~finally~~ *[found]* *[1]* ⟨discovered⟩ two great auks. He promptly killed them both. Soon after, he returned to *[1]* ~~Reykjavik~~ *[Reja]* to collect his reward; 100 crowns ($60) for the last two great auks on earth. *[✗ 0 *]*

* Miscues occurring more than twice were not counted.

FIGURE 4.7 Record of oral reading: Tanya

SOURCE: From *Exploring Paths: Skills Reader*, HBJ Bookmark Reading Program, by Margaret Early, Donald Gallo, and Gwendolyn Kerr, published by Harcourt Brace Jovanovich, Inc., 1979. Passage by Mark Wexler, copyright 1974 by the National Wildlife Federation. Reprinted from the April–May issue of *National Wildlife Magazine*.

Comprehension

½ **1.** What is this passage about? (the great auk; its extinction)
RESPONSE: About two auks.

✗ **2.** In what part of the world did the great auks live? (Newfoundland, Scandinavia, Iceland, etc.)
RESPONSE: On an island. [Do you know where it was?] No.

✗ **3.** When did the events in the story take place? (1500–1800)
RESPONSE: Don't know.

½ **4.** ✗ a. What did the great auks look like? (penguins)
RESPONSE: Like hawks; big birds.
✓ b. How big were they? (3 feet)
RESPONSE: Three feet.

½ **5.** What problem did these birds have? (hunted and killed)
RESPONSE: They couldn't stay in one place. The place where they were at would disappear under the ocean.

½ **6.** Why were the birds hunted and killed? (for food, cooking oil, skins)
RESPONSE: For the money. If they caught two hawks, they get $50 worth, get 50 coins each. So they got 100 coins, they got $60.

½ **7.** What happened to Penguin Island in 1830 and what did the birds do? (it sank into the ocean; the birds swam to another island)
RESPONSE: It disappeared under the ocean. [What did the auks do when this happened?] They flew away.

½ **8.** Why did Carl Siemson offer a large sum of money for the birds? (he was an agent for prospective buyers of skins)
RESPONSE: He wanted to get some money for himself for the birds. So if he got 'em, then he would kill them. Then he would get some money for them and they both would have been even about the money.

✓ **9.** How much were the hunters paid for the last two great auks? ($60)
RESPONSE: (not asked; answered in response to item 6)

✗ **10.** What happens when animals are hunted and killed with no protection from the law? (extinction)
RESPONSE: They'd be kind of scared. They'd be dead. Men would go to jail.

Vocabulary Knowledge

✗ **1.** *specimens*
RESPONSE: Leaves. [Tell me more about it.] Not sure.

✓ **2.** *slaughtered*
RESPONSE: Kill someone.

✓ **3.** *surviving*
RESPONSE: They lived on.

✗ **4.** *refuge*
RESPONSE: Don't know.

✗ **5.** *prospective*
RESPONSE: You're looking at it . . . thinking about it.
Teacher: Can you use it in a sentence?
RESPONSE: The prospective was easy.

✗ **6.** *immense*
RESPONSE: Clever.

✗ **7.** *extinct*
RESPONSE: Don't know.

FIGURE 4.8 Responses to comprehension and vocabulary knowledge questions: Tanya difficulty with both comprehension and word knowledge, is there evidence that her inadequate knowledge of word meanings accounts for her comprehension difficulty?

PAUSE AND REFLECT.   Look at Tanya's responses in Figures 4.8–4.10. How would you analyze her print skill, comprehension, and vocabulary knowledge? What would you assess further?

Preliminary Analysis

Print Skill. The results from Tanya's oral reading are summarized in Figure 4.9, which shows a total of 18 oral reading errors. Of these, five were sight word errors, mainly insertions and omissions. A few of the sight word errors seemed to result when she was attempting to pronounce a difficult name; the others are typical of mature readers and do little harm to meaning. The majority of miscues were in response to content words, and almost half of these were responses to somewhat unusual names. The others involved important content words (e.g., *extinct, rendered, refuge, prospective*). These errors may indicate some difficulty with the pronunciation of multisyllabic words. On the other hand, she pronounced many difficult content words accurately (e.g., *Scandinavia, specimens, slaughtered, frigid*). Thus, her apparent print translation difficulty may actually reflect unfamiliarity with these words.

Comprehension. The results from Tanya's comprehension questions are summarized in Figure 4.10. Of the nine text-related comprehension questions she was asked, she answered only one (item 9) correctly and six only partially correctly, yielding a comprehension score of 44 percent. Tanya showed some understanding of the destruction of the last two great auks but seemed unaware that this was the culmination of a series of destructive events. Her grasp of the details of time and place and the auks' resemblance to penguins was also quite limited.

It is not always possible to identify specific words that might be implicated in failures of comprehension. And so it was in Tanya's case. An examination of the passage in relation to the questions she answered incorrectly provided a few good leads regarding specific words that might be sources of difficulty for her. There were, however, two words central to the general topic or theme of the passage that could have interfered with her overall comprehension. The word *specimens* in the first paragraph provided an important clue that the birds were not extinct; unfamiliarity with this word would certainly make the rest of the passage more difficult to understand. Similarly, the word *extinct* in the last paragraph, if unknown, would represent a significant loss of information about the topic at large. In addition a number of place names mentioned in the passage could have been unfamiliar to Tanya; and the auks' resemblance to penguins would have little meaning if she had no knowledge of penguins. Paul planned to explore these items

ORAL READING ANALYSIS

Name Tanya Grade 7 Date Oct.

Book/Page Exploring Paths Level 13

A. Difficulty

18 / 342 95 % Correct

Level: Independent (Instructional)
Borderline Frustration

B. Word Learning: Sight Word Errors

Printed Word	Oral Response	Further Exploration	Evaluation
of	at		No problem
finally	found		
the	[omitted]		
were	[omitted]		
at	[inserted]		

C. Word Identification: Content Word Errors

Printed Word	Oral Response	Further Exploration	Evaluation
great	greatest	✓	generally little difficulty
throughout	through	✓	with word identification
prospective	prospect	✓	when meanings and
			pronunciations of words
refuge	rē-uge	re-fuge	are known.
rendered	reneered	✓	
Napoleonic	Nupolentlc	Nā-pol-e-nic	
② Reykjavik	Reja	Rē-ka-vik	
② Eldey	Italy	✓	
Siemson	Simmons	Simson	
extinct	estic	✓	
discovered	[omitted]	✓	

D. Integration–Fluency

Integration: Most sight word and affixed word errors are contextually appropriate. No use of correction strategies.

Fluency: Rate 342 / 3.5 = 98 wpm Evaluation Slower than average

Phrasing Fluent except when she encountered unknown words.

FIGURE 4.9 Analysis of oral reading responses: Tanya

COMPREHENSION–VOCABULARY KNOWLEDGE SUMMARY

Name __Tanya__ Grade __7__ Date __Oct.__

Book/Page __Exploring Paths__ Level __13__
                   __334-335__

COMPREHENSION

__4__ / __9__ __44__ % Correct

Level: Independent   Instructional
      Borderline   (Frustration)

A. Retelling: Complete   Main Idea   Partial   (Inadequate)

Comments: __Remembered only minor details__

B. Text-Related Comprehension

Item #	Response	Further Assessment (Comments)	Item #	Response	Further Assessment (Comments)
1	½		6	½	
2	X		7	½	
3	X		8	½	
4	½		9	√	
5	½				

C. Beyond-Text Generalization

Item #	Response	Further Assessment (Comments)	Item #	Response	Further Assessment (Comments)
10	X				

VOCABULARY KNOWLEDGE

__2__ / __8__ __25__ % Correct

Item Tested	Response	Comments	Item Tested	Response	Comments
specimens	X		extinct	X	unknown concept
slaughtered	X		penguins (P)*	X	"tiny creatures" unfamiliar
surviving	√				
refuge	X		sums (P)	X	could not
prospective	X		reward (P)	√	use context
immense	X		agent (P)	X	to find clues

* P indicates a probe item

EVALUATION

A. COMPREHENSION: __Not probed because basic concepts were unfamiliar__

B. Vocabulary Knowledge __Lacks much background knowledge presumed by this material (e.g., didn't know what penguins looked like; could not locate Newfoundland, Scandinavia or Iceland on globe; completely unfamiliar with concept of animal extinction)__

FIGURE 4.10 Summary of responses to comprehension and vocabulary knowledge question: Tanya during further assessment. In the meantime, he examined the results of the vocabulary assessment.

Vocabulary Knowledge

As summarized in Figure 4.10, Tanya was able to define or use in a sentence only two of the seven words she was asked about. On this basis, her vocabulary knowledge was definitely an area of weakness. However, the unknown words alone could not fully account for her low comprehension score, since they were not directly related to incorrectly answered questions. Additional questioning was undertaken, therefore, during the further assessment that followed, to determine whether Tanya's general information and conceptual knowledge were adequate for this passage.

Further Assessment

This stage focused on Tanya's knowledge of a few key words (e.g., *penguins* and *extinct*) and on her knowledge of the places mentioned in the passage. When asked if she knew anything about penguins, Tanya replied they were tiny creatures but she did not know what they looked like. When shown a picture book of types of birds, she could name the dove and pigeon in English and did recognize the penguin and label it in Spanish. With regard to the problem of extinction, Tanya did not know of any other animals that had been hunted and killed until none were left on earth; and she was unaware that anything was currently being done to protect wildlife from extinction. For example, she assumed that hunting and fishing licenses were primarily for the purpose of raising money and that wildlife preserves were designed to make it easy for people to see the animals. Further, she did not know where Newfoundland, Scandinavia, or Iceland could be found on the globe. Finally, she could not use context to suggest clues to the meanings of *sums* or *agent.*

Interpretation and Instruction

Tanya's comprehension of the diagnostic passage was extremely limited, as was her knowledge of important words in it. Her problem in vocabulary knowledge was lack of the appropriate terms in English for concepts she knew. However, she did lack some of the basic concepts necessary for understanding the significance of the events described. Paul decided that passages at this level of difficulty were inappropriate for Tanya and began to look for simpler books on the topics under study to use with her. He also planned to focus on important concepts, background knowledge, and comparison of English–Spanish vocabulary during pre-reading instruction.

INSTRUCTION TO SUPPORT VOCABULARY DEVELOPMENT

Within the framework of effective instruction outlined above, a wide variety of techniques and activities are possible. In most instructional situations, you would negotiate among various objectives and constraints and make a number of instructional choices based on elements such as the student's initial knowledge level, the importance of the word to the study at hand, and the time available for instruction. All those factors make up what have been called the cost and benefits of instruction (Graves & Prenn, 1986). Both the nature of the vocabulary words chosen for instruction and your purpose, as well as the student's prior knowledge about the words and their base concepts, can influence your decision to choose one technique over another.

Your purpose in working with vocabulary is twofold. A first goal is the development of independent word-learning strategies, such as use of context, references, and word structure. Your students need to build habits of self-reflection and monitoring of vocabulary and concept knowledge. "Do I know anything about this?" and "Is my definition adequate for this context?" become important questions for students to ask.

A second consideration is enlarging the student's conceptual base and recognition vocabulary so that impediments to effective comprehension are removed. If this is a major objective, prereading instruction on key concepts may be called for, especially for those terms that are not well developed by the context, such as the words chosen as assessment words in the case studies of Raymond and Tanya. This goal suggests an alternative instructional decision. Words can be highlighted before readings and predictive activities generating tentative meanings can be emphasized, so that the reader has a focus for contextual learning. Postreading monitoring, evaluation, refinement, and verification of meaning then become essential elements in the instructional cycle. The words that have well-developed contextual references in a reading selection lend themselves to this focus.

Your task then is to help the students "contextualize" the word in a relevant way. The context created should be drawn from, or related to that provided by the text and should draw on what the student already knows to mediate the new learning. For example, when discussing equipment for the unfamiliar game of pelota that is the subject of a reading selection, you may wish to contextualize the words by using the student's knowledge of racquetball or other racquet sports. In a situation where a concept is completely unfamiliar, you may choose to build knowledge firsthand before teaching by analogy. In creating these contexts, students can "hypothesize" the meanings of unknown words from sentence or paragraph contexts before reading the selection or consulting a reference. Alternatively, the concept underlying each unknown word can be discussed before the word itself is introduced. For example, to introduce *assassination,* discussion would begin with the idea of "kill" or "murder" and lead toward the murder of a political figure (Vaughan, Castle, Gilbert, & Love, 1982). Described below are a number of additional strategies for introducing, hypothesizing about, and helping students manipulate words and relate them to real-world contexts. They are designed primarily for showing the interrelationships among word meanings and include opportunities for self-questioning and monitoring.

Learning Word Meanings from Context

Many of the words we know—perhaps most—have probably been learned spontaneously in the course of general reading and listening experience (Nagy & Herman, 1987). Yet research suggests that vocabulary building is a slow and gradual process

(Eller, Pappas, & Brown, 1988; Gray & Holmes, 1938). This is not really surprising. When we encounter unfamiliar words in a text we are not, in general, inclined to develop and commit to memory precise meanings for them. Because we are attending to passage meaning rather than to individual words, we are more likely to infer vague meanings consistent with the text, or else read around unknown words as long as the passage remains comprehensible. In unusual circumstances we may consult a dictionary or a friend.

McKeown (1985) has documented the basic steps involved in learning from context: noting that an important word is unknown; generating hypotheses about meaning; cross-checking by reading on, going back or consulting a friend or reference. Variations of the cloze procedure (Blachowicz, 1977) may be employed or direct instruction with natural contexts or teacher-prepared sentences may be used (Blachowicz, 1993; Buikema & Graves, 1993). In all cases, the process should involve students in predicting and monitoring meanings with a process involving the following:

- Look—before, at, and after the word
- Reason—to connect what students know with the clues from the author
- Predict—a possible meaning
- Resolve/Redo—use what you know, the clues from the author, a reference, to confirm your prediction or start the cycle again (Blachowicz & Zabroske, 1990, p. 506)

Reference use can also be an important tool in learning from context. If reference materials are used *after* a word is encountered in context, students have identified a specific domain ("This word is some kind of animal") or questions to answer ("Could this be a type of deer?") that will help them use the dictionary effectively.

Schwartz and Raphael (1985) have suggested that employing a "concept-of-definition" template can provide a framework for approaching and evaluating contextual learning. His instructional methodology focuses on having students develop expectations for adequate definitions through the process of filling out a concept-of-definition frame (see Figure 4.11) and models a step-by-step approach to achieving and utilizing such frameworks. A related process, the PAVE (*Predict, Associate, Verify, Elaborate*) procedure, can assist teachers in strategically connecting contextual and reference learning. With PAVE, students make predictions about a word's meaning which they verify from context and references (Bannon, Fisher, Pozzi, & Wessel, 1990). Such processes appear productive for the development of context-sensitive independent learning strategies.

Building Conceptual Networks

Along with becoming effective independent users of context, readers must be encouraged to learn and retain new words by connecting them to concepts and words they already know. Methods to help them activate what they already know, establish connections, organize their knowledge, and manipulate it are suggested below. Many of these can also be incorporated into a metacognitive approach to instruction, one

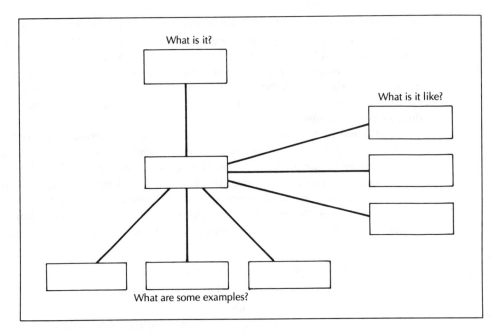

FIGURE 4.11 Word map

SOURCE: R. Schwartz and T. Raphael, "Concept of Definition: A Key to Improving Students' Vocabulary." *The Reading Teacher, 39,* 1985. Reprinted by permission of the International Reading Association.

that asks students to evaluate what they know before reading, make tentative connections to new words, establish predictions about words they know something about, and construct questions about those that are unfamiliar. Then, after reading, students can go back and evaluate their earlier predictions about word meaning and establish or refine meanings for words they have questions about. Note that all these examples are intended to be applied within the context of a selection being read or a content area being studied. This connection to the topic of their reading provides the contextualization necessary for true vocabulary development.

1. *Brainstorming and Classification.* In activities of this type, students create what might be called a **concept map**, a representation of what they already know in relation to a given word. Working in small groups, students are given a limited amount of time to list as many related words as they can. You then combine the students' contributions into a master list, and the students group the words on the list into categories. You may provide the categories, or the students may derive their own. This technique is often recommended as an interesting way of introducing a major concept related to a unit of study. Concepts associated with terms such as *propaganda, pollution, nutrition,* and *revolution* lend

themselves to this technique, since students are likely to have a degree of knowledge in these areas.

Many other options such as exclusion brainstorming, knowledge rating (Blachowicz, 1986), and concept ladders (Gillet & Temple, 1982) are useful as formats for prereading of new vocabulary. You can design all these with a cognitive monitoring component by focusing on some works for prereading prediction and some for postreading evaluation and refinement.

2. *Using Graphic Organizers.* Structured overviews (Barron, 1969), semantic maps and webs (Johnson & Pearson, 1984), and vocab-o-grams (Blachowicz, 1986) all utilize a graphic model to present new words and make explicit the connections among new and already known concepts and structures. You identify the words to be taught and in a diagram show how they are related to each other. You do not present a finished diagram to the students, however. Rather, you build the diagram *with* the students as you explain and discuss each new word. Students participate by recalling prior knowledge, relevant experiences, examples, and so on. The diagram then remains on display as a reference point and an aid to memory while instruction proceeds. Thus the structured overview is actually an "advance organizer" for the key concepts, as represented by the technical vocabulary, to be taught in a content area lesson or unit. As such, it may contain familiar as well as unfamiliar words, relating what is to be taught to what is already known about a particular topic.

3. *Creating Personal Contexts.* Along with techniques stressing semantic and categorical relatedness noted above, the creation of personal contexts for words is another way to explore and develop meanings. Developing importance ratings for words (Sloan, Trathen, & Dole, 1993), creating and enacting dramatic contexts (Duffelmeyer, 1980), creating analogies (Bean, Singer, & Cowan, 1985), and self-selection and explanation (Fisher, Blachowicz, & Smith, 1991; Blachowicz, Fisher, Pozzi, & Costa, 1992) are also useful ways to relate new words to what students already know. In these instances, as in the ones above, you must provide scaffolding and feedback to the learner in the form of information or questions that help monitor and refine meaning.

Extending and Elaborating Word Meaning

Once words have been introduced and discussed, students need opportunities to experiment with them in meaningful ways. This helps them to refine, extend, and elaborate their meanings and to become comfortable with nuances of usage. Use in oral language and writing are the best ways for students to explore with words as well as going back to refine graphic organizers, concept maps, or other structures used before or during reading. There are also some simple postreading activities that can help students extend and elaborate meaning. As in all good vocabulary activities, discussion, explanation, and use are critical to real learning.

1. *Insult or Compliment?* (Lake, 1971). This activity works well with adjectives, since it deals with the favorable or unfavorable connotations of words. You prepare a list of words and give it to the students. The words may be unfamiliar, in which case students will use a dictionary, or they may be words that have already been defined and discussed, in which case the activity may be considered an application of word meanings. The students' task is to decide whether the use of these words to describe them personally would be a compliment or an insult. You follow these with a discussion.

2. *Choose and Use.* Have students think about the features of words to answer questions that make them think, For example:
   Would a *street urchin* be well dressed?
   Should you trust someone who *bamboozled* you?
   Discussion and explanation should follow along with further use of the words (Hafner, 1977; Beck, Perfetti, & McKeown, 1982).

3. *Word Sorts.* In this activity students organize words into categories. You can provide the categories, or the students may be required to search for the relationships among word concepts in order to derive their own.

4. *Post-Structured Overviews.* This activity is somewhat similar to a word sort, but it allows greater freedom in portraying relationships. Students must be familiar with structured overviews or various diagram formats, however, before they can exploit this freedom. Small groups are each given a list of words and a set of 3 × 5 cards; each word on the list is written on a card. The students then "work together to decide upon a spatial arrangement among the cards which depicts the major relationships among the words" (Vacca, 1981, p. 251). Discussion of each group's solution follows. You should recognize that more than one solution is possible.

5. *Create Keywords.* Students can generate a "keyword," which will serve as a mnemonic for the definition of the word to be learned (Pressley, Levin, & Miller, 1981). The keyword is a familiar word that is in some way similar in sound to the target word. It may, for example, rhyme with it or begin with the same syllable. The keyword is then used to construct an image (or verbal cue) that represents the meaning of the target word. For example, to remember the definition of *carlin* (an old woman), one might select *car* as the keyword and visualize an old woman riding in (or atop) a car. Then, the word *carlin* would bring to mind *car*, and this in turn would bring to mind the image of the old woman and, hence, the meaning of *carlin*. Keywords and images are sometimes difficult to create, especially for abstract words. However, the activity is likely to be interesting as well as useful to students, at least for some words or in some learning situations. The procedure should be introduced to students accordingly—as one possible strategy for remembering definitions.

SUMMARY

We have described procedures for investigating the influence of unknown words on reading comprehension. We have also illustrated the application of those procedures in two case studies. The studies demonstrate how the assessment of word knowledge is related to the diagnostic process as a whole; they also highlight the way in which unknown words may underlie incorrect responses to comprehension questions. The first case study showed that specific words may lead directly to incorrect answers. In the second case study, however, the relationship was less direct, and unknown words took their toll in fragmentation of overall comprehension. This latter phenomenon reflects the important principles discussed in the first part of the chapter regarding the nature of word knowledge. It reflects the fact that we ordinarily know much more about word referents than just their definitional attributes and that it is this sum total of knowledge that "drives" the comprehension process. If this knowledge is inadequate with respect to the major theme of a passage, overall comprehension is likely to be disrupted. (In other words, had Tanya been aware of the *problem* of extinction, even though she did not know the word itself, she might have been able to recognize the events described in the passage as instances of that problem.) This view of word knowledge has clear implications—supported by recent research—for the design of instruction. In general, instruction in word meanings must go beyond definitions and include experiences in which the learner constructs relationships between new words and what he or she knows. The process must be one of active learning, in which self-monitoring of word knowledge and relating this knowledge to real-world situations and events are important components.

TRY IT OUT

1. Select a student from your class who might have a problem with vocabulary knowledge. Take a reading selection your students will be using next week and choose a diagnostic passage such as the ones chosen for Raymond and Tanya. Select key vocabulary and assess. What is your conclusion?

2. Find one of the standardized tests noted in this chapter, or any one you use in your school that has a vocabulary subtest. Look over the vocabulary subsection and answer some of the items. Are the words chosen reflective of your curriculum? Is vocabulary presented in context? Are the students asked to respond in a clear and sensible way? Also, find the most recent review for this test in the *Mental Measurements Yearbook* (Buros, 1938–1985) to give you other views on strengths and weaknesses. What is your overall evaluation of this measure? What insights do you have for its use and interpretation as a vocabulary measure?

3. **Student Portfolio Ideas:** You might ask students to create semantic maps or webs relating some of the central vocabulary in a selection or chapter to keep in their portfolios. This is particularly useful for content area chapters. Another

portfolio addition might be an "importance list," a short list of words they choose as key vocabulary from a selection they are currently reading. Along with the list, have students give a short explanation of *why* each word is central to their reading. This helps students develop the habit of self-selection for study and can give you insight into their interpretation of their reading.

 4. For Your Teaching Portfolio: Add to your teaching portfolio from this chapter. You might include

- your responses to "Pause and Reflect" on Raymond and Tanya
- "Try It Out" #1 and #2 above
- a sample vocabulary instructional lesson that you tried and evaluated
- a response to one of the "For Further Reading" selections for this chapter

FOR FURTHER READING

Blachowicz, C. L. Z. & Lee, J. (1991). Vocabulary development in the whole literacy classroom. *The Reading Teacher, 45,* 188–195.
Describes a framework for vocabulary selection and instruction in whole literacy classrooms.

Irvin, J. L. (1990). *Vocabulary knowledge: Guidelines for instruction.* Washington, DC: National Education Association.
Good short overview with teaching ideas.

Johnson, D. D., & Pearson, P. D. (1978). *Teaching reading vocabulary* (2nd ed.). New York: Holt, Rinehart and Winston.
Excellent ideas for lower elementary grades.

Nagy, W. E. (1989). *Teaching vocabulary to improve reading comprehension.* Urbana, IL: National Council of Teachers of English.
Excellent ideas for content reading.

chapter 5

Reading Comprehension: Its Nature and Development

CHAPTER GOALS FOR THE READER

To understand the strategic, constructive nature of good reading

To understand the interaction between reader and author that underlies comprehension

To appreciate how readers' prior knowledge, language, and text organization influence their comprehension

To develop a framework for questioning and develop skill in analyzing text and composing questions

CLASSROOM VIGNETTE: ONE CLASSROOM

As soon as Sandra, a new teacher, got over the initial shock of her first year of teaching, she began to observe the different ways in which her fourth-grade students comprehended the same passages. Omar, one of her bilingual students, had trouble understanding how pronouns connected one sentence to another. He told her they "didn't have all those little words" in his native language. Julia found it difficult to recognize transitions from one sentence to another when the author didn't put in clear transitional words. In her oral reading, she phrased these as if the author were starting a new idea. Laticia was excellent at stating the facts of the passage but wasn't likely to add any new information. She focused on "what the author said" and didn't add information from her own knowledge. All of Sandra's students struggled when a selection wasn't clearly organized, particularly in their content texts.

Sandra also noticed that her own questions were sometimes unfocused and seemed to confuse her students rather than help them focus on something important in what they were reading.

Sandra's observations could apply in most classrooms. Some students will show good understanding when they are reading about a topic they already have considerable knowledge of, but they are less effective when the topic is unfamiliar. Others do well when the author's language is like their own but have difficulty when the language is more diverse. Still others can comprehend parts of what they read but have difficulty in seeing or constructing an organizational pattern for their reading. And then there are some students who have well-developed strategies for understanding most things they encounter. Strategies, knowledge, language, and organization—these are key words for understanding comprehension. This chapter examines these four important aspects of comprehension and provides a foundation for assessing comprehension in Chapter 6.

CHAPTER OVERVIEW

This chapter has three parts. The first section presents an overview of the constructive nature of comprehension by focusing on the characteristics of students who comprehend well. This approach reinforces not only the general importance of the reader's prior knowledge but also focuses on strategic and constructive processes for using that knowledge. The second section explores different factors that influence instruction: the knowledge and language of both the reader and the author, the need to make inferences and elaborations during reading, and the importance of informational organization to comprehension. The third section stresses the importance of questioning and retelling to assessment of comprehension. An awareness of all these issues is critical to the reflective assessment of comprehension, which is discussed in Chapter 6.

CHAPTER OUTLINE

Comprehension: A Strategic and Constructive Process

What Influences Comprehension?
   The Knowledge and Language of the Reader
   The Knowledge and Language of the Author
   Case 5.1: Omar and Laticia
   The Need to Make Inferences
   The Organization of Information
   Personal Response

Questions and the Development of Comprehension
   Beyond Levels of Thinking
   Text-Related and Beyond-Text Questions
   Questions and Prior Knowledge

We observe comprehension by listening to what students say in discussion, by reading what they write in response to reading, by probing with questions, and by interpreting what they tell us about their own introspection and understanding. If students have difficulties in understanding that do not seem to depend on print or word knowledge, we begin to examine the process of comprehension itself, the process of integrating and organizing information across a text and connecting it with what is already known. Assessing comprehension plays a central role in the diagnostic process. It enables you, the teacher, to estimate the level of materials that are appropriate for instruction and also serves as a backdrop against which word-level skills and knowledge may be evaluated.

The purpose of this chapter is to examine those aspects of comprehension that most directly affect the assessment process: the nature of comprehension as a strategic and constructive activity and as revealed in the behaviors of good readers; factors with the reader and within the text that affect comprehension; and a framework for questions and retellings that reflect what we know about texts and their structures.

COMPREHENSION: A STRATEGIC AND CONSTRUCTIVE PROCESS

There are many ways to view comprehension. It is "thought-getting and thought manipulating" (Huey; 1908/1968); it is "reasoning" (Thorndike, 1917); it is the "construction . . . and progressive refinement of hypotheses in order to comprehend, interpret, or evaluate text information" (Mason et al., 1984, p. 31). These are all apt descriptions of reading and they share the characteristic of being process oriented. This redefinition of reading as an active, constructive process has stimulated a major strand of reading research over the last two decades. Central to this redefinition has been the emphasis on reading as a process by which the reader interacts, or "transacts" (Rosenblatt, 1985), with the text being read.

From this perspective, the process of making meaning is a constructive one (Blachowicz, 1984) in which the reader connects what he or she already knows to information and clues supplied by the author in a text. Significant for **comprehension** then, is what the reader already knows (commonly referred to as prior knowledge), what the author supplies, and the strategies the reader employs to construct something meaningful through interaction or transaction with the text. Making meaning involves interactions with others; therefore, comprehension is also viewed as a process of social construction (Bakhtin, 1981). We work out meanings based on our own community backgrounds, goals, and values. Because of this, teachers must put themselves inside the cultures of the children they teach to understand their comprehension difficulties.

The strategic aspect of reading is central to understanding comprehension, as it is to all the issues considered in this book. One way to get a "feel" for the strategic nature of reading is to focus on what good readers do. Good and poor readers have been observed and compared in many reading situations: in classroom and experimental reading tasks (Spiro, 1980); while thinking aloud during reading (Meyers & Lytle, 1986); when faced with reading difficulty that they must repair (Garner, 1987). While terminology and research methods differ, there is an emerging consensus about strategic processes that seem characteristic of good readers:

1. Good readers use what they know. They realize that reading is more than remembering exact wording from the text; it also involves reasoning, and adding their own knowledge is a critical component of the comprehension process.

2. Good readers self-question to establish what they *don't* know and what they want and need to know. For many things they read, their knowledge is limited. Asking good questions helps them make hypotheses, draw analogies from experience, and set some purposes and guidelines for reading.

3. Just as good readers read with purpose, to answer their questions, to fill in knowledge, or to confirm a hunch, they integrate information across the text, add information by making inferences to build cohesion, and use structure to organize their comprehension.

4. Good readers monitor their reading. They keep track of their hunches, change them, reread, look for more evidence, but generally keep a sense of "How am I doing? Do I understand this?" as an ongoing evaluative standard. This process is called **metacognition**, the idea that good readers are aware of their own cognitive behavior while reading and know how to use and control their strategies to read, learn, and remember ideas and information. Metacognitive theory suggests that good readers have some awareness of these processes and can call on a repertoire of strategies when something goes wrong with their comprehension. How explicit or tacit this awareness may be, however, is still a subject of debate.

5. Good readers respond thoughtfully to what they have read. Newly emerging research suggests that readers who respond personally to what they read exhibit high degrees of critical and analytical thinking (Galda, 1990; McGee, 1992).

PAUSE AND REFLECT.   Observe your own reading as you continue this chapter. Which of the five characteristics of good readers do you exhibit? Keep track of the ones you don't understand to see how the chapter clarifies them.

WHAT INFLUENCES COMPREHENSION?

From previous chapters describing the emergence of literacy and the development of print skills and vocabulary and concept knowledge, we have seen that influences on the comprehension process can come from many sources—from the reader's knowledge and experience of the world, books, and literacy; from the ways the author writes and structures the text; and from the context or social situation within which the reading is done. This section examines reader language, author language, inferencing to connect the two, text organization, and reader response to determine their influence on comprehension.

The Knowledge and Language of the Reader

We noted earlier in this text the importance of experience for the development of the conceptual knowledge on which all comprehension is based. In Chapter 2 the significance of early literacy experiences, such as dramatic play and storytelling, being read to, and early experimentation with writing and reading, were noted. In Chapter 4, the development of the reader's conceptual and vocabulary knowledge were emphasized. All these help readers develop an awareness of the transactional nature of reading and writing, and give them pleasure that motivates them to become independent readers and capable users of language, for it is this intertwining of all language functions that is a major developmental influence on reading performance.

Certainly reading is intimately related to language. Words that look alike tend to sound alike, and words and sentences have the same meaning when they are written as when they are spoken. Indeed, reading is commonly characterized as "a language process." But what is language? Is it the words we use when we speak? Or the sounds that make up the words? Or is it the organization of words in sentences? The very fact that we can ask these different questions suggests something about the answer: Language involves all of these—sounds, words, and sentences.

Words, of course, have both sound (i.e., phonemes) and meaning. Thus we can say that language is a system of sounds that conveys meaning. To know a language is to know that system, its *phonology*.

But the sequence of sounds that make up a word conveys meaning only to those who already know what thing, or action, or quality of things or actions the word stands for. Knowing a language, then, involves some knowledge of its *lexicon* as well as its phonological workings.

Finally, the sequence of words that make up a phrase or sentence is meaningful only if one knows the third component of language, its *syntax*. Language, then, is not speaking or listening; these are language *behaviors*. It is, rather, a three-level system of *knowledge* that we use when we speak or listen (and when we write or read as well). It is this knowledge that enables us to express our thoughts and feelings (in speech or writing) and to understand others (in listening and reading). In other words, we use our *knowledge* of language in reading and writing just as we do in speaking and listening. And it is in this sense that we can say, "Reading is a language process."

Because reading and language are so closely related, we sometimes think that reading comprehension—the comprehension of written language—is neither more nor less than the comprehension of spoken language. That is, we assume that a student should have no difficulty understanding a written passage as long as the words and sentence structures in it are familiar and express ideas that are within his or her cognitive grasp. But this is only partly true. Reading differs from listening in a number of important ways, and accommodating these differences is part of the process of learning to read. Except in the special case of oral reading in the classroom, reading is a solitary activity whereas spoken language generally involves the presence of another human being. This may be one reason many children find it difficult to concentrate during independent (silent) reading. In addition, written language provides less information: The stress, pause, and intonation of spoken language are absent in reading, as are the relevant social and physical contexts, which supply important nonlinguistic clues. Thus, reading places the burden of comprehension more squarely on language alone. Finally, children must become aware that written language is processed in much the same way as spoken language—that it relates to real-world situations and can be understood by reference to prior knowledge and experience. A primary purpose of language experience stories is to help children develop this awareness.

For the child in the primary grades, the transition from spoken to written language entails a major adjustment over and above the adjustment to the print translation task. This adjustment is facilitated by the traditional practice of simulating in beginning reading materials the language of ordinary conversation. Later on, in the intermediate grades and beyond, students must adjust to written language that is more precise and tightly organized, more closely reasoned, and more complex in style and content than the language they are likely to hear in ordinary discourse. At all stages of learning to read, therefore, students need language and literacy experiences that will help them make the necessary adjustments and develop skill in reading comprehension.

The Knowledge and Language of the Author

Not only the language of the reader but also the language of the author—the author's lexical, linguistic, and structural decisions—affect the processes a reader must call into play to understand a selection. That what we read should make sense is self-evident. What is not so evident, perhaps, is that coherence is constructed through the cooperative effort of the reader and the writer; readers need to employ specific strategies to connect the language of the author with their own knowledge and language. Critical to all these strategies is the need to integrate information and to make inferences. The term **integration** is used here in a somewhat broader sense than in Chapter 2. It refers to the process of combining information across sentences.

CASE 5.1: OMAR AND LATICIA

Sandra was interested in getting a clearer picture of Omar and Laticia, two students in her fourth-grade class. To learn how they used their own knowledge when they read, she asked them to read the following paragraph:

Father said, "Happy birthday!" as he handed Jimmy a box. Jimmy opened up the box. There he saw a small brown puppy.

Sandra asked each student three questions:

1. Where was the puppy?
2. Whose birthday was it?
3. How does Jimmy feel?

As we progress through this chapter, you will learn how Omar and Laticia dealt with these questions and what conclusions Sandra drew about their need for instruction.

Omar was unable to answer the question, "Where was the puppy?" He needed to integrate the information across all three sentences in order to understand that the puppy was in the box. For Omar, that meant understanding that "the box" of the second sentence was the same as "a box" the father had handed over. He also needed to connect "there" in the third sentence to "the box" in the second. These types of integration are second nature to mature readers but can cause problems for younger or less mature readers.

Besides integrating information based on author cues such as referents, readers must also make **inferences** by using their own knowledge to provide what the author leaves unsaid. In the sample above, for example, the reader can infer that the puppy is Jimmy's birthday present, something not explicitly stated by the author but an inference that would make sense from what the author tells us.

In general, the integrative process enables the reader to store information more efficiently (in condensed form), and the inferential process determines the particular way in which information is interrelated (and thus the form in which it can be condensed). In the example above, inferences involved linguistic elements, spatial relations, and cultural knowledge. But inferences may also involve temporal and causal relations, not to mention many others.

As the example shows, integrative and inferential processes are by no means unique to written language. Linguistic linkages and spatial, temporal, and causal relations all inhere among statements in ordinary conversation as well as in connected text. And these relations are inferred on much the same basis in both cases—on the basis of general knowledge and previous experiences with the contextual situation. Perhaps it is because these processes are so much a part of the ordinary flow of everyday language that they have so long been taken for granted and only recently have become the object of serious study. In any event, like other aspects of spoken language that are important to reading progress (e.g., vocabulary knowledge and knowledge of sentence structure), it is largely through reading that these processes develop; and it is through their development that a student is able to understand more and more "difficult" prose.

Linguistic Devices.   The processes of integration and inference are highly dependent on the reader's store of general knowledge and personal experience. There are, however, certain linguistic devices used by authors, most notably those related to text structure and coherence, that appear to facilitate the integration of information. A few of these devices are described below. You will find that some familiarity with them is useful in examining instructional materials either to determine their general appropriateness or to pinpoint possible sources of difficulty for students. Comprehension is most likely to break down at those points in a text where these devices have not been used effectively by the reader (or writer).

1. *Topic Sentences.* A well-known technique for assisting the reader in integrating information involves placing a topic sentence at the beginning of a paragraph. This "points" the reader's attention to the topic of the paragraph and also to certain concepts in his or her knowledge store. The concepts thus activated serve as sources of information for making inferences (to the extent necessary) about how subsequent sentences are related to the first and to each other. For example, consider an opening sentence that reads as follows: "Tom slammed the door as he came out of the house wearing old clothes and carrying a bucket of paint." This points the reader to the idea that someone was or will be painting something (as suggested by the old clothes and, of course, the bucket of paint) and that he may be angry, possibly about having to paint. With these ideas in mind, the reader can understand the next sentence—"The barn was a long way off"—as probably telling what was to be painted. Then, if the paragraph is well structured, subsequent sentences will relate back to the slamming of the door as well as expand on the significance of the location of the barn. Thus, the opening sentence establishes a situational or conceptual context within which each sentence may be related to what has gone before.

2. *Pronouns.* Another linguistic device that signals how a sentence is related to earlier material is the pronoun. Typically, an author will make repeated references to the same object, event, or idea. The use of a pronoun in such instances alerts the reader to the commonality of reference and thus facilitates (at least for adults) the integration of incoming information with prior information. The pronoun in effect signals that something is related to "old" information and directs the reader to search his or her memory (or the text) for the previous mention of its referent in order to integrate the new information with the old. For example, in the following paragraph,

> It was a perfect *day* for flying. The air was still and there wasn't a cloud in the sky. He couldn't have asked for a better *one*.

the pronoun *one* facilitates integration of the information in the final sentence with the "old" information about *day*.

3. *Synonyms and Synonymous Expressions.* Repeated reference to a topic that has already been introduced may also be made through synonyms. This device is a more difficult one for the reader than the pronoun. Although the antecedent of a pronoun may be ambiguous at times, the pronoun itself always clearly signals that the referent has been mentioned before. A synonym, on the other hand, is not marked as another word or expression for something previously mentioned and hence does not instruct the reader to search for its previous mention. If the reader does not recognize,

from the referential context, that a word or expression refers to an item mentioned earlier, the integrative process will be disrupted and there will be some loss in comprehension. For example, notice the word *victims* in the second sentence below:

> During the past century nearly one hundred kinds of living creatures have disappeared from the face of the earth. . . . Some of the better known victims have been the European wild ox, . . . (Gilbert, 1959, p. 97)

The reader must infer that the word *victims* refers to "living creatures [that] have disappeared from the face of the earth." This understanding requires an awareness that extinction comes at the hands of others, so that extinct creatures can be termed "victims." Thus, familiarity with the important facets of a referential situation is often required for the reader to recognize coreferents.

4. *Definite Article.* The use of the definite article *the* in a text also marks a distinction between old and new information and thus facilitates comprehension. "*The* implies that the item now mentioned has a unique and specific referent that has previously been established, and therefore cues the listener/reader to match this item with one already in memory" (Gourley, 1978, p. 177). The following pairs of sentences illustrate how dependent we are on this device:

a. Yesterday Beth sold her old Ford to a dealer. Jack bought *the* car [the one Beth sold] today.
b. Yesterday Beth sold her old Ford to a dealer. Jack bought *a* car [*not* the one Beth sold] today.

5. *Syntactic Structure.* The structure of a sentence is itself a device by which information may be tagged as new. In general, the information at the end of a sentence is assumed to be the new information. Thus, in the simple active sentence *John loves Mary*, "the fact that John loves someone is interpreted as old information and the identity of that someone is interpreted as new" (Carpenter & Just, 1977, p. 232). Similarly, in the passive counterpart of that sentence (i.e., *Mary is loved by John*), Mary's being loved by someone is marked as old information and the identity of that someone, John, which appears in the last part of the sentence, is the new information being conveyed. When new information is given at the beginning of a sentence, it is often marked as such in the syntactic structure, for example, through "*it* clefts": *It was Mary whom John loved. It was John who loved Mary.*

6. *Connective Terms.* The vast majority of words in a language—the nouns, verbs, adjectives, and adverbs, or so-called content words—are **referential** in nature. That is, they refer directly to particular objects, actions, attributes, and qualities. Every language includes, as well, a small set of words that are **relational**, sometimes called "function words." Unlike the linguistic devices described above, which simply signal the *advent* of new information that is related to what has gone before, relational words specify the *way* in which new information is related to the old:

> Causal relations, for instance, are typically marked by causal conjunction (e.g., "since," "because," "due to"). The description of a process may often

include such temporal inter-unit links as "first," "next," and "then." Contrastive elaborations may be marked by adversative conjunctions (e.g., "however," "on the other hand"). List-like elaborations are marked by additive conjunctions such as "in addition," "likewise," and "furthermore." Conclusions are typically preceded by temporal conjunctions such as "in conclusion" or "to sum up." Finally, examples are signaled by the additive conjunctions "for example" and "for instance." (Geva, 1983, p. 385)

Thus, while nouns, verbs, adjectives, and adverbs represent the propositional content of a passage, the relational words express its structure, the connections between propositions.

The Need to Make Inferences

The linguistic devices described above help the reader relate incoming information to information previously given, and inferential processes play an important role in this aspect of comprehension. There are, however, certain types of inferences required for text coherence that are not directly motivated by linguistic cues. These might be considered "high-level" inferences. High-level inferences require the reader to add information to a text—to make certain connections that are implicit not so much in the language as in the ideation. They are necessary when a text does not contain all the information needed for a reader to understand it fully. Writers—like speakers—must make assumptions about the range of knowledge and social sophistication their readers—or listeners—already possess in order not to burden them with unnecessary detail. Thus, matters of common knowledge or shared cultural values and experiences tend not to be made explicit. This means that there is almost always an implicit as well as an explicit text; understanding the implicit text is what is sometimes referred to as "reading between the lines."

The implicit text, however, does not consist of *all* inferences that *can* be made; it consists of those that must or should be made for purposes of coherence. For example, if we read that "Mike's brother took Mike to a quiet street to teach him to ride his new bike," we may infer that Mike's brother is kind and helpful and that a quiet street in this context is one with little traffic. But these inferences may not be required for text coherence; they may be only incidental, in the same way that certain details found in the explicit text—the color of the bike, perhaps—may be incidental to the story. Only if inferences are connected in some way to what has gone before or what is to come after can they be considered part of the implicit text and necessary for text coherence.

There are two general types of inferences the reader must typically make in constructing a coherent text. Both types involve adding information that relates to more than one proposition in the explicit text. In one, the information added is a connective showing how one proposition in the text is related to another. In the other, the information added is itself a proposition linking two other propositions in the text.

1. *Making Connective Inferences.* The temporal, causal, or other connections between sentences are frequently left implicit in discourse text. In these cases, the

reader must make connective inferences. Such connectives can usually be made explicit by familiar terms such as *and, but, or, since/because, so/therefore/that is why, for example, this means,* and *namely.* Note how this type of inference (shown in brackets above the line of actual text) clarifies the information in the following paragraph that caused difficulty for Julia in the chapter opening vignette.

> Most people believe that earthworms are of little use except for fish
> [for example]
> bait. But scientists have found that they are very important. /Earth-
> [In this way]
> worms eat soil./They make the soil better by grinding it up as it passes
> [For another example]
> through their bodies./The holes that earthworms make as they burrow
>
> in the earth make it easier for the roots of plants to enter the soil.
> [For still another example]
> /Earthworms use leaves to line their underground homes. These leaves
> [Thus]
> make the soil richer./Scientists have found that earthworms are the
> [because]
> earth's plowmen./They keep stirring up the soil which helps to raise
> better crops.[1]

2. *Making Propositional Inferences.* These are "additions of new propositions to the text base" (Crothers, 1978, p. 63). They add the information and ideas that are plausible as "reasons, causes, effects, and the like" (p. 63). The preceding paragraph on earthworms states that the leaves the earthworms use to line their underground homes "make the soil richer." Since this information represents an example of how earthworms make the soil better, the propositional inference may be drawn that "richer soil is better soil."

In the "birthday gift" example used earlier, Laticia was able to correctly answer the question about the location of the puppy ("in the box") that stumped Omar. However, she had difficulty answering questions like, "Whose birthday was it?" "How did Jimmy feel?" "What kind of dad did Jimmy have?"—questions that required her to connect her knowledge of the world, birthdays, feelings, and motivation with the text. She would answer, "I don't know," or "It doesn't say." Sometimes this inability stems from the reader's lack of prior knowledge about the topic under discussion— birthdays, for example. At other times it can reflect the reader's hesitancy to take a risk or lack of awareness that such risk taking is not only allowed but desirable.

> **PAUSE AND REFLECT.**　　Stop and think. What kind of instruction would help Omar? What types of instruction might be useful for Laticia? Propose and discuss.

---

[1] Reproduced by permission from the Metropolitan Achievement Tests, 3rd ed. Copyright © 1959 by Harcourt Brace Jovanovich.

In any event, integration and inferencing are two critical strategic behaviors for connecting the language and knowledge of the author with the language and knowledge of the reader.

> **PAUSE AND REFLECT.**   Choose a chapter or selection that your class is working on this week (or from this or another textbook). Scan through it and note places where integration and inference are required. Do you see examples of the types of structures noted above?

The Organization of Information

Beyond the processes of integration and inference, reading also involves the organization of information (both stated and implied) across many sentences—that is, at a more global level, such as that of whole paragraphs or even passages. This type of organization is made possible by what are called internal frameworks or **schemata**. Internal to the individual, these schemata are built up over relatively long periods of time out of acquired knowledge, experience, and understanding. But they are more than a simple store of information and ideas. They represent the high-level order an individual has imposed on his or her experiences (including school experiences), and at the same time, they represent the order an individual can *bring* to new experiences. New experiences are "assimilated" into existing schemata, and schemata are always in the process of changing as a result of new experiences. It may be that acquiring certain kinds of new knowledge takes a long time because they demand the development or rearrangement of whole systems or networks of knowledge.

Schemata are hypothetical constructs that help us understand and explain many of the cognitive behaviors we observe. In terms of reading comprehension, they help us understand why (or how) people remember certain things and forget others, or why certain things are distorted in memory. Since people tend to remember the information in a text that is important or relevant to the central theme, we assume that they have available some internal mechanisms for sorting and organizing incoming information. These mechanisms can be thought of as generalized ideas about the high-level organization of information. Thus, we probably have a schema that guides our reading of news stories in the daily newspapers, a different schema for reading editorials, and still different ones for mystery stories, romantic fiction, and so forth.

Educational experiences are surely an important factor in the development of an individual's schemata—in the way an individual comes to organize and understand social and natural phenomena. At present, we are not sure how educational practices should be modified, if at all, to facilitate this development. It seems reasonable, however, that the high-level organization of knowledge in a text should be reflected in the questions we ask if these questions are to develop and assess our students' ability to understand discourse.

Narrative Structure.   In general, we seem to remember best the parts of a story that "make up" the story; they are the "structurally important units." They represent the kinds of information commonly found in most stories, and this commonality is probably the reason they tend to be remembered so well. What we call a story is normally made up of certain basic elements, and when people are asked to recall a story, they usually remember something about each of these elements. Apparently, through the experience of reading (or hearing) many stories, people develop a set of expectations about them. These expectations are like "slots," which people fill as they read. A story that conforms to these expectations, and thus permits the reader to find the information for each slot with relative ease, is easier to follow than one that does not. We can say that such a story is well formed.

The idea that stories are made up of certain common elements and that these elements are represented in the mature reader's system of knowledge is an important one. It is part of the more general theory of comprehension discussed in the preceding section—the theory that organized systems of knowledge, called schemata, play a central role in discourse comprehension by serving as "advance organizers" for incoming information. Schemata are akin to the background knowledge and experience a reader brings to the reading task; in schema theory, knowledge and experience are further conceptualized as highly organized and abstract. A story schema, it is theorized, represents the reader's generalized knowledge of the elements common to most stories.

A number of investigators in the field of cognitive psychology have attempted to describe the basic elements of a well-formed story (Fitzgerald, 1989). Such descriptions are called **story grammars**. These grammars categorize story events in much the same way that traditional grammar categorizes words (nouns, verbs, adjectives, etc.) and sentence parts (subject, predicate, complement, etc.). The grammars that have been developed thus far apply only to very simple stories and are often highly complex, so a detailed study of them would not be useful for our purposes. However, we describe a simplified version of a story grammar in the belief that it may prove useful to teachers in charting the main line of a story and writing questions that pertain to it.

In grammar, a story consists of a setting and one or more episodes. The **setting** includes the time and place in which the events occurred, the introduction of the main characters, and any additional information that might be necessary to make the ensuing events understandable. An **episode** consists of (1) an initiating event, (2) the reaction of the main character to that event, (3) an action on the part of the main character that is motivated by his reaction, and (4) a consequence that is a direct outcome of the action. The **initiating event** is what sets the story in motion. It may be a sudden change in the external environment (e.g., "Mary heard a strange noise in the kitchen"; "Bob came to Jill with the news that the ice was too thin for skating") or it may be some internal event (e.g., "Joe remembered that today was Lisa's birthday"; "Bill remembered he hadn't seen Joe in a long time"). In either case, the initiating event sets up a situation to which the main character responds. His response is both internal and external. More specifically, the character's **internal reaction** involves some feeling, thought, desire, or goal ("Joe knew she wanted a gold necklace") and this in turn motivates him to take some **external action**. The action itself may be simple and direct ("He told his secretary to pick out a gift at Tiffany's"), or it may involve some subsidiary goals, plans, and attempts to carry them out (canceling a luncheon engagement, borrowing money from a friend, etc.). The action is likely to be the most elaborated part of the story. Finally, the action is responsible for (i.e., initiates, causes, or allows) some **consequence**, and that ends the episode. The consequence (or any other part of the episode) may then serve as the initiating event of another episode.

This story grammar, then, identifies five broad categories of story information—setting, initiating event, internal reaction, external action, and consequence. The amount of detail in each category will naturally vary from story to story, and certain categories may be omitted. Setting information may involve only a simple introduction of the protagonist (e.g., "Jenny was on her way to the library"). This is often the case in stories concerning the routines of daily life. Internal reactions are also sometimes expressed only vaguely or not at all. A character may simply take some action in response to an external (initiating) event, as in the following example: "Mary heard a loud crash outside. [initiating event] She hurried to the window. [action]" In this example we may infer that the internal reaction was one of curiosity, or perhaps fear. When, as here, the internal reaction is obvious given the nature of the initiating event, its omission does not interfere with comprehension. The consequence of an action may be self-evident as well (e.g., "He threw the glass across the room [and it broke]"). Finally, there may be no overt initiating event; a story may begin with a desire or goal of the protagonist—for example, "Sara was determined to win the race." In this example, the initiating event (the announcement of the race, perhaps) occurs prior to the beginning of the story and is not mentioned in the story.

In addition, the order in which story information is given may deviate from that described above. Setting information may be postponed and introduced in an episode at the point at which it is relevant, or a consequence may be described before its antecedent action: "They couldn't find the ball anywhere. Judy had hit it as hard as she could."

What story grammars do is describe in general terms the basic outline of a simple, well-formed story in Western societies. They suggest that the reader not only expects a story to be about some action or series of actions taken by a main character, but the reader also expects those actions to be purposeful. In other words, an action is expected to have both an antecedent (in the form of some initiating event and/or internal reaction) and a consequence. We believe that this view of stories can serve as a guide to you in the process of writing questions. If the basic outline of a story typically involves five broad categories of information, we can think of a story as providing the answers to five categorical or generic questions, somewhat like the following:

[Setting]	1. Where and when did the story take place? Who were the main characters in the story?
[Initiating event]	2. How did it all begin? [What was the predicament of the main character(s)?]

[Action]   3. What did the main character(s) do?
[Internal reaction]   4. Why did he (she, they) do it?
[Consequence]   5. What happened as a result?

These generic questions reflect the idea of a story as a progression of related events—one thing leads to another, which leads to still another, and so on. With these questions in mind, following the initial reading of the story, the teacher should be able to derive a set of questions that reflects the main story line. There may, of course, be more than one question in any category, and some categories may be too sparsely represented in the story—too vague or nonspecific—to be questioned. Thus, the generic questions should make us sensitive to any ambiguities, missing information, or other weaknesses of the story structure.

Expository Structure.   While the structures of stories are familiar to most school-age readers, the structures of expository text, such as those of social studies and science textbooks, are much less predictable. Not only is there greater variation in expository structures, but many differing structures can be used and intermixed within a single article or chapter.

As is true with narrative structure, familiarity with expository structures enhances comprehension (McGee & Richgels, 1985) and can also form the basis for asking sensible, structurally coherent questions. When you analyze expository structures, it is sometimes useful to ask three basic questions:

1. What is the topic?
2. How does the author organize the information about the topic?
3. How could I summarize the author's message?

A conventional or informal outline or map of selection content can help isolate the topic and the organizational pattern (see Figure 5.3, p. 157, for an example). The most common patterns of overall expository organization, sometimes called macrostructures, are the following:

1. Chronological order—shows a sequential pattern of ideas as they happened in time.
2. Cause and effect—indicates interaction of at least two aspects of a situation, one of which causes the other to come about.
3. Comparison and contrast—looks at the similarities and differences of at least two items.
4. Problem and solution—indicates an interaction of at least two aspects of a situation, one of which is the problem and the other the solution.
5. Argument—presents the positive and negative aspects of a situation.
6. Category and example—presents a superordinate category with subordinate members; sometimes linked with description.
7. Simple listing—gives a list in which order is not relevant. Can be descriptive.

Looking at the topic, at the information presented, and at its organization is essential to making a clear summary of the author's message and is a prerequisite for the critical thinking necessary to evaluate that message. As we will see later in this chapter, it is also essential for developing good diagnostic questions or retelling formats.

Personal Response

Another factor that affects students' comprehension is the depth and intensity of their response to what they have read or heard. Children respond to literature in different ways, and the nature of their response can shape and color what they comprehend (Martinez & Roser, 1991). Students who are encouraged to respond personally have exhibited an enhanced level of critical thinking about what has been read (Galda, 1990; McGee, 1992). While the importance of this emerging field is just beginning to be understood by practitioners, it is clear that asking for students' responses to what has been read prior to undertaking any formal retelling or questioning can often reveal preconceptions and insights that affect their comprehension.

QUESTIONS AND THE DEVELOPMENT
OF COMPREHENSION

The use of questions in instruction has a significant effect on both the development and assessment of students' comprehension strategies. The focus of direct teacher questioning affects the thinking strategies that students develop. Also, when your instructional activities use good questioning and model the process of self-question-ing you help your students develop into effective independent comprehenders (Palincsar & Brown, 1983). Further, strategies directed toward the metalinguistic aspects of asking and responding to the questions "What are they really asking here?" "How should I go about finding and integrating information in the text with what I know?" are critical to independent content learning (Raphael, 1986).

It is clear that assessment involves asking good questions, interpreting responses to them, and using probing questions to follow free response and recall. You may ask yourself, "Of the many questions that may be asked about any given text or selection of text, which one will assess fairly the comprehension of the reader?"

Beyond Levels of Thinking

This question has engaged the attention of experts in reading, and in education generally, for a very long time; much as been written about the kinds of questions teachers should ask. In general, you are urged to ask a variety of questions in order to give students the opportunity to respond in a variety of ways to the materials they read. You are also advised, more specifically, to avoid overemphasizing questions that require only memory for directly stated information. You are encouraged, above all, to focus on questions that require high-level thinking in order to develop high-level cognitive processes. In short, questions have traditionally been approached from the standpoint of the mental processes required to answer them.

A major problem with this approach is that it is difficult to implement. A number of question-classification schemes based on this approach have been developed over the years, but even the simpler ones require distinctions between levels or types of thought that are both difficult to make and "not warranted by the current state of our knowledge about language and cognition" (Anderson, 1972, p. 149). Moreover, questions that appear to elicit high-level thinking because they cannot be answered from directly stated information may actually be quite trivial. Sanders (1966) points out that "thinking" questions cannot really be derived from insignificant subject matter, and he gives the following examples to illustrate:

TEXT: This little pig went to market.

QUESTIONS: Why? Did he go to buy or to be bought? . . . If to buy, what and for whom? Is he an informed buyer, the sort who would study the Buyers' Index and Consumers' Guide? . . . If he is to be sold, what price will he bring? What will be the effect on the market price . . . ?

TEXT: This little pig had roast beef.

QUESTIONS: Would you consider roast beef proper food for a pig? Which is better, nutritionally speaking, rare or well-done meat? (p. 171)

Sanders's caution is particularly relevant for the field of reading, where the "instructional diet" of simple story materials may provide little "food for thought." That is, the stories designed for developing basic reading skills do not always lend themselves to thoughtful discussion, and attempts to use them for this purpose may be unproductive.

Another problem with the mental-process or levels-of-thinking approach to questions is that it does not recognize a distinction between literal questions that pertain to important information and those that pertain to incidental detail, a point raised by Beck and McKeown (1981). Guszak (1967) alluded to this problem in his now-classic study of the kinds of questions teachers actually ask. He found that approximately 70 percent of the questions were of a literal nature, requiring only recognition (locating information in the passage) or recall (answering from memory) of factual information. While this result is frequently cited as evidence that teachers ask too many literal questions, Guszak himself was more critical of the quality of the questions. That is, he did not feel that a 7-out-of-10 proportion of literal questions was necessarily objectional; his objection was that many of the questions involved "retrieval of the trivial factual makeup of stories." It appeared to him that students were likely to miss "literal understanding" of story plots, events, and sequences "in their effort to satisfy the trivial fact questions of the teacher" (p. 233). But Guszak recognized, at the same time, that teachers could not employ more appropriate questioning patterns without clearer guidelines.

In sum, the traditional focus on levels of thinking in the design of questions does not effectively guard against trivialization of either nonliteral or literal questions. We believe, therefore, that questions should be approached from the standpoint of their relationship to the text as a whole rather than from the standpoint of the mental processes they elicit. Accordingly, we consider questions as either *related* to the text or *beyond* the text, according to whether they pertain to the information and ideas set down by the author. We also recommend that text-related questions be designed to follow the author's train of thought—that text-related questions as a whole reflect the story as a coherent whole. Beyond-text questions, on the other hand, will be those that take off where the author left off, so to speak. They will go "beyond the lines" and generalize about the author's ideas, extending them to other contexts or relating them to other ideas and issues. In a sense, these questions will relate to the ultimate purposes of reading—the enjoyment and appreciation of literature and the acquisition of knowledge and insight into human affairs. They will consist largely of the types of questions generally categorized and valued as thought provoking.

Text-Related and Beyond-Text Questions

The rationale for our approach to questions is not just that mental process taxonomies are difficult to work with or that good thinking questions are difficult to derive from simple story materials. It lies also in recent insights into comprehension as a discourse process. These insights (described more fully in a later section) suggest that understanding "what it says" is not a trivial matter. In order to understand the communicative intent of a passage, readers must engage in levels of thought that are as simple or complex as the ideas communicated. They must select, combine, and integrate passage information, including information that is not explicitly stated. This means that text-related questions will generally require both literal and nonliteral (inferential) comprehension and that they must reflect the author's general intent as expressed in the passage as a whole.

In addition, our approach preserves the basic distinction between the ideas of the author **(text related)** and those of the reader **(beyond text)**, thereby emphasizing that what is written must be understood in its own right before it can be explored in greater depth. The beyond-text questions will stimulate the reader to use the text as a springboard for reflection and conjecture. These questions will also draw on information and ideas that, while peripheral to the text, may be important to the reader.

A good set of questions, then, will consist of at least two basic parts or distinct types. One part will be text related, in the sense that it will adhere closely to the significant content of the text, including the inferences directly motivated by text coherence. The other will go beyond the text as a communicative entity and explore its general implications and incidental detail (Sadow, 1982). The first part will assess the student's comprehension of the passage as a whole—of the story told therein or the aspect of human knowledge conveyed—and will be a major factor in determining the suitability of like materials for instruction. The second part will assess the student's ability to use textual detail to broaden his or her knowledge and understanding of physical and social phenomena. The difference between these two parts is illustrated by the following example.

In the opening of *Charlotte's Web* (White, 1952), Fern learns that her father is on his way to the barn, carrying an ax, with the intent of "doing away" with the runt pig that was born the night before. Fern's mother explains that the pig would probably die anyway. Outraged at the "unfairness" of killing the pig "just because it is weak and little," Fern runs after her father and pleads for the pig's life. He gives in to her plea, saying, "I'll let you start it on a bottle, like a baby. Then you'll see what trouble a pig can be" (p. 3). The text-related questions on this passage would establish the facts of the story qua story—who did what, why they did it, and what happened as a result:

1. What is a runt pig? Who is Fern? Where does she live?
2. What was Fern's father going to do?
3. Why was Fern's father going to "do away" with the pig?
4. How did Fern feel when she learned that her father was going to kill the pig?
5. What did Fern do about it?
6. How did her father respond to her?

Notice that the questions follow the sequence of the story and that they are relatively independent of each other. That is, inability to answer (2), for example, does not preclude the possibility of answering (3) and (4). In fact, (3) and (4) give the answer to (2).

The beyond-text questions, on the other hand, might explore the conflict between Fern's point of view and her father's in terms of the more universal conflict between a child's point of view and an adult's. They might also (or alternatively) address the conflict between the father's point of view as a farmer and as a father. For example:

1. Why did Fern's father "give in" to her plea? (Was he convinced that it would be unjust to kill a runt pig or was he merely being kind to his daughter?)
2. Why would Fern's father believe that it was all right to kill the pig?

It is clear that these questions cannot be answered from a reading of the passage, and it is in this sense that they are beyond the text, or reader based. It is also clear that they represent what might be called "literary analysis." If the students have read another story in which there is a similar conflict between young and old or between the dual roles and responsibilities of an individual, the teacher may ask that it be recalled and contrasted with this one. Other beyond-text questions that might be asked include these:

3. What was Fern's mother's reaction to the father's intention to kill the pig?
4. Fern's mother said, "It will probably die anyway." Why would that be likely to happen?
5. Fern's father said, "A weakling makes trouble." What is a weakling? In what way would it make trouble?
6. If you were Fern, would you be willing to take care of the pig?

Questions and Prior Knowledge

The insights discussed above are important for several reasons. They highlight the reading process as a global one in which the reader is actively engaged in constructing a unified representation of text information, and they heighten our sensitivity to the "connectedness" of written prose. They strongly imply that there can be no subsitute for "real" reading experiences, that is, for experiences with a variety of types of discourse text. Another important implication is that materials may be difficult to understand if they require inferences that are beyond the reader's experiential or knowledge base. Finally, these insights provide a rational basis for the design of text-related questions. They help us recognize that while such questions do not pertain to the deepest levels of meaning or the ultimate purposes of reading in the way that beyond-text questions do, they are an important intermediary step.

Recent insights emphasize, further, that text-related questions should pertain to the ideas and information that contribute in some way to the text as a whole, for it is a mistake to confuse comprehension with memory for incidental detail or even for incidental inferences. In fact, these insights suggest that such details are frequently forgotten because they bear so little connection to other textual information and, therefore, are only superficially processed. For example, it may make no difference, in terms of other events in a story, whether a certain incident took place in the morning or afternoon, last week or this week, or whether it was first noticed by one story character or by another. If it does not, the reader has no opportunity to relate these items of information to subsequent events nor any need to relate them to earlier ones. Similarly, in an adventure tale about a series of incidents, if it makes little difference whether the incidents occurred in one order or another, there will be minimal processing of, and little memory for, the sequence of events.

In short, the process of following the main story line or thread of an argument does not tend to reinforce or "activate" nonessential facts, and memory for them is likely to be spotty and idiosyncratic. Such facts may or may not be remembered, but good comprehension of discourse does not imply that they are likely to be. Rather, good comprehension means grasping the vital information in the text and the train of thought (the low-level and high-level inferences) that binds this information together.

If text-related questions involve both "reading the lines" and "reading between the lines," then beyond-text questions may be conceived as "reading beyond the lines." These questions also involve inferential processes, but the inferences are more in the nature of "grand conclusion[s] from a number of explicit and implicit propositions combined" (Crothers, 1978, p. 55). That is, they are not cued by specific linguistic devices nor by any specific inferences that are motivated by text coherence—they do not "connect" specific statements in the text with each other. It is in this sense that beyond-text questions may be said to involve the "deeper" levels of meaning. And as with text-related inferences, the reader must draw on his or her fund of general knowledge to arrive at these deeper meanings.

In the case of story materials, beyond-text questions generally call on the reader to apply his or her knowledge of human events, actions, and feelings to a given situation. For example, in a story about a young boy whose father and brothers are all fishermen, we learn that what the boy wanted most was to go fishing with his father. We can understand this desire in terms of boys in general—most boys would think going fishing is fun. But we can also understand it, with reference to this boy in particular, in terms of boys' desires to do what their fathers and older brothers do, to be like them, to feel grown-up, and so on. In other words, we understand the story character's feelings and appreciate the story more fully because we recognize those feelings as consistent with what we know about little boys in general. Beyond-text questions should assess this application of knowledge.

Another example is provided by Miriam Schlein's (1966) story, "The Big Cheese." In this story a farmer decides to give his finest cheese to the king. Here we recognize the farmer's pride in his work, and it is through knowledge of this type of pride that we understand why the farmer would elect to give his cheese to the king instead of selling it in the open market and allowing "just anyone" to eat it. Also involved, of course, is the special feeling that citizens may have toward their leaders. And parallel to the farmer's pride is the pride shown by a goatherd, who insists that goats' milk makes better cheese than cows' milk. For this story, too, beyond-text questions require an examination of the actions and reactions of story characters from the point of view of their consistency with certain general ideas about human events. As we ask such questions, we help students develop these ideas, and we help them see the relevance of these stories to the "human condition."

A particular question may be either text related or beyond the text, depending on the answer that is expected (or given) (Pearson & Johnson, 1978). A text-related answer can be justified with specific reference to the text. A beyond-text answer is one that is based on insights or logical reasoning that is not clearly implied in the text. Consider the following question and some possible answers concerning "The Big Cheese" (Schlein, 1966).

QUESTION: Why did the goatherd suggest that he and the farmer taste the cheese?

ANSWER A: Because it was lunchtime and he was hungry.

ANSWER B: Because he didn't believe it was the best cheese (because it was not made from goats' milk).

ANSWER C: Because he thought the farmer should be sure it was the best cheese before he gave it to the king.

Answers B and C pertain directly to the goatherd's own statements: "Then how can it be the best cheese ever made? The finest . . . cheeses are always made from goats' milk" (p. 80), and "How can you present the king with a cheese you do not know tastes the best?" (p. 81). So answers B and C are text related and, as such, show good comprehension of the story line. Answer A goes beyond the text, since there is no clear implication in the text that the goatherd's motives are not as he represents them. This answer, then, is ambiguous with respect to the student's comprehension of the text itself. It could represent good insight into the fact that people sometimes have ulterior motives. On the other hand, it could be that the student simply failed to understand the persuasive arguments of the goatherd, as given in the text, and that his or her answer is really a "stab in the dark."

However, beyond-text questions need not be confined to issues involving human goals, desires, and feelings. There is much information of a factual nature to be gained from stories. Teachers' questions should help students "pull" this information out and make it part of their general fund of knowledge—part of the background knowledge they will be able to bring to subsequent stories. For purposes of assessment, these questions may help the teacher evaluate the adequacy of the student's background knowledge in relation to story content. This is important, since it is often a lack of some specific information that leads to misunderstanding of story events. In "The Big Cheese" (Schlein, 1966), for example, students must understand that farmers *sell* their products at a "market" (many city children may think of "markets" only as places where families buy food). They must also grasp the fact that cheese may be made of milk from goats as well as from cows and that in "olden" days a farmer might transport his products by wheelbarrow.

Constructing Comprehension Questions

In general, text-related questions recapitulate the main story line or central ideas in a text. Unfortunately, there are no simple prescriptions or rules to follow in construct-ing these questions, no objective methods for determining that one idea or piece of information is essential or more important than another. Here teachers must rely on their own clear understanding of the text to be used, based on a careful reading, rereading, and analysis of it. One way to proceed, though not necessarily the only way, is as follows.

You should first read the text for an overview of its content and organization, much as you would for any other material of its kind. On this reading, you will also gain insight into what the passage is like, which parts stand out in memory, and which are readily lost. You should then try to construct a set of questions whose answers will represent a broad outline of the story's significant content. A second reading of the text will enable you to "fill in" the outline. A third and final reading will suggest some beyond-text questions. These are described more fully below, then illustrated with the questions that would result from a typical passage. Because of their differences in form, content, and purpose, story materials and nonfiction are treated separately.

Story Materials.   On the first reading, simply follow the story line (i.e., find out who did what, why they did it, and how it all came out). This reading will help you form the intuitive base for the group of questions that will reflect the causal essence of the story and assess story comprehension. Highly relevant to this step are the results of some recent investigations into story structure and story recall.

The derivation of text-related questions based on story structure constitutes the first step in the process of writing questions. For the second step, a second reading of the story will usually be necessary. In this step, the story outline constructed in Step 1 will be rounded out with important details. With very short stories, all or most of the details may be important for the story line. In fact, the shorter the story, the less likely it is to include incidental detail. With longer stories, however, readers are likely to forget many details, particularly if the details do not carry the story forward.

This process of question construction is illustrated for the third-grade story, "The Restless Kangaroo," shown in Figure 5.1.

PAUSE AND REFLECT.   Compose a set of questions for "The Restless Kangaroo." Then compare them with the ones in Figure 5.2. Where did you tap the same knowledge and processes? Where were your choices different? Discuss and evaluate.

A typical set of questions that might result from the first and second steps of question writing is shown in Figure 5.2. While the questions derived during Step 1 are quite predictable, those written during Step 2 result from a less systematic process. There are no hard and fast rules regarding questions of detail; you must be guided by your own sense of story cohesiveness.

In examining the questions generated for "The Restless Kangaroo," note the relationship between Step 1 and Step 2 questions. There is usually only one correct answer to a Step 2 question, whereas Step 1 questions give the student more latitude in framing his or her answer. More important, Step 2 questions are often implicit in one or another Step 1 question, so that Step 2 questions will often be answered in response to a Step 1 question. Thus, Step 2 questions often serve as clarifying "probes" when the answer to a Step 1 question is incomplete or vague or suggests a slight misunderstanding of the question. For example, in response to question S10 (Figure 5.2), one child said, "They put him in a box," suggesting that he did not understand the zoo's final solution to the problem. However, in answering question D4, this child said, "There was no straw to put in the pouch," showing clear understanding of the solution.

The third and final step in the question-writing process is the creation of beyond-text items. As already explained, these deal with the story as an exemplar of something interesting and important about the way people live, work, play, and otherwise conduct their affairs, or with some thematic issue or communicative intent of the author. In searching out ideas for these questions, it is useful to look to each of the five story elements for suggestions. The zookeeper's internal reaction (worry) on finding the joey on the floor of the cage suggests that he is knowledgeable regarding the care of animals. A good question would be, "From this story, can you tell what a good zookeeper must know or be able to do?" The zookeeper's knowledge and devotion to duty, evident in the action he took to find out about the problem, suggests the following question: "If you were in charge of a zoo, would you hire Pete as a zookeeper? Why (or why not)?"

Expository Materials.   Questions concerning expository texts are constructed on the same principle as narrative questions, but here it is the traditional outline form that guides the procedure. An outline shows the relative importance of text ideas and ideally, it also specifies how ideas are related to one another. That is, it depicts, in

The Restless Kangaroo

The zoo had a problem. The problem was Tanga who was the mother kangaroo.

She had begun to take her joey, as kangaroo babies are called, out of her pouch in the night. For two mornings Pete, who is the head keeper at the zoo, had found the cold little joey on the dirt floor of the kangaroo pen.

Each time Pete rubbed the joey with a towel until he was warm. Then he tucked him back into Tanga's pouch. And Tanga stood still because she was a gentle kangaroo.

But on the third morning the joey was found on the floor again.

"This is a problem," the zoo director said. "The joey is too young to be out of Tanga's pouch."

"It is a new problem," said Pete. "Tanga has been a good mother. She always kept her other joeys safe until they were older."

"We must find out why she does this now," said the director. "If this goes on the joey might catch a chill. He may even die."

"Tonight I will stand watch at Tanga's pen," said Pete. "Perhaps I can learn why she puts her joey on the floor."

"That is a good idea," said the director.

When night came to the zoo, Pete went to the animal barn where Tanga lived. He sat down on a chair in front of her low gate.

In the next pen the great elk, with its wide antlers, snorted. On the other side of Tanga's pen a zebra stamped its feet and then a deer sneezed.

The llamas and camels and the buffalo gazed over their gates at Pete for a long time. It was plain that they were surprised to see him there at that time of night.

But at last they all became used to him and, one by one, they went to sleep.

And Tanga lay down on her side in her own pen on her clean straw bed and went to sleep also.

The big barn was quiet and dark but for the soft glow of one light up near the roof.

Pete yawned and leaned back in his chair. He had worked hard all day. He was sleepy and it was hard to keep awake. But he did keep awake.

After a while he heard a "scritch-scratch" in the stillness. He stood up and looked into the shadows of Tanga's pen.

Tanga was sound alseep. But something was moving. It was the joey's tiny paw.

It waved back and forth, back and forth, out of the opening of Tanga's pouch. Then it dug down into the straw and Pete could hear the same "scritch-scratch" that he had heard before.

When the joey pulled a pawful of straw into her pouch, Tanga kicked her long back feet. But she did not wake up.

Soon the joey pulled another pawful of straw into the pouch. This time Tanga gave a loud sigh.

Without opening her eyes she turned on her back. She lifted the joey with her front paws and dropped him into the straw. Then she turned over on her side and was still again. And she hadn't waked up at all.

The joey scratched around a bit and then he too was still.

"I have found the answer to our problem." Pete whispered to himself. "Tanga's joey is a naughty baby."

He tip-toed into the pen and picked up the shivering joey and tucked him in his jacket. Then he felt inside Tanga's pouch with gentle hands. Besides the straw, he found sharp pebbles from the dirt floor of the pen.

"Poor Tanga!" Pete said. "No wonder you put your joey out in the cold! No kangaroo likes to be scratched by straw and pebbles!"

He cleaned her pouch and Tanga opened her eyes and blinked her long lashes as if she were saying "Thank you."

FIGURE 5.1 Narrative passage

SOURCE: From *With Skies and Wings*, Level 9, pp. 207–213. In *Reading 360*, published by Ginn and Company, 1969. Story by Edythe R. Warner, reprinted by permission.

"There, Tanga," said Pete when he was through. "Go back to sleep. Things will be better from now on."

He took the joey to the zoo office. There he rolled him in a towel and put him in a box to keep warm.

When morning came Pete told the zoo director what happened.

"You see," he said, "when Tanga's joey wakes up he likes to play with the straw and pebbles. Then he takes them into his own pouch-bed. He is a naughty little kangaroo."

The director smiled. "I don't think he is naughty," he said. "He is just a restless little kangaroo. But we will fix it so this will not happen again."

As soon as all the other zoo keepers heard the story about Tanga and her restless kangaroo, they went right to work.

They moved Tanga and her joey away from the animal barn and into a big cage in the zoo's main building. The cage had a smooth floor with no pebbles. And instead of straw for a bed Pete gave Tanga a blanket.

From then on there was no more trouble. When the restless joey awoke at night he pulled and tugged on the blanket until he was tired. Then he went back to sleep.

The zoo's problem was solved. The joey was not found out of Tanga's pouch again until he was old enough to climb in and out by himself—which he did, over and over again, until he finally grew so big that he could no longer fit.

graphic form (the indentation and letter–number system), the superordinate–subordinate structure of passages and expresses, in words, the particular kind of superordinate–subordinate relationship that inheres between each topic and its subtopics.

For example, Figure 5.3 gives three possible outlines of an expository passage on trees. Outline 1 shows only the superordinate–subordinate relationships. There are, however, two different *kinds* of relationships between the subtopics (A, B, C, and D) and the major topic, trees. Clearly, subtopics A and B are *kinds* of trees whereas C and D are *uses* of trees. A third type of relationship inheres between each set of minor subtopics, that is, each (1) and (2), and their superordinates, A, B, C, and D: subtopics (1) and (2) are *examples* of their superordinate topics. Thus, the subtopics of an outline are always elaborations of a topic, but there are many different kinds of elaborations. A good outline makes these explicit in some way or other. Two possible ways are shown in outlines 2 and 3 in Figure 5.3.

In addition to the relationships exemplified here—kinds, uses, and examples—subtopics may be related to their topics as causes, effects, functions, parts, characteristics, procedural steps, chronological sequence, and so on.

The first step, then, in formulating expository questions is the preparation of a complete outline. This is a relatively easy step with well-organized, clearly written passages, such as the one on forest fires in Figure 5.4.

PAUSE AND REFLECT.   Construct an outline for "Forest Fires" (Figure 5.4). Then compare it with the outline in Figure 5.5. After evaluating your choices, compose questions for the passage and compare with those in Figure 5.6. Where did you tap the same knowledge and processes? Where were your choices different? Discuss and evaluate.

Story Structure Category	Story Structure Questions (Step 1)	Detail Questions (Step 2)
Setting	S1. Where did this story take place? S2. Who is Pete? S3. Who is Tanga?	D1. What is a joey? [What is a baby kangaroo called?]
Initiating event/ problem	S4. What was the problem that the zoo was having with the kangaroos?	D2. What did Pete do with the joey each time he found him on the floor of the pen?
Internal reaction	S5. Why was that a problem? [Why were the zookeepers worried about the baby kangaroo being out of the mother's pouch during the night?]	
Action	S6. What did Pete, the zookeeper, do to find out about the problem? [Why did Pete stay up all night watching the kangaroo pen?]	
Consequence	S7. What did Pete find out when he watched the kangaroos all night? [What did the joey do in the middle of the night?] S8. Why did Tanga take the joey out of her pouch at night? S9. Why did the joey put the straw in the mother's pouch? S10. What did Pete do to solve the problem for the kangaroos?	D3. What did Pete find when he felt inside the mother kangaroo's pouch? D4. How did the new pen solve the problem? [How was the new pen different from the old one?] D5. What did the joey do in the new pen when he woke up in the middle of the night?

FIGURE 5.2 Questions based on narrative passage[a]

[a]The questions shown in brackets suggest some alternatives in terms of wording and/or emphasis that seem to be equally appropriate.

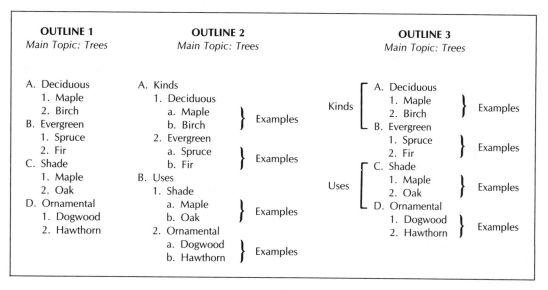

FIGURE 5.3   Possible outlines of an expository passage on trees

FIGURE 5.4   Expository passage about forest fires

SOURCE: From "The Influence of Metacognitive Knowledge of Expository Text Structure on Discourse Recall" by L. M. McGee in J. A. Niles and L. A. Harris (Eds.), *New Inquiries in Reading Research and Instruction* [Thirty-first Yearbook of the National Reading Conference. Rochester, NY: National Reading Conference, 1982].

Forest Fires

An important problem for forest rangers is how to protect forests from being ruined by fire. Each year thousands of trees are destroyed by fire. Careless campers do not put their fires completely out. Cigarettes are left to burn on the dry ground. These small fires in dry forests can burn thousands of trees. One solution to the forest fire problem is to man lookout stations and use helicopters to spot fires. Fires that are spotted right away can be put out before they get too big to handle. Then fires will cause less damage to the forest. A second solution to the problem is to have experts and bulldozers ready to move in quickly to fight the fire. Bulldozers can throw huge amounts of dirt on a fire in a short time. The dirt helps put the fire out quicker. A third solution is to build fire lanes in the forests. Fire lanes are long breaks in the forest where there are no trees. These breaks prevent the fire from spreading and getting too large.

MAIN TOPIC: How forest rangers protect forests from fire damage

- **A.** Causes of fire
  - 1. Camp fires
  - 2. Cigarettes
- **B.** Solutions to Problem
  - 1. Early detection
    - a. Lookout stations
    - b. Helicopters
  - 2. Quick extinction
    - a. Bulldozers—throw dirt on fire
    - b. Experts
  - 3. Preventing spread of fires
    - a. Fire lanes

FIGURE 5.5   Outline based on expository passage about forest fires

The next step is to derive questions from the outline using procedures similar to those described for the questions based on narrative selections. Typically, one question may be written to focus on the main topic and one or two questions may be developed to explore each of the subtopics in the outline. We encourage you to develop questions based on the passage outline and compare them with those shown in Figure 5.6.

FIGURE 5.6   Questions based on outline of expository passage about forest fires

1. What is the important problem that forest rangers must deal with? (protect trees from fire damage; forest fires)
2. How do many forest fires get started? (cigarettes and campfires)
3. How are lookout stations and helicopters used in solving the problem of forest fires? (spot fires in early stages)
4. How are bulldozers used in fighting fires? (throw dirt on fire)
5. What are fire lanes? (areas that are bare of trees)
6. How do fire lanes prevent fire damage to forest? (prevent spread of fire)
*7. The passage mentioned that "experts" are needed in fighting fires. What sorts of things might experts know that would be helpful in fighting fires? (wind conditions; how and where to approach fires; methods of fighting fires)
*8. What might be done to prevent fires from getting started in the first place? (punish wrongdoers; supervise campgrounds; educate people)

*Beyond-text question

Free and Elicited Recall

As an alternative to direct questioning, you might consider an aided recall procedure (Morrow, 1988). The student is instructed to recount everything he or she can remember about the passage. The free, or unprompted, retelling reflects the student's assessment of the important story elements, and the order in which they are told gives you a clue to the organization the reader has abstracted from or imposed on the passage. It is also possible for you to evaluate the reader's oral language and vocabulary use based on the language he or she uses to retell the selection.

Then you help the student fill in missing information by asking specific questions about important ideas or events that were not mentioned. This means you must be prepared with a list or outline of the main passage content against which you can check and evaluate the student's retelling. It would be much the same kind of outline as was recommended for the preliminary step in constructing questions. **Open-ended questions** (e.g., "Tell me more about ___"; Explain what you meant by ___") can be used to elicit more information following free recall, or the questions can be more directive. It is important to include this step since several investigations have found that students, particularly poor readers, normally store much more information than they produce in a free recall task (e.g., Bridge & Tierney, 1981).

SUMMARY

In this chapter we have presented a theoretical overview of current conceptualizations of comprehension, emphasizing that it is an active, constructive process. We have also examined some reader and textual variables that affect this process. Last, we have applied this knowledge to the issue of what makes good questions, stressing both their connection to the text (the story map and the central story issue of the author) and the need for questions to go beyond the text to foster inference and develop literary appreciation.

TRY IT OUT

1. Find passages from standardized tests used in your school. Are inferencing and integration required? What background knowledge is needed for the inferences? Do your students have it?

2. Select a student in your class who has comprehension difficulties. Observe her during a reading lesson. Can you relate any of her behaviors to issues raised in this chapter? (If you don't have a class, try doing this with your own reading this week.)

3. Choose a passage from a favorite novel. Indicate where the author expects you to make inferences (where all the information is not given—you must supply some). Bring your passage in and share with the group.

4. **Student Portfolio Ideas:** (1) Have your students analyze a chapter or selection from their assigned reading. Then ask them to construct the questions they think would be good to ask. Have them compare their questions with others in their group and come up with a master list. (2) Ask students to monitor their own reading on the next assigned reading and indicate where they have trouble understanding. Share as a group and discuss why the sections are difficult. Is it knowledge, language, organization, or some combination of all three that makes sections difficult?

5. **For Your Teaching Portfolio:** Choose a selection from a textbook and analyze it using a map, web, or outline. Construct questions based on your analysis. Then compare your questions with those suggested in a teacher's manual. Contrast strengths and weaknesses.

FOR FURTHER READING

Irwin, J. W. (1991). *Teaching reading comprehension processes.* Englewood Cliffs, NJ: Prentice-Hall.
An excellent overview of comprehension with ideas for instruction.

Jones, B. F., Palincsar, A. S., Ogle, D. S., & Carr, E. G. (1986). *Strategic teaching and learning: Cognitive instruction in the content areas.* Alexandria, VA: Association for Supervision & Curriculum Development.
Excellent ideas for strategic instruction in the content areas.

Pearson, P. D., & Fielding, L. (1991). Comprehension instruction. In R. Barr, M. L. Kamil, P. Mosenthal, & P. D. Pearson (Eds.), *Handbook of reading research.* White Plains, NY: Longman.
A timely review of research on comprehension instruction.

chapter 6

Reading Comprehension: Assessment and Instructional Support

CHAPTER GOALS FOR THE READER

To understand the variety of ways readers can experience difficulty in understanding

To learn how to gather data about a reader's comprehension

To work through three cases using questioning, retelling, and think-alouds for
data gathering

To develop some alternatives for instruction related to assessment

CLASSROOM VIGNETTE: SOLVING CLASSROOM PUZZLES

Jim, a middle school language arts teacher, is puzzled by the performance of
three of his students. Bob is a methodical student and excellent oral reader
who answers factual questions with great accuracy. Yet he is silent and
unresponsive whenever class discussion or written assignments move on to
bigger issues. Though Andrea finishes her class reading assignments quickly,
her performance in class discussions and on written work is uniformly poor.
Her typical strategy is to pick some words out of the teacher's questions on a
reading guide and rephrase them into an answer. Yet her oral reading is
accurate if somewhat expressionless. Jake, another capable oral reader, is
energetic but inconsistent in discussion and is frequently the first to want to
answer questions or offer opinions. Sometimes he is right on target, but at
other times his responses are way off base.

In this chapter, we will see how Jim went about gathering data on each of these students to develop a more detailed profile of their comprehension strengths and weaknesses. First he had to establish a baseline by answering the question, "What is adequate comprehension?" Next, he gathered data on these students using the selection they were reading in their literature anthology. Finally, he analyzed their performances and decided on specific instructional strategies to use with each student. By working through the cases of Bob, Andrea, and Jake, you can begin to develop an understanding of the multifaceted nature of comprehension and build a framework for assessment and instruction.

CHAPTER OVERVIEW

This chapter has three parts. The first section discusses the variety of comprehension difficulties that can be observed and the concept of "instructional level." The second segment focuses on data gathering and presents cases using questioning, retelling, and think-alouds to gather data on and analyze student reading performance. The third section presents instructional recommendations for developing interactive strategies, for developing the ability to reorganize information in large segments of text, and for developing sentence-level comprehension, relating these to the student cases presented earlier.

CHAPTER OUTLINE

Comprehension in the Classroom
    Instructional Level
    Common Problem Areas

Gathering Authentic Data
    Preparation
    Administration
    Evaluation
    Case 6:1: Bob—Using Questions
    Retelling
    Case 6.2: Andrea—Using a Retelling
    Think-Alouds
    Case 6.3: Jake—Using a Think-Aloud

Comprehension Instruction
    Developing Interactive Strategies
    Developing the Ability to Reorganize Information
    Reflecting on the Cases: Instructional Recommendations

Try It Out

COMPREHENSION IN THE CLASSROOM

An assessment of reading comprehension serves a twofold purpose. It enables you to make an informed decision regarding the level of materials that would be appropriate for instruction, and it alerts you to a student's specific instructional needs. You would generally undertake such an assessment when you have some question concerning a student's current placement in instructional materials or the type of instructional emphasis that would enable the student to make better progress. For the most part these questions arise when a student is not performing well during daily lessons. However, they can also arise when a student is performing extremely well, for instructional materials should be neither so difficult that the student can have little success with them nor so easy as to require little thought or attentional effort. Thus, the student who is always able to answer your questions may need more challenging materials, while the student who can seldom answer questions correctly may need less demanding ones. You must make every effort to see that instructional materials are optimal from this point of view.

In addition, you must be aware of the area(s) of reading in which a student is relatively weak and consequently requires special attention. A student is considered to need special attention in the area of comprehension when his or her performance on a comprehension test is inadequate (below a certain level) *and* the assessment procedures described in preceding chapters indicate that the student's print skills and vocabulary knowledge—the areas of reading underlying comprehension—are not prime sources of difficulty.

We first discuss criteria for establishing whether materials are at an appropriate level of difficulty for a student's use in reading instruction. Then we describe the general types of comprehension problems that students may encounter and a procedure for assessing an individual student's major problem along with alternative diagnostic possibilities. Finally, we suggest some instructional techniques for helping students gain proficiency in comprehension and for carrying out further diagnostic teaching.

Instructional Level

When selecting materials for use in the classroom, teachers use many types of criteria. Content, format, and language are all important elements for establishing whether materials are at an appropriate level of difficulty for a student in reading instruction. Standardized reading formulas using sentence length and word frequency are commonly used to scale commercial materials and trade books as to readability (Weaver & Kintsch, 1991). Yet teachers make these determinations without a particular child or group of children in mind; and their estimations do not take into account what the readers already know or don't know about the subject being discussed and their prior experiences with reading materials of the type and organization under examination.

A more classroom-sensitive concept is that of **instructional level**, a level at which a student can comprehend adequately in a challenging but teacher-supported situation.

In general, materials are considered suitable for instruction when the student, after reading them, can answer correctly a certain proportion of the questions asked. Unfortunately, there is no firm agreement among reading authorities regarding what this proportion should be. Recommendations range from 60 percent to 75 percent. Harris and Sipay (1985) suggest that 60 percent is "marginal." They also note that a 50–60 percent criterion may be used with students of limited experiential background if "more time than usual will be spent [by the teacher] developing the concepts and vocabulary necessary for understanding the stores" (p. 185). Betts (1954), on the other hand, recommends 75 percent comprehension for oral reading and a substantially higher percentage for "silent reading to locate specific information." In the procedures recommended by Betts, however, the oral reading of a passage is *not* the student's first encounter with the text; it is a rereading after silent reading. (Betts is a strong advocate of the principle that silent reading should precede oral reading, although he acknowledges that oral reading at sight provides valuable information regarding word recognition skills.) Nevertheless, we believe that, with well-designed questions, a criterion of 75 percent is not unreasonable even for a first reading. We also believe, with Harris and Sipay, that this criterion should be applied flexibly. Under certain conditions, a student who scores below 75 percent on a diagnostic passage may benefit from instruction in materials at the same level of difficulty. In general, such conditions exist when a student is relatively strong in vocabulary knowledge and, if given an opportunity to reinspect the passage, is able to answer correctly several questions that he or she initially missed. That is, the student would be proficient in basic language skills but lacking in the ability to interrelate and organize passage information. In addition, you must be in a position to provide instruction that would take account of the student's relative difficulty with this aspect of comprehension.

We note that a teacher usually undertakes assessment to explore difficulties he or she observed in a student's reading during classroom activities. It is, therefore, puzzling when students who have been selected for diagnosis perform well on a diagnostic passage that is at the same level of difficulty as their classroom materials. In such cases, you may want to consider first whether the reading selection used in the diagnosis is in fact typical of classroom materials. It could be considerably easier in style, structure, and content, even if it came from the same reader level. If the passage appears to be typical, then the student's classroom difficulties could be due to inattention, disinterest, difficulty in working in a group setting, differences in topic and type of reading material, and the like. You must also recognize that the student has probably put forth a higher level of effort during the diagnosis than can reasonably be expected during daily classroom routines. Still, the diagnostic performance gives evidence of available strength. You should therefore discuss the results of the diagnosis with the student and elicit his or her interpretation or views on the matter. Your expression of interest and concern will undoubtedly be important to the student and may, in itself, help the student become more deeply involved in reading activities.

Alternatively, the student may have some insights into his or her own difficulty that will be useful to you in planning and implementing classroom activities.

If a student selected for diagnosis scores extremely well in comprehension—90 percent or better—the passage should be considered at a level appropriate for independent reading. You may then administer a more difficult passage to determine the student's instructional level; or the student may simply be assigned to more difficult materials on a trial basis.

A 75 percent level of comprehension, then, indicates that the reader is gathering enough of the important information in a text for reading to be a satisfying and productive experience: The reader not only is successful but has a sense of accomplishment as well. At a much higher level of comprehension, say 90 percent or above, particularly if the answers to questions are full and unhesitating, the reader is processing information so efficiently that there is little to be gained from the instructional efforts of the teacher; materials that present so little difficulty can be read independently.

On the other hand, when comprehension is below 75 percent, the student is normally gaining too little of the information in the text for reading to be a comfortable experience under ordinary instructional conditions. It is often possible, however, to adjust instruction to accommodate a student who scores at least 50 percent in comprehension. A student who scores below 50 percent is following the text so poorly that even with strong instructional support in the form of extensive prereading discussion and activities, he or she will find reading a frustrating experience. Thus, comprehension scores between 50 and 75 percent represent borderline situations in which the teacher must consider the nature of the student's problem and decide whether instructional support would increase his or her comprehension to a level that would be acceptable (75 percent or greater). For example, instructional support focused on the identification and/or meaning of words contained in reading selections may solve enough problems for the student to enable him or her to read with adequate comprehension.

Word recognition proficiency must also be taken into account in determining instructional level. A student who performs well in comprehension and poorly in word recognition may need to work with easier materials for a time while developing greater print skill. Easier materials may facilitate progress in this aspect of reading. On the other hand, a student may derive psychological or social advantages from working with the higher-level materials that would outweigh his or her difficulty with word recognition. An important consideration in this regard is the type of word recognition difficulty involved. If sight word fluency and accuracy is a major problem for the student in addition to content word difficulties, the easier materials are likely to be the better solution. If, however, identification of unfamiliar content words constitutes his or her prime difficulty, then the higher-level materials can probably be used. In the latter case, of course, you must plan to provide the student (along with other members of the reading group) prereading assistance by identifying difficult words. In addition, you must make some provision for the student to receive help with specific word identification skills.

The way to use diagnostic information regarding vocabulary knowledge and print skill in making instructional decisions is described more fully in the next chapter. In this section we examine the implications of a specific difficulty in the area of comprehension.

Common Problem Areas

We noted in Chapter 1 that poor comprehension is often related to inadequate print skills and/or vocabulary knowledge. Sometimes, however, comprehension is poor (below 75 percent) even though the reader can identify the important words in a passage and their meanings are reasonably familiar. In such cases, the reading difficulty is considered to be specific to comprehension. In general, this means that the reader fails to see how ideas fit together—how one idea builds on another or is constrained by it. Often it is causal chains that go unrecognized, but other types of relationships give rise to difficulty as well. For instance, the reader might not recognize that one statement is an amplification of another, or that it is a summary of a series of preceding statements or an example in support of a general statement.

We do not yet have a more precise formulation of the nature of individual problems in comprehension. In the past, teachers often attempted to determine which subskills of comprehension were weak in individual cases by analyzing students' comprehension test performance. The belief was that the types of questions students missed frequently would indicate the specific areas of comprehension in which they were deficient. However, we believe that this procedure is not really defensible. No one passage, or even a series of passages such as those found in a standardized test or informal reading inventory, can provide a sufficient number of questions of each type to yield reliable results. Moreover, even if there were sufficient questions of each type, there is little evidence that the question types represent distinct and independent subskills. Analyses of responses to standardized test items have generally shown that the ability (or inability) to answer one type of question tends to be correlated with the ability (or inability) to answer other types (Davis, 1944, 1968; Thorndike, 1973–74; Thurstone, 1946). That is, there is little tendency for students to show strength (or weakness) in one aspect of comprehension independently of strength (or weakness) in most other aspects.

Research tends to corroborate the view that students' specific difficulties in comprehension cannot be identified through analysis of question types. In a study of sixth graders, the poorer readers, as was expected, answered fewer questions correctly than the good readers; but they were similar to the good readers in that they answered more main idea questions than detail questions (Meyer, 1977). A similar result was observed with good and poor readers at the college level (Marshall & Glock, 1978–79). With regard to inferences, Bridge and Tierney (1981) found that the proportion of total information recalled that was inferential in nature was the same (approximately 40 percent) for poor readers as for good readers at the third-grade level. And, among a group of poor comprehenders at the seventh-grade level, Palincsar and Brown (1983) found no tendency for questions about implicit information to be more difficult than questions about explicit information.

At the same time, there is a growing body of evidence, consistent with the view of comprehension presented in the preceding chapter, that poor comprehension arises from difficulty with the integrative processes necessary for understanding discourse. For instance, Marshall and Glock (1978–79) found that intersentence relationships were a major stumbling block for poor readers at the college level. These relationships may be made explicit through various signaling devices (*however, because, in contrast, instead, in other words, for example, first, second,* etc.) or they may be implicit. Whereas the better readers did equally well under both circumstances, the poor readers suffered a significant reduction in recall of passage information when these relationships were implied rather than directly stated. Moreover, the poorer readers tended to include fewer interpropositional relations in their written recalls. Further evidence that the absence of signaling devices can be detrimental to poor readers was obtained in a study of ninth graders (Meyer, Brandt, & Bluth, 1980).

In addition, research indicates that poor readers are generally insensitive to the high-level organization of passage information. That is, in recalling information after reading, poor readers are much less likely than good readers to follow the overall argument or pattern of discourse used by the author. While awareness of textual organization at the discourse level is rarely directly relevant to classroom comprehension tasks, it evidently facilitates the processing of lower-level information, for there is a high correlation between a student's ability to use the top-level structure of text in organizing his or her recall and the total amount of information recalled (Meyer et al., 1980). In addition, instruction in the main types of expository discourse (e.g., main idea–supporting details; problem–solution; comparison–contrast) leads to marked increases in the amount of information students recall (Bartlett, 1978; McDonald, 1978; both cited in Meyer et al., 1980).

Finally, there is considerable evidence that poor readers have difficulty monitoring their mental processes while reading and that they do not make appropriate adjustments when they encounter obstacles to comprehension (Kimmell & MacGinitie, 1985). For example, poor readers often fail to recognize that something does not make sense or that they do not know the answer to a question. Nor do they regularly reread portions of text in an attempt to gain clarification. In an investigation of the question-answering strategies of good and poor readers in grades 4–10, a passage was used that required the student to look back to the text for the answers to certain questions. Researchers found that the good readers in grades 6 and 7 (although not in the lower grades) showed some awareness of comprehension difficulty on at least 50 percent of the questions that required lookbacks. That is, they indicated uncertainty or dissatisfaction with a response by shrugs, grunts, hesitations, and the like, and by such verbal expressions as ". . . I think"; ". . . or something"; and "that's a hard one." By contrast, the poor readers in these grades showed such behaviors on less than 7 percent of the questions. However, contrary to expectation, the sixth- and seventh-grade good readers did *not* look back to the text with great frequency for the answers to the targeted questions. It was only among the good readers in eighth grade and beyond that this strategy was observed with considerable frequency (79 percent of the questions that required lookbacks). Thus, while poor readers at all grade levels tend to be unaware when they do not understand or know the answer to a question, even good readers do not employ lookbacks to resolve difficulties until they reach the upper grades (Garner & Reis, 1981).

Given this evidence, it is useful to view poor comprehension as arising in relation to difficulty with the integration of text information, both at the intersentence level and at higher levels of text structure. Underlying this difficulty are poorly developed strategies for utilizing background knowledge and recognizing and responding to failures of comprehension as they occur.

However, for some students, poorly developed strategies for interacting with text and organizing information represent only part of the problem. Instruction in such strategies can be effective only if students already possess the basic capacity for understanding the ideas and information with which they must interact. Therefore, in order to provide appropriate instruction once you have determined that a student's difficulty is in comprehension, you must decide whether the student has this basic capacity. You would assess his or her comprehension for this purpose. You would provide the student with an opportunity to reread relevant portions of the diagnostic passage and answer the questions that were incorrectly answered on the initial administration of the comprehension test. If the student corrects several answers on this second trial, you can conclude that he or she has the ability to acquire basic text information and can profit from instruction in interactive and organizational strategies. On the other hand, if the student is essentially unable to correct his or her answers, then the difficulty is either at a conceptual level or at the level of acquiring basic text information, necessitating instruction in intersentence and intrasentence relationships. This latter type of instruction focuses on the anaphoric relations and linguistic devices that interrelate sentence information. It also involves the modeling of certain thought processes or interactive strategies believed to be second nature to proficient readers.

In reading the above statements, which suggest distinctions among comprehenders, it is necessary to consider what information becomes available to you early in your investigation. While the print skills required across a variety of reading situations are fairly stable and determinable by a thorough initial diagnosis, comprehension skills are not. Differences in content, organization, style, and length can make dramatically different demands on the reader, making initial diagnosis of comprehension problems more tentative and qualified (Wixson, Peters, Weber, & Roeber, 1987). It is therefore less possible to make what is called a differential diagnosis with respect to comprehension from one or two diagnostic encounters. Rather, ongoing diagnostic instruction manipulating the type and complexity of material used and degree and mode of teacher support can both pinpoint a student's abilities and disabilities and guide the appropriate sequence of instruction. We discuss these variables later in our section on instruction.

GATHERING AUTHENTIC DATA

If assessment of comprehension is to provide authentic data, it must involve observing students in the act of comprehending. You can gather information by interacting with readers in postreading discussion, by having them recall what they have read (a retelling), or by involving them in oral or written introspection and retrospection as they read. Whatever the initial data-gathering choice, all comprehension assessment techniques call on the examiner to respond to the reader through direct, indirect, or probing questions at some point in the diagnostic cycle. Questioning is essential to all diagnosis, either as an initial stimulus or for later probes of what is spontaneously presented in a retelling, in an introspection, or in a guided reading lesson. Further, the guidelines for designing a set of questions to accurately represent the content of a selection, presented in Chapter 5, also provide the standard for analyzing a student's free recall, introspection, or instructional contribution.

In this section we show how Jim used a classroom selection, "Two Were Left" to gather data on his students' comprehension. To carry out the assessments within the context of normal classroom routine, Jim needed to analyze the selection the students would be reading, prepare questions or a retelling format, decide on some administrative and evaluative guidelines, and decide how to work with each student. For Bob, postreading questioning was used for assessment—perhaps the most common approach to gathering data. With Andrea, a retelling was used. For Jake, an introspective think-aloud provided a promising option for assessment. Jim frequently gave one student attention while the larger group worked independently, so he took Jake aside and worked through the selection with him. For Bob and Andrea, Jim scheduled some individual time after reading while the larger group worked on extension activities.

Preparation

Jim read "Two Were Left" (Cave, 1969) using the process we illustrated for "The Restless Kangaroo" in Chapter 5 (see Figure 6.1). He then constructed a set of questions that represented the important information in the selection.

> **PAUSE AND REFLECT.**   Read "Two Were Left" (see Figure 6.1) and design a set of questions that you think reflect the important information and issues of the selection. Also choose some important vocabulary terms to analyze. Compare your questions and terms with those in Figure 6.2 (p. 174) and to the list of important information in the retelling protocol in Figure 6.3 (p. 178).

In constructing questions or a retelling protocol, Jim quite naturally has specific responses in mind. These are recorded in parentheses next to each question on the prepared question list or as entries on the retelling protocol (see Figures 6.2 and 6.3) for easy reference during testing. Then Jim can make a quick judgment regarding the quality of the student's response and assess further when doing so seems appropriate. Often an answer is correct under a slightly different interpretation of the question. For example, in connection with the story of "The Restless Kangaroo" (p. 154) one of the questions is "What did the zookeeper do to find out about the problem [that the zoo

Two Were Left

On the third night of hunger, Noni thought of the dog. Nothing of flesh and blood lived upon the floating ice island with its towering berg except those two.

In the breakup Noni had lost his sled, his food, his fur, even his knife. He had saved only Nimuk, his devoted husky. And now the two marooned on the ice eyed each other warily—each keeping his distance.

Noni's love for Nimuk was real, very real—as real as the hunger and cold nights and the gnawing pain of his injured leg. But the men of his village killed their dogs when food was scarce, didn't they? And without thinking twice about it.

And Nimuk, he told himself, when hungry enough would seek food. One of us will soon be eating the other, Noni thought. So . . .

He could not kill the dog with his bare hands. Nimuk was powerful and much fresher than he. A weapon, then, was essential.

Removing his mittens, he unstrapped the brace from his leg. When he had hurt his leg a few weeks before, he had made the brace from bits of harness and two thin strips of iron.

Kneeling now, he stuck one of the iron strips into a crack in the ice and began to rub the other against it with firm, slow strokes.

Nimuk watched him intently, and it seemed to Noni that the dog's eyes glowed more brightly as night came.

He worked on, trying not to remember why. The slab of iron had an edge now. It had begun to take shape. Daylight found his task completed.

Noni pulled the finished knife from the ice and thumbed its edge. The sun's glare, reflected from it, stabbed at his eyes and for a moment blinded him.

Noni steeled himself.

"Here, Nimuk!" he called softly.

The dog watched him suspiciously.

"Come here," Noni called.

Nimuk came closer. Noni read fear in the animal's gaze. He read hunger and suffering in the dog's labored breathing and awkward, dragging crouch. His heart wept. He hated himself and fought against it.

Closer Nimuk came, wary of his intentions. Now Noni felt a thickening in his throat. He saw the dog's eyes and they were wells of suffering.

Now! Now was the time to strike!

A great sob shook Noni's kneeling body. He cursed the knife. He swayed blindly; flung the weapon far from him. With empty hands outstretched he stumbled toward the dog, and fell.

The dog growled. He warily circled the boy's body. Noni was sick with fear.

In flinging away his knife he had left himself defenseless. He was too weak to crawl after it now. He was at Nimuk's mercy, and Nimuk was hungry.

The dog circled him and was creeping up from behind. Noni heard the rattle of saliva in the savage throat.

He shut his eyes, praying that the attack might be swift. He felt the dog's feet against his leg, the hot rush of Nimuk's breath against his neck. A scream gathered in the boy's throat.

Then he felt the dog's hot tongue licking his face.

Noni's eyes opened, staring, not believing. Crying softly, he put out his arm and drew the dog's head down against his own. . . .

The plane came out of the south an hour later. Its pilot, a young man of the coastal patrol, looked down and saw the large, floating ice island with the berg rising from its center. And he saw something flashing.

FIGURE 6.1   Diagnostic reading selection

SOURCE: From *New Worlds Ahead* by I. Willis and R. E. Willis, pp. 409–411, published by Harcourt, Brace, and World, 1969. Copyright 1942 by the Crowell-Collier Publishing Co. Reprinted by permission of the author, Hugh B. Cave.

It was the sun gleaming on something shiny which moved. His curiosity aroused, the pilot banked his ship and descended, circling the ice. Now he saw, in the shadow of the peak of ice, a dark, still shape that appeared to be human. Or were there two shapes?

He set his ship down in a water lane and investigated. There were two shapes, boy and dog. The boy was unconscious but alive. The dog whined feebly but was too weak to move.

The gleaming object which had trapped the pilot's attention was a hand-made knife stuck point first into the ice a little distance away and quivering in the wind.

was having with the kangaroos]?" The expected answer is that the zookeeper stood watch over the kangaroo's pen one night while the animals slept. If a child answered, "He gave them a different pen," one must allow for the possibility that the child did not quite catch the words *to find out* and for this reason answered as if the question pertained to what was done *about* the problem. In such a case, it seems reasonable to clarify the question, for example, by saying, "Yes, he did that in the end. But how did he find out what the problem was?"

In other cases, the answer given might relate to an aspect of the story problem that is different from the one the teacher had in mind. In response to the question, "What was the problem the zoo was having with the kangaroos?" a student might answer, "The baby kangaroo kept putting straw into the pouch." This is, of course, the "ultimate" or underlying problem in the story, but the initial problem, in terms of the story structure, is that the baby kangaroo was found on the floor of the pen on several occasions. Again, the question should be clarified: "Yes. But they noticed a problem before they found out about that. What was the problem they noticed?" Then, if necessary, further clarification might be given: "What kept happening to the baby kangaroo because it kept putting straw into the pouch?" In general, answers that give information that is correct in terms of the story but slightly oblique in relation to the question should be probed further, either at the time of the initial response or after all the questions have been asked.

Another type of problematic response is one that is too broad or narrow. In Chapter 4 we saw that Raymond gave too narrow an answer (namely, specific examples in response to the question of what determines the kinds of housing people build), apparently because he did not fully grasp the idea that external conditions can determine what people do. He was given partial credit, however, for recognizing the examples as relevant to the question. An answer that is too broad should also be given partial credit if it represents a reasonable generalization from the evidence.

In addition, it is good practice to give students an opportunity to sharpen their answers. For answers that are too narrow, Jim may ask for a general statement about the specific facts or examples given (e.g., "What does the use of logs from a nearby forest show about the housing people build?"). For answers that are too broad, he should ask for more precise information. Take as an example a passage about the problem of oil spills on the ocean, which discusses the fact that the oil kills animals, birds, and microscopic plant life. A student who says, in response to the question of why oil spills must be prevented, that they "cause pollution" should be asked for some specification of the harmful effects of this pollution.

Administration

A basic principle of instruction in reading is that the reader should be given some general purpose or guiding statement before reading. This principle should be followed in assessment as well. Jim prepared the entire group for reading "Two Were Left" by setting the stage for the excerpted selection they were to read. The group hypothesized about life for the Inuit and the dangers of being stranded in the wild. He then took Jake aside for the think-aloud process, coming back to work with Bob and Andrea immediately after silent reading. For each of them, he had a "right after reading" session to tap their immediate comprehension and worked with each of them a second time to further assess their understanding.

As the procedure is teacher designed, the teacher can, whenever advisable, repeat, reword, or clarify questions. He or she must acknowledge that some questions may be ambiguous, permitting more than one interpretation, or they may elicit unanticipated, though correct, responses. For this reason, taping of the sessions is advisable so that the teacher can devote his attention to listening to the reader and asking thoughtful questions.

Evaluation

After working with each student, Jim prepared an analysis. For Bob and Andrea, he used the following procedure:

1. Initial analysis: Calculate a comprehension score by determining the percentage of text-related questions that the student answered correctly. If a retelling has been used, calculate the percentage of important elements he or she recalled. If the comprehension score is less than 75 percent, analyze print skill and vocabulary knowledge to see whether these areas have interfered with comprehension. If poor comprehension is *not* attributable to either of these underlying areas, look further at comprehension.

2. Further assessment of comprehension: For each question that was answered incorrectly, have the student reread the portion(s) of the passage that are relevant and give him or her a second opportunity to answer the question or provide retelling information. The purpose is to gain insight into the student's thinking and text-processing strategies. When the student can correct his or her initial response, assume that the first difficulty was relatively superficial—the student is able to grasp basic information but has difficulty identifying or extracting the relevant information. In some cases, the student may have misunderstood the question or failed to include it in his or her retelling.

When the student is unable to respond correctly after reexamining the text, the difficulty is considered to be more severe. In such cases, a more detailed assessment should focus on the cohesive elements of the selection and the reasoning and prior knowledge necessary to make inferences. Let's look at Bob's case in more detail to see how Jim conducted his diagnostic process.

CASE 6.1: BOB—USING QUESTIONS

Bob, a seventh-grader, read "Two Were Left." (See Figure 6.1.) This story was about an Inuit boy, Noni, who was marooned with his dog on an ice island. Since there was no wildlife or vegetation on the island, within a few days the two were near starvation. With much anguish, the boy concluded that he must kill the dog for food.

Bob showed excellent print skill when he read the story aloud. Further, the vocabulary knowledge assessment, shown in Figure 6.2, indicated that he was familiar with the key words in the story (e.g., *marooned, essential, wary, descended, intention*). The questions that Bob's teacher, Jim, developed to measure his understanding of the story are also shown in the figure, along with his responses. As you can see, Bob's comprehension score was only 60 percent. Thus, because his print skill and vocabulary knowledge were both highly satisfactory, his main difficulty was considered to be in the area of comprehension. You should examine the questions that Bob answered incorrectly to identify possible reasons for his comprehension difficulties.

Further Assessment for Comprehension

The first question that Bob missed in the comprehension test was drawn from the following paragraph:

> He could not kill the dog with his bare hands. Nimuk was powerful and much fresher than he. A weapon, then, was essential.

The question was "Why did Noni think a weapon was essential?" Bob had initially answered, "To kill wild animals for food." (The correct answer would refer to the fact that the dog was too powerful to be killed barehanded; partial credit could be given for referring to the need to kill the dog for food.) Further assessment with regard to this question was as follows:

JIM: I'd like you to read this paragraph again and see if you can tell why Noni thought a weapon was essential.

BOB: [after reading]: To kill the dog, for food.

JIM: Yes, but why did he need a *weapon?*

BOB: Can't kill a dog without a weapon, with bare hands.

JIM: And why not?

BOB: It could kill you, too big.

One interpretation of this result is that Bob had initially answered as he did—"to kill wild animals for food"—because he conceived of the question as a generic one—as pertaining to weapons in general, rather than to the story in particular. Another possibility is that he had forgotten—or was never really certain—that there were no wild animals on the ice island. (That information appears in the second sentence of the story, several paragraphs before the one under discus-

Comprehension

✓ 1. Where were Noni and Nimuk marooned? (on an ice island)
RESPONSE: Ice island.

✓ 2. How did Noni feel about Nimuk? (loved him very much)
RESPONSE: Liked him.

✗ 3. Why did Noni think a weapon was essential? (Nimuk was too powerful to kill with his bare hands)
RESPONSE: To kill wild animals for food.

✗ 4. From what did Noni make a weapon? (strips of iron from his brace)
RESPONSE: Knife.

✓ 5. Why were they wary of each other? (they were both starving—might kill the other for food)
RESPONSE: 'Cause one might eat the other.

✓ 6. Why was Noni unable to attack the dog? (loved him too much)
RESPONSE: Noni like the dog; did not want to kill him.

✗ 7. What did Noni do with the knife? (threw it away—"far from him")
RESPONSE: Tried to kill Nimuk and left it there.

✗ 8. When did Noni know that the dog would not attack him? (when he felt the dog licking his face)
RESPONSE: The dog came closer and closer.

✓ 9. Who rescued them? (a pilot in a plane)
RESPONSE: A plane.

✓ 10. What was quivering in the wind which caught the pilot's attention? (the knife)
RESPONSE: Knife.

Vocabulary Knowledge

✓ 1. What is a *husky*?
RESPONSE: An Eskimo sled dog.

✓ 2. What does *marooned* mean?
RESPONSE: Deserted on an island.

✓ 3. What does *gnawing* mean?
RESPONSE: A dull pain that doesn't stop.

✓ 4. What does *essential* mean?
RESPONSE: Necessary.

✓ 5. In the story, it says that Noni "steeled" himself. What does *steeled* mean?
RESPONSE: Got his nerve up.

✓ 6. What does *wary* mean?
RESPONSE: Careful-cautious.

✓ 7. What does *descended* mean?
RESPONSE: Go down.

✓ 8. What does *feebly* mean?
RESPONSE: Weakly.

✓ 9. What does *quivering* mean?
RESPONSE: Shaking.

✓ 10. What does *intention* mean?
RESPONSE: Going to do something.

FIGURE 6.2 Responses to comprehension and vocabulary knowledge questions: Bob sion.) Nevertheless, he was able to answer the question correctly on rereading, showing that he could, at least, understand the intersentence relationships in the paragraph.

Jim continued with another question that Paul had initially missed. This related to the part of the story that described how the Inuit boy made a knife with two strips of metal taken from a brace he was wearing on his wounded knee. The relevant paragraphs read as follows:

> Removing his mittens, he unstrapped the brace from his leg. When he had hurt his leg a few weeks before, he had made the brace from bits of harness and two thin strips of iron.
>
> Kneeling now, he stuck one of the iron strips into a crack in the ice and began to rub the other against it with firm, slow strokes.
>
> Nimuk watched him intently, and it seemed to Noni that the dog's eyes glowed more brightly as night came.
>
> He worked on, trying not to remember why. The slab of iron had an edge now. It had begun to take shape. Daylight found his task completed.

In answer to the question "From what did Noni make a weapon?" Bob had responded, "a knife." After rereading, he responded as follows:

BOB: Oh. A slab of iron.

JIM: And where did he get the iron?

BOB: His brace for his knee.

JIM: Can you explain how he made a knife out of the iron?

BOB: He rubbed it until it had an edge.

JIM: What did he rub it with?

BOB: Not sure . . . on the ice?

This was a rather difficult sequence of text. It required the reader to visualize a step-by-step procedure, and Bob was evidently unable to do this. Still, on a second reading he had gleaned the essential idea that the knife was made from a part of the brace.

The third question that Bob missed involved a crucial element of the story. Just as the boy was about to strike the dog, he was overcome with grief and "flung the weapon far from him." Bob evidently understood the boy's reluctance to kill the dog; in answer to the question, "Why was Noni unable to attack the dog?" he had replied, "Noni liked the dog; did not want to kill him." Yet, in answering the next question, "What did Noni do with the knife?" Bob had stated that Noni "tried to kill Nimuk and left it there." Thus, Bob seemed to have two conflicting ideas about a dramatic story event. Jim explored further by having Bob reread the following segment.

> Now? Now was the time to strike!
>
> A great sob shook Noni's kneeling body. He cursed the knife. He

swayed blindly; flung the weapon far from him. With empty hands outstretched he stumbled toward the dog, and fell.

Then Jim asked the question again, "What did Noni do with the knife?"

BOB: Tried to kill Nimuk. Threw it far.
JIM: Did he throw it at the dog?
BOB: Yeah. But he missed him.

Since the student did not answer correctly on this second trial, the assessment then took the form of a detailed analysis of the text.

JIM: Show me the part that tells what Noni did; read it aloud.
BOB: [from passage]: "Flung the weapon far from him."
JIM: Yes, I suppose that could mean that he threw it at the dog and missed. But I think it means something else. Do you know how I know?
BOB: No.
JIM: Well, let's look at what happened before that, right after Noni finished making the knife. [The teacher points to the preceding paragraph and the student reads it aloud: "Closer Nimuk came, wary of his intentions. Now Noni felt a thickening in his throat. He saw the dog's eyes and they were wells of suffering."] Okay, so where was Nimuk when Noni threw the knife?
BOB: [No response.]
JIM: [clarifying]: Where was Nimuk in relation to Noni? How close was he?
BOB: Well, he came closer . . . Oh, he saw the dog's eyes.
JIM: Yes, so the dog had to be pretty close to Noni. Do you see now what it means that Noni "flung the weapon far from him"?
BOB: He wasn't trying to kill the dog?
JIM: Right. We have to assume that he wasn't trying to kill the dog—that he changed his mind at the last minute and threw the knife "far from him"—far from himself and the dog.

There was, then, some plausibility to Bob's interpretation of the story character's action, at least when that action is taken by itself, out of context. It only becomes implausible that the boy meant to kill the dog when he "flung the weapon far from him" when one takes into account the dog's proximity. Thus, as may have occurred with the first question, Bob had failed to keep one fact in mind while considering another. And, as with the first question, he did seem able to understand the language of the text at both the sentence and intersentence levels.

The fourth and final question that Bob missed involved the next event in the story. After the Inuit boy threw the knife "far from him" he lay on the ground in fear that the dog would now attack him:

He shut his eyes, praying that the attack might be swift. He felt the dog's feet against his leg, the hot rush of Nimuk's breath against his neck. A scream gathered in the boy's throat.

Then he felt the dog's hot tongue licking his face.

In response to the question, "When did the boy know the dog would not attack him?" Bob had answered, "The dog came closer and closer." After rereading, he was able to answer correctly, "When he felt him licking his face."

Taken together, Bob's responses on further assessment suggest that his main comprehension difficulty is in integrating story events. He seemed to consider each event an isolated phenomenon. As a result, his grasp of the story line was initially vague and impressionistic. Nevertheless, he was able to correct three out of four of his responses, indicating that he had the capability to grasp the basic information in the text. Therefore, Jim diagnosed Bob's comprehension problem as poorly developed strategies for interacting with information and for recognizing its overall structure. We comment on instruction for Bob later in this chapter.

Retelling

Jim used some of the same assessment strategies with Andrea that he had used with Bob. However, because he wanted to assess Andrea's comprehension without the clues that questions sometimes provide, he used a retelling. **Free recall**, more commonly called **retelling**, is a process in which the student is asked to retell the story or reproduce information in his or her own words. Following a prereading orientation, the examiner does not ask specific questions but rather asks the reader to retell the selection. Working with a prepared checklist (see Figure 6.3 for an example for the selection "Two Were Left," introduced earlier), the examiner records the information supplied by the reader in the order in which it is presented. Following the student's unprompted recall, the examiner uses questions to assess further for any information the student did not supply. During or after the retelling, the assessor can also make anecdotal notes on the student's oral language.

You can score aided recall easily if the checklist of information you prepare in advance is precise and well ordered. Give the student points for each idea or fact recalled, as you would with questions. One advantage of this procedure is that it gives you some idea of the student's verbal clarity and fluency. It is more time-consuming than direct questioning, however, at least at the point of administration, and the added information may be superfluous if you have many other opportunities to observe students' verbal proficiency.

Retellings have been used extensively as a research tool and less frequently for assessment and instruction (Gambrell, Pfeiffer, & Wilson, 1985; Irwin & Mitchell, 1983; Morrow et al., 1986). They have the advantage of showing the examiner what the student sees as important without the prompt of teacher questions. Further, the sequence in which the student retells the information and the language he or she uses to express it also provide more diagnostic information.

Diagnostic use of the retelling procedure can bring certain problems, however.

Information	Spontaneous	Prompted
1. Noni and Nimuk	√ (no names)	½
2. marooned on ice island		
3. Both were becoming hungry	√	
4. Noni considers killing Nimuk	√	
5. Nimuk too strong to kill with bare hands		—
6. Noni began to make a knife from knee brace		—
7. Both were wary because each might harm other		—
8. Noni unable to kill Nimuk because he loved him		—
9. Noni threw knife far from him		√
10. Nimuk approached Noni	} (whole	—
11. Noni feared Nimuk would attack him	sequence	—
12. Nimuk licked Noni, didn't harm	missing)	—
13. Pilot found boy and dog	√	
14. because of blade's reflection		—
Percentage of comprehension:	$\frac{5.5}{14} = 39\%$	

FIGURE 6.3   Retelling response checklist for "Two Were Left": Andrea

Morrow et al. (1986) found that students often have trouble with the process if it is unfamiliar but that repeated attempts produce more elaborated retellings. Further, children respond differently to different directions. For example, if both the reader and the examiner have read the story, students will often omit important information, assuming the examiner already knows it (Golden & Pappas, 1987). Moreover, the quality of the retelling or reproduction may reflect the student's verbal and expository skills as much as his or her comprehension. Students vary widely in their ability to organize and verbalize information. Like other integrative and language skills, this one depends a great deal on practice. Since questions serve as "cues" or "prompts," readers can usually remember much more about a passage in response to questioning than they can reproduce in a free recall. For example, Stein and Glenn (1979) report that in retelling a story, young children tended to omit information about the goals and motives of story characters and yet they were able to answer questions about these story elements.

   More significantly for our purposes, the tendency to provide additional information in response to questioning is much more pronounced among poor readers than among good readers. Bridge and Tierney (1981) found that of the total number of items of information that were ultimately remembered by a group of low-achieving third graders, over 40 percent were given during the further assessment task that followed free recall. Therefore, while it may be well to give students an opportunity to retell the story in order to assess their ability to do so, a good set of questions will be needed to obtain a valid estimate of their comprehension skill.

CASE 6.2: ANDREA—USING A RETELLING

Andrea, a seventh grader with good print and fluency skills, read the same story introduced earlier, "Two Were Left," about the dilemma of an Inuit boy marooned with his dog. Jim began the retelling process.

JIM: Can you tell me the story as if you were telling it to someone who hadn't read it?

ANDREA: There was a kid and his dog and because nobody could live in the cold they had to keep going. So he was going to kill his dog because the dog was creeping around him. But a plane saved them in time.

JIM: Anything else you'd like to tell someone who hadn't read it.

ANDREA: [pausing a long time]: Well, the kid wanted to use his knife to kill the dog.

JIM: Why was that?

ANDREA: Well, it's a good weapon for killing.

JIM: Where did he get the knife?

ANDREA: He carried it in his leg pocket.

JIM: Do you have any idea where this is happening?

ANDREA: In the winter someplace.

JIM: How did Noni and Nimuk feel on the ice?

ANDREA: Cold and hungry.

JIM: Was this a problem?

ANDREA: Sure, they'd starve or freeze.

JIM: Any other problems?

ANDREA: Well, that would be enough.

JIM: Why do you think he didn't kill Nimuk?

ANDREA: He'd need his dog for pulling his sled later.

JIM: What happened to the knife?

ANDREA: He threw it away.

JIM: Why?

ANDREA: He wasn't going to use it.

JIM: How did the pilot find them?

ANDREA: He must have looked around for a long time and then saw two little black dots on the ice.

PAUSE AND REFLECT.   Cover up the right-hand side of the retelling checklist in Figure 6.3 and score Andrea's responses. Then compare with Jim's scoring. Discuss differences. How would you assess her comprehension?

Further Assessment for Comprehension

Following the first retelling and questioning, Jim did further assessment by asking Andrea to reexamine the selection. Simple reexamination did not help Andrea do a better job of answering some of the questions. For example, the issue of the knife is an important one for the selection. Jim then led Andrea through this series of questions:

1. Did Noni have his knife at the beginning of the story? What does the author tell us? (the knife was lost in the breakup of the ice)
2. Why did he need a knife? (Nimuk too big to kill with bare hands)
3. How did he get the knife? (made it from knee brace)
4. What happened to the knife? (he threw it far away)

Then Jim related the knife's reflection in the sun to the pilot's discovery of the two survivors. In doing this, he needed to go paragraph by paragraph, and sometimes sentence by sentence, through this short selection helping Andrea identify important information, sequence it, and make connections.

Unlike Bob, Andrea seemed to grasp only the most obvious information provided by the author and was unable to improve her performance without Jim's considerable support and segmenting of the selection. Andrea's problem is much more severe and requires attention to extraction of basic information as well as its integration across the text. We will comment on her instructional plan later in the chapter.

Think-Alouds

In the **think-aloud** procedure (Lytle 1982) the student is asked to introspect and verbalize before, during, and after reading a selection. The teacher asks the student to reflect and comment on what he or she is reading as the text is exposed line by line. In the introspection process, Lytle has noted that students comment on what they understand (signaling understanding), indicate what is causing them problems (monitoring of doubts), analyze parts of the text (analyzing) or verbally try to figure things out (reasoning), relate the author's ideas to their own knowledge (elaborating), and evaluate aspects of the author's message and style (judging).

Readers exhibit strategies when they combine the "moves" noted in parentheses above for a particular purpose, such as to remove a doubt. Characteristic strategies in certain situations may define a student's style, which may be consistent across various texts. Though this process is still an exploratory one, having a student "talk through" a selection may provide diagnostic insights and instructional leads.

CASE 6.3: JAKE—USING A THINK-ALOUD

Here we consider an excerpt from a think-aloud protocol of Jake, a seventh-grade student, reading "Two Were Left." Jim noted that Jake is very inconsistent in his reading group. Sometimes he seems to have a good grasp of what is being read; at other times he is very confused or seems to have very different interpretations from those of the rest of the group. Jim decided to try to think-aloud with his next lesson.

JIM: Jake, I'm going to show you this story sentence by sentence and I want you to think out loud as you read it.

JAKE: What do you mean?

JIM: You can tell me about what you think the author is saying, what it makes you think of, where you think the author is going, what puzzles you, how you figure things out, anything that comes into your head.

JAKE: Okay.

TEXT: "Two Were Left."

JAKE: It must tell about two people left off somewhere. I don't know where.

TEXT: On the third night of hunger, Noni thought of the dog.

JAKE: One person is Noni and he's probably worried that no one will take care of his dog while he is stuck somewhere.

TEXT: Nothing of flesh and blood lived upon the floating ice island with its towering berg except those two.

JAKE: They're somewhere near an island but nobody lives there. They're left.

TEXT: In the breakup, Noni had lost his sled, his food, his fur, even his knife.

JAKE: He's really stuck but I still don't know who the other guy is. Maybe the other guy wants to kill this guy. But he's got a knife.

TEXT: He had saved only Nimuk, his devoted husky.

JAKE: Well, his dog's okay. I'll bet the dog will find the other guy first and get him and save Noni.

TEXT: And now the two marooned on the ice eyed each other warily—each keeping his distance.

JAKE: Well, the other guy is near enough to see him. I'm sure the dog will save him.

It is clear from the think-aloud protocol that Jake has made a conclusion from the title concerning who the "two" were and is retaining this schema, causing himself a bit of confusion as he reads on in the selection. He keeps waiting for the other person to attack and interprets each of the sentences in light of this overriding schema. Also he has not attended to some essential signal words in the selection: *except,* indicating they are on the island; *even,* signifying his knife is gone.

After the protocol was finished, he said, "This is a really crazy story and I don't understand it at all." Jim took him back to the beginning and worked through the first paragraph again. In their repeating the protocol, the selection made sense. Jim concluded that Jake does not have much difficulty with narratives if he begins by clearly establishing the characters and their problems or goals. Diagnostically, working through a selection in this manner gives Jim insight into strategy use, misuse, and overuse that can help students better approach a reading assignment. We will comment on his instruction later.

Besides its obvious diagnostic implications, Jim can use think-aloud protocols for intervention. If a student's style is nonfunctional, he can provide the types of responses *they* would make as modeling and feedback (Huffy, Roehler & Herrmann, 1988, Palincsar & Brown, 1983), can interrupt the reader and focus them on his own processes (Brown, 1986), or can have students write their responses in a reading journal (Mayers, 1993) for later reflection, comparison, and discussion. Students can do a rereading of a selection along with an earlier audiotape to reflect on an earlier reading. Further, Jim can structure group think-alouds by using an overhead projector on which a selection is revealed chunk by chunk for group analysis and discussion.

COMPREHENSION INSTRUCTION

We turn now to instruction in comprehension. How can we improve instruction for students with comprehension difficulties? Some years ago the answer would have been that we must identify areas of specific weakness and strengthen those areas through direct instruction. Educators believed that comprehension was made up of a number of subskills and that remedial efforts should be directed toward improving one or another of them. Thus, some students might need help in noting and recalling details while others might need help in following sequences of events or grasping main ideas. This approach is now generally perceived as unduly limited and not entirely consistent with what we know about the nature of comprehension and the research on its development. Therefore, we recommend a somewhat different approach.

We noted earlier the difficulty in making a differential diagnosis for comprehension. What frequently can be determined for each reader is the degree of teacher support, the explicitness of instruction, and the length and complexity of material used in the instruction for productive comprehension. If comprehension problems are severe, adjustment may be needed in all these conditions; if problems are minimal, fewer changes may be needed. For example, some students, like Bob, require a small degree of teaching intervention and guidance to discover ways to interact better with whole texts. Others, like Jake, need heavy intervention at the start of a new selection to help them develop a schema for completing the selection unaided. Still others, like Andrea, need to be focused on very small units of text with explicit instructional demands to develop their strategies. Therefore, what differentiates comprehension instruction at the beginning of diagnosis are these three dimensions: length of the unit of text used for instruction, degree of teacher intervention, and explicitness of teacher direction.

Given these differing dimensions, we recommend two types of instructional procedures for helping all students with poor comprehension. The first introduces the students to various strategies, such as self-questioning, predicting, and self-monitoring, which foster an interactive approach to reading. Presented in this section are four techniques representing varying degrees of teacher intervention, instructional explicitness, and length of text units (though this last can obviously be varied within each model). The Directed Reading-Thinking Activity (DR-TA) (Davidson & Wilkerson, 1988), and Know-Want-Learn (K-W-L) (Ogle, 1986) combine implicit modeling and low-to-moderate teacher directness in consideration of larger chunks of text. The ReQuest Procedure (Manzo, 1969) combines a gradually increasing text size with implicit modeling and high directiveness. Reciprocal Teaching (Palincsar & Brown, 1983) is the most intensive of the four, combining small text chunks with high directedness and explicit modeling.

A second type of instruction examines relationships within a text, the structure and organization of material, the connections within and across sentences, and the relationships between questions and the text from which they are derived. The need for this focusing on organization and relationships is often revealed during some of the text interaction instruction noted above. For example, with Jake's think-aloud, which in our model would be characterized as focusing on small text units with low teacher directiveness and low modeling, revealed a problem with signal words such as *except* and *even,* suggesting that he needed to pay greater attention to the words that make connections within sentences.

Developing Interactive Strategies

The directed reading lesson format common to basal reading materials has a familiar and predictable structure. You prepare concepts and vocabulary, set a prereading purpose, have the student read part or all of the selection, and ask the student discussion questions after reading. Skills are introduced and practiced at one or more places in the lesson and reteaching, extension, and enrichment activities complete the cycle. While this is a sensible and legitimate structure, there are many reasons to modify it for comprehension enhancement.

At the core of interactive reading is the active use of what the reader already knows to learn something new. Analyses of classroom instruction (Beck, McKeown, McCaslin, & Burkes, 1979; Durkin, 1978–79) have suggested that too little time before reading is devoted to developing and activating the prereading schemata necessary for effective comprehension. A second concern about the directed reading lesson is that the major part of the "work" is done by the teacher, relegating the students to the role of passive responders, not building those strategies needed to approach text independently (Stauffer, 1969). We offer several instructional alternatives to the directed reading lesson, all of which view your role as that of expert guide in leading students through a strategic approach to text. Both tacitly and explicitly these procedures call on the reader to control and monitor the reading situation.

The Directed Reading-Thinking Activity.   The **Directed Reading-Thinking Activity** approach models the comprehension process by participants' walking through a selection bit by bit rather than locating all discussion after reading. In this way you help the student experience the thinking processes that an expert reader uses in comprehending a text (Davidson & Wilkerson, 1988). The basic processes to be modeled are as follows:

1. Before I read a section of text, I use clues to make predictions about what the author will tell me.
2. I stop as I read to refine or reformulate my predictions.
3. I repeat steps 1 and 2 throughout the selection.

To plan a DR-TA you select an appropriate reading selection, one about which students can make predictions and that is at an appropriate instructional level. After analyzing the selection, you choose several points at which the reader might be stopped and asked for a prediction about subsequent content. The title, picture, caption, first paragraph, or some combination of these often serve as the basis for the first prediction.

After each chunk is read, you and your students discuss their prediction in the light of the clues the author has given them. Probing questions are the norm for the teacher in the DR-TA, questions such as, "What makes you think so?" "What did the author say that confirms (or disconfirms) that?" "What will _____ do about _____ ?" "Why do you think the author said that?" Students go back to the selection to find more information, to clarify a point, and to resolve conflicts, and oral reading is used to substantiate their opinions.

In the process of reasoning through the text with the author, the reader comes to a full construction of the message so that the final discussion can focus on evaluating the author's message and craft. Writing also fits naturally into the DR-TA in that students can write predictions and evidence at various points, and they frequently want to rewrite sections of narratives that they find unsatisfactory.

The K-W-L.   The **K-W-L** (Ogle, 1986) is a predictive approach to expository material. Like the DR-TA, it asks students to become active readers by specifying a purpose for reading. It has three basic strategies:

1. Brainstorm. Before reading, ask myself: What do I **K**now?
2. Set purpose. What do I **W**ant to know after I read?
3. Consolidate after reading. What did I **L**earn?

You would lead the students through brainstorming on the topic before reading, then have them list what they would like to find out. At this point you can also participate as a contributor of relevant questions. After reading, students go back to see which questions were answered by the selection, refine their knowledge, and frequently set reference goals for themselves to search out information that interests them and that is not provided by the author.

ReQuest Procedure.   In Manzo's (1969) **ReQuest Procedure,** you would not only model questions but also provide some feedback on the quality of students' questions by praising those that are good and withholding comment on those that are not. The procedure is one of turn taking, which gives it an attractive gamelike quality. After a sentence is read, first the student asks you questions and then you ask the student questions. All questions must be answered without either of you referring to the passage, though the responder may ask for clarification or rephrasing of the question. (Students are told to try to ask questions that a teacher might ask.) You and your students continue in this fashion with succeeding sentences until you feel that enough information has been established for students to make reasonable predictions about the remainder of the story. At that point, predictions are made and students read to verify them.

Reciprocal Teaching/Modeling.   Palincsar and Brown (1983) developed the Reciprocal Teaching/Modeling procedure in which students and teacher take turns leading a dialogue. The "leader" asks an important question about a small segment of text—no more than a paragraph—and is also responsible for (1) **summarizing** what has been read; (2) **predicting** what might be discussed next; and (3) offering **clarification** of anything that seemed confusing. You guide students in these activities by a variety of prompting and modeling techniques (e.g., "Remember that a summary doesn't include a lot of detail"; "What question would a teacher ask?"). The help and participation of other students in the group may also be solicited on occasion. In addition to prompting the student leader, you provide praise and feedback specific to the student's conduct of the dialogue. You might offer corrective feedback by saying, "That was interesting information. It was information that I would call detail in the passage. Can you find the most important information?" (Palincsar & Brown, 1983, p. 14). Then, at the conclusion of each student-led discussion, you model any portion of the discussion that you feel needs improvement (e.g., "I would summarize by saying . . .").

An important element of this instructional procedure is informing students of its self-monitoring purpose: "Being able to say in your own words what one has just read, and being able to guess what the questions will be a on test, are sure ways of testing oneself to see if one has understood" (p. 14). The role of self-questioning, predicting, summarizing, and clarifying in enhancing comprehension, and the need for using these strategies during independent reading, must also be made explicit. Palincsar and Brown report that although seventh-grade students had considerable difficulty with the role of dialogue leader during the first few instructional sessions, by the end of 10 sessions they were able to produce questions and summaries of "some sophistication." Therefore, a teacher who wishes to use this procedure should plan to use it regularly for several weeks.

An attractive feature of the reciprocal teaching format is that it emphasizes certain processes of reading while focusing on the *meaning* of segments of text. Instruction is provided within the context of "real reading" and by repeated modeling. This is in sharp contrast to the more traditional "skills" method of helping students with comprehension difficulty. Typically, in the more traditional method, specific aspects of text processing (e.g., sequencing events, recognizing causal relations) are isolated, directly taught through explanation and illustration, and then practiced by students on specially prepared materials and exercises. Students' performance on these materials is then evaluated as correct or incorrect. A major weakness of this method, aside from the isolation of particular aspects of meaning from the holistic process of reading, is that students are not *shown how* to arrive at correct solutions to the problem of meaning. Reciprocal teaching, as we have seen, directs students' attention to specific elements of text with a general focus on meaning. Therefore, we believe the method may be adapted to instruction in other features of text, particularly connective terms, as noted below.

Developing the Ability to Reorganize Information

Recognizing that text information is interrelated is fundamental to comprehension. We have already discussed the role of postreading questions in this connection, arguing that they should recapitulate the orderly progression of events and ideas that make up the story line. Similarly, students can be focused on overall selection organization, the connection across sentences, the relationships between questions and the text that generates them. Again the length of textual units to which the strategies are applied, amount of teacher directedness, and explicitness of instruction are significant variables.

In this section we do not try to present a comprehensive range of these techniques but rather offer a selection reflecting the dimensions of teacher support and intervention discussed earlier. For example, the strategy fostered in the Question-Answer Relationship procedure (Raphael, 1986) requires explicit instruction, as do the Guided Reading Procedure (Manzo, 1975) and the instruction on connective terms. In contrast, graphic organizers can be used as the basis for implicit instruction utilizing discovery techniques, but direct instruction of text structures is also possible. The ultimate goal of all these methods, however, is to pass the control of the process from teacher to learner.

Question-Answer Relationships.   Students need to respond to questions throughout their school careers, yet Durkin (1978–79) noted that little if any instruction focuses on the strategic processes needed to answer questions. Raphael's **Question-Answer Relationship** method (QAR) (1986) focuses students on the different strategies they can employ in answering a question. Her work is based on the idea that questions have several definable relationships with the selections from which they are drawn (Pearson & Johnson, 1978) and that each of these relationships suggests a different strategy for responding.

Some questions ask you merely to locate information that an author has given you explicitly and all in one place. Raphael (1986) terms these "Right There" questions; the author has answered them right there in the text for you. Other questions can be answered by looking for clues, implicit and explicit, scattered across a text; for these you must "Think and Search." A third type of question necessitates that you add your own knowledge to what the author tells you; these are "Author and You" questions, calling for analysis, synthesis, and evaluation. A fourth type of question can be answered by you alone; these are "On My Own" questions.

For example, for the selection, "Two Were Left," some possible QARs would be these:

QUESTION: Where were Noni and Nimuk when the selection began?

ANSWER 1: Marooned on an ice flow. (*Right There:* The student just searched for an answer given directly by the author.)

ANSWER 2: Maybe in Alaska (*Author and You:* The student used the clues of climate, terrain, sled, and husky to connect with what he knew about various locales.)

The above is a good example of two possible correct answers for the same question, each with a different procedure for answering.

QUESTION: Would you say Noni loved Nimuk? Support your answer.

ANSWER: Yes, because he worried about him but he couldn't kill him. (*Think and Search:* The reader had to collect clues across the text.)

QUESTION: Have you ever had to make a hard decision that scared you?

ANSWER: (Varies) (*On Your Own:* The student doesn't need to refer back to the story to answer this one.)

Raphael suggests making these categories and strategies explicit to students and having them classify and answer questions as a group. You can structure this activity as a game in which students gather evidence for a set of questions and discuss how they answered them (Sentell & Blachowicz, 1989).

Guided Reading Procedure.   As originally developed by Manzo (1975), the **Guided Reading Procedure** is designed to enhance students' recall of expository materials. It also increases the level of student participation in class and provides challenge as well as variety. It consists of the following steps:

1. A passage of appropriate length is selected. The length is best judged in terms of the reading speed and attention span of the average reader in the group. As a rule of thumb, primary grade students might be expected to read for 3 minutes and to read a 90-word passage in that time (30 words per minute); intermediate grade students might read for 5 minutes at approximately 100 words per minute—a 500-word passage; junior high students might read for 7 minutes at 125 words per minute—an approximately 900-word passage; and high school students could probably read for 10-minutes at 200 words per minute—a 2,000 word passage.

2. The teacher prepares students for the selection by introducing the general topic—relating it to previous classroom instruction as well as to students' personal experiences—and by introducing vocabulary, new concepts, and so on. A general purpose for reading is established, and students are directed to remember as much of the passage as they can.

3. After reading, students tell whatever they remember, and all information is recorded on the chalkboard by the teacher in the order in which it is recalled. (It may be abbreviated in form to save time.) One teacher found that having students write the information in their notebooks while the teacher recorded it on the chalkboard helped sustain students' attention and interest.

4. After students have contributed all the information they can remember, the teacher directs their attention to any inconsistencies, inaccuracies, or inadequacies that may be present. Students are encouraged to consult the text for necessary corrections and additions.

5. The group is then asked to organize the information they have compiled. This may take any form that is familiar to the students—a diagram, an outline, a chronological sequence, or even a semantic web. The teacher guides this process by raising questions, making suggestions, and so on.

6. The teacher then raises some final questions to help students gain full understanding of the passage.

7. For the final step, a conventional, teacher-made comprehension test is administered. The test items can be of any kind, but they should reflect the ideas and information that were brought out during class discussion. Manzo cautions against omitting this step: "It is important to the overall design because it provides an opportunity for evaluation, feedback, and reinforcement." He also notes that "students . . . come to look forward to these tests as opportunities to show what they have learned—a just reward for effort."[1]

Although Manzo's procedure was originally designed to be used following silent reading of an entire passage, you may also use it as a prereading activity. In this case, students first survey the passage by reading the title, headings, pictures, charts, introductory and summary paragraphs, and so on. Then they recall as much as they can, organize their recall, and check it for accuracy and completeness (as in Steps 3, 4, and 5 above). They then read the entire passage and take the final comprehension test (Step 7). When used as a prereading activity, the procedure demonstrates the value of surveying materials before reading and thus serves to combine the teaching of surveying skills with the teaching of specific content. After reading, the students contribute ideas while you record them on a chalkboard. Each idea is enclosed in a circle, and lines are drawn to connect the circles as appropriate. Students are permitted to refer to the text to refresh their memories or resolve conflicts.

For example, for a story about triplets, the teacher wrote the name of each triplet in a separate circle and the names of all three in a fourth circle. The four circles radiated from a central circle, the core of the web, which was left blank. The students were directed to "remember important things about each sister." After the story was read (by the teacher in this case, as a listening activity), the children recalled

---

[1]From "Guided Reading Procedure" by A. V. Manzo, 1975, in *Journal of Reading, 18,* 291. Reprinted by permission of the author.

information on how each sister differed from the others as well as on the characteristics they all shared. The core of the web, representing the central idea, was filled in after the four strands had been completed; an appropriate statement of the central idea was arrived at through brainstorming "sisters who do same and different things." The completed web then served as a springboard for a group discussion of individuality, family relationshps, and the like.

Direct Instruction in Text Structure.

Instructional techniques that focus student attention on the structure of what they read have been shown to increase comprehension, learning, and remembering if the task matches the way comprehension will later be measured (Anderson & Armbruster, 1984; Weaver & Kintsch, 1991). That is, if students will be asked to summarize a text, instructional tasks that ask them to build a schematic representation will be useful. Such tasks would be less useful if students needed to prepare for a multiple-choice test.

Sentence-Level Comprehension.

While most instructional intervention is carried out with whole selections or large segments of text, some instruction may need to focus on sentence-level comprehension and instruction. Though children come to school with fairly sophisticated knowledge of the syntactic system of their language, this competence continues to develop over the elementary school years with exposure through reading, writing, speaking, and listening as the prime avenues of this development. Therefore, we do not suggest that extensive instruction with isolated sentences be included in the instructional program. Rather, the following techniques may be tried with sentences that proved difficult within the context of a larger selection.

Highlighting Anaphoric Relations.   **Anaphoric relations** refer to the way in which certain words can be used as substitutes for words or groups of words that occurred previously in the text. In addition to personal pronouns, anaphoric devices include pronouns that substitute for places *(here, there)* and for things and ideas *(it, this, that)*. One of the more difficult types of anaphora involves the substitution of pro-verbs *(does, can, will)* for previously mentioned verbs or verb phrases. *Mary* **skates well.** *John* **does** *too. Mary* **does figure eights.** *So* **can** *John.*

An experienced clinician (Daskal, 1983) reports that students with poor comprehension are generally responsive to instruction in anaphora. Not only do they become proficient in identifying the antecedents of anaphoric words but they learn to attend more closely to the succession or "flow" of ideas in written materials. The procedure she follows begins with oral discussion. The student is simply asked questions that require the identification of pronoun or pro-verb antecedents. For example, given the following text,

> Harry and Josh went to the store to buy hot dogs, potato chips, and soft drinks for the picnic. But *they* were so expensive that the boys didn't have enough money to pay for *them.*

the student would be asked, "What was expensive?" or "What couldn't they pay for?" Next, the student learns to draw lines between pronouns and their antecedents. (With nonconsumable materials, a sheet of acetate is clipped to the page of print and the student uses a china marker.) This activity enables the teacher to monitor the student's accuracy in identifying antecedents, and it helps the student develop awareness of these cohesive text elements. After several weeks of this type of instruction, students automatically relate anaphoric terms to their antecedents.

Focusing on Connective Terms.   Daskal's procedure can also be applied to connective terms. These specify how ideas are related to one another. Geva (1983) provides a useful four-way classification of these terms. She points out that some of them simply *add* ideas to other ideas (e.g., *and, also, as well,* and *in addition*) whereas others express contrastive or adversative relations (e.g., *but, however,* and *on the other hand*). A third type signals causal relations (*because, so, therefore, as a result, consequently*), and the final type pertains to temporal sequence (*before, after, first, next, then*). The relationships signaled by these terms can, of course, apply to information in any unit of text—to information contained in individual clauses or sentences, or in a series of sentences within a paragraph, or in several paragraphs or even larger stretches of text.

Instruction in these relationships must be conducted, quite obviously, in the context of the kinds of situations to which they refer. For example, to show students what specific temporal words mean, you need to look at situations that can be temporally sequenced. For this reason, reciprocal teaching appears to be a promising format for highlighting connectives and the relationships they signal. A series of sessions could incorporate specific emphasis on these relationships into the procedure; each time a signal word occurred in a passage segment, the dialogue leader would be expected to discuss its informational value. The particular signal words that students should look for would be introduced beforehand and displayed in a prominent place for quick reference.

Signal words can also be systematically highlighted during regular reading lessons. You simply examine the lesson materials to locate these terms and then plan interesting and appropriate ways to call attention to them during postreading discussion. The purpose is to help students become aware of the terms and attend to them without external guidance.

Sentence Combining.   Another type of exercise, one that can be presented as a game, is sentence combining. This process can be used to engage students in the construction of complex sentences from two or more simple sentences (Froese & Kurushima, 1979; Straw & Schreiner, 1982). Another alternative is a sentence anagram task (Weaver, 1979) in which students learn to organize words into groups within a sentence and then into complete sentences.

Reflecting on the Cases: Instructional Recommendations

PAUSE AND REFLECT.   Review the cases of Bob, Andrea, and Jake. What instructional suggestions from this chapter would you make for each of them? What other ideas do you have about appropriate instruction? Discuss and then compare with Jim's choices, described below.

Surveying the range of instructional possibilities, Jim decided on these courses of action for his students:

For Bob, who was able to improve his comprehension with some general rereading directions from Jim, the DR-TA would be a good choice, helping him to break a selection into slightly more manageable chunks and focusing him on monitoring his own reading more closely.

For Jake, who formed an early, unproductive schema about reading that colored the rest of his comprehension, the ReQuest technique might provide a good starting point. He needs to be held closely to the text at the beginning of a reading selection to help him get on the right track. Within this process Jim needs to help Jake attend to small signal words to help build an appropriate initial schema to guide the rest of his reading.

Andrea had greater difficulty with her comprehension; Reciprocal Teaching could be a good starting point for her, focusing on sentences or short paragraphs. Because she also has great difficulty with vocabulary and using contextual information, much of the questioning and clarification could focus on these needs. Having Andrea work with graphic organizers might help her organize her concepts more effectively.

Like all instructional recommendations, these are tentative, to be modified as you observe more lessons and learn more about each student's abilities and problems. This is the nature of diagnostic instruction.

SUMMARY

You can generally make a diagnosis of difficulty in the area of comprehension once you have determined that print skill and vocabulary knowledge are not underlying sources of poor comprehension. Having made this decision, you should explore further to identify the nature of the comprehension problem. In order to provide appropriate instruction, you must determine whether a student's difficulty stems from poorly developed strategies for interacting with text and organizing text information or from the inability to understand the information the text contains.

Case studies utilizing postreading questioning, retelling, and the think-aloud procedure were presented along with a framework for specifying instruction. Variables such as level of teacher support, explicitness of instruction, and the length of the instructional text unit were identified and used to construct a framework for describing instructional strategies and for selecting the type of intervention that would be appropriate for the comprehension problems of the three cases. Examples are given of interactive instructional strategies such as The Directed Reading-Thinking Activity, ReQuest, Reciprocal Teaching, Question-Answer Relationships, Guided Reading Procedure, and Direct Instruction of Text Structure.

TRY IT OUT

1. Choose a passage from an upcoming lesson. Prepare questions and a retelling protocol for it. Try it with one student, using the retelling protocol first and then asking any questions not dealt with. What do you learn from each? What type of information did the questions tap that the student didn't offer independently? Compare and discuss.

2. Write a diagnostic report on one of the students analyzed in this chapter. How would you communicate, in writing, what you found out to Jim, the student's regular teacher? What examples from the student's performance would be helpful? What instructional ideas would you suggest for Jim, going beyond those in the chapter? Compare and discuss with others. What categories of information should be in such a report? What kinds of styles are appropriate?

3. **Student Portfolio Ideas:** (a) Ask students to retell a selection to one another and analyze their own retellings. Have them reflect on how they chose important ideas and how these were communicated. What insights did they gain into their own retellings as well as those of their classmates? (b) Ask students to construct a graphic or other form of retelling. Have students compare, contrast and display their examples.

4. **For Your Teaching Portfolio:** (a) Add retelling protocols for the selections chosen for "Try It Out" in Chapter 5. Build a portfolio of sample selections of various grade levels. (b) Add a case analysis to your portfolio. Compile one for your own students or do a simulation with one of the students from this chapter.

FOR FURTHER READING

Klein, M. L. (1988). *Teaching reading comprehension and vocabulary: A guide for teachers.* Englewood Cliffs, NJ: Prentice-Hall.
Full of practical classroom applications.

McNeil, J. D. (1992). *Reading comprehension: New directions for classroom practice* (3d ed.). New York: HarperCollins.
Provides a good theoretical base with practical examples.

Wilson, R. M., & Gambrell, L. B. (1988). *Reading comprehension in the elementary school: A teacher's practical guide*. Newton, MA: Allyn & Bacon.
Very clear descriptions of basic instructional strategies.

chapter 7

Writing: A Window on Reading

CHAPTER GOALS FOR THE READER

To become knowledgeable about current perspectives on writing and its development

To develop strategies for assessing writing

To develop strategies for integrating writing and reading assessment

To develop a framework for assessing the reading–writing classroom

CLASSROOM VIGNETTE: USING WRITING FOR AUTHENTIC ASSESSMENT

Keisha is a teacher with a combined second and third grade. She has been experimenting with integrating strategic reading and process writing instruction in her classroom and believes that doing so has improved her instruction. Currently she wants to go further and develop assessment strategies that are consistent with her instructional philosophy. Keisha's principal is committed to an accountability model that requires teachers to have written records to support their instructional and evaluative decisions. Yet she is flexible and willing to accept a variety of types of documentation if it is thoughtful, organized, and can be used to communicate clearly with a parent. So Keisha's challenge is to develop an analysis system that will be both personal and clear to students, parents, and administrators. Analysis of writing plays an important part in this process. This chapter presents some of the structure, strategies, and models of assessment that Keisha developed to learn from her students' writing. Specifically, she is interested in using writing to find out more about three of her students. She wants to look at Ken's and Jennifer's writing to help her plan appropriate spelling and word study instruction for them. Further, she wants to look at Cal's written summaries to provide a focus for his comprehension work.

CHAPTER OVERVIEW

This chapter has three parts. The first section discusses contemporary perspectives on writing, including developmental and process-focused views. The second segment focuses on assessing writing—from data gathering, to holistic scoring, to collecting integrated data—ending with a framework for analyzing what goes on in the reading–writing classroom. The third section suggests types of instructional support that help a teacher integrate reading and writing instruction.

CHAPTER OUTLINE

UNDERSTANDING WRITING DEVELOPMENT

Perspectives on Writing

Our knowledge of the writing process and of writing instruction has changed dramatically over the last decade. Luckily for the readers of this chapter, there are now numerous volumes devoted to enriching our knowledge about writing (see For Further Reading at the end of this chapter for some starting points). Our focus in this chapter is to sketch a general outline of what we know about reading and to suggest how this knowledge relates to classroom assessment. Important for our purposes, research suggests that reading and writing are two aspects of language use that emerge at about the same time, are interrelated, and depend on similar or overlapping knowledge, skills, and strategies (Kucer, 1985; Shanahan, 1984; Tierney & Pearson, 1983). For some children who are involved in early experimentation with writing, writing development may precede reading development. Further, children with literacy exposure generally display print awareness beyond what was recognized in times past (Sulzby & Teale, 1987; Clay, 1975).

While clear-cut relationships between writing and reading competence are not always easy to draw (Stotsky, 1984), examples of students' writing can provide insights into their concepts of print and written texts, their strategies for constructing meaning, and their general language development. Beyond awareness of the functions of print and of sound–symbol relationships, students' writing can reflect their awareness of structure, organization, genre, intention, purpose, point of view, vocabulary concepts, and many other aspects related to comprehension. With these notions in mind, we first present an overview of current views of writing, then look at ways to assess writing, and examine the ways in which writing can provide insights about a student's knowledge of print, comprehension, self-monitoring, and interest. Finally, we discuss classrooms in which writing flourishes and connects readily to reading.

Historically, educators focused on the products of writing, what was written, the grammar and mechanics of writing, and so forth. Evaluation of writing focused on these products, with assessment typically made of composition, grammar, usage, and mechanics. Current views give more emphasis to writing as a process that has strategic components, much as current views of reading value and stress the development of reading strategies. So good instruction, and therefore, assessment, must deal with not only the products of writing but its strategic processes as well. It is important to remember that writing, like all aspects of literacy, is a developmental process.

Stages and Processes

> **PAUSE AND REFLECT.**   Before reading this section, jot down on paper the types of reading you have seen done by preschoolers, by primary graders, and by developing writers. Compare this with what is described in Figure 7.1.

Any teacher planning to carry out good assessment must understand the developmental stages of the process being studied. Work by many researchers who watched the growth of literacy in young children (Baghban, 1984; Bissex, 1980; Hannan, 1984) suggests that learning to write in an environment that supports early learning, proceeds through three typical stages (see Figure 7.1). The *emergent writer*

Stage	Behaviors
1. The Emergent Writer	Draws or "writes" communications and shares with others Shows intention and planning with drawings and writing Produces scribble writing Shows interest in words and letters Uses letters in writing and drawing Writes names and may use some invented spelling
2. The Beginning Writer	Begins to label drawings and writes longer sentences and captions for them Writes pattern stories and lists of sentences (e.g., James is my friend. Jake is my friend. Jesse is my friend.) Uses invented spelling showing awareness of initial spelling patterns Writes longer pieces with personal content and dialogue; becomes conscious of beginning, middle, end Shows awareness of audience Shows concern with spelling (asks for correct ways) and handwriting (erases, crosses out, rewrites)
3. The Developing Writer	Begins to use different forms of writing (e.g., inform, persuade, describe) Begins to use concepts, ideas, and vocabulary from other reading and content areas Becomes aware of author's style from reading and from other students Shows greater awareness of need to revise and edit for audience

FIGURE 7.1   Stages of writing development

experiments with print and shares these experimentations with others. The child who "scribble writes" a grocery list, gives love letters to her parents, and points to letters on a sign is in the emergent stage. The *beginning writer*, usually in the primary grades, gives pictures elaborated labels, writes stories with invented spelling, and shows a developing knowledge of sound–symbol relationships. In later grades, the *developing writer* writes longer pieces in a variety of genres, experiments with vocabulary, and begins to develop his own voice. These stages are not discrete; they ebb and flow into one another as writers move toward greater control, fluency and competence.

Besides the developmental stages of writing, teachers are also concerned with the stages in the writing process itself and observe students in this process to assess whether they need support in approaching writing strategically. Though their terminology may vary, students of writing typically describe various stages in the writing process with strategies for getting started, for making an initial draft, for reflecting on and revising a piece of writing, and for bringing a piece to conclusion (see Figure 7.2).

Stage	Strategy
1. Prewriting	Conceptualizes a theme or topic "Brainstorms" ideas Makes a personal record Envisions an audience Uses resources as needed (e.g., other people for trying out ideas; other treatments; self-reflection)
2. Drafting	Rehearses with composing, drawing, or talking Takes risks in composing and spelling Considers audience Self-reflects Uses resources (e.g., others)
3. Revising and Editing	Self-evaluates Takes perspective of audience Seeks response to drafts/shares Seeks other information/opinions as needed Is willing to change/rewrite Edits for grammar, usage, mechanics, spelling, legibility
4. "Publishing"	Produces a product of sustained effort Presents in final form Shows development of voice/style Shares with others

FIGURE 7.2   Stages in the writing process

Teachers also realize that the instructional environment of the classroom can make a big difference in how students develop as writers. Generally, classroom climates that help writers develop include writing as a regular part of the daily routine, usually connected with reading and the other language arts. Daily activities in a "writing intensive" classroom often feature writing and reading of the individual's own writing. Students keep journals and logs; they write in response to reading and to help them study in all content areas. They are involved in structured writing activities that help them develop all aspects of the writing process as well as in spontaneous, self-sponsored writing for the recording and expressing of personal ideas. In reading–writing classrooms, students are helped to see the connection between the author and the reader at all times. When they read, they ask questions about the writer's purpose and point of view, and recognize how style develops. When working in content areas, they ask questions about the qualifications of the authors, the currency of ideas, and possible bias of texts. All these types of issues contribute to classrooms where writing and reading are seen as two sides of the same coin. Recognizing that writing is both developmental and a strategic process, we now turn to issues of how to assess writing in a way that both reveals its richness and assists you in planning instruction. It is clear that we must go beyond standardized measures of grammar and mechanics toward measures that are indicators of process and of development.

ASSESSING WRITING

To assess students' writing thoroughly, you should collect information on both the development of students' control of the writing process and samples of their writing products. Analysis of writing samples along with observational checklists and anecdotal record keeping can give you a well-rounded picture of a child's performance. Because teachers are interested in change and development, they need to collect both types of information over time; many teachers compile portfolios of writing and of class data.

Portfolios are being used for evaluation in many K–12 classrooms (Valencia, 1990), special education classrooms (Bartoli & Botel, 1989), and college classrooms (Elbow, 1986). Different types can be compiled depending on the purpose of the portfolio—for example, to give information on writing products, processes, or even on programs. Simmons (1992) has researched the use of portfolios in wide-scale assessment and has proposed a schematic for different types and levels of portfolio information, including process, product, and programs (see Figure 7.3). His research compared the perceptions teachers formed about students by using standardized test results and by using portfolio information. Simmons found that portfolio assessment gave teachers much more detailed information about student writing performance. Often, timed essay writing and exams failed to reveal the real strength of some students and overestimated the competence of others who were adept at multiple-choice exams but were unable to do much real writing. This type of research, along with a groundswell of teacher support for classroom assessment, has encouraged many teachers, schools, and districts to investigate the use of portfolios.

Portfolios usually contain process data which show how a student's writing has developed as well as writing products such as drafts, responses, lists of personal questions, practice activities, final drafts, and completed projects. Portfolios can contain self-evaluation information such as students' reflections on their writing products and their personal development. Teachers can compile their own class portfolios of data relevant to larger views of assessment. For these, teachers may interview their students about their writing and reading, or have students interview one another (Hansen, 1987). We discuss both student and class portfolios at greater length in Chapter 10. For this chapter, we want to consider how you would collect portfolio data about the writing process, how writing samples from the students can be generated and collected, and how you might analyze both the process of writing and the products. We also give examples of how some teachers have collected specific types of reading-related writing samples.

Observing Writing

PAUSE AND REFLECT.   Before beginning this section, brainstorm the ways you know to observe students' writing and to record what you observe. Compare your suggestions with those to follow.

Level of Information	Purpose	Traits	Contents
Product	Assessment of written products	Ideas Organization Wording Mechanics Flavor	Best pieces: • Student choice • Teacher choice • Joint selection Required pieces
Process	Assessment of writing abilities	What I do, know, think How I do it, know it, think it What I feel How I see myself How I approach work How I use/give feedback How I challenge myself	Ordered pieces: • Student ranking • Drafts Notes, journals, logs Labels Conversations Experiences Readings Teacher notes Self and peer evaluations Conference logs
Program	Assessment of development of writing abilities	Chances to • Discover topic • Use many forms • Confer • Keep task open • Vary length How do students and teachers • Agree on standards • Understand the other Change over time Impact on ability, socioeconomic status	Assignment lists Conference logs Interview data: • Length • Duration • Range • Evaluations • Expectations • Socioeconomic status Scores

FIGURE 7.3   Levels of portfolio information

SOURCE: Reprinted by permission of Jay Simmons. In *Portfolio Portraits*, Donald H. Graves and Bonnie S. Sunstein, eds. (Heinemann, A Division of Reed Publishing [USA] Inc., Portsmouth, NH, 1992.

There are many ways to collect information about the writing process students engage in. A common method is to observe students during process writing instruction and practice and to record your observations in a log or on a checklist. You want to observe them in various stages of the composing process to see where their strengths and needs lie. By keeping dated records of observations focused on the writing process, you will have a better measure of the way individual students develop writing strategies. Observational checklists are good tools for collecting and organizing classroom data. To be useful, checklists must be short and simple, relate to both long-term and short-term goals, and have room for qualitative as well as quantitative data (Heller, 1991). Figure 7.4 displays an example of a teacher-designed checklist for observing writing.

Student _____   Date observed _____

I = does independently   S = does with support   N = needs development

1. Can choose topic
      Can focus a topic
      Has diversity in topics

2. Can write in different genres
      Shows diversity in genre choices
      Has knowledge of conventions of that genre

3. Can brainstorm before writing
      Alone
      With group
      Keeps a record

4. Can select relevant details to include

5. Is willing to revise
      Can be selective about adding or deleting text
      Can use input of others
      Can self-reflect
      Can consider audience

6. Is willing to edit
      Mechanical aspects to work on

7. Can bring a piece to publication
      Has persistence
      Has production values

Comments/instructional goals:

FIGURE 7.4   Observing the writing process

By setting up a systematic approach for observing students over the school term, you can compare growth and set instructional goals as the term progresses. It is important to understand that process observation and the setting of process goals are important to the development of literacy.

We are not suggesting that you should ignore what students are writing. Along with observing students in the process of writing, as they develop strategies, you need to look at the writing they produce for other clues to their strengths and needs. Collecting and analyzing *writing samples* is the most common approach to this need. Samples of student writing collected over time can provide powerful data on both process and product growth. Both finished and draft materials can provide insights into the student's writing. You can also keep *anecdotal records* on writing and may choose to do some sort of *holistic scoring* to help get a global view of a student's progress.

Holistic Scoring

PAUSE AND REFLECT.   Before reading this section, jot down the things you think are important to evaluate in your students' writing. Then compare your list to those in the examples that follow.

Holistic scoring is being increasingly used to evaluate students' writing samples. **Holistic scoring** aims at an overall evaluation of the writer's ability to communicate ideas to a particular audience. The rater takes a piece of writing and either matches it to another piece in a set of samples or scores it for certain features he or she has determined to be important for that type of writing. The rater does not make corrections or revisions in the paper but ranks, scores, or grades it based on a scoring evaluation guide. Many varieties of scoring protocols and guides have been developed, with more or less direction for the evaluator, who is assumed to have practiced scoring and to have developed reliability with other raters. Typically these guides describe various aspects of a type of written work and rank the author's performance based on an evaluative scale. They can be simple (Deiderich, 1974; see Figure 7.5) to more complex (see, for example, Cramer, 1989).

FIGURE 7.5   Holistic Scoring Scale

SOURCE: Adapted from Diederich, P. (1974). *Measuring growth in English.* Urbana, IL: National Council of Teachers of English.

1—Poor 2—Weak 3—Average 4—Good 5—Excellent		
	Reader _____	
Quality and development of ideas 1 2 3 4 5		
Organization, relevance, movement 1 2 3 4 5		
	_____ × 5 = _____ Subtotal	
Style, flavor, individuality 1 2 3 4 5		
Wording and phrasing 1 2 3 4 5		
	_____ × 3 = _____ Subtotal	
Grammar, sentence structure 1 2 3 4 5		
Punctuation 1 2 3 4 5		
Spelling 1 2 3 4 5		
Manuscript form, legibility 1 2 3 4 5		
	_____ × 1 = _____ Subtotal	
	Total grade: _____ %	

Some evaluators believe that rubric use should also involve a clear and uniform way to collect similar samples from students in various grades. In this type of rubric use, local samples are collected at designated grade levels. These local samples are selected as typical of levels of writing development at that grade. In subsequent years, students in the designated grades are asked to produce particular types of writing at predetermined times in the school year. This writing is compared to the local samples to give consistent and comparative measures across the year (see Figure 7.6). While

FIGURE 7.6   Scoring rubric—Persuasive writing—Grade 6

LIBERTYVILLE PUBLIC SCHOOLS
District No. 70
Libertyville, Illinois

COMPOSITION COMPETENCIES EVALUATION

Grade Six   PUPIL _____

DATE _____   SCORE _____

Persuasive	Pass	Fail
ORGANIZATION • Writes a persuasive assignment, giving 3 valid reasons to support stance • Addresses audience and stays on topic • Uses a topic sentence		
GRAMMAR/MECHANICS (majority of time) • Uses complete sentences • Uses correct capitalization and punctuation • Uses correctly quotation marks (if appropriate) • Uses correct agreement (subject-verb, pronoun and antecedent)		
STYLE • Varies word choice (uses different words) • Varies sentence length and patterns		
EDITING/REVISING • Uses legible handwriting • Uses correct spellings • Revises to make changes in draft • Checks for and corrects errors in draft		
APPEAL • Was composition interesting, readable?		

PLEASE NOTE:

• Every subtopic must be correct in order for that main area to be marked as passing.
• Four out of five main areas must be marked pass in order for this writing piece to be evaluated as passing.

standardized measures have typically focused on evaluating grammar and mechanics, holistic assessments allows a broader look at writing and the processes and strategies involved (Hammil & Larsen, 1988).

Integrated Assessment

Teachers interested in integrated instruction are also interested in **integrated assessment**. This involves collecting assessment data as students are performing authentic language tasks and using writing as a "window to reading." In this section, we show how Keisha collected information on her students during their regular classroom activities and how she looked at writing to help her answer three important questions about some of her students:

What can students' spelling tell about their print knowledge?

What can students' writing tell about their vocabulary, concept knowledge, and comprehension?

What can their writing tell about students' self-evaluation and metacognition?

CASE 7.1: KEISHA'S CLASSROOM

For her own classroom, Keisha found some observational checklists devised by Heller (1991) particularly useful as models for recording oral and written responses in a class lesson (see Figure 7.7). Companion checklists kept by students gave a second perspective on the reading and writing in the classroom (see Figure 7.8). Keisha also decided to keep an **anecdotal journal** on each of her reading and writing classes and to reflect on each entry to help her plan instruction. One of her entries looked like this:

> February 17
>
> The class is really having trouble with compare and contrast. Only Lashana, Joe, and Marty were able to make some good comparisons between Yeh-Shen and Cinderella. We need to construct some graphics to help. I had Pat, Tyrone, and Sella make a list of the important aspects of Yeh-Shen: setting, characters, problem, etc. Then Lou, Jason, and Marianne made a list of the elements in Cinderella. I had a hard time getting Reno to work on task—I wonder if I need to have him read a bit to see if he is struggling at this level. I'll make him partners with Bette to see if that provides enough support. They work well together. Tomorrow we are going to first work on putting the list together for "same"—then "different." I need to get the librarian to help me find some more Cinderella-type books *(Mufaro's Beautiful Daughter?)* and to make up some Venn-diagram charts. I need to do a mini lesson on compare and contrast and relate those terms to same–different.

Keisha's observation focused on what occurred in her class, on some specific students and on planning for instruction. She could watch how students' knowledge and strategies developed from lesson to lesson.

Basic Lesson Plan Scenario: Listen to story, discuss, decide on writing topic, compose first and final drafts.

Objective: After listening to (or reading) *Alexander and the Terrible, Horrible, No Good, Very Bad Day* (Viorst, 1972), the students will contribute to a discussion of the story. The students will write and illustrate a personal narrative about the worst or best day they or someone they know ever had (or imagined). The narrative will be revised for publication in a class collection.

Name	*Oral Contributions* + ✓ o		*Written Narrative (1st/2nd)*
Emily	+	Very talkative	1st ✓ "My Birthday" 2nd ✓ " Ill. ✓ Child & birthday cake
Sarah	+	Lots to say - Just lost a tooth	1st ✓ "The Lost Tooth" 2nd ✓ " Ill. ✓ Wanted to glue "lost" tooth on paper.
Mark	+	"Christmas & New Year" - Best Days	1st ✓ "Trains" 2nd none Ill. ✓ Trains & RR tracks.
Kevin	✓	"Summertime" best days	1st ✓ "Camping Out" 2nd ✓ "Yellowstone Park" Ill. ✓ Change title in revision
John	o	Sad today. Doesn't know why	1st ✓ "My Dog" - About a dog John once had. 2nd Resisted revision Ill. ✓ Excellent drawing.
Brad	o	Inattentive today	1st ✓ "The Special Day" 2nd none Ill. ✓ Picture of a circus tent.
Cynthia	✓	Good response	1st ✓ "Saturdays" 2nd ✓ Ill. ✓ Picture of child "sleeping in".
Robert	+	Great ideas!	1st ✓ "The Shopping Trip"

FIGURE 7.7 Instructional group observational record

SOURCE: From *Reading-Writing Connections: From Theory to Practice*. By Mary F. Heller. Copyright © 1991 by Longman Publishing Group.

L 12-1-89
R
Ⓦ

My Trip To space.

Beucase it is my novel.

L 11-17-89
Ⓡ
W

The Astronauts

Because I ingoy it.

Ⓛ 11-10-89
R
W The big orange spot.

because it is funny.

L
R
W

L
R
W

FIGURE 7.8   Student self-evaluation

SOURCE: From *Reading-Writing Connections: From Theory to Practice.* By Mary F. Heller. Copyright © 1991 by Longman Publishing Group.

Keisha also decided to use student journals, which can be helpful, especially when students are encouraged to ask questions, to help assess reading. While the writing in these journals can be very revealing about writing strategies and processes, research on students' responses to literature indicates that what they say about books can give real insights into their comprehension and development (Studier, 1981; Kiefer, 1988). She found that she could analyze journal writing to get information on her students' knowledge of print and on their comprehension.

Analyzing the Spelling in Children's Writing.   As we discussed in Chapter 2, experimentation with writing is an important component of beginning literacy. Children's spelling can be a powerful clue to their internalization of the regularities of the sound–symbol system. In this section, we review the developmental stages revealed through an analysis of young writers' spelling. Then we examine the spelling of Ken whom you met in Chapter 3. You will remember that his parents were concerned about his progress during first grade and had asked Eileen, his teacher, whether he should be tutored during the summer months before he was to enter Keisha's 2–3 classroom.

The developmental framework is also useful in examining spelling in the extended texts that children write. We consider the writing of one of Keisha's students, Jason. We also introduce an analysis sheet that you can use for students in your class.

Developmental Stages of Spelling.   In Chapter 2, we described how the spelling strategies of children change over time. As they read and write, their knowledge of orthography or spelling increases. They develop greater knowledge of the elements of words, and they do so in a fairly predictable manner. Refer to Figure 2.1 on page 33 and you will see that Anne, who is in kindergarten, writes only the beginning consonants and sometimes the ending consonants of words. Jonathan, who is in first grade, represents the beginning and ending consonants and sometimes the medial vowel sounds, yet his spellings differ in predictable ways from standard English spellings. In contrast, it is easy to "read" Silvia's writing because she represents most of the sounds in words and writes many in standard form.

It is challenging to read the writings of Anne and Jonathan, but teachers at the kindergarten and first-grade level acquire the necessary skill to do so. To help you learn how to read these invented spellings, it is useful to have students read their writing aloud.

You can collect writing samples in one of two ways. You may wish to have children write a set of words or you may wish to examine the writing that children produce daily in your classroom. The advantage of the spelling task is that you have the opportunity to observe how children write words that include a representative set of consonants, consonant blends, short vowels, and long vowels. The advantage of the more natural writing task is that it shows how children select and spell words to represent the meanings they wish to communicate.

A Developmental Spelling Task.   Although many different lists of one-syllable words can be used, the Developmental Spelling Test which we describe here (Ferroli & Shanahan, 1987; Morris & Perney, 1984) is particularly useful because it includes words of various complexity and it is sensitive to changes that occur in the beginning stages of spelling (see Figure 7.9). The spelling task has been used with kindergartners (Ferroli & Shanahan, 1987) and first graders (Morris & Perney, 1984) and found to be a good predictor of later first-grade achievement.

The list is composed of twelve words as shown in Figure 7.9. Before administering the list, you must prepare children through a demonstration of spelling. First they should be asked to listen for the letter names they hear in a few sample words not found on the list such as *mat* and *dip*; you should then write these letters on the blackboard, supplying unknown letters if the children offer only a partial spelling. For example, if the children hear only the *m* and *t* in *mat*, you might say "Good," write M_____T on the board, and say "there's an 'A' in the middle." Following this modeling, children should be encouraged to spell the list words as well as they can by writing the letter names they hear. It is important to praise them for whatever spellings they produce. Give the list as you would a spelling test.

Figure 7.9 also includes typical spellings generated for these words by children at different stages of development. On the basis of these spelling responses, you can

FIGURE 7.9   Developmental Spelling Test items and illustrative spelling at each stage

SOURCE: L. Ferroli and T. Shanahan, 1987. Kindergarten spelling: Explaining its Relation to First-rate Reading. In J. E. Readance and R. S. Baldwin (Eds.), *Research in Literacy: Merging Perspectives.* Thirty-Sixth Yearbook of the National Reading Conference. Rochester, NY: National Reading Conference. Based on D. Norris and J. Perney, 1984. Developmental Spelling as a Predictor of First-rate Reading Achievement. *Elementary School Journal, 84.* Copyright © 1984 by the University of Chicago Press. Reprinted by permission.

Correct	Preliterate	Initial Consonant	Consonant Frame	Phonetic	Transitional
BACK	RE	BET	BC	BAK	[a]
SINK	E	C	SE	SEK	SINCK
MAIL	A	MM	MOL	MAL	MAEL
DRESS	S	DN	JS	GAS	DRES
LAKE	AH	L	LAE	LAK	LACE
PEEKED	TTT	PF	PT	PECT	PEKED
LIGHT	IEIX	LSIE	LAT	LIT	LIET
DRAGON	ATJA	JK	GAN	DAGN	DRAGIN
STICK	F	S	STC	SEK	STIK
SIDE	TC	ST	CI	SID	CIDE
FEET	V	F	FT	FET	[a]
TEST	ABT	TS	TST	TAST	TEEST

[a] No transitional spellings were produced by the subjects for these words.

determine whether the majority of a child's responses are preliterate, initial conso-nant, consonant frame, phonetic, transitional, or correct. Instruction in word ele-ments should be geared to the child's stage of development. For example, for a child in the preliterate stage, you should check his or her knowledge of letter names to determine which, if any, need to be taught; similarly, for a child in the consonant frame stage, you should test consonants and consonant blends in final positions and short vowels to determine what word elements need to be taught.

To demonstrate this procedure, look at the cases of Ken and Jennifer, two of Keisha's students. Ken's parents have been concerned about his progress in reading. Also, Jennifer often gets discouraged when editing her own work. Keisha decided to look more closely at the developmental spelling test she had administered to Ken to assemble more information on his knowledge of word elements. Then she examined Jennifer's writing portfolio for the same reason.

CASE 7.2: KEN'S SPELLING

In order to describe Ken's spelling knowledge more precisely, Keisha adminis-tered the Developmental Spelling Test. She began the test by demonstrating how to spell two basal words: *mat* and *dip*. She first had Ken listen to *mat* to see what sounds he could hear. He heard the phoneme corresponding to *m* at the beginning and that for *t* at the end. Keisha encouraged him to write the letters associated with these sounds. Then she had him first say *dip* slowly to himself and then write the letters he heard. Then she presented the test words, encouraging him "to write them as well as he could." The results are shown in Figure 7.10.

PAUSE AND REFLECT.   Study Ken's spelling. How do you assess his developing knowledge of English orthography? At what stage of development is he? What ideas does this give you for Ken's instruction?

Keisha studied Ken's spelling and concluded that he has good command of consonants at the beginnings and endings of words, but that he is not yet able to represent consonant blends and vowels. In terms of his underlying knowledge, Ken is in command of the consonant frame of words. From this Keisha concluded that he was ready to be sensitized to words' medial sounds. She decided to include activities involving sound boxes during the remaining months of his small-group instruction. That is, when the children are composing an experience story and have agreed on what they want to write, she will have them participate in the spelling. If, for example, they wish to write the word *run*, she will create a sound box with three empty squares (☐☐☐), and the children will be encouraged to tell the sound they hear first, the sound they hear second, and the sound they hear last. As children identify the sound, Keisha will ask for the letter that goes with the sound and write it in the box. Other children in Ken's group are also ready for this activity.

b K [back]   S K [stick]

S K [sink]

S [side]

M l [mail]

i [dress]   f s t [feet]

l K [lake]   p t [peeked]   T a [test]

l T [light]

___ [dragon]

FIGURE 7.10 Ken's spelling

CASE 7.3: JENNIFER'S WRITING

Keisha encourages her students to write on a daily basis. Often she reads a story aloud to them and asks them to write their thoughts and reflections on the story. Although Keisha often reads Jennifer's writing, she has not recently undertaken a systematic analysis of her spelling. The sample that Keisha decided to study is shown in Figure 7.11.

PAUSE AND REFLECT.   Read what Jennifer has written. In general, is she able to convey the message she wishes to communicate? Now look carefully at her spelling. Which examples are particularly revealing? Study these examples; what does your analysis lead you to conclude about her knowledge of word elements? Given this tentative conclusion, what instructional support might you want to provide?

JeNNiFeR

THiR was a bird Namd
Joyiss. He livd IN tHe bqc
yIRD of a Hiws. a 7 YeR owld
GiRl livd IN tHe Hiws and
SHe loved Loyiss.

FIGURE 7.11   A sample of Jennifer's writing

When Keisha looks at the writing samples of students in her class, she uses a simple analysis sheet that she staples to the writing samples in her portfolio (see Figure 7.12). On this sheet, she summarizes what she learns about the knowledge of each child. It also allows her to keep track of what she sees, form small groups of children with similar spelling needs, and plan instruction in word study based on student mastery of spelling patterns in writing. On the basis of her study of Jennifer's writing, Keisha wrote the spellings on the summary sheet shown in Figure 7.12.

On the basis of her analysis, Keisha concluded that Jennifer shows many signs of spelling strength. She does need encouragement to notice the standard spellings of words, however. There are several other children in her class who are at the same stage. Keisha will form these children into a study group to focus on words from their writing that are close approximations of standard spelling. Simply helping children to become aware of how words are spelled in standard English is usually sufficient to encourage them to move from the transitional stage to standard spelling.

Developmental Spelling Analysis Sheet

Student Jennifer   Date 10/15

Sample: From writing time following the reading of stories on pets.

Relevant examples: thir yird hiws yer bac
namd livd (note also: loved)

Analysis: Represents most sounds appropriately, but not all
in standard form — Is in the transitional stage.

Comments/instruction: A nice beginning to her story. Has learned
a lot about spelling words. Needs to learn standard
spellings.

FIGURE 7.12. Keisha's notes on Jennifer's writing

CASE 7.4: CAL'S SUMMARY WRITING

Many analyses use summary writing and question generation to help analyze students' comprehension. Look at Cal's summary of "Perfect the Pig" and Keisha's analysis sheet (see Figure 7.13).

Based on Cal's summary, Keisha decided to probe Cal's understanding of the motivation of one of the main characters. She also wanted to learn whether Cal was familiar with the concepts related to courtrooms and trials. Last, since he usually had more detailed comprehension of nonfictional selections, she wanted to verify that he realized the fantastic aspects of "Perfect the Pig" and to give him some strategies to use for skimming to separate fact from fiction.

Analyzing Writing for Vocabulary, Concepts, and Comprehension

Writing from Models.   Besides summary writing, teachers can use students' own writing from models and use their interpretation for analysis. For example, for a class studying fables, Keisha had students read several fables and discuss them. Then she used their writing samples to analyze what they had internalized about the genre and structure. The analysis system she used (shown in Figure 7.14) was drawn from Pappas, Kiefer, and Levstik (1990). She can then analyze the fables and other genres of writing that her students produce to learn which elements of each genre are clear to them and which are yet to be internalized.

Using Writing to Look at Self-Evaluation and Metacognition.   In addition to teacher observations of students in the process of reading and writing, student self-evaluations can provide insights into reading. Keisha uses a strategy interview for students at the start of the year to get a picture of what strategies they employ. These,

Name: Cal

Book **summary**—Perfect the Pig.

The lady found the little pig and loved it a lot. She saved her money and took care of perfect. She was an artist and painted lots of pictures too. She lost perfect and another guy found it and took care of it. He got money by charging people to look at perfect. She wanted her pig back and went to the court guy and he let her have it back. They lived happily ever after.

Questions I have:

1. Why was she so mad at the guy? He found her pig and took care of it.
2. Could you go to court about a pet?

Reaction: This seemed kind of dumb. I like animal books but not this one.

Keisha's Analysis of Cal's Summary

Is it:

Accurate: In general

Complete: Skimpy about action, setting

Characters: Doesn't have any names

Plots (Actions/Motivation) Resolution: Does he understand that man mistreated the pig for own gain?

Concepts/Vocabulary: "Court guy"—probe about court concepts memory or knowledge?

Comments/Instruction: I need to ask Cal about the man's motivation to see if he understood what man was doing. His question indicates he didn't get the fact that man was exploiting Perfect. Cal really doesn't like these fantasy animal type books very much. Need to help him choose more realistic ones. Make sure he can skim to use pictures, etc., to separate fantasy from more realistic books when choosing.

FIGURE 7.13 Summary, question, reaction sheet

along with her observations of class performance, help her understand her students' metacognitive strategies (see Figure 7.15). She also asks students to self-evaluate their comprehension monitoring strategies (see Figure 7.16) and uses these surveys not only to help her plan instruction but also to get her students to think about their own learning.

These are only a few of the types of integrated assessment strategies that Keisha and other teachers use to turn students' writing into information for reading instruction. Many other options exist, such as student critiques of assignments, best work/least satisfying work choices in portfolios, and others detailed in the many resources now available to teachers interested in reading and writing connections (see For Further Reading at the end of this chapter).

Child: _____	Date: _____

Context	
How well does the child control the genre being attempted? Are there certain beginnings, endings, sequences present to indicate a certain genre?	
Is the text complete? Are details or elaborations included?	
Interesting vocabulary used? Use of cohesive ties? Ambiguous terms?	
Any missing information? Is information ordered to make sense?	
Interesting repairs used?	
Attention to transcription of medium aspects of text?	
Fluency in composing?	

INSTRUCTIONAL IDEAS:

FIGURE 7.14   Observing genre and structure

SOURCE: From *An Integrated Language Perspective in the Elementary School: Theory into Action*, by Christine C. Pappas, Barbara Z. Kiefer, Linda S. Levstik. Copyright © 1990 by Longman Publishing Group.

INSTRUCTIONAL SUPPORT FOR WRITING

Many of the strategies we have presented earlier in this book naturally connect reading and writing instruction. For example, predictive reading instruction, described in Chapter 6, involves writing down predictions, collecting ideas as we read, and writing responses or refinements of our predictions after reading. Use of developmental spelling, discussed in Chapter 3, is based on writing. Because there are

Reading Strategies

1. What do you do before reading to help you understand?

2. While you read, what do you do if you don't understand something?

3. What do you do when you come to a word you don't know?

4. After you read, what can you do to help you understand better?

FIGURE 7.15   Metacognitive survey

FIGURE 7.16   Metacognitive rating sheet

Reading Strategies

Name _____   Date _____

Reading selection:

Before reading
   I use pictures, titles, and headings to help me think about what I'm going to
      read.   Fiction?   Nonfiction?   What type?
   I think about what I already know about this type of reading selection.
   I set my purpose and/or make predictions before reading.

During reading
   I think about what might come next.
   I revise my predictions and/or make new ones.
   I imagine pictures of what I'm reading.
   I look for author clues to what will happen/be coming.
   I pick out important ideas; keep track of the "drift."
   I skip hard words/parts and try to go on.
   I notice when something doesn't make sense.
   I go back and reread.
   I ask myself questions.

After reading
   I ask myself what I understood.
   I compare what I read with what I predicted.
   I discuss with others or write for myself.

This self-evaluation form is designed for teachers involved in the Reading/Writing/Learning Staff Development coordinated by the Elementary Reading and Language Development Department of the Orange County Public Schools.

	Implemented	Goal for next year
Classroom environment		
I increased print in the environment	_____	_____
I increased shared decision making	_____	_____
I provided a risk-free environment	_____	_____
I increased the variety of genre and levels of difficulty of the books in the library corner	_____	_____
Schedule		
I refined the schedule to provide adequate time daily for children to read and write	_____	_____
Teachers as learners		
I read professionally	_____	_____
I read for pleasure	_____	_____
I read new children's books	_____	_____
I wrote with students for authentic purposes	_____	_____
Readers' workshop		
I provided a predictable structure	_____	_____
I conducted minilessons	_____	_____
I provided a block of time daily for self-selected and self-paced reading	_____	_____
I held literature discussion groups	_____	_____
I conferred with individual students	_____	_____
I provided opportunities for children to respond to reading	_____	_____
Reading aloud		
I read aloud to students	_____	_____
Sharing		
I conducted shared reading (big books, charts, multiple copies)	_____	_____
Guided reading		
I met with small groups for guided reading sessions	_____	_____
Comprehension		
I activated children's prior knowledge	_____	_____
I modeled strategies good readers use	_____	_____
I provided opportunities to integrate new knowledge (summarize, evaluate, synthesize)	_____	_____
Writers' workshop		
I provided a predictable structure	_____	_____
I conducted minilessons	_____	_____

FIGURE 7.17 Reading/writing/learning self-evaluation form

SOURCE: Reprinted by permission of Janet Speer Johnston and The International Reading Association.

I provided a block of time for independent writing
   (student-selected topics)   _____   _____
I conferred with individual students   _____   _____
I provided opportunities for students to share their writing   _____   _____

Assessment
  I gathered data for students' portfolio   _____   _____
  I analyzed writing samples   _____   _____
  I took anecdotal records   _____   _____
  I used running records to evaluate miscues and strategies _____   _____
  I made instructional decisions based on the data collected _____   _____

Communication with parents
  I reported student progress through use of portfolios   _____   _____
  I established a method for sharing information   _____   _____

so many excellent resources for connecting reading and writing instruction (see For Further Reading at the end of this chapter for ideas), we have framed our discussion in this section within the notion of teacher self-assessment. How can you look at your own *classroom* to evaluate whether you are providing instructional support for writing?

> **PAUSE AND REFLECT.** Based on what you already know about writing, what things would you expect to see in a classroom that offers appropriate instructional support for writing? Jot down a list and compare with lists made by others or the list in Figure 7.17.

Effective Integration in Classrooms

Research and good practice suggest that classrooms that effectively integrate reading and writing instruction have some shared characteristics. These are presented in a summarized form in Figure 7.17.

Classroom Environment. In reading–writing rich classrooms, the environment not only supports the development of literacy skills, but encourages and stimulates literacy as well. Classrooms are rich and full of print with many types of reading materials available. Student writing is also shared and "published," and the environment encourages students to take chances in their reading and writing. Students also need to have plenty of time to read and write and time to persist in all their activities.

Reader's and Writer's Workshop. Classrooms that stimulate literacy have a predictable approach to reading and writing. Teachers offer minilessons on skills and strategies and also meet with small groups for teacher-involved guided reading. Teachers also confer individually, in pairs, and in small groups about students' reading and writing. Blocks of time are provided for self-selected reading and self-sponsored writing. Rich discussions take place about reading, and writers share and respond to each other's writing. Sharing of reading and writing takes place in many forms.

Comprehension.   Comprehension and communication are central to many types of reading and writing lessons. Students use what they already know in prereading and prewriting; teachers scaffold good strategies for both reading comprehension and process writing. Students are encouraged to integrate what they are learning, to synthesize, and to respond both personally and critically.

Teachers Are Models.   In a reading–writing classroom teachers are also learners. They read for pleasure and for professional growth and keep up with children's books. They also write along with their students. Teachers share their love of reading and writing by reading aloud to students and by sharing their own writing.

Assessment.   Teachers in reading and writing classrooms make instructional decisions based on real reading and writing. They collect portfolios of work along with anecdotal records.

Communication with Students and Parents.   In a reading–writing classroom, teachers encourage students to take control of their own learning. They establish good methods of sharing information with parents and do so with portfolios of work.

One of the most significant changes in literacy education in the last 10 years has been the change in the instruction of writing. The characteristics noted above are hallmarks of classrooms where teachers are not only integrating instructional goals but are interested in more realistic and integrated assessment as well.

SUMMARY

In this chapter, we have presented a perspective on writing that emphasizes writing as a process with developmental and procedural stages. Knowledge of developmental stages—what characterizes an emergent, beginning, and developing writer—can help a teacher observe students meaningfully during the process of writing and use information gained from this observation to shape more sensitive instruction in both reading and writing. The chapter presented cases centered around spelling and summarizing to provide examples of classroom decision making based on writing. Further, teacher self-assessment of instruction and the instructional climate can help the teacher structure a classroom in which writing flourishes in close connection with reading and the other language arts.

TRY IT OUT

1. Brainstorm with other teachers to create a holistic scoring rubric for your students. Use the examples in the chapter as your starting point or consult some of the books in For Further Reading.

2. **Student Portfolio Ideas:** Ask your students to do one of the metacognitive activities in Figure 7.13 or 7.14 or one you devise yourself. Then have them share what they learned and set goals for the future.

3. **For Your Teaching Portfolio:** Choose one student you'd like to know more about and compile a folder of observations on him or her using some of the examples in this chapter. What can you learn about this student from writing?

FOR FURTHER READING

Hansen, J. (1989). *When writers read*. Portsmouth, NH: Heinemann.
An excellent, classroom-focused overview of the interconnections between reading and writing.

Heller, M. F. (1991). *Reading-writing connections: From theory to practice*. White Plains, NY: Longman.
Detailed classroom applications and ideas for integrating reading and writing instruction.

Zemelman, S., & Daniels, H. (1988). *A community of writers*. Portsmouth, NH: Heinemann.
A framework for establishing a community of writers in the classroom. Many excellent examples for middle and secondary schools as well as for primary classrooms.

chapter 8

Dynamic Assessment: Case Studies of Assessment and Instruction

CHAPTER GOALS FOR THE READER

To understand the construct of reading difficulty levels and how this relates to materials selection and instruction

To learn how to undertake dynamic assessment using classroom materials

To focus the diagnostic strategies presented in earlier chapters by working through two cases of diagnosis using instructional passages

CLASSROOM VIGNETTE: FOCUSING FOR INSTRUCTION

Monica is the junior and senior high school reading specialist in a small midwestern town. She is responsible for working with individuals and small groups and for helping teachers work with all students in the mainstreamed regular classrooms. Part of her job is to carry out simple diagnostic procedures with curriculum-based materials and to help focus instructional planning for the classroom.

Sharon, a seventh grader, and Patricia, a ninth grader, are two students Monica sees in special reading sessions. Both are cooperative students with good attendance and participation. Patricia enjoys reading her self-selected mystery books but Sharon rarely chooses to read in her free time. Both have difficulty with assigned reading in school. In this chapter, we describe the ways in which Monica integrated the diagnostic procedures presented in earlier chapters into two full-scale diagnoses of these two readers. We also describe the instructional planning that resulted from her analyses.

CHAPTER OVERVIEW

The previous seven chapters of this text have introduced ways of thinking about and investigating the development of reading proficiency. Chapter 1 described a model for diagnosis that focuses on the relations among print skill, vocabulary knowledge, and reading comprehension. Chapters 2 and 3 discussed ways to understand and diagnose students' print strategies. Chapter 4 focused on the development of vocabulary knowledge and described procedures for assessing students' knowledge of concepts and terms included in their reading materials. Chapters 5 and 6 discussed ways of thinking about reading comprehension and described procedures for developing questions and diagnosing comprehension problems. Chapter 7 looked at writing in the diagnostic process. These various topics and diagnostic procedures were developed in separate chapters because of their complexity. In this chapter, the procedures are combined into a comprehensive diagnosis of reading proficiency in accord with the basic model described in the first chapter.

Although we do not expect you to perform a comprehensive diagnosis of the reading strategies of each of your students, conducting intensive case studies is a useful way to consolidate the diagnostic knowledge that was presented in previous chapters and to learn to think about reading development in terms of the diagnostic model. After conducting several case studies, you can begin to use the procedures more informally, during the course of daily instruction. The training procedures should increase your sensitivity to the pattern of oral reading responses and to the demands of comprehension questions as well as the appropriateness of student answers. There will always be students whose reading difficulties are extremely perplexing and for whom you may have to undertake an extensive diagnosis. But for most students informal observations during daily instruction over a period of time will suggest ways in which instruction can be more effective.

This chapter has three parts. The first section focuses on the construct of reading levels as benchmarks for determining whether the materials used for instruction are at an appropriate level of difficulty for students, and for planning instructional support when materials prove too difficult. The second segment presents a methodology for preparing for, implementing, exploring further, and interpreting diagnosis with an instructional passage and using the information gained for instructional planning. The third section offers two case studies as examples of instructional diagnosis and planning.

CHAPTER OUTLINE

Levels of Reading

Diagnostic Procedures
    Preparation
    Administration

LEVELS OF READING

One of the more important instructional issues you will confront is whether the instructional materials you are using in your classroom are of appropriate difficulty for your students. Betts (1954) found it useful to characterize the appropriateness of the match between students and materials in terms of levels. The **independent** reading level is the highest level at which students can read fluently with good comprehension without instructional assistance. The **instructional** level is the highest one at which students are able to read with adequate comprehension once they are provided with appropriate instructional support. Finally, at the **frustration** level the text is so difficult that even with appropriate support, students may be unable to comprehend. In this last case, students may comprehend inadequately because of problems with print processing, vocabulary knowledge, or comprehension strategies. Figure 8.1 is a graphic representation of the difficulty levels of reading materials.

While these levels have proven historically useful to teachers looking for appropriate materials for instruction, remember that it is rarely possible to determine an exact reading level for a child, particularly for one reading beyond the primary levels (Powell, 1984). Familiarity or unfamiliarity with content, genre, and structure can cause great variability in a student's ability to read a selection with understanding. Further, for instructional purposes, different situations will require different levels of reading difficulty. For example, reading that is assigned as homework or as independent seatwork should pose almost no print or comprehension problems for students. They should be able to read the material orally with good intonation and phrasing or silently with ease; they should readily comprehend the main ideas and important facts. When students have difficulty correctly identifying 2 or more words in every 100, they may have problems focusing on the meaning and these problems may hinder them from developing mature reading strategies. Failure to answer more than 1 question in every 10 is another indication that the material is probably too difficult for independent reading. Be sure that the questions you use in making this assessment are appropriate and nontrivial. There are some disabled readers for whom no reading material is easy and who therefore should not read unless the teacher has prepared them for the passage or provides direct support.

Given the range in reading proficiency in most classes, you should assign for homework and independent reading materials that represent a comparable range in

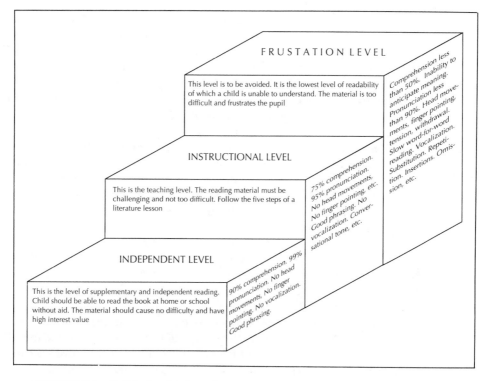

FRUSTRATION LEVEL

This level is to be avoided. It is the lowest level of readability of which a child is unable to understand. The material is too difficult and frustrates the pupil

Comprehension less than 50%. Inability to anticipate meaning. Pronunciation less than 90%. Head movements, finger pointing, tension, withdrawal. Slow word-for-word reading. Vocalization. Substitution. Repetition. Insertions. Omission, etc.

INSTRUCTIONAL LEVEL

This is the teaching level. The reading material must be challenging and not too difficult. Follow the five steps of a literature lesson

75% comprehension. 95% pronunciation. No head movements, etc. No finger pointing. No Good phrasing. Conversational tone, etc.

INDEPENDENT LEVEL

This is the level of supplementary and independent reading. Child should be able to read the book at home or school without aid. The material should cause no difficulty and have high interest value

90% comprehension. 99% pronunciation. No head movements. No finger pointing. No vocalization. Good phrasing.

FIGURE 8.1   Betts's levels of reading.

SOURCE: From E. A. Betts, *Foundations of Reading Instruction* (p. 448), New York: American Book Company, 1954. Reprinted by permission.

difficulty. Students can best develop their reading strategies through contextual materials that they can read fluently with good comprehension. Unfortunately, some students never experience the pleasure of problem-free reading and are thereby deprived of appropriate reading practice.

When your students read under your direct supervision, more problems in print skill and comprehension can be tolerated. As a rule of thumb, if a student is reading aloud, he or she should have difficulty with no more than 1 word in every 20. Comprehension should be good, with at least three out of every four questions answered correctly.

You need to keep in mind not only the average performance of the group with which you are working but also the performance of individuals in your group. When individual students are missing more than half the questions posed or having difficulty with more than 1 word in every 10, the materials are inappropriate, representing frustration-level work. Instructional support cannot help a student who is reading frustration-level material to the point that he or she can perform at acceptable levels of print processing and/or comprehension.

By contrast, students who perform in the borderline region between frustration level and acceptable instructional level may be helped by instruction that has been developed with their particular needs in mind. Support reading, partner reading, use of taped materials, reading guides, or group guided reading can help them comprehend materials that might be too difficult without such support. This borderline region is characterized by an accuracy of 90 to 94 percent on oral reading and of 50 to 74 percent on comprehension. Table 8.1 presents some simple criteria for determining the reading difficulty levels of materials. The frequency of borderline determinations is a strong indicator that informed judgments are required as part of a thoughtful diagnosis. (See For Further Reading at the end of the chapter for more on this topic.)

Consider the case of Eva, discussed in Chapter 3. Martha had her read the next story in her basal reader with little instructional support. Eva's oral reading accuracy score of 91 percent indicates performance in the borderline range. However, her comprehension was quite good at the instructional level, as she answered correctly 8 out of 10 questions. Eva was in the lowest reading group and Martha wanted her to remain there. However, the analysis of print skill difficulties indicated that her problems were severe. Martha's alternatives were either to give Eva reading instruction on an individual basis with easier materials or to try to eliminate some of the print-processing problems posed by her current basal reader through increased instructional support.

Martha decided to try the second alternative, spending more time on word identification and discussion of key story terms prior to reading. After providing such preparation, Martha listened to the quality of Eva's oral reading and found that it was more fluent than it had been, with less than 5 percent of the words causing problems. Martha then proceeded to offer this increased support to Eva's reading group as part of their regular instruction. Other students in the group seemed to profit as well. At the same time, Martha helped Eva select easy reading material for independent reading. If Eva's comprehension of the story had not been so complete, Martha might not have found it possible to keep her with the reading group.

For most teachers, the students who cause most concern are those for whom the reading materials are too difficult. When frustration-level reading is indicated, in terms of either oral reading accuracy or level of comprehension, the teacher must find more appropriate materials. If the student's performance is in the borderline region, it may be possible to make the materials accessible through appropriate instruction. Usually, the teacher must further diagnose the student's reading strengths and

TABLE 8.1.   Criteria for determining reading levels

	Passage Reading	
Level	Oral Reading Accuracy (%)	Compehension Accuracy (%)
Independent	98–100	90–100
Instructional	95–97	75–89
Borderline	90–94	50–74
Frustration	below 90	below 50

difficulties to pinpoint the nature of the problem and to experiment with instructional support.

In the next section of this chapter, we describe specific procedures for diagnosing reading strengths and difficulties. Again, we illustrate with individual case studies in order to consolidate the diagnostic strategies introduced in prior chapters.

DIAGNOSTIC PROCEDURES

To judge the appropriateness of instructional materials and the reading development of students, you should take the following steps. As these steps were described in previous chapters, they are presented in summary form here.

Preparation

Select from the student's instructional materials a passage that seems to pose some difficulty for her and that is similar in length to those you typically use for instruction. Prepare a photocopy or double-spaced typewritten copy of the passage.

Next, study the passage and create a set of vocabulary knowledge and comprehension questions according to the procedures described in Chapters 4 and 5. Order the comprehension questions in the sequence of the story and type or write them, leaving enough space between them to record the student's responses. The vocabulary knowledge questions should follow the comprehension questions.

Use a system like the one described in Chapter 3 to record the student's oral reading responses. You should also tape-record the session so you can check the time the student required to read the passage and the accuracy of your handwritten oral reading record.

Administration

Make sure the student is comfortable and relaxed. Discuss your reasons for the diagnosis with her (e.g., to learn more about how to work with her on reading) and describe the procedures you will use. Tell her you will ask her to read a passage and answer some questions about it and that next time her reading strategies will be explored more informally. When you ask her to read the selection aloud, give some version of the following directions:

> This is a story in which . . . [theme-related preparatory statement]. Please read this story aloud for me. If you come to a word you don't know, try to figure it out, or skip it. I will not be able to help you, so do the best you can. After you finish, I will ask you some questions.

Before the student begins reading, test the tape recorder. You might let the student record her voice and then listen to the replay. Record the student's oral reading on the photocopy or typed version of the story as well as on tape. Keep the tape recorder running while you ask her the comprehension questions so her responses won't be lost if she answers more rapidly than you can write. Use the tape recording to check the amount of time she needed to read the passage.

Analysis

Study the student's performance on the first part of the diagnosis to determine the area(s) of reading you should explore further. If his print skill accuracy is below 95 percent, select sight and/or content words and develop procedures for examining his underlying resources for identifying words. If his comprehension is below 75 percent, examine the questions he answered incorrectly and plan questions that may facilitate further exploration. At the same time, consider the influence of vocabulary knowledge on his comprehension and print skill; when appropriate, select additional words or phrases for presentation during this stage.

Further Exploration

During a second session with the student administer items for further exploration according to the procedures summarized in Figure 8.2. If you suspect the student is having difficulty with print skill, regardless of the adequacy of his comprehension performance, you should focus first on content word identification and then on content word meaning. The reason for this order is that presenting the vocabulary knowledge items first would invalidate the exploration of word identification. If sight words are also a problem, explore these after identifying the content words. Record the student's responses to the print skill exploration in writing as well as on tape. It is important to make complete notes since it is often difficult on the basis of a tape recording to reconstruct the questions or word parts to which the student was responding.

Next, present the vocabulary knowledge items you selected for obtaining further evidence if you have not already presented them in exploring print skill. Conduct further exploration of comprehension last. You may omit this stage if, by then, you are convinced that print skill and vocabulary knowledge are interfering with the student's comprehension.

Interpretation

In analyzing a student's performance on a diagnostic passage, it is useful to focus first on print skill, then on vocabulary knowledge, and finally on comprehension. Then, when you have achieved an understanding of the student's strategies in each of these areas, examine his relative strength using the model presented in the first chapter.

Print Skill.   The evidence concerning a student's print strategies comes from two sources: her oral reading of contextual materials and her identification of isolated words and word parts. The first source tells you about the student's integrated approach to print; the second yields evidence about her underlying knowledge of

These procedures may be used after the student has read a passage and responded to comprehension questions.

If Student Demonstrates Difficulty Identifying Content Words

1. Select content words that the student missed during the oral reading. Write them on a blank page in list form. For each word, first see if the student can pronounce it without help. If not, use the procedures described in Chapter 3: See if the student can divide the word into syllables and pronounce them. If not, see if the student can pronounce just the first syllable (cover the remainder of the word with a finger). If not, see if the student knows the sound corresponding to the first consonant or consonant cluster, then the vowel and final consonant(s). For syllables that lend themselves to visual analogy, test to see if the student can think of a word that ends the same and on that basis identify the syllable; if not, provide such a word and see if the student can use it to identify the syllable. Test a sample of consonants, consonant clusters, vowels, word endings, and word families. Continue with successive words on the list as long as the procedure yields new information and the student is responsive.

2. Ask the student to define the words missed, using the procedures described in Chapter 4.

If Student Demonstrates Difficulty with Sight Words:

1. Select sight words that the student misread during oral reading. Write them on a blank page in list form. See if the student can pronounce each word. Note whether the response is immediate or delayed. Continue further exploration only as long as it yields new information and the student is able to respond attentively.

If Student Demonstrates Inadequate Comprehension:

1. Explore the student's knowledge of word meanings and/or concepts that may be interfering with comprehension, as described in Chapter 4. If vocabulary knowledge is adequate, explore comprehension further as described in the next two steps.

2. Note those questions that were answered incorrrectly. Have the student reread the portion of the passage on which the question is based and reask the question. Continue this procedure for the remaining incorrectly answered questions.

3. If the student fails to answer a question correctly after rereading, explore further using the informal interview technique illustrated in Chapter 6. Note intersentence and sentence-level problems of the text that may interfere with the student's comprehension, and use informal procedures to explore these areas.

FIGURE 8.2　Summary of procedures for further exploration

print. Though the two sources of evidence complement each other, the analyses are done separately.

The analysis of contextual reading involves four steps. First, examine the student's response to the entire passage in order to characterize her general proficiency. Then, focus your analysis on her responses to high-frequency sight words and, subsequently, on responses to content words so that you can determine how she identified words that were unfamiliar. Finally, assess her reading integration and fluency. Record the results of this four-step analysis on the oral reading analysis form.

Your analysis of the student's performance on isolated words (further exploration) may focus on sight words, content words, or both. Exploring sight words should reveal whether the student recognizes them on sight when other problems involved in contextual reading are removed. Exploring content words provides answers to the following questions: Can the student divide multisyllabic words into syllables? Can she identify simple syllables and more complex syllables (those containing blends, digraphs)? Can she identify word endings (*-ing, -es, -ed*)? Does she know vowel pronunciation and markers? Can she blend letter sounds?

Next, you consolidate on the oral reading analysis form the results obtained from the oral reading analysis and further exploration in order to answer the following questions:

1. Is the passage of appropriate difficulty in terms of the student's print skill and instructional needs?
2. What is the student's strength in rapid sight word recognition?
3. What resources does the student possess for identifying unknown words?
4. Are the student's print-processing skills integrated and fluent?
5. What, if any, aspect of print skills should be the focus of instruction?

In answering these and subsequent questions you should note any supporting evidence.

Vocabulary Knowledge.   You can use informal questioning and discussion to ascertain whether the student has the background experiences needed to understand the passage. However, word knowledge questions and further exploration will be needed to assess his knowledge of the specific words that pertain to these experiences. This step also provides evidence of whether the student is able to select the particular meaning of a word that is appropriate to the sense of the passage. This evidence concerning vocabulary knowledge should answer three questions:

1. Does the student have command of the concepts used in the passage?
2. Is this knowledge explicit and clear (definitions) or implicit and somewhat vague (sentence use)?
3. Can the student use context to select the appropriate word meaning?

Comprehension.   Interpretation should begin with the evidence concerning the student's ability to respond correctly to text-related comprehension questions. In completing the comprehension–vocabulary knowledge summary form, look for answers to the following questions:

1. Did the student understand the essential information contained in the passage and the import of the message? Is the passage at an appropriate level for the student for instructional purposes?
2. If not, what are the student's strengths and weaknesses in comprehension?
3. Is the student's problem mainly in the area of comprehension, or do difficulties with print skill or vocabulary knowledge contribute to his comprehension difficulties?

4. Based on your exploration of the student's comprehension, what, if any, instruction in comprehension does he need?

Summary/Integration.   First, summarize your conclusions about the student's print skill, vocabulary knowledge, and comprehension. Then determine whether his vocabulary knowledge or print skill difficulties interfere with his comprehension. Finally, discuss with the student his major strengths and difficulties in reading.

Instructional Planning

On the basis of the summary and final integration of diagnostic information, you should be able to answer the following questions:

1. Is the instructional material of appropriate difficulty for this student under ordinary conditions? Would certain forms of instructional intervention help the student to cope with the material?
2. What forms of instruction will help this student further refine his reading strategies?

Your recommendations for instruction should follow directly from the final summary/ integration of results and should be listed in order of priority.

It is extremely important to discuss your diagnosis and recommendations with the student. It is also important to ascertain how the student feels about the recommendations. The instruction can be successful only when the student becomes a part of the planning and implementation.

CASE STUDIES

The two case studies described in the remaining sections of this chapter demonstrate how these procedures can be applied. A teacher using this form of diagnosis may wish to prepare the student for reading the passage in the manner he or she normally follows in the classroom, rather than, as we have suggested—to have the student read with only a brief introduction.

CASE 8.1: SHARON

Sharon is 12 years old and in seventh grade. She has difficulty in reading and is in a remedial reading class. She works hard and is very cooperative in school. She is a shy student with very little experience outside of her lower-class neighborhood. Her mother is dead, and she lives with an older sister, who is her guardian, and other sisters and brothers. She does not have many interests—"just likes to stay home and watch TV or play outside with her younger sister." Her teacher, Monica, noticed that she often had difficulty comprehending assigned materials and decided to learn more about Sharon's reading strategies.

Preparation

Monica selected a passage that she thought might be of interest to Sharon. It was entitled "Bringing Light to the Blind" and was taken from a high fourth-grade reading workbook called *Adventure Trail* (Charles E. Merrill). Monica's first step was to study the passage in order to derive comprehension and word knowledge questions.

PAUSE AND REFLECT.   Analyze "Bringing Light to the Blind" shown in Figure 8.3. What questions would you ask? What vocabulary knowledge would you tap? Compare these with Monica's choices in Figure 8.4.

Figure 8.4 shows Monica's comprehension and vocabulary knowledge questions and the responses that she expected. The first six comprehension questions involve text-related comprehension, while question 7 encourages the student to generalize beyond the text.

FIGURE 8.3   Diagnostic reading passage: Sharon

SOURCE: From *Adventure Trail*, Diagnostic Reading Workbook, Grade 4, by E. M. Johnson, p. 46. In *New Diagnostic Reading Series*. Columbus, Ohio: Charles E. Merrill Publishing Co., 1969. Reprinted by permission.

Bringing Light to the Blind

Only about one-fourth of the blind people in our country can read. They read Braille (brāl). As you know, Braille is a way of printing by raised dots. The blind run their fingers over the raised dots.

Did you ever shut your eyes and run your fingers over a page of Braille printing? All the little raised dots seemed to run together. Even if you knew the Braille alphabet, your fingers could not pick out each separate dot. But the boys and girls who cannot see read stories in Braille. Their fingers are trained to be their eyes.

A Frenchman, Louis Braille, made it possible for those who cannot see, to read. When he was a small boy, he used to play around his father's harness shop. One day, he was trying to punch holes in a piece of leather with a big awl. The tool slipped and hurt Louis' eye. Before long, he became blind.

When Louis was ten years old, he was sent to a school for the blind in Paris. There he began to study music and learned to play the organ. He became a very fine musician.

Louis did not just want to become famous. He wanted to help all those who could not see. So he set to work to find an alphabet which could be read with the fingers. Today that system of writing is known as Braille.

Some books and magazines are printed in Braille for boys and girls. "My Weekly Reader Number Four" is one of them. Every week, the American Printing House for the Blind prints Braille copies of this newspaper.

There are even books that "talk." The books are like phonograph records that talk to the blind. When a blind person wants to read, he turns a key and then listens. It is as if someone were reading a book aloud to him. Our government sends the talking books free to blind people in all parts of our country.

Comprehension

1. How do blind people read? (They run their fingers over raised dots, or by Braille.)

2. What do blind people train to be their eyes? (fingers)

3. How did Louis Braille become blind? (He was hit in the eye with a tool [awl] while punching holes in leather in this father's harness shop.)

4. When Louis Braille was at school, what did he study? (music; playing the organ)

5. What did Louis Braille do for the blind? (made it possible for blind people to read by inventing an alphabet that could be read with the fingers, etc.)

6. What are books that "talk"? (like records that talk to the blind)

*7. Do you think that Louis Braille was a brave person? Why?

   *Beyond-text question

Vocabulary Knowledge

1. What is *Braille*? (printing by small raised dots that can be read by touch)

2. What is an *awl*? (a tool for punching holes)

3. What does *raised* mean? (higher; above)

4. What is a *system*? (a method)

FIGURE 8.4   Comprehension and vocabulary knowledge questions: Sharon

Administration

Sharon was quite relaxed when she read the passage orally and responded to the prepared questions. The record of her oral reading is shown in Figure 8.5.

Following the oral reading, Sharon was asked to retell as much of the selection as she could remember. Here is what she said: ". . . about blind people . . . reading and stuff. About this boy . . . he was doing something and something hurt his eye. That's all I remember." Because Sharon's retelling was so incomplete, it was necessary for Monica to administer the questions she had prepared. Sharon's responses are shown in Figure 8.6.

PAUSE AND REFLECT.   Before reading Monica's first analysis, analyze Sharon's reading as recorded in Figures 8.5 and 8.6. Is there a problem with print? What are Sharon's strengths and difficulties? What would you explore further?

Analysis

On the basis of Sharon's oral reading of the passage and her responses to the comprehension questions, Monica decided to explore two areas: Sharon's content

Bringing Light to the Blind

^③*Brälly* — 21 / 1
^① *Bra*

Only about one-fourth of the blind people in our country can read. They read ~~Braille~~

Brälly
(bräl). As you know, ~~Braille~~ is a way of printing by raised dot(s). The blind run their finger(s) — Ɓ 1 *

over the raised dot(s) — ✗ 0

paget Brä-alky
Did you ever shut your eyes and run your finger(s) over a ~~page~~ of ~~Braille~~ printing? All the — Ɓ 1

s *Brāley*
little raised dots seem(ed) to run together. Even if you knew the ~~Braille~~ alphabet, your — ✗ 1

see-per-s
finger(s) could not pick out each ~~separate~~ dot. But the boys and girls who cannot see read — Ɓ 2

Brāky
stories in ~~Braille~~. Their fingers are trained to be their eyes. — ✗ 0

Brāley
A Frenchman, Louis ~~Braille~~, made it possible for those who cannot see, to read. When — ✗ 0

he was a small boy, he used to play around his father('s) harness shop. One day, he was — ✗ 0

a
trying to punch hole(s) in a piece of leather with a big awl. The tool slipped and hurt Louis' — ✗ 1

eye. Before long, he became blind.

© *sent*
When Louis was ten years old, he was ~~sent~~ to a school for the blind in Paris. There he — 1

begin *ing* *could become*
~~began~~ to study music and learned to play the organ. He ~~became~~ a very fine musician. — 4

a
Louis did not just want to become famous. He wanted to help all those who could not — 1

see. So he set to work to find an alphabet (which could be read with the fingers). Today that — 1

simple *it* *s* *Brāley* *skipped entire line in passage*
~~system~~ of writing (s) known as ~~Braille~~. — 3

Brāley
Some books and magazines are printed in ~~Braille~~ for boys and girls. "My Weekly Reader — ✗ 0

Number Four" is one of them. Every week, the America(n) Printing House for the Blind — 1

Brāley
prints ~~Braille~~ copies of this newspaper. — ✗ 0

s *s*
There are even books that "talk." (The) books are like phonograph records that talk to (the) — 1

blind. When a blind person want(s) to read, he turn(s) a key and then listens. It is as if — 1

someone were reading a book aloud to him. Our government sends (the) talking books free — ✗ 0

a
to blind people in all parts of ~~our~~ country. — 1

* *Dialect-based miscues occurring more than twice were not counted.*

FIGURE 8.5 Record of oral reading: Sharon

SOURCE: From *Adventure Trail*, Diagnostic Reading Workbook, Grade 4, by E. M. Johnson, p. 46. In *New Diagnostic Reading Series*. Columbus, Ohio: Charles E. Merrill Publishing Co., 1969. Reprinted by permission.

Retelling

. . . about blind people . . . reading and stuff. About this boy—he was doing something and something hurt his eye. That's all I remember.

Comprehension

✓ 1. How do blind people read? (They run their fingers over raised dots, or by Braille.)
Response: They read from Brā-ley.

✓ 2. What do blind people train to be their eyes? (fingers)
Response: They use their hands, don't they?

½ 3. How did Louis Braille become blind? (He was hit in the eye with a tool [awl] while punching holes in his father's harness shop.)
Response: He was doing something and he knocked something over and it made him blind. [Q.: What hit him in the eye?] That harness stuff.

✓ 4. When Louis Braille was at school, what did he study? (music; playing the organ)
Response: Music.

✗ 5. What did Louis Braille do for the blind? (made is possible for blind people to ready by inventing an alphabet that could be read with the fingers, etc.)
Response: He helped them learn and put up this thing about blind.

✗ 6. What are books that "talk"? (like records that talk to the blind)
Response: Don't know.

✗ *7. Do you think that Louis Braille was a brave person? Why?
Response: Yes, he was brave. He helped people that were blind to read and write.

*Beyond-text question

Vocabulary Knowledge

✗ 1. What is *Braille*? (printing by small raised dots that can be read by touch)
Response: Like a thing that goes through a line or something. [Q.: can you explain that?] Well . . . not sure.

✗ 2. What is an *awl*? (a tool for punching holes)
Response: Don't know.

✓ 3. What does *raised* mean? (higher; above)
Response: You raise it . . . raise it up.

✗ 4. What is a *system*? (a method)
Response: Don't know.

Figure 8.6 Responses to comprehension and vocabulary knowledge questions: Sharon word errors, in order better to assess her word identification skill, and her vocabulary knowledge in areas pertinent to the passage.

Further Exploration

The results from Sharon's oral reading analysis and further exploration are summarized on the oral reading analysis form in Figure 8.7. Sharon's answers indicate that she has good knowledge of basic phonics concepts but has difficulty applying this knowledge during contextual reading.

The summary of Sharon's comprehension performance and the results from the vocabulary knowledge exploration are presented on the comprehension–vocabulary knowledge summary in Figure 8.8. Because Sharon's word knowledge was so limited, Monica felt there was no point in exploring her comprehension skills further.

PAUSE AND REFLECT.   What do you see as areas of difficulty for Sharon? What are the implications of this diagnosis for Sharon's instruction?

Interpretation

Print Skill. Sight words do not seem to be a problem for Sharon, and she possesses good phonics and structural skills. It is difficult to know whether her failure to apply these skills during contextual reading occurred because of the large number of unfamiliar words in the passage or because the general meaning of the passage was difficult for her to grasp. Most of the substitutions that did not make sense occurred in sentences that were too technical for her. While it is clear that Sharon's reading of this passage was neither integrated nor fluent, the number of problems posed may simply have overwhelmed her. It will be important for Monica to have Sharon read an easier passage with fewer unfamiliar words in order to have a more valid test of her integration and fluency.

Some affixed words and verb forms posed problems for Sharon. Dialect substitutions where the final *s* was either omitted or inserted were eliminated from consideration. But Sharon's problem seems to extend beyond that of pluralization and possession to other affixes. Her oral language differs in certain respects from standard English; further, at times she appears to be overcorrecting for dialect. It is important to determine the extent to which Sharon's problems with affixes arise from dialect influence as opposed to lack of knowledge. Exploration results suggest that she understands affixes but during difficult oral reading becomes confused about their pronunciation.

Vocabulary Knowledge. Sharon's vocabulary and understanding of words seems to be quite limited for a seventh grader. She does not know some words typically known by students her age (*harness, system, volume*) and has vague or limited concepts of others (*separate, raised*). The possibility that she is in command of

ORAL READING ANALYSIS

Name *Sharon* Grade *7* Date *Feb.*

Book/Page *Adventure Trail* Level *4ᵗʰ Grade*

A. Difficulty

30 / *329* *94* % Correct

Level: Independent   Instructional
~~Borderline~~   Frustration

B. Word Learning: Sight Word Errors

Printed Word	Oral Response	Further Exploration	Evaluation
is	it	✓	*Immediate and correct recognition of sight words. Sight words are probably not a problem with the easier materials.*
our	a	✓	
② the	[omitted]	✓	
③ a	[inserted]	✓	
could	[inserted]	✓	
[a line]	[omitted]		

C. Word Identification: Content Word Errors

Printed Word	Oral Response	Further Exploration	Evaluation
② Braille	Bră/Brăly/Brāley Brăley		*Good knowledge of phonics. Application may be more of a problem. Has some knowledge of affixes and syllabication. Well developed word identification skill; need to check application during easier contextual reading.*
page	paget	✓	
known	knows	✓	
sent	seen ⓒ	✓	
seemed	seems	✓	
learned	learning	✓	
separate	seper ⓒ	✓	
began	begin	✓	
became	become	✓	
system	simple	✓	
American	America	✓	

D. Integration–Fluency

Integration: *Errors are generally not contextually appropriate; infrequent correction of errors; highly dependent on graphic cues.*

Fluency: Rate *329* / *6.1* = *54* Evaluation *Slow, even for a foorth grader.*

Phrasing *Choppy — does not read with appropriate phrasing.*

FIGURE 8.7 Analysis of oral reading responses: Sharon

COMPREHENSION–VOCABULARY KNOWLEDGE SUMMARY

Name **Sharon** Grade **7** Date **Feb**

Book/Page **Adventure Trail** Level **High 4th**

COMPREHENSION

3½ / **6**   **58** % Correct

Level: Independent   Instructional
(Borderline)   Frustration

A. Retelling: Complete   Main Idea   Partial   (Inadequate)

Comments: _She had a difficult time expressing herself – limited vocabulary, problems with sentence structure._

B. Text-Related Comprehension

Item #	Response	Further Exploration	Item #	Response	Further Exploration
1	✓		6	NR *	
2	✓	(mentioned hands, not fingers)			
3	½				
4	✓				
5	X				

* NR = no response

C. Beyond-Text Generalization

Item #	Response	Further Exploration	Item #	Response	Further Exploration
7	X				

VOCABULARY KNOWLEDGE

1½ / **6**   **25** % Correct

Item Tested	Response	Comments	Item Tested	Response	Comments
Braille	X				
awl	X				
raised	✓	Knows verb form			
system	X				
separate dot (P)*	½				
harness (P)	X				

* P indicates a probe item

EVALUATION

A. Comprehension: _Vague understanding of ideas in passage. Her comprehension is inadequate – the materials are inappropriate._

B. Vocabulary Knowledge _Very limited word knowledge – even unable to use words in a sentence_

FIGURE 8.8 Summary of responses to comprehension and vocabulary knowledge questions: Sharon more knowledge than she is able to express was not supported by exploration, but Monica should undertake further observation of her vocabulary knowledge.

Comprehension. The results from Sharon's retelling and the text-related questions are consistent, and they reveal that she had difficulty understanding this selection. Even when her responses were correct or partially correct, they indicated serious limitations. She seemed to have particular difficulty describing major concepts explained in the passage. The main underlying problem seemed to be her failure to understand the technical concepts (raised dots, awl) necessary for understanding the central concepts (Braille) and events (the eye injury). However, print-processing problems may have also interfered with her understanding of *books that "talk."*

Summary/Integration. The analysis shows that Sharon's sight recognition and her phonics and structural skills are strong even though she sometimes fails to apply this knowledge during contextual reading. Given the difficulty of the passage for her, it was not possible for Monica to evaluate Sharon's reading integration (use of context) and her fluency. On this fourth-grade selection, she showed poorly integrated strategies and extremely slow reading.

Sharon's main problem is her extremely limited vocabulary knowledge. Monica assumes that her poor reading comprehension is a direct reflection of her vocabulary deficiency.

Instructional Plan
Materials. High fourth-grade level material is too difficult for Sharon unless the reading is preceded by extensive instructional support focused on the development of word meanings. Sharon should be reading from easier material (level to be determined) to enable her to attend to meaning, use context, and increase her reading rate.

Instructional Priorities. The major focus of Monica's instructional support should be on developing Sharon's vocabulary and her reading integration and fluency. This instruction can be provided in a group that includes other students with similar problems.

1. Before Sharon reads a selection, Monica should identify concepts that may be unfamiliar and encourage Sharon to speculate about their meaning and relationship to the theme of the selection. Monica should explain unfamiliar or partially known concepts. Because the goal of vocabulary development is the improvement of comprehension, thorough discussion should follow the reading of each selection in order to develop comprehension and establish its importance.

   Monica can use other procedures to expand Sharon's vocabulary knowledge. For example, she can read stories to her (along with other students), and discuss new concepts, with suggestions for their use in alternative contexts. Sharon may also profit from working with another student on synonym, antonym, and root word–affix activities.

2. To improve Sharon's reading rate, integration, and fluency, Monica can give her short selections that are easy for her. Sharon should be encouraged to concentrate on gaining meaning from everything she reads.

CASE 8.2: PATRICIA

Patricia is in ninth grade. Like 80 percent of her freshman class, she is in a double-period basic English class for students reading on a second-to-fifth-grade level. On this year's California Achievement Test, she scored a grade equivalent of 5.2 on vocabulary and 3.2 on comprehension. In contrast to many other students in her class, Patricia attends regularly and does all the assigned work. She understands and enjoys the mysteries that she reads on her own but has difficulty with most of her school reading. Because Monica is able to spend some extra time with Patricia, she decided to undertake a more systematic diagnosis of Patricia's reading strategies in order to determine which should be the areas of instructional focus.

In the testing situation, Patricia was relaxed, friendly, and eager to proceed. She was asked to read a fifth-grade-level passage entitled "Rescue in a Burning Building." The record of Patricia's oral reading is shown in Figure 8.9.

She was then asked to retell the selection and to respond to the questions that Monica had prepared. Patricia's responses to the comprehension and vocabulary knowledge questions are shown in Figure 8.10.

PAUSE AND REFLECT.   Look at Figures 8.9 and 8.10. What would you explore further?

Analysis and Further Exploration

On the basis of Patricia's responses to the passage and the comprehension and vocabulary knowledge questions, Monica decided that further exploration should examine her comprehension responses and her word knowledge. In addition, Monica decided to have Patricia respond to several of the content words that she had had difficulty pronouncing in order to confirm that print skill was not an area of difficulty. When questioned, Patricia responded quickly and accurately to words such as *adjoining, escape,* and *motioning.* Thus, Monica made no further analysis of her oral reading responses.

Comprehension and vocabulary knowledge responses and the results of further exploration are given in the comprehension–vocabulary knowledge summary form in Figure 8.11.

Rescue in a Burning Building

NEW YORK, June 17—A fireman rescued a 76 year old woman from a burning apartment building yesterday by tossing her off a fire escape. The woman, Mrs. Mary Rogers, landed safely in the arms of another fireman waiting on the roof of an adjoining building.

Fireman Edward Lane had risked his life to reach the woman, who was trapped in her smoke-filled top floor apartment in the five-story building. The fire was blazing out of control as Lane carried the almost unconscious woman onto a fire escape.

As flames threatened them, Lane tried without success to first climb to the roof and then to go below the height of the flames. He could not do so while carrying the dead weight of the helpless 115-pound woman.

Then he saw another fireman, Mike Mays, motioning to him with his arms held out. Mays was on the roof of the next building, which was level with the fire escape. A space of only four feet separated the two buildings, but there was a fifty-foot drop to the ground. Lane tried to pass Mrs. Rogers over to Mays, but the gap was too wide.

Then the two men decided that the only chance to save the woman was to try something very dangerous. Lane reached back and threw Mrs. Rogers across the space between the buildings. For a moment the woman was not supported above the ground. Then Mays caught her by the neck and shoulders, and pulled her safely onto the roof. Mrs. Rogers was uninjured.

Lane then climbed to the roof of the burning building, went down another fire escape and back to fighting the fire.

FIGURE 8.9   Record of oral reading: Patricia

SOURCE: From *Real Stories*, Book 1, pp. 200–202, Milton Katz, Michael Chakeres, and Murray Bromberg (Eds.), New York: Globe Book, 1969. (Originally published in *Newsday*; reprinted by permission of the publisher, Newsday, Inc., Melville, NY)

Retelling

Response: It was a fire. He had to get this lady out of the building. They had to use the fire escape to get the lady out of the building.

Comprehension

√ 1. Where did Fireman Lane find the woman? (in her smoke-filled apartment, on the top floor of the building)
Response: In the building, in the house (*house means apartment*).

√ 2. How serious was the fire? (It was blazing, out of control)
Response: Real serious.

✗ 3. Why couldn't Fireman Lane carry the woman up or down the fire escape? (She was too heavy in her unconscious state—"dead weight.")
Response: Because it was too hard. [Q.: Explain how.] Just too hard.

✗ 4. Where was the other fireman, Mike Mays? (on the roof of the next building, level with the fire escape)
Response: Trying to get the fire out.

✗ 5. Why couldn't Fireman Lane pass the woman to the other fireman? (The gap between the buildings was too wide—four feet.)
Response: (Could not answer.)

✗ 6. What did Fireman Lane finally do with the woman? (threw her across the space between the two buildings; Mays caught her)
Response: (Could not answer.)

√ *7. Why do you think the woman was "almost unconscious"?
Response: Because of the smoke.

*Beyond-text question

Vocabulary Knowledge

√ 1. What does *risked* mean, as in "He risked his life"?
Response: Took a chance.

√ 2. What does *unconscious* mean?
Response: Knocked out.

√ 3. What does *tossing* mean?
Response: You throw it.

✗ 4. What does *adjoining* mean?
Response: Like you join a club.

FIGURE 8.10 Responses to comprehension and vocabulary knowledge questions: Patricia

PAUSE AND REFLECT.   What do you see as areas of strength and difficulty for Patricia? What are the implications of this diagnosis for Patricia's instruction?

COMPREHENSION–VOCABULARY KNOWLEDGE SUMMARY

Name Patricia   Grade 9   Date Nov,

Book/Page Real Stories   Level 5th gr.
200-202

COMPREHENSION

2 / 6   33 % Correct

Level: Independent   Instructional
Borderline   (Frustration)

A. Retelling: Complete   Main Idea   Partial   (Inadequate)

   Comments: Incomplete and inaccurate retelling; she had only the barest understanding of story.

B. Text-Related Comprehension

Item #	Response	Further Exploration	Item #	Response	Further Exploration
1	✓		6	✗	
2	✓				
3	✗				
4	✗				
5	✗				

C. Beyond-Text Generalization

Item #	Response	Further Exploration	Item #	Response	Further Exploration
7	✓	possesses some background knowledge of fires			

VOCABULARY KNOWLEDGE

6 / 8   75 % Correct

Item Tested	Response	Comments	Item Tested	Response	Comments
risked	✓		motioning (P)	✓	
unconscious	✓		gap (P)	✗	
tossing	✓				
adjoining	✗				
blazing (P)*	✓				
dead weight (P)	✓				

* P indicates a probe item

EVALUATION

A. Comprehension: Does not seem to understand the situation — e.g., where the second fireman was and what the problem was. May need to work on visualizing situations. Dense prose and expository materials may be particularly difficult for her.

B. Vocabulary Knowledge Some concepts are unknown, but generally she shows good strength in word knowledge.

FIGURE 8.11   Summary of responses to comprehension and vocabulary knowledge questions: Patricia

Interpretation

Print Skill. Patricia seems to have almost no problems with sight word recognition and word identification. Most of her errors on content words involved word endings (*-ed, -ing, -s*). Examination of the passage shows that typically she does pronounce these endings. In fact, she often pronounces endings that she drops during oral conversation. When words were presented in isolation during further exploration, she pronounced the affixes according to standard English. Thus, it is clear that Patricia possesses knowledge about word endings. Print processing does not appear to be a problem area that interferes with her comprehension. Nevertheless, her reading rate is slower than the average range for fifth graders, so some improvement in integration and fluency may be needed. It is difficult for Monica to evaluate her use of context since her word attack skills are strong but her comprehension is low.

Vocabulary Knowledge. Patricia knew three-quarters of the vocabulary items tested. The two she missed, while not key words, would definitely have aided her comprehension. They also indicate that Patricia probably does not know many words typically known by ninth graders. Verbal knowledge is a possible area of weakness that may contribute to Patricia's comprehension difficulties. Nevertheless, as is also suggested by the results from the standardized reading test, her comprehension is lower than might be expected on the basis of her vocabulary knowledge.

Comprehension. Patricia's retelling (incomplete and inaccurate) showed that she had only the barest understanding of the situation in the story. Her answers to the factual questions (two correct out of six) support this. Even her two correct answers were not specific. In further exploration, where she had an opportunity to reread most of the text orally and silently, she still did not grasp the point of the story. She reread the key paragraph many times before she comprehended it.

Summary/Integration. Patricia's main area of reading difficulty lies in comprehension. Since she could not answer the questions after rereading, her problem appears to be at the sentence and intersentence level. Her vocabulary knowledge is relatively strong and does not seem to account for the comprehension difficulty. Print processing represents an area of strength, although work may be needed to improve integration and fluency.

Instructional Plan

Materials. While the currently used fifth-grade-level material is appropriate for Patricia for instructional purposes with respect to print-processing demands, it represents frustration level (below 50 percent) with respect to her comprehension. Given the test results, her instruction should begin with material with very familiar concepts or with a lower-level selection.

Instructional Priorities. Instruction should focus directly on the development of basic text-processing strategies, particularly those that are useful for expository materials. Key terms should be discussed as needed.

1. Patricia's comprehension may be improved through individual work. She needs instructional materials (on a third- or fourth-grade level) that ask specific questions about information presented and provide corrective feedback. At least once a week Monica should review Patricia's work with her. At this time, Monica may wish to engage in reciprocal teaching of comprehension strategies (as described on page 185). Patricia should then be encouraged to concentrate on comprehending what she reads, paraphrasing sentences to herself, and interacting with the text as described in Chapter 6. Work on anaphora and connectives is also appropriate.

2. Students with comprehension problems similar to Patricia's should be brought together into a group. The group should learn to speculate—on the basis of titles, headings, and initial paragraphs—what a selection may be about. Discussion should follow each main segment of the article to check the accuracy of group predictions. For both expository and narrative selections, the group should be given help in organizing information as described in Chapter 6.

3. Patricia should be encouraged to read on her own and to expand her reading interests. She could be given mysteries or exciting biographies that are slightly harder than the ones she presently reads. Her integration and fluency should be checked on these high-interest materials.

SUMMARY

One purpose of diagnosis is to establish the level of materials that students can read easily (independent level) and the level students can read with teaching support (instructional level). It is also important to identify those materials that are extremely difficult and should be avoided (frustration level). We have described criteria for oral reading accuracy and comprehension accuracy that will be helpful to you in making judgments about the reading levels appropriate for your students.

By combining and interpreting information that you obtain concerning student skill with print, vocabulary knowledge, and reading comprehension, you can draw conclusions about the levels of materials that are appropriate for students and the type of teaching support they need. A formal analysis of reading involves six steps: (1) preparation of the reading selection and questions, (2) administration of the task, (3) analysis of the results, (4) further exploration of reading strengths and difficulties, (5) interpretation of results, and (6) instructional planning. In the classroom setting, your procedures will be more informal as you gather and interpret relevant information over a period of time.

We have shown, through detailed presentation of two case studies, how the procedures introduced in preceding chapters may be used to diagnose students' reading problems and modify your instruction in accordance with students' needs. While the process of acquiring expertise in using these procedures may be time-consuming, it leads to deeper understanding of the various facets of reading and provides you with a framework for making sense of students' successes and failures and for refining your instructional approaches.

TRY IT OUT

1. Do a dynamic assessment of a child in your class. Tape-record the assessment and share with one of your classmates. Compare and contrast your procedures and conclusions about instruction. List shared questions or problems and how you resolved them.

2. **For Your Teaching Portfolio:** Prepare a Guidelines Sheet for carrying out dynamic assessment, a sample passage, and record sheets. You can also append an example, as in #1 above. Include a sheet of questions that arose and suitable answers.

3. **Student Portfolio Ideas:** Share your assessment with a student and discuss your findings. Have the student reflect, in writing, on your assessment and plans or steps *he or she* might take to improve performance.

FOR FURTHER READING

Johnston, P. H. (1983). *Reading comprehension assessment: A cognitive basis.* Newark, DE: International Reading Association.
Views reading as a process through which students actively pursue meaning and describes appropriate assessment strategies.

Pikulski, J. J., & Shanahan, T. (Eds.). (1982). *Approaches to the informal evaluation of reading.* Newark, DE: International Reading Association.
Describes methods for informally assessing reading in the classroom.

Powell, W. R. (1980). Measuring reading performance informally. *Journal of Children and Youth, 1,* 23–31.
Discusses criteria that are useful in the informal assessment of reading.

chapter 9

Using Informal Reading Inventories for Assessment

CHAPTER GOALS FOR THE READER

To understand the nature and classroom uses of informal reading inventories

To develop a framework for evaluating an informal reading inventory

To develop guidelines for administration and interpretation of informal reading inventories

To work through three cases of assessment using informal reading inventories

CLASSROOM VIGNETTE: ADDING TO YOUR ASSESSMENT TOOLKIT

Laura is a reading teacher in a small, two-school district. Her work takes her into elementary and high school classrooms where she works with both students and teachers. Because she sees such a wide variety of students, she needs materials on many levels to make initial assessment decisions. She also works with teachers in small workshop sessions to help them develop their observational and analytic skills. As Laura emphasizes observing students in actual reading and listening situations, she is investigating informal reading inventories as materials for her assessment library. She wants to know:

What is an informal reading inventory (IRI)?

What guidelines can be used to evaluate IRIs?

How is an informal reading inventory administered and interpreted?

This chapter address Laura's needs and her questions. You will also be able to work through three cases of students she assessed with informal reading inventories.

CHAPTER OVERVIEW

Informal reading inventories are useful tools for teachers who need to meet with a wide range of students. Because they are composed of reading selections and word lists that cover a large developmental span, they can be especially helpful to the teacher who assesses students who are not in her regular classroom. In this chapter we look at the ways informal reading inventories (IRIs) can be used for assessment. First, we describe informal reading inventories and comment on their history and development. Second, we share guidelines for evaluating informal reading inventories. Third, we present procedures for administering and interpreting informal reading inventories, describing three divergent cases of assessment using these tools.

CHAPTER OUTLINE

The Informal Reading Inventory (IRI): Description, History, and Development

Guidelines for Evaluating IRIs

Administering IRIs
   Administering the Word Recognition Task
   Administering the Oral Reading Task
   Administering the Silent Reading Task
   Administering the Listening Task
   Case 9.1: Chuck

Interpreting Results of IRIs
   Level of Materials
   Areas of Strength and Need

Case Studies
   Case 9.2: Sara
   Case 9.3: James

Try It Out

THE INFORMAL READING INVENTORY (IRI): DESCRIPTION, HISTORY, AND DEVELOPMENT

Informal reading inventories (IRIs) are among the most widely used forms of instructionally based reading assessment. Typically, an **IRI** consists of sets of graded word lists and passages (see Appendix C for examples). Teachers use these in a systematic way to determine an individual's independent, instructional, and frustration reading levels and analyze them to provide a profile of a student's strengths and needs. Though there has been much rich dialogue surrounding these inventories their popularity in both classroom and clinic (Harris & Lalik, 1987; Masztal & Smith, 1984) attests to their power as assessment tools.

The development of informal reading inventories is commonly attributed to Betts (1946) although similar diagnostic processes were used in earlier clinical assessment. The original procedure was designed to help teachers construct their own inventories from their classroom instructional materials with the idea of evaluating student performance in activities that were as much like classroom activities as possible. In many ways, the original IRIs reflected the model for assessment with instructional passages that we have proposed in this book. For that reason, IRIs are often useful for drawing conclusions about reading that could easily be connected to instruction.

Besides being closely tied to classroom reading, the informal nature of the inventories encouraged teachers to take control of decision making about their use and interpretation. Criteria for evaluation in an IRI are not norm-referenced criteria but rather criteria for mastery of such aspects of reading as word recognition and comprehension. As the popularity of IRIs grew, standards for mastery and placement were proposed. Though there has been a rich and spirited dialogue about the boundaries of these criteria and issues of the reliability of IRIs (Johns, 1993; Lipson, Cox, Iwanowski, & Simon, 1984), shared ranges of interpretation have emerged such as those presented in Chapter 8 (see Table 8.1).

GUIDELINES FOR EVALUATING IRIs

As IRIs grew in popularity, commercial inventories began appearing (see Table 9.1), with developers paying some attention to selecting passages that reflected mastery by representative samples of students. Further, attention was given to aiding users in making decisions about passage reading that reflected broader, more qualitative and strategic views of reading (Goodman, Watson, & Burke, 1987; Leslie & Caldwell, 1990). Whether purchasing a commercial inventory or designing one of your own, you might consider several issues:

1. The passages ought to represent the type of reading you do in your classroom. They should be of good literary quality with language that sounds natural. Topics should be of interest to the student to be assessed and the selection should be of sufficient length and integrity to stand alone. Word lists should reflect the types of words your students will encounter in regular classroom reading.
2. Questions should be clearly worded, they should be both divergent and convergent, and they should be organized to tap the important aspects of the selection. They should be "passage dependent," that is, the reader should need to read the selection to answer the questions. Good

TABLE 9.1.   Selected list of published Informal Reading Inventories

Title/Publisher/Date	Word List Grade Ranges	Passage Grade Ranges	Forms
Analytical Reading Inventory (Woods, M. L. & Moe, A.) Charles E. Merrill, 1989	P–6	1–9	3
Bader Reading and Language Inventory (Bader, L. A) Macmillan, 1983	PP–12	PP–12	3
Basic Reading Inventory (Johns, J. J.) Kendall-Hunt, 1991	PP–8	PP–8	3
Classroom Reading Inventory (Silvaroli, N. J.) Wm. C. Brown/Benchmark, 1994	PP–6	PP–8	3
Ekwall Reading Inventory (Ekwall, E. E.) Allyn & Bacon, 1986	PP–9	PP–9	4
Information Reading Inventory (Burns, P. C., & Rose, B. D.) Houghton Mifflin, 1989	PP–12	PP–12	4
Reading Inventory for the Classroom (Flint, E. S., & Cooter R. B., Jr.) Gorsuch Scarsbrick, 1993	PP–9	PP–9	3
Qualitative Reading Inventory Scott, Foresman, 1990	P–7	P–7	4

questions should call on readers to provide elaborated answers, not simple "yes" and "no" responses. (Review Chapter 5 for more ideas on questions.)

3. In commercial IRIs, the formats and directions for use should be clear and convenient and the information the author provides about philosophy, use, and field testing should be relevant to your own school situation.

Throughout the discussion of administration and interpretation that follows, we assume that you have chosen a commercial inventory and choose to use its scoring standards, or you have constructed your own and will use the scoring standards we described earlier. In any of these cases, the judgment of the administrator is an important decision factor in how administration and interpretation will take place. The guidelines we offer should be interpreted as generic ones for dealing with IRIs.

ADMINISTERING IRIs

The general method for administering a standardized IRI is as follows: First, the word recognition test is administered and scored according to the instructions in the test manual. This provides you the basis for determining the level of the first passage to be read orally by the student. The student then reads progressively more difficult passages aloud until her performance falls below the oral reading accuracy and comprehension criterion levels. Next, she begins reading a passage silently at the instructional level established through oral reading. She then reads progressively more difficult passages until her comprehension falls below the criterion level. For silent reading, it is also important to establish the student's independent reading level; thus, she must also read progressively easier passages until she achieves 90 percent comprehension or higher. On some tests, this standard may be unrealistic; if there are nine questions or fewer, it means that no questions can be missed.

Finally, beginning one level above the student's instructional level established during oral or silent reading, you read progressively more difficult passages aloud to the student until her comprehension falls below the specified criterion. Figure 9.1 summarizes these steps in administering an IRI and the general considerations for starting and discontinuing each task.

The administration of the IRI allows you to identify the level of material that can be read easily by the student at his independent level, the levels that may be appropriate for alternative instructional purposes, and the levels that are too difficult for him. Testing usually continues until each of these levels has been established. There may be times, however, when you may wish to use the IRI to answer a more limited question (e.g., to determine a student's independent level of silent reading or instructional level for print processing). Obviously, in such cases, the procedures described here for the systematic use of the IRI would not be followed; only the relevant portion of the IRI would be used. This is an important point, since diagnostic work should never blindly follow an established set of procedures. Although it is necessary for you to be familiar with the procedures involved in a comprehensive

FIGURE 9.1   Criteria for administering informal reading inventory tasks

---

Word Lists
  Begin with the easiest list.
  Discontinue when the student scores below 75 percent correct on the untimed administration.

Oral Reading Task
  Begin with a passage at the highest level on which the student achieved 90 percent correct on the flash administration of the Word Lists.
  Discontinue when the student's instructional and frustration levels are established.

Silent Reading Task
  Begin with a passage at the highest level on which the student met the criteria for instructional level in oral reading accuracy and comprehension on the Oral Reading Task.
  Discontinue when the student's independent, instructional, and frustration levels are established.

Listening Task
  Begin with a passage one level above the highest level on which the student met the criterion for instructional level in comprehension on the Oral Reading or the Silent Reading Task.
  Discontinue when the student's frustration level is established.

approach, it is equally necessary to know when to follow only a portion of these procedures.

Administering the Word Recognition Task

The word lists measure the student's instantaneous sight vocabulary (flash presentation) and word identification skills (untimed presentation). In Chapter 3, we described procedures for assessing the "basic" sight vocabulary of students through oral reading analysis. While the primary and first-grade word lists provide a similar measure of basic sight vocabulary, the subsequent lists show how well students are incorporating other words into their store of words that are quickly recognized. Proficient readers are in command of a large store of sight words, and students during the elementary grades expand their set of sight words beyond the basic set to include most other words that they encounter frequently during contextual reading. Flash performance on the more advanced word lists shows whether the students' development of this larger sight vocabulary is grade appropriate.

The procedures for flash administration consist of using two rectangular cards, one placed just above the word to be flashed and the other covering the word. When the student is ready, quickly move the bottom card down, exposing the word. After a half-second exposure, move the top card down to cover the word. Mark correct responses on the student record form with a check (✔); record incorrect responses phonetically. When the student fails to respond, record this as "NR" (no response), "DK" (don't know), or "x." No corrections are given.

When the student fails to recognize a word during the flash presentation, let him reexamine it immediately, with no time limitation, to see whether he can identify the word. Use the further exploration procedures described in Chapter 3 for determining the knowledge a student possesses about phonics. Use structural analysis with words the student reads incorrectly on an IRI as well as on a diagnostic passage.

Administering the Oral Reading Task

The first passage the student reads is determined by her performance on the word lists. If the student's performance on this first passage is at or above the prescribed criteria, she reads progressively more difficult passages until her performance falls below the criteria. If, on the other hand, her performance falls below the criterion for either accuracy or comprehension, this level represents the borderline or frustration level. In this case, she reads increasingly easier passages until her instructional level is established (acceptable comprehension and oral reading accuracy).

As the student reads each passage aloud, record any errors made, using the procedures described in Chapter 4. Count the number of errors. When the student finishes reading a passage, ask the comprehension questions, record the answers, and determine a comprehension score. On occasion you may wish to assess comprehension by having the student retell the passage prior to asking the comprehension questions, as described in Chapter 6.

Administering the Silent Reading Task

Following the oral reading task, ask the student to read certain passages silently. The point of this task is to determine whether he is at least as proficient in silent reading as in oral reading. Although many normal readers achieve greater comprehension when they read silently than when they read aloud, this is not the case with most disabled readers. Therefore, the first silent reading passage administered is at the *same* level of difficulty as the one the student was able to read orally with good comprehension (the instructional level). After he reads the passage silently, ask the comprehension questions and record and score the answers. If the student's comprehension is below the criterion, administer successively easier passages until he achieves adequate comprehension when reading silently. On the other hand, if his comprehension score on the first silent reading passage is at or above the criterion, administer progressively more difficult passages until the frustration level is established. It is particularly important during silent reading assessment to establish the level at which the student's comprehension is extremely high (about 90 percent) for independent reading.

Administering the Listening Task

The **listening task** measures a student's comprehension and underlying verbal knowledge when print skill difficulties (if any) are eliminated. As a rule, a listening task is administered only with passages that are more difficult than those the student is able to comprehend through her own reading. It is unnecessary to administer as a listening task passages that represent a level of difficulty the student can read and understand through reading on her own.

The listening task usually begins with a passage one step higher in difficulty than the most difficult passage the student was able to read orally or silently with adequate comprehension. Read the passage aloud to the student, ask the comprehension questions, and record and score the student's answers. If her comprehension score is below the criterion, discontinue the listening task. The reason for discontinuing at this point is that under normal circumstances the next lower-level passages will have been read by the student with adequate comprehension during oral or silent reading. If her listening comprehension score on the first passage is adequate, read the next higher-level passage to her, ask the questions, and record and score the answers. Read progressively more difficult passages until her comprehension falls below the criterion. Then discontinue the listening task.

If the particular IRI materials being used provide only two passages at each level of difficulty, both passages at the level that would be appropriate for the listening task may have already been administered—one for oral reading and the other for silent reading. In this case, the listening task should proceed to the next higher level.

Laura presented the case study of Chuck, a fourth grader, to a group of teachers with whom she was working on assessment procedures. First, we work through Chuck's case to see how an IRI is administered. Then we examine two more cases—Sara, a second grader, and James, a high school student—to get an idea of the range of information an IRI can provide.

PAUSE AND REFLECT. Look at Case 9.1: Chuck, which follows. Compare it with the procedures you just read. Does it make sense? Bring questions to group discussion.

CASE 9.1: CHUCK

To illustrate the comprehensive procedures, we use the case of Chuck, a fourth grader, tested with the Ekwall Reading Inventory (1986). Laura first administered the preprimary-level word recognition list to Chuck. She exposed the words for a half-second interval (flash). If Chuck did not recognize a word, it was presented for an untimed interval. As shown in Figure 9.2, he quickly recognized all words on the preprimer list, but he failed to recognize 1 word out of 10 on the primer list. He was able to identify that word when it was presented without the pressure of time. Laura continued administering the lists, up through and including the fifth-grade list, on which Chuck's untimed score fell below 75 percent.

Second, Laura asked Chuck to read a passage aloud and answer comprehension questions. The passage selected was at the highest level at which Chuck recognized 90 percent of the flashed words, the first-grade level. Chuck's oral reading and comprehension on the first-grade passage were good, and Laura then asked him to read the second-, the third-, and finally the fourth-grade passages. Oral reading was discontinued after the fourth-grade passage because both his oral reading accuracy and comprehension dropped below the test criteria.

Third, Laura assessed Chuck's silent reading comprehension by having him read a passage at the third-grade level, his instructional level on the oral reading task.

FIGURE 9.2 Summary of performance on IRI: Chuck

INFORMAL READING INVENTORY SUMMARY

Test _Ekwall R.I._ Child _Chuck_ Age _9_ Grade _4_ Date _Jan._

Level	Recognition Test		Informal Reading Inventory					
			Oral Reading Task			Silent Reading		
	Flash (%)	Untimed (%)	Accuracy (%)	Comprehension (%)	Rate (wpm)	Comprehension (%)	Rate (wpm)	Listening Comprehension (%)
Preprimer	100	100						
Primer	90	100						
First	90	100	97	100	95	100	105	
Second	80	90	95	100	81	85	84	
Third	80	90	95	75	73	50	87	
Fourth	40	80	89	50	62			75
Fifth	—	60						50
Sixth								
Seventh								
Eighth								
Ninth								

His comprehension of this passage fell below the criterion. Laura then administered easier passages. Testing proceeded down to the first-grade passage in order
to establish Chuck's independent level for silent reading comprehension.

Finally, Laura administered the passages as a listening test. That is, she read the
passage aloud to Chuck and then asked him to answer comprehension questions.
Testing began at the fourth-grade level, the level where Chuck's oral reading
comprehension fell below the instructional level. Because he demonstrated
adequate listening comprehension (75 percent) on the fourth-grade passage, she
administered the fifth-grade passage. Since his comprehension was not acceptable
at this level (50 percent), the listening task was discontinued.

These procedures work well for younger disabled readers and older disabled
readers suspected of having print skill problems. However, for some older readers
for whom silent reading proficiency is of particular concern, it is useful to test
silent reading comprehension first and to sample oral reading second in order to
obtain a more valid measure of their silent comprehension. For most readers the
complete IRI can be administered at one time, but for younger readers the silent
reading tests, when administered last, may not be valid because of fatigue.
Therefore, it is advisable to break the testing into two sessions if fatigue is noted in
the students.

INTERPRETING RESULTS OF IRIs

For the teacher-constructed series of graded passages, consisting usually of a single
passage per level, the interpretation was similar to that for diagnoses made with
individual reading passages. In contrast, the standardized inventories allow for a
variety of comparisons, which provide a comprehensive basis for understanding a
student's reading strength and difficulty. For example, in addition to comparing a
student's performance from level to level, as was possible with the teacher-constructed inventory, it is now possible to compare oral and silent comprehension and
reading rates. The student's identification of isolated words on the graded lists can be
compared with his print processing during oral reading. Further, a student's level of
vocabulary knowledge as estimated from the vocabulary questions following each
passage can be compared with his listening comprehension. This variety of comparisons is complicated, but it does increase the precision of the diagnosis. Such a
comprehensive diagnosis should be unnecessary for most students in a class.
Occasionally, however, there is a particularly perplexing problem that requires a
comprehensive reading inventory.

Like teacher-constructed inventories, comprehensive IRIs are interpreted in two
stages. First, the teacher makes a judgment about the level of materials appropriate for
reading instruction and independent reading. Then she examines concerning print
skill, vocabulary knowledge, and comprehension in order to determine relative
strengths and weaknesses. Her recommendations concerning the appropriateness of
alternative materials are based on the first analysis; the establishment of instructional
priorities is based on the second.

Level of Materials

Instructional Reading Level.   The level of instructional materials you select depends on the nature of instruction. For example, the level of material that is sufficiently challenging to foster the further development of word identification skills may be higher than the level of materials appropriate for the development of silent comprehension strategies. The instructional level for word identification is based on the student's oral reading accuracy, whereas selecting instructional material for group-based comprehension instruction is based on the student's oral reading comprehension. For instruction that emphasizes the monitoring of silent reading comprehension, material selection is based on silent reading comprehension.

Independent Reading Level.   The silent reading task determines the highest level of materials the student can read silently with good comprehension. This will normally be her independent reading level. It represents the level at which she can recognize and identify words without pronouncing them aloud and at which she can concentrate on meaning without instructional support.

Areas of Strength and Need

Print Skill.   The listening task measures the strength of the student's comprehension skills unconfounded by her ability to process print. In general, if a student can, through listening, understand materials that are too difficult for her to read, you may infer that print skill difficulty interfered with her reading comprehension. A detailed analysis of oral reading of one or two passages at the instructional or borderline level (as outlined in Chapter 4) should confirm this inference and reveal the specific nature of the difficulty and appropriate instructional emphasis. Evidence from the word lists (flash and untimed), the oral reading, and the reading rate scores (silent versus oral) should all be considered in drawing conclusions about a student's print-processing skill.

Vocabulary Knowledge.   Information about a student's vocabulary knowledge comes from two sources. First, asking specific questions about vocabulary and phrases provides you with information on whether the student understands the key terms of a passage. Vocabulary knowledge performance on any of the three tasks (oral reading, silent reading, listening) that you administer at any one level should be combined to determine the percentage of terms the student defines or describes correctly at that level. Second, the listening comprehension score reflects a student's underlying vocabulary knowledge. A high score indicates good verbal development whereas a low score is ambiguous since it may reflect limited vocabulary knowledge, poor comprehension strategies, or both.

Comprehension.   Evaluation of reading comprehension begins with a comparison of oral versus silent reading comprehension. If the student's silent reading comprehension is a grade or more lower than his actual grade, this indicates that he has not yet internalized strategies to monitor comprehension during silent reading. He is able to comprehend but, because of limited practice or for some reason, has not learned to attend to meaning without the added support of pronouncing words aloud. Once a reader becomes proficient, it is not unusual for his silent comprehension to exceed his oral comprehension; a discrepancy in this direction is not viewed as a problem.

Next, compare the highest level of reading comprehension (oral or silent) with listening comprehension. A discrepancy here indicates that the student has print-processing problems. At the same time, the higher listening comprehension score suggests that once the print problems are solved, his reading comprehension will be similar to his listening comprehension.

Finally, analyze the student's responses to the reading comprehension questions. When you determine that his major problem is in comprehension, further explore his strategies, using the procedures described in Chapter 6.

CASE STUDIES

The cases described show how diagnosis using an informal reading inventory was undertaken by Laura. The case of Sara provides an overview of the diagnostic thinking involved in the interpretation of the inventory. The case of James goes into much greater detail, presenting passage-by-passage evidence from an informal reading inventory.

CASE 9.2: SARA

Sara is in the middle reading group in a second-grade class. The basal program being used in her class is the Houghton Mifflin series, and her group currently reads from the second-grade reader. Laura, the teacher we introduced at the beginning of the chapter, decided to take a closer look at Sara's reading because of her poor comprehension of stories in the reading group in contrast to her relatively good performance on seatwork assignments. Laura decided to administer the Basic Reading Inventory by Johns (Kendall/Hunt Publishing Co., 1993) to gain a better understanding of Sara's reading strategies. She administered the word lists and the oral reading passages on the first day and the silent reading and listening passages on the second day. Sara worked hard and was involved in these reading activities. The results from the administration of the word lists are shown in Figure 9.3.

PAUSE AND REFLECT.   What level of task should be administered first as an oral reading task?

| | Recognition Test | |
Level	Flash (%)	Untimed (%)
Preprimer	95	100
Primer	95	95
First	80	90
Second	70	95
Third	55	70
Fourth		
Fifth	.	
Sixth		
Seventh		
Eighth		
Ninth		

FIGURE 9.3   Summary of performance on the word recognition tests: Sara

PAUSE AND REFLECT.   As you read through the description of Laura's assessment of Sara, stop at each number in parentheses. Ask yourself the questions below:

Stop 1. What would you do next? Should testing be discontinued or proceed to the next level? Compare your choices to Laura's.

Stop 2. Given Sara's performance the previous day, on what level should Laura begin her reading?

Stop 3. On what level should Laura begin the listening task?

Stop 4. Given these results, what tentative conclusions can you draw about the nature of Sara's reading difficulty? What level of material should Sara be reading?

Administration of the oral reading passage should begin at the highest level at which the student obtained at least 90 percent correct on the flash administration of the word lists. Thus, for Sara, oral reading should begin on the primer-level passage. When given this passage, she made only one oral reading error and got all the comprehension questions correct. Laura then gave Sara the first-grade passage. On this she made 4 oral reading errors on the 100-word passage; and she missed 2½ out of 10 passage questions. (1)

According to the scoring guide of the test, up to 5 oral reading errors and up to 2½ comprehension errors represent the instructional level. Thus, oral reading should continue at the next higher level. On the second-grade passage, Sara made 8 oral reading errors (8 percent of the words) and missed 6 of the 10 questions. Because the comprehension score shows that the second-grade passage is in the frustration range for Sara, oral reading was discontinued.

The next day Laura had Sara read silently at the highest level on which she last demonstrated instruction-level oral reading and comprehension. (2) This was the first-grade level. Sara read this passage and knew the answers to all the passage questions.

Laura had her read the next more difficult passage, which was at the second-grade level. On this passage, Sara read with good comprehension, missing only 1 of 10 questions. Consequently, Laura asked her to read the third-grade-level passage. On this passage she knew the answers to only 3 of 10 questions. Since this performance indicated the material was at Sara's frustration level, Laura discontinued the silent reading and instead had her listen to a passage that Laura read aloud. (3)

The administration of the listening task should begin at the level above the highest level successfully comprehended when the child read either orally or silently. For Sara, this means the third-grade level. (Since Sara could comprehend at the second-grade level when reading silently, there was no need to test her listening comprehension at that level or below). When Laura read the third-grade passage aloud, Sara missed only 1 question. Thus, Laura proceeded to the next more difficult passage. On the fourth-grade passage, Sara missed only 3 of 10 questions. Therefore, Laura read the fifth-grade passage to her. On this passage Sara was able to answer only 4 of the 10 comprehension questions. The results from the inventory are summarized in Figure 9.4.

Scores in the vocabulary column are based on answers to passage questions. Since for each passage there were two questions about word meaning, it was possible to tabulate the total number of correct answers on these questions at each level. For example, on the second-grade level, the vocabulary knowledge

FIGURE 9.4 Summary of performance on IRI: Sara

INFORMAL READING INVENTORY SUMMARY

Test J. John's BRI Child Sara _____ Age 8 Grade 2 Date Dec.

| | Recognition Test | | Informal Reading Inventory | | | | | | | |
| | | | Oral Reading Task | | | Silent Reading | | | Vocabulary | |
Level	Flash (%)	Untimed (%)	Accuracy (%)	Compre-hension (%)	Rate (wpm)	Compre-hension (%)	Rate (wpm)	Listening Comprehen-sion (%)	N	%
Preprimer	95	100								
Primer	95	95	99	100	111				2/2	100
First	80	90	96	75	91	100	100		4/4	100
Second	70	95	92	40	67	90	77		3/4	75
Third	55	65				30	71	90	4/4	100
Fourth								70	1/2	50
Fifth								40	0/2	0
Sixth										
Seventh										
Eighth										
Ninth										

percentage was based on the results from the passage read orally and that read silently. On the third-grade level, it was based on the passage read silently and the one read to Sara by her teacher. (4)

Tentative Instructional Conclusions

Areas of Reading Difficulty. Sara's reading diagnosis is complicated in several ways. Because her reading profile does not conform to typical patterns, it is important for Laura to understand the nature of Sara's reading strengths and difficulties before specifying the levels of materials that she should read.

With respect to reading comprehension, Sara's silent reading comprehension is better than her oral comprehension by one grade level. It is not unusual for silent reading to be better than oral reading comprehension when a reader is proficient. But other evidence from the word lists and the oral reading accuracy indicates that Sara is not a proficient reader. For example, on second-grade-level materials, where her silent reading comprehension was good, she is in the borderline region for oral reading accuracy, and the flash presentation of second-grade words indicates some problems with sight recognition. The discrepancy between oral and silent comprehension would seem to indicate that Sara can compensate for poorly developed print skills when she reads silently, but when faced with the additional demands of oral reading, she is not able to process print accurately and also comprehend at the same time.

Sara's listening comprehension shows that she possesses the necessary background knowledge to understand third- and even fourth-grade-level material. The vocabulary knowledge evidence confirms her strength in this area, at least through the third-grade level. Laura concludes that Sara's difficulty in oral reading comprehension is not a reflection of poorly developed word knowledge.

It is in the area of print skill that Sara's difficulties appear to lie. The results for the word lists, for example, indicate that she had difficulty with immediate recognition of some first-grade-level words. While a single error (95 percent) may occur by chance, the four errors (80 percent) on the first-grade-level list suggest that some first-grade words are not familiar to her. Even when given more time, Sara was able to correct only two of the four errors. She had even more difficulty with the flash administration of the second-grade list, although here she was able to correct all but one of her errors with time. Laura concluded that Sara's performance on the third-grade list is at the frustration level.

In addition to her problems reading isolated words, Sara made four errors on the first-grade passage and eight on the second-grade passage (each 100 words in length), and her reading rate diminished from a relatively fast rate on the first-grade passage to a slow-average rate on the second-grade passage.

These results point to print processing as the area in need of further study. Laura should analyze the errors that Sara made on the second-grade passage and explore some of her responses to the passage and word lists. Given the discrepancy between her flash and untimed scores on both the first- and second-grade lists, Laura can conclude that Sara possesses knowledge about word identification but has not done enough easy reading to consolidate this knowledge and expand her sight vocabulary. Because of this lack of experience, she is able to read orally with a high degree of accuracy only when she focuses mainly on print and somewhat superficially on meaning. And as materials become more difficult (second grade), she is no longer able to avoid errors. When reading silently, primary focus on meaning and probably less stringent monitoring of print allow her to comprehend second-grade material. However, this strategy is no longer functional at the third-grade level, where she encounters many more print problems. Thus, on the basis of the evidence Laura concludes that Sara's major problem is in the area of print skill. Further, she speculates that the problem pertains to the consolidation and application of Sara's existing knowledge about print as well as to the development of new knowledge about word identification.

Levels of Materials. If taken alone, Sara's silent reading comprehension might suggest that her independent reading should be at the second-grade level. However, her difficulty processing print at this level suggests that it might not be the appropriate place to begin if Sara is to develop good reading strategies. Indeed, even first-grade-level material may pose print problems that require her undivided attention. The level of material that appears to pose no print skill or comprehension problems is the primer level. Although Sara may soon progress to first-grade-level materials, at the present time primer is her independent reading level and the level that will be effective in helping her consolidate good reading strategies.

To determine Sara's instructional level, Laura focuses on the area of her greatest need and then asks what level material would best serve to develop this area. She has tentatively concluded that Sara's main reading problem involves print skill. Not only does she need to consolidate and expand her sight vocabulary through extensive reading at her independent reading level (primer and then first grade), but she needs further to develop her word identification strategies. Whereas first-grade materials may be appropriate for instructional purposes, second-grade materials may be too difficult. Following further study of her print-processing strategies (oral reading analysis for the second-grade passage and exploring responses), Laura should examine her response to second-grade-level materials when instruction is specially designed to prepare her for the reading. If Sara shows better print strategies with instructional preparation, it is appropriate to keep her with her present reading group, which is working with second-grade material, and to offer appropriate instructional support that will further develop Sara's word identification skills and permit her to focus on comprehension.

Sara's performance on the third-grade-level passage indicates that this is her frustration level. Even though she is able to understand materials at this level when they are read to her, her print-processing problems are so great that she cannot comprehend them when she is reading.

CASE 9.3: JAMES

James is a freshman in high school and is in an intensive reading program. He is ranked 31st among 50 disabled readers. He was referred by Laura to the class on the basis of teacher recommendations and diagnostic reading test results. On the most recent standardized reading test, he scored a grade equivalent of 5.3 in comprehension and 6.8 in vocabulary. These scores reflect an average gain of 2.5 grade equivalents over the prior year's test. This achievement is a result of his desire to improve his reading so that he might go to college. Because of his extremely high motivation, Laura asked him if he would like to have an inventory made of his reading skills so that she could better advise him as to how he might improve his reading even further. He agreed that this would be of interest to him.

During the testing with the Analytical Reading Inventory by Woods and Moe (Charles E. Merrill, 1989), James was pleasant and responsive. Between passages he talked about the books he likes to read, the movies he has seen, and one of his favorite authors, Edgar Allan Poe.

Administration

First James read all the word recognition lists. He achieved 90 percent accuracy on flash administration at the fifth-grade level but 95 percent at the sixth-grade level (the highest level list). He then read the sixth-grade passage orally, followed by the passages for grades 7 through 9. Next he read the seventh-grade passage silently. Laura selected this level because it corresponded to the highest oral reading passage for which his comprehension score was at the instructional level. Because of his low comprehension on this passage, he next read the sixth- and then the fifth-grade passages silently. Finally, he was administered the eighth-grade listening passage, on which he correctly answered seven out of eight questions. Although James scored 81 percent on the next higher passage (grade 9), Laura discontinued the testing because there are no higher level passages on this IRI. (The IRI records from James's performance are shown in Appendix C.)

Analysis and Further Exploration

The first step in the analysis is for Laura to examine the test records and score them (see Appendix C). On the word lists it is necessary to determine the percentage of words correctly recognized for the flash and the untimed administrations.

The next step is to score the passages. It is useful for Laura to keep the passages in the order in which they were administered and to identify them as "oral," "silent," or "listening." For orally read passages, the number of errors is recorded line by line and then the total determined. The total number of errors in relation to the total number of words read and the percentage of errors are then recorded following the passage. On the sixth-grade passage (see Appendix C) James made 3 percent errors and thus read with 97 percent accuracy. In this example, it would also be important to note that the problems were concentrated in the first three sentences, with few occurring thereafter.

Next, Laura scored the comprehension questions using the expected answers as a guide. When ambiguous responses occur, it is important to ask the student to "explain further" during the administration of the test so that credit may be given if the information has been comprehended. The total number of questions answered correctly out of the total asked and the corresponding percentage figure were recorded on the passage next to the number of oral reading errors. For example, as shown for the Level 6 passage, James correctly answered eight out of eight questions, for 100 percent comprehension.

Finally, Laura determined James's rate of reading. For example, James read the Level 6 passage in 1 minute and 36 seconds, which is equivalent to 96 seconds or 1.6 minutes (96 divided by 60). Because the passage is 192 words in length, 192 is divided by 1.6 to yield a reading rate of 120 words per minute. This information was recorded next to the comprehension percentage score.

After all the orally read passages had been scored, Laura determined comprehension and rate scores for the silently read passages. These scores were also recorded following the passage. The comprehension of the passages administered as listening tasks were then scored and recorded. The final step was to transfer all accuracy percentages, comprehension percentages, and reading rates to the summary sheet, as shown in Figure 9.5.

Once the results had been summarized, the next step was to consider each area of James's reading to determine whether any of his responses should be explored further. The results pertaining to oral reading accuracy, reading rate, and isolated word recognition accuracy suggest that James is experiencing some difficulty with word identification. The Level 7 passage was selected for further analysis, and further exploration was undertaken to explore his recognition of sight words and content words presented in isolation.

Laura's comparison of James's oral reading comprehension with silent reading comprehension suggests a problem in silent reading. Since James is able to comprehend, but not without the support of oral reinforcement, the interactive and monitorial strategies described in Chapter 6 represent appropriate instructional approaches.

FIGURE 9.5 Summary of performance on IRI: James

INFORMAL READING INVENTORY SUMMARY

Test __Woods – Moe__ Child __James_____ Age __14__ Grade __9__ Date __March__

| Level | Recognition Test | | Information Reading Inventory | | | | | | |
| | Flash (%) | Untimed (%) | Oral Reading Task | | | Silent Reading | | Listening Compre-hension (%) | Vocabulary (%) |
			Accuracy (%)	Compre-hension (%)	Rate (wpm)	Compre-hension (%)	Rate (wpm)		
Primer	100	100							
First	100	100							
Second	100	100							
Third	95	100							
Fourth	95	100							
Fifth	90	100				100	109		100
Sixth	95	100	97	100	120	81	97		100
Seventh			95	88	105	56	111		25
Eighth			92	63	91			88	50
Ninth			93	25	87			81	25

The results from the listening task suggest that James's vocabulary knowledge is sufficiently well developed for the comprehension of ninth-grade material. However, the vocabulary-related comprehension questions suggest otherwise. These results, summarized in Figure 9.5, show that many terms from the seventh-grade level and up are unknown to him. Thus, exploration of the Level 7 content words needs to focus on word meaning as well as recognition.

The analysis of miscues made on the seventh-grade-level passage and exploration based on this analysis are shown in Figure 9.6. The results show that James's knowledge of sight words and word identification is strong but that his application of this knowledge is inconsistent. Further exploration of his knowledge of word meaning reveals inconsistent understanding of vocabulary items (for example, he knew the meanings of such words as *terrifying, miserable, wretched,* and *vaguely* but he did not know the meaning of *independent* and *belligerent*).

Interpretation

Print Skill. Laura's analysis and exploration based on the seventh-grade passage reveal that James possesses considerable knowledge about phonic and structural analysis and that his basic sight vocabulary is well developed. Whether the larger stock of sight words that he recognizes instantaneously is grade appropriate cannot be determined from the evidence because lists beyond the sixth-grade level are not included in the text. But the fact that he experienced some difficulty with the flash presentation beginning at the third-grade level suggests that his broader sight recognition vocabulary is not as large as it should be. Indeed, some of the difficulty he experienced during passage reading may have been based on the unfamiliarity of many words that are typically recognized by students his age.

Though James is able to apply his knowledge about print effectively when he is not under the time pressure of contextual oral reading or flash presentation, he does not do so easily when he *is* under pressure. If he were more proficient reading silently than orally, these difficulties might be attributed to nervousness and be overlooked. However, because his comprehension is less adequate during silent than oral reading, Laura infers that his silent print-processing strategies are no more efficient, and probably less efficient, than his oral reading strategies.

Further exploration indicates that James does not need special instruction to learn about print but, rather, needs considerable practice with easy materials in order to consolidate and apply what he already knows. His slow reading rate reflects his current difficulty in application and should improve once he does more reading; if his reading rate does not improve spontaneously, then it may need to be the focus of special instructional intervention.

However, James's print skill difficulties may not simply be a function of too little practice. Recently, James has seen several eye doctors because of blurred vision. The conclusion from the examination is that the blurred vision stems from eyestrain and that James must learn to relax while reading. Glasses were not recommended. The eyestrain may actually be the result of his difficulty in reading print fluently rather than the cause, but in any case, James's visual difficulties should be kept in mind.

ORAL READING ANALYSIS

Name _James_ Grade _9_ Date _March_

Book/Page _IRI Woods Moe_ Level _7_

A. Difficulty

_13_ / _262_ _95_ % Correct

Level: Independent (Instructional)
Borderline   Frustration

B. Word Learning: Sight Word Errors

Printed Word	Oral Response	Further Exploration
run	return	✓
did	had ⓒ	✓
had	[omitted]	✓
from	[omitted]	✓
a	[omitted] ⓒ	✓
the	[insertion]	✓

Evaluation

Sight words are known when presented in isolation. Given the number of such errors, James should be encouraged to do more easy reading to consolidate his sight recognition.

C. Word Identification: Content Word Errors

Printed Word	Oral Response	Further Exploration
turn	to ⓒ	✓
friend	friends	✓
terrifying	terrific ⓒ	✓
miserable	miserably ⓒ	✓
wretched	wretcher ⓒ	✓
picnic	band ⓒ	✓
vaguely	vă|vā-goly ⓒ	✓

Evaluation

Ability to correct miscues indicates strong knowledge of phonics and structural analysis. Systematic syllable-by-syllable word attack, but slowness of process indicates little reading practice.

D. Integration–Fluency

Integration: Good use of content — both graphic cues and context serve as a basis for correction.

Fluency: Rate _262_ / _2.5_ = _105_ Evaluation _Below norms for 7th gr._
Phrasing _Many repetitions and pauses for word identification and perhaps comprehension._

FIGURE 9.6 Analysis of oral reading responses, Level 7: James

Vocabulary Knowledge. James's listening comprehension is good at the ninth-grade level (81 percent comprehension). The passage, about Pygmies, develops a topic with which James is unfamiliar and contains many difficult words (e.g., *equatorial, Ituri Forest, Zaire, contagious, blasphemy*). It would seem that when James is not faced with the task of print skill, he may be better able to compensate for not knowing the meaning of some key terms. His listening comprehension is better than might be expected on the basis of his knowledge of specific terms.

Comprehension. James's retelling of selected passages is comprehensive: He reported the sequence of events accurately and related many details. While his comprehension following oral reading is adequate through the seventh-grade level and borderline at the eighth-grade level, his silent reading comprehension is near frustration at the seventh-grade level. These results indicate that he will have considerable difficulty reading grade-appropriate (i.e., ninth-grade) materials, particularly when he is reading silently. Within the area of comprehension, Laura decided that silent reading should be the focus of instruction for James.

Summary/Integration. On the basis of the listening test results, Laura determined that James should be able to read ninth-grade-level materials with comprehension. Currently, however, he experiences problems with eighth-grade materials and even seventh-grade material that he reads silently. Two separate problems contribute to his reading comprehension difficulties. First, his print-processing strategies are not adequately developed and thus he reads slowly with many repetitions and corrections of miscues. Second, his knowledge of key terms is limited. While he is able to compensate for this limited knowledge when materials are read to him, when he is faced with print-processing problems as well, his comprehension fails. The fact that his comprehension failure is more severe under silent reading conditions suggests that in addition to developing his vocabulary and refining his print-processing strategies, he must learn to monitor his comprehension during silent reading.

Instructional Plan

Materials. Laura found that materials above the seventh-grade level yielded borderline or poor comprehension results on the IRI. With instructional preparation (discussion of the meaning and pronunciation of key vocabulary), James should be able to comprehend course materials that he reads at the seventh-grade level and perhaps at the eighth-grade level when topics are familiar.

Special reading instruction should focus on three areas: consolidation of print-processing skill, development of vocabulary, and development of silent reading comprehension. For the first, the material should be easy for James when he reads silently. Thus, fifth- (and somewhat later, sixth-) grade materials should be used. The selections should be about topics of high interest to James. Vocabulary development may be undertaken along with content area instruction and should reinforce the concepts being presented in his course materials. He should begin silent reading of short passages of sixth-grade-level material followed by comprehension questions, and, as rapidly as comprehension warrants, proceed to seventh- and then eighth-grade-level passages.

Instructional Priorities. Laura advised James's content area teachers that James will have difficulty reading materials independently above the sixth-grade level but that if they provide appropriate instructional support, including the discussion of the meaning and pronunciation of key terms, James can cope with seventh- and perhaps even eighth-grade-level materials.

James also needs help in improving his vocabulary. He should be taught how to prepare vocabulary cards for words from his courses that are unfamiliar and how to review and use these words orally. If possible, he should be paired with another student who could profit from vocabulary instruction so that they can discuss words together.

For James, the development of print-processing skills will be a major priority. James needs to learn to apply his good knowledge efficiently and to enlarge the set of words that he recognizes instantaneously. His fluency can best be developed by extensive reading of easy and highly interesting materials. These materials should initially be at the fifth-grade level although James may soon progress to more difficult material. In conjunction with this reading, James should be taught a system for recording and evaluating his reading rate. Charts should be kept of the number of pages read to provide a tangible record of his accomplishments.

Finally, Laura recommended that James be taught study strategies, such as those described in Chapter 6, for monitoring his comprehension during silent reading. It is important that the passages for this purpose be limited to several pages at most and be followed by comprehension questions so that James can have immediate feedback on the effectiveness of his comprehension strategies.

SUMMARY

The standardized informal reading inventory has many advantages over a diagnosis based on oral reading of a single passage. It allows for the comparison of silent and oral reading and for an assessment of fluency and word recognition proficiency at various levels of difficulty. These comparisons make it possible for you to determine more precisely the level of materials that a student should read under various conditions. Perhaps its greatest strength lies in the assessment of listening comprehension, which allows a more definitive conclusion to be drawn regarding the influence of word recognition on a student's comprehension. However, many of these comparisons are available to you on a more informal basis. For instance, you will note that many students have greater difficulty with silent than oral reading. What is important is that you understand the significance of these comparisons in relation to the kinds of problems students encounter in becoming proficient readers.

TRY IT OUT

1. Collect as many commercial informal reading inventories as possible. Working in a group or with a partner, use the evaluation criteria presented in this chapter to select those that you think might be useful to you. Add them to Table 9.1 and update with a column of personal comments.

2. **For Your Teaching Portfolio:** Use a commercial informal reading inventory to assess a child in your class. Tape-record the assessment and share with a classmate. Compare and contrast your procedures and conclusions about instruction. List shared questions or problems and how you resolved them.

3. **Student Portfolio Ideas:** Share your assessment with the student and discuss findings. Have students reflect, in writing, on your assessment and plans or steps *they* might take to improve performance.

FOR FURTHER READING

Johns, J. L. (1993). *Informal reading inventories: Annotated reference guide.* DeKalb, IL: Communitech International Corp.
Describes the characteristics and coverage of many commercial IRIs.

Johnson, M. S., Kress, R. A., & Pikulski, J. J. (1987). *Informal reading inventories.* Newark, DE: International Reading Association.
A standard overview of the theoretical and historical development of the IRI process.

Pikulski, J. J., & Shanahan, T. (1982). *Approaches to the informal evaluation of reading.* Newark, DE: International Reading Association.
Includes many excellent and well written ideas and examples for using IRIs in assessment.

chapter 10

Decision Making: Organizing, Using, and Communicating Assessment Information

CHAPTER GOALS FOR THE READER

To understand the nature and classroom uses of standardized tests

To understand the nature and uses of class and student portfolios

To develop a framework for using assessment information in forming flexible, need-based groups, selecting materials, and developing appropriate instructional strategies

To develop an understanding of how to share information with parents, students, and specialists.

CLASSROOM VIGNETTE: ASSESSMENT IN DIANE'S CLASSROOM

Diane is an experienced teacher recently reassigned to fourth grade in an inner-city school. Her classroom contains fourth-grade and third-grade basal readers and a small library of trade books on many levels. Many of her students are new to the school and the records on some of them are sketchy, although these contain for most of them a standardized test score as well as their third-grade reading group placement. Diane also has a student teacher and wants to help him frame some basic questions for starting the school year. Together they list their questions:

What kinds of information can help us get started?

How can we best interpret and use standardized test data?

How should we develop our portfolio records?

On what basis should we organize students for instruction, select appropriate materials, and provide appropriate instruction?

About what should we be communicating with students, parents, and specialists?

These are questions related to basic classroom decisions that must be made to get instruction under way at the start of a new school year.

CHAPTER OVERVIEW

In this final chapter we consider how the model for curriculum-based assessment informs and is informed by the testing program of the school; instructional decisions made at the beginning of the school year; and communication with parents, students, and specialists. Because standardized reading tests are particularly useful to the classroom teacher for making decisions at the beginning of the school year, and because they are routinely administered in most schools, we believe teachers should be knowledgeable about them. In addition, various portfolio systems provide a means of organizing information that will inform instructional decision making and communication with others.

The first section of this chapter considers the kinds of standardized tests available, characterizes their strengths and limitations, and discusses how to evaluate and interpret results from them. The second section describes two forms of portfolio assessment—class portfolios and student portfolios—that are useful in organizing information about student progress. The third section discusses strategies for (1) assessing students' individual reading needs at the beginning of the school year in order to form initial pairs, teams, or groups for instruction, (2) selecting appropriate materials, and (3) developing appropriate instruction. The fourth section describes procedures for communicating with students, parents, and professionals about student needs and progress.

CHAPTER OUTLINE

Organizing Assessment Information
   Understanding Standardized Tests
   Problems with Standardized Tests
   Case 10.1: Interpreting Standardized Test Information

Portfolios
   Building a Class Portfolio
   Building Student Portfolios

Using Information
   Organizing Students for Instruction

ORGANIZING ASSESSMENT INFORMATION

We strongly believe that for you to obtain information that is directly relevant to planning instruction for your students, you must learn to undertake curriculum-based assessment. That is, you must learn to observe and interpret oral reading responses and to construct vocabulary and comprehension questions and interpret students' responses to them, ideally with existing materials and instructional tasks. Such evidence provides a valid basis for shaping instruction to better meet the needs of your students.

When such observation is conducted over time, it provides a reliable basis for planning instruction. However, if this information is gained through interaction with students over a period of time, how can you make good decisions about grouping and instruction at the beginning of the school year? Some teachers undertake reading assessment of all their students at the beginning of the school year, using such instruments as informal reading inventories, oral reading of selected passages, word lists, and phonics inventories. Others prefer to rely on recommendations of teachers from the prior year. Some use the results from standardized tests. Still others wish to see none of this evidence, relying on the information they derive from their interaction with students during the first weeks of instruction.

Is there a "right" way? Each of the solutions that are traditionally followed has advantages and limitations. The first approach, assessing all students at the beginning of the school year, has the advantage of providing a wealth of information about students' reading, but there are also several disadvantages. The evidence is derived from specially contrived testing situations, which are not closely related to instructional tasks. Further, some of the evidence gathered early in the school year may not be valid or accurate, because students at that time are more interested in solving other problems such as figuring out what their teacher is like and getting acquainted with other students in the class. Finally, because individual testing takes an enormous amount of time during school hours, the students not being tested must undertake much work without the direct supervision of the teacher.

The second approach, relying on the recommendations of the previous year's teachers, also has several advantages and disadvantages. Information concerning students' reading levels at the finish of the school year is useful, particularly for students in the primary grades. However, successful progress in the primary grades, which is heavily dependent on the development of print skills, may not be closely related to students' later progress in the middle and upper grades, which is highly dependent on background knowledge and comprehension proficiency. Thus, for teachers to perpetuate the reading group structure of the previous year may hinder the progress of students who had difficulty learning print skills but who are good comprehenders. Further, there can be changes in reading proficiency over the summer, as well as changes in the instructional materials and approach from one year to the next. Thus, while we believe that the reading level from the prior year should be considered, it should not be the only information used.

Moreover, some teachers use the results from standardized reading tests, administered the prior year or at the beginning of the current year, as the basis for grouping and planning instruction. This approach has the advantage of being efficient in that students are usually tested for less than an hour or two and tests are easily scored. At the same time, the tests yield relatively little evidence: single scores in such areas as word recognition, vocabulary, comprehension, and/or reading rate. Careful interpretation of patterns of test results, however, can indicate areas of a student's reading that need further exploration.

Finally, some teachers prefer not to use existing information from standardized tests and prior teachers, but instead wish to gather information during instruction that enables them to learn more about their students' reading. Indeed, this book has emphasized such strategies. We believe that such an approach is most effective when teachers have developed observational and interpretive skill and work within a model of reading that serves to guide the diagnosis. We do not agree, however, that information from standardized tests and other teachers must distort your own judgment. We believe that it is possible for you to treat standardized test results and teacher reports as additional sources of information, important but not definitive. However, the results from standardized measures should not be allowed to override your conclusions based on curriculum-based measures of reading.

We recommend an approach in which you are the central decision maker who considers information from several different sources. At the beginning of the school year, information from standardized tests, teacher recommendations, and student records will tend to be more important than later in the year, when you have had the opportunity to collect information on an ongoing basis during instruction. We do not recommend massive testing of individuals at the beginning of the school year with such measures as informal reading tests or other informal measures. Individual testing should be necessary for only a few students who are experiencing extreme difficulty or who are particularly perplexing to you. Time during the beginning weeks of school should be devoted to instruction rather than assessment, though good instruction is always diagnostic to a certain degree.

Given this perspective, we believe it is important for you to be familiar with the characteristics of standardized tests and to understand both the advantages and limitations of this form of assessment information. Thus, in this section, we first consider the nature of standardized tests: the kinds of tests there are, their problems, and how to use information from them at the beginning of the school year. As the year progresses and as you have the opportunity to observe the reading and writing of your students, standardized test information becomes much less important. But as you gather information on your students, you need to develop systems for organizing this information. We recommend two procedures: a class portfolio in which you gather the information on your students, and student portfolios, kept by each student in your class, containing samples of their reading and writing. In this section, we describe these class and student portfolios, illustrating them by showing you the ones that Diane and her students developed.

Understanding Standardized Tests

In this book we have proposed a framework for curriculum-based assessment in which teachers use instructional materials and curriculum tasks to structure classroom diagnosis. The term *testing*, however, refers to a much larger realm of school assessment. In this section we describe the types of formal measures with which you must be familiar, explain some concepts basic to these measures, and give examples of how you might adapt more formalized assessment instruments to provide instructional information.

Formal measures are basically of two types: criterion-referenced and norm-referenced, the latter frequently referred to as "standardized" tests. It is important to understand the ways in which these two types of tests differ.

Criterion-Referenced Tests. The goal of **criterion-referenced tests** is to compare a particular student's performance with mastery goals set by a curriculum program, or predetermined body of knowledge. These instruments provide qualitative information on the skills and knowledge considered basic for progressing in a particular curriculum. For example, a curriculum goal might be that students should be able to divide compound words into their constituents. Figure 10.1 shows a criterion-referenced test item designed to assess achievement of this goal.

FIGURE 10.1   Criterion-referenced test item: Division of compound words

Goal: Students will divide compound words into their constituent words.

Direction: Give each student a duplicated sheet with the following words.

Say: These words are all made up of two or more words. Draw a line between the words that make up the compound.

Example: mail/man

Items:

truckload	railroad
dishpan	baseball
fireman	joystick

Along with the curricular goal, criterion-referenced tests (CRT) frequently indicate a performance standard to be met. While 70 to 80 percent is a common mastery standard, criteria vary by age of student and by item being tested. For example, an appropriate mastery level for naming the letters of the alphabet for first graders might be 100 percent. Though this type of testing is very much like teacher-created informal testing, many CRTs are part of larger, purchasable instruction and management systems such as the Wisconsin Design (Otto & Askov, 1972) or those provided by basal programs.

You must address several issues when you use criterion-referenced measures for either assessment or placement. Questions to ask include the following:

1. Are the objectives related to essential skills, strategies, and knowledge? Frequently the items most essential to the reading task are the most difficult to conceptualize as discrete objectives, and the items most easily tested may not be essential for effective reading.
2. Is the performance required a real measure of the goal? Does circling a digraph on a worksheet, for example, measure how well a student can use graphophonic knowledge of that cluster for reading or is it just an isolated measure? How genuine is the reading in the testing situation?
3. Is the criterion level appropriate for the age and ability of the student?

All of these relate to the larger issues of reliability and validity, which we discuss later in this section. In sum, CRTs can provide specific information about the particular skills of a particular student. However, in their use you must be sure that you are not just assessing one-time mastery of peripheral behaviors but rather focusing on knowledge, skills, and strategies important to the reading act.

Norm-Referenced Tests. The purpose of **norm-referenced tests** is to allow the evaluator to compare the performance of a student or group of students to a larger group for the purpose of identifying potential problems or for assessing group achievement. Most norm-referenced tests are group tests, but a small number are individually administered both for achievement estimates (e.g., the Peabody Individual Achievement Test) or for diagnostic purposes (e.g., Woodcock Reading Mastery Test, Gilmore Oral Reading Test). Most group reading tests are called "survey" tests and give an overview of global reading performance. Diagnostic tests are designed to give a profile of student strengths and weaknesses.

A standardized test is an *objective, normed* measure of a *sample* of behavior. Let's look at each of these key words to try to understand some basic concepts about this type of test.

Objective. When we say a friend is objective in deciding arguments, we mean that that person treats everyone the same way and does not show favoritism. The same sense of the term applies to *objective* in standardized tests. In order to treat each test taker alike, these tests are designed with a set of answers from which test takers select so that the answers can be scored impartially. Time limits, specific directions for explaining and administering the test, and answer sheets all help ensure that the test taking, answering, and scoring process is as much alike as possible for all students.

Normed. Tests that are **normed** are developed and tested on a large group of diverse students so that the test designers are able to calculate the average performance of many students in differing age and geographic groups. Tests can have *nationwide* norms, norms that reflect a broad spectrum of geographic and ethnic diversity, or they can provide *local* norms so that the user can compare the performance of a particular group of students with closely matched peers, such as, for example, rural midwestern students.

Normed scores are used to place a value on the *raw* score (the number right), which, since there is no standard for comparison, cannot by itself tell the teacher how well a group has performed. For example, a raw score of 24 out of 26 might seem good. However, it becomes very clear that such a score is not good when you know the task is naming the letters of the alphabet and the test taker is applying for graduate school.

The most common normed scores are stanines, percentile scores, and grade-equivalent scores. The word **stanine** is a contraction of standard-nine, because stanines represent divisions of the normal curve divided into nine equal or standard parts. Stanines place students in a broad performance band and allow comparisons across tests, with stanines 4 to 6 considered average, 5 being the mean; stanines 1 to 3 are below average, and stanines 7 to 9 are above average.

Percentiles, better called percentile ranks, are often confusing for teachers and parents, who confuse them with percentages, indicators of the number of items correct. Ranging from 1 to 99, **percentile rank** indicates a student's relative position in the norming group. For example, a score of 60th percentile means a student did better than 60 percent of the other students taking the test; it does not mean that the student scored only 60 percent correct.

Grade scores indicate a level of achievement in terms of years and months in school; for example, 6.3 would indicate an average level of performance for a sixth grader in the third month of school. Such scores assume great importance because grade organization is most familiar to parents, children, and teachers. There are some very significant problems in the use of grade scores, however.

The first of these is the question of growth across the school years. Consider the observable changes in reading from the beginning of first grade to the beginning of second grade. Normally these are significant changes in what we would call reading performance. Then imagine the change from junior to senior year of high school. These changes would be harder to detect and harder to describe. A year's growth at earlier levels may not indicate the same amount of change as at later levels, and using grade scores to discuss growth can have similar problems of equivalence.

A second problem is typified by interpreting a high score gained by a young child. For example, a good second-grade reader may score 4.6 on a standardized test, but when placed on fourth-grade materials, the child is unable to function. Why? It is important to remember that the score of 4.6 was obtained on a test meant for second graders. That indicates that the able second grader did as well as a fourth grader in the sixth month of school would do *on second grade material*. Both the reporting and interpreting of grade scores require care.

Sample.   When you have your blood tested, the technicians and doctor don't require that all the blood be removed from your body and analyzed. Rather, they work with a sample that they assume represents that quantity. In the same way, reading tests take a short **sample** of what you do and extrapolate to a larger estimate of your performance. Like a medical test, there are two important requirements: that this test be reliable and that it be valid.

Reliability.   **Reliability** refers to the degree of consistency a test has. If a particular blood-testing technique is correct 9 times out of 10, it is fairly reliable; tests must also be reliable in the way they rank students who take them. Tests are also checked for consistency of items across the test and for equivalency of different forms. Every test manual describes one or more ways in which reliability is estimated, and expresses this reliability as a decimal, a coefficient of reliability; the closer to 1.0 a coefficient of reliability is, the more consistent a test is.

Along with a high reliability, look for a low **standard error of measurement (SEM).** This figure indicates how accurate given scores on a test are and emphasizes that no score is absolute, that each is subject to a certain degree of error. For example, with a raw score SEM of 2 points, a child whose obtained raw score is 43 can be estimated to have an actual raw score between 41 and 45 with about 70 percent surety. If we double the value of the standard error of measurement to 4, we can be 90 percent sure that the score is between 39 and 47. The smaller the standard error of measurement, the more likely that the child's obtained test score and actual score are close together. SEM can also be useful in helping report scores as ranges, often with grade-level variations of .3 to .6 a year, rather than an absolute, to give parents and others a better picture of the student's performance.

Reliability alone, however, is not sufficient to make a test good. Consider our initial metaphor of a blood test. A blood test can give us the same data each time and be highly reliable. Yet it is useless as a test for vision since it has no real connection with that trait.

Validity.   A test is **valid** when it measures what it is intended to measure. For a reading test to be valid, it must measure those things that we think are important to reading. For example, a test that assesses only decoding might better be called a decoding test than a reading test, since no comprehension is involved. Validity is assessed by evaluating the content of the test and comparing it with one's own definition of or curriculum for reading. Frequently tests are deemed valid by testimony of experts or by a comparison of their content with that of other, more established tests. Nothing substitutes, however, for examining and taking a test oneself.

PAUSE AND REFLECT.   Before reading the next section, "Problems with Standardized Tests," reflect on your own test-taking history. What problems have you experienced with standardized tests? What problems have you encountered in classrooms? List and compare with those that follow.

Problems with Standardized Tests

Standardized tests are useful for gathering large-scale statistics but may often be misleading when used for analyzing a particular student. In addition to the difficulties inherent in reliability, error of measurement, and reporting, teachers are normally aware of other problems, a few of which we discuss here.

High Floor Problem.   You may have received a new student into your class with records suggesting that he has a low but measurable reading level, yet he is unable to read at the primer level. How is it that a nonreader can receive a score, one that goes up each time he or she is tested? The answer lies in the way increasing grade forms of tests are designed. It is almost impossible for any student to receive a zero raw score. By chance a few of the answer marks will find the right space, giving the students the lowest possible score on the test. While this score will remain in stanine 1 over the years, the lowest grade possible becomes *higher* on each higher level of a test. Therefore, a student who can't read gets a score, one that goes up each year.

Test–Question Independence.   In the 1970s, Tuinman (1974) did some interesting research on test construction. He allowed students to see the comprehension questions on some standardized tests without having read the passages to which the questions referred. Then they were asked to answer the questions as well as they could. Tuinman found that many questions on tests were test independent, that is, they tested a student's knowledge and reasoning rather than the reading of the passage. For example, a question, "What did the monkey eat?" is very likely to elicit the answer "bananas" regardless of whether you have read the selection. Since the publication of Tuinman's work, test questions have undergone more stringent evaluation but it is still possible for students with specific prior knowledge to answer from their knowledge base rather than from their reading of material.

Task Validity.   The formats of most standardized reading tests have received major criticism. The passages are generally short and unrelated, switching from narrative to exposition, from topic to topic. Further, unlike real-life comprehension tasks, test tasks look for one right answer. Developments in state-based assessment (Valencia & Pearson, 1986; Wixson, Peters, Weber, & Roeber, 1987) have recognized these as serious difficulties. The current decade is an interesting one as test designers search for more valid assessment devices.

Specific Sources of Test Information.   *The Mental Measurement Yearbooks* provide an invaluable aid to the practitioner. Begun by Oscar Buros in 1938, the yearbooks are issued and revised periodically and contain reviews on most standardized instruments. Their index volumes, *Tests in Print I and II* (Buros, 1961, 1974), can be used to locate initial and subsequent surveys of particular tests. Separate volumes, *Reading Tests and Reviews* (Buros, 1968, 1975, 1978) are excerpted from the yearbooks. In addition, professional journals such as the *American Psychologist, Journal of Educational Measurement, Psychological Bulletin, The Reading Teacher,* and *The Journal of Reading* contain regular test reviews.

CASE 10.1: INTERPRETING STANDARDIZED TEST INFORMATION

Teachers typically receive standardized test results as part of the portfolio of information for an incoming class. The major purpose of such assessment is for schoolwide or districtwide assessment; however, these results can also provide a starting point for a teacher to get to know a new class and can serve as a screening instrument for the initial formation of instructional groups.

Let's return to Diane's class, introduced at the beginning of this chapter, to understand how teachers can use the information from standardized tests to start their instructional planning at the start of the school year. Diane's goal for the first month of school is to begin learning the reading and writing strengths of her students and the areas in which they need support. She and her assistant initially look over the test scores shown in Figure 10.2. This information may help them form questions about the reading of certain children that can be answered through informal conversations with them and observation of their reading and writing during instruction.

FIGURE 10.2 Standardized test results: Fourth grade/tested at 3.9

Student	Reading Vocabulary	Reading Comprehension	Third-Grade Group
Ann	3.4	3.7	L
Candy	4.1	3.8	M
Carol	3.0	4.3	L
Connie	4.3	4.0	M
Cornelia	4.1	3.9	H
Daniel	4.1	3.8	H
David	4.0	4.3	M
Denise	4.5	4.0	H
Donald	4.8	3.7	H
Dorothy	4.3	5.1	M
Dottie	3.1	3.1	L
Gary	3.4	3.9	M
Gordon	3.7	3.0	M
Grace	3.5	3.0	H
Greta	4.4	3.9	H
Jean	2.9	2.0	M
Jeff	5.7	4.9	H
John	3.1	2.8	L
Kay	4.3	4.0	H
Lois	3.4	3.3	M
Lottie	2.7	1.8	L
Tia	4.5	3.9	H
Walter	1.9	2.2	L
Wanda	2.2	2.7	L

PAUSE AND REFLECT.   Look at the vocabulary and comprehension scores of the students listed in Figure 10.2. Which children raise questions in your mind, suggesting that you should learn more about them? What are your questions? Are the differences you see between the vocabulary and comprehension scores significant? Consider the basal group placement of the students when they were in third grade. How does this information lead you to modify some of your tentative conclusions? What further information would you want to obtain?

Typically, in examining test scores, you first see that some children receive low scores and others high scores relative to their peers. Remember that these scores are only estimates and that the children's true levels of performance may be somewhat higher or lower. Diane and her assistant are particularly concerned about Lottie because of her low comprehension score. In addition, they want to observe the reading of Dottie, Grace, Jean, John, Walter, and Wanda. They note the relatively high scores of Dorothy and Jeff and want to observe how independent they are when they do their class work. Finally, they note the high discrepancy between vocabulary and comprehension scores for Carol, Donald, and Dorothy.

When they consider the third-grade group placement, they are puzzled by Carol's placement in the low group. Further, the low group placement of Ann surprises them. On the other hand, two of the children they are concerned about, Grace and Jean, were in the high and middle groups last year—so perhaps, the test scores are not valid.

Obviously, Diane cannot draw conclusions solely on the basis of this information. It does, however, raise some questions and suggest which children may need special support and more challenging work.

PORTFOLIOS

Building a Class Portfolio

This section on building a class portfolio may be among the most important in the book, for if you do not find a way to record and organize the information and insights you develop, they will be of limited use to you. A class portfolio differs from a teacher portfolio: In the first, you organize your reflections about the students in your class; in the second, you gather samples and reflections about your own life as a professional.

How should you go about developing a system to organize the knowledge you are developing about your students? There are many different systems; although we describe some, the system you develop may turn out to be a unique hybrid.

There are several steps you should use as guidelines in developing a class portfolio. These include specifying your goals in the areas of reading and writing, thinking about the activities in your class that may yield valuable information, selecting the type of information you want to include in the class portfolio, determining the physical form of the portfolio, and finally, making sense of your portfolio records.

Specifying Your Goals.   Your goals in the areas of reading and writing will directly reflect the prior learning of your students. If you are teaching first grade, your goals will differ somewhat from those of a sixth-grade teacher. Further, the children in your class will differ from each other and your goals must reflect these developmental differences. In Diane's case, for example, the goals she will set for Walter will differ considerably from those for Dorothy and Jeff.

Yet, there is general learning in the area of literacy that will apply to all children: knowledge of print, reading fluency, vocabulary development, comprehension strategies, love of reading, knowledge of types of writing (narrative and nonfiction), writing fluency, and ability to organize ideas. The Upper Arlington City Schools include among their assessment guidelines for teachers four main categories that capture many of these areas. Their guide is shown in Figure 10.3.

From the large set of possible goals, you must select the subset (from 4 to 10) that you will evaluate during the year. Some teachers prefer to define a limited number of

---

UPPER ARLINGTON CITY SCHOOLS
Holistic Reading Assessment
Observation Form

Date _____   Holistic Reading Score _____

Student's Name _____   Grade _____

Teacher _____   Observer _____

BOOK SELECTION FOR HOLISTIC READING ASSESSMENT

Book Title _____

Child selected _____   Teacher selected _____

WIDE READING

• *May I see your book list?* (comment on books read)
  Book List: Limited _____   Adequate _____   Extensive _____
  Comments:
• *How do you choose a book to read?*
• *What is one of your favorite books? Why?*
• *What are you reading now?*
• *What do you think you will choose to read next? Why?*

FIGURE 10.3 A holistic reading assignment observation form

CONSTRUCTING MEANING / RESPONSE

* *Tell me about the book you have selected for this conference.*

Student discusses story idea _____ major events _____ characters _____
story ending _____

(Prompting may be used to elicit additional information; i.e., Tell me more about the story idea.)

Prompted with additional questions _____   No additional prompting necessary _____

* *Why do you think the author wrote this book?*
* *Would you recommend this book? Why or why not?*

SILENT / ORAL READING / USE OF STRATEGIES

* *Find a passage in your book to read aloud. You can read it to yourself first if you like.*

Estimated Accuracy: 95–100% _____   90–95% _____   Less than 90% _____

Do miscues interfere with meaning? yes _____ no _____

Rate: slow _____ adequate _____

Fluency: (Intonation, phrasing, repetitions) fluent _____ some fluency _____
        nonfluent _____

Observation of student strategies: (self-correction, prediction, use of cues) Comments:

* *Tell me in your own words about what you've just read?* (Comment on reading and retelling).

ATTITUDE / SELF-ASSESSMENT

* *Do you like to read? Why or why not?*
* *What are your strengths as a reader? (What do you do well as a reader?)*
* *What would you like to improve about your reading?*

PLANNED INTERVENTIONS:

general goals; others identify a larger number of more specific goals. But whatever the number, they will be the areas in which you gather information in an ongoing fashion.

Thinking About Class Activities.   Another way to define your assessment activities is to think about the activities that your children do each day or week and to identify those that may lend themselves to evaluation. Diane's class includes large and small group reading instruction, reader's workshop, independent reading and writing time, and book club activities. During the independent reading and writing time, she meets individually with students to discuss their recent work and to enter selected work into their literacy portfolios. Each of these activities offers Diane different opportunities to increase her understanding of her students' reading and writing. During the individual conferences, for example, she can explore her students' understanding of and reflection on books they have recently read, she can study samples of their writing, and she can ask questions and listen carefully to assess their feelings and reflections about their literacy activities. During reader's workshop, she can note who works with whom and the reading activities they undertake.

Selecting Portfolio Information.   The information gathered in a class portfolio should represent areas of literacy that coincide with instructional goals (i.e., that are important aspects of literacy) and that permit assessment of learning over time. Pils, a teacher in a first-grade whole language classroom (Pils, 1991), for example, gathers the following:

- Writing samples (considered for their content, number of known words, sentence structure, and punctuation)
- Number of words read aloud in one minute (assessed in September, January, and May)
- Ten-minute writing samples (at three-month intervals throughout the year)
- Lists of books read and to be read (kept during buddy reading time)
- Challenge cards (lists of unknown words and their sources)
- Conference records (students' interests in reading, how themes of books are alike and different, what they are currently writing about)

These samples are either easily obtained (number of words read aloud in 1-minute and 10-minute writing samples) or can be gathered during the course of instruction. All are in keeping with Pils's literacy goals for her first graders. Some samples that are gathered may be kept best in student portfolios (discussed in the following section) and some in a class portfolio. For example, from the samples listed above, students should keep in their portfolios the writing samples, the list of books already read and to be read, and the challenge cards. The other information (1-minute word reading sample, 10-minute writing sample, and conference records) may be kept best in the class portfolio.

You must decide how to record the observations you make during ongoing instruction, and two systems that have been developed by teachers may work for you. One involving anecdotal records is described by Rhodes and Nathenson-Mejia (1992). They offer three guidelines: "Describe a specific event or product. Report rather than evaluate or interpret. Relate the material to other facts that are known about the child" (adapted from Thorndike & Hagen, 1977, p. 503). A sample provided in Figure 10.4 illustrates the nature of anectodal records.

A somewhat different system is described by Pils (1991). Her portfolio materials include strips of blank mailing labels attached to a clipboard. Each morning she dates several of these; then as she walks around the room she records her observations of children's works. For example, her records on Stacy might include the following:

(9/24) Stacy: I can read Hop on Pop all by myself.

(10/5) Stacy: Stacy and Alan very good buddies. Stacy helps Alan with words. She read all of helper chart when she selected her job. (p. 48)

Eleanor

STRDAIPADENBSNO
(Yesterday I played in the snow)

STRDA = yesterday
I = I
PAD = played
EN = in
B = the (said "du" and thought she was writing "D")
SNO = snow

Showed her how to stretch her words out like a rubberband—doing it almost on own by SNO. E does have a fairly good grasp of sound/letter relationships. However, has a hard time isolating words and tracking words in sentences in her mind. That may hold up progress for awhile. Asked her—at end—what she did in writing today that she hadn't done in previous writing. She said, "I listened to sounds." Told her to do it in her writing again tomorrow.

FIGURE 10.4   An anecdotal record of Eleanor's reading

SOURCE: Rhodes, L. K., & Nathenson-Mejia, S. (1992). Anecdotal records: A powerful tool for ongoing literacy assessment. *The Reading Teacher, 45,* 503.

Pils has a three-ring binder with a section for each child. At the end of the day, she places the labels on the sheets named for each child she observed and recorded.

While it is important to use some more formal observational procedures such as the Upper Arlington City Schools Holistic Reading Assessment form (see Figure 10.3), it is also important to ensure that your daily observations are represented in your class portfolio.

Determining the Physical Form of the Portfolio.   The portfolio may take many forms. It may be a set of manila folders, one for each child, to be kept in your file drawer. It may be a loose-leaf notebork with a section for each child. It may be an accordion file with a section for each of your children. The form should be one that will be easy for you to use. You should have the physical form of the portfolio established before the beginning of the school year.

Making Sense of Your Portfolio Records.   The final step is the most important. The best-kept records in the world will do you little good if you fail to reflect on what you have observed over time and make sense of the patterns you see. Your records should be descriptive rather than interpretive. At least once a month, read over your portfolio entries for each child in your class and ask what they tell you about the child's literacy development. You will begin to see recurring patterns in some areas and marked departures in others. When we do this sort of study, we usually record our thoughts and ideas in writing as we read the record. It is possible to identify patterns and inconsistencies in our insights and emerging understandings.

On the basis of the patterns you see and the changes that have occurred, identify the current reading and writing strengths and weaknesses of the child. These tentative conclusions will form the basis for setting new short-term goals. During your next conference with the child, you will be able to discuss and confirm the patterns you believe you see and use this as the basis for discussing goals for reading and writing.

The insights and new understandings you derive from your study of the portfolio entries should be recorded in brief form in the portfolio. The study will better prepare you for your next observations of the student's reading and writing.

> **PAUSE AND REFLECT.**   Select a grade level that you either currently teach or would like to teach in the future. Describe your goals for student reading and writing. What are the activities you will undertake to help your students achieve these goals? What type of information will you want to include in your class portfolio? Describe the procedures you will follow and the physical form of your portfolio recordkeeping approach.

Building Student Portfolios

A student portfolio is like the portfolio of an artist, which contains a representative sample of the artist's work, revealing the essence of who she is and what she is trying to accomplish. A similar collection of work can be developed by students in your class. Building a portfolio is important for two reasons. It becomes a window into the student's thinking, revealing his or her aspirations, interests, and goals. It is a powerful educational tool that can encourage students to assume control of their own learning.

Paulson, Paulson, and Meyer (1991) and colleagues developed the following definition: "A **portfolio** is a purposeful collection of student work that exhibits the student's efforts, progress, and achievement in one or more areas. The collection must include student participation in selecting content, the criteria for selection, the criteria for judging merit, and evidence of student self-reflection" (p. 60). Although portfolios can be defined in other ways, we have selected this definition because it captures what we believe are several important aspects of them.

First, the collection of student work must be purposeful; it must relate to the goals that you and the student have established in the area of literacy. Do not assess too many areas. For example, it may be sufficient to collect work in three areas: writing; a list of books read, with brief entries; and writing that relates to reading activities. More activities related to the development of print may be included for younger children (spelling samples, words known, challenge words, and the like).

Second, the work collected must show the "efforts, progress, and achievements" of the child. The samples must be judiciously selected to show work reflecting effort (e.g., multiple drafts of the same paper) and must be collected over time to show progress. Not all the child's work should be included or the task of examining the collection will become overwhelming. The work should be selected with a purpose in mind. More samples will be collected at the beginning of the year to represent the year's starting point; some of these may be eliminated as the year progresses. The portfolio is organic in nature and may profit from being pruned periodically.

In addition, the student will be involved in selecting content, establishing the criteria for selection, and judging merit. Part of the value of student portfolios lies in the student's assuming responsibility for his or her own reading and writing development. This can occur only if the student's goals and values influence what is kept in the portfolio and influence the criteria by which merit is judged. For many teachers, the interactive process of considering work, discussing its strengths and weaknesses, and judging its merits is a new one. Those who have been doing it for some time have learned to become very good listeners when they interact with their students. Teachers who wish their students to keep portfolios must set aside time for individual conferences every week or two for younger students and at least every three weeks for older ones. Conferences should be more frequent at the beginning of the year than later. Usually the focus of the conference is on the new work the student has placed in his or her portfolio. On the basis of the conference, some of this work will be kept in the portfolio and other work will be sent home, displayed, shared, or discarded.

Finally, evidence of student self-reflection will be included in the portfolio. By encouraging students' self-reflection on their work, the portfolio collection gives students opportunities to take charge of their own learning. Prior to several conferences with their teachers (for example, at mid-year and a time or two thereafter), students can be encouraged to study the work they have recently collected, compare it with previous work, and draw conclusions about their progress. Paulson, Paulson, and Meyer (1991) provide some useful illustrations of student reflection. These are shown in Figure 10.5. Writing about what they have learned becomes an important part of the process for students and a valuable part of the record.

The sort of informal assessments that we have described must be recorded and organized in some ways. The procedures for building class portfolios and student portfolios represent solutions to the problem of organization. They become useful educational tools for assessing student learning and progress and for planning instruction. In the following section, we consider how the information that you have gathered and organized helps you make informed instructional decisions.

USING INFORMATION

Gathering information and making observations are useful only if you learn to make good decisions based on the understanding that you are developing about each of your students. As you reflect on the characteristics of each child, you must pose certain questions:

1. How will I organize my class for various instructional activities?
2. What level of materials can each of my students read independently and with support?
3. What kind of support should I provide each of my students?

5-11-90

At the beginning of the year.
I heivit been yoosng periods
and I am now.
At the beginning of the year.
I havit been yoosng sentence
and I am now.
At the beginning of the year.
I havit been yoosngelaboration
and I am now ~~the End~~

Today I looked at all my
stories in my writing folder
I read some of my writing since
September. I noticed that I've
impaved some stuff. Now I edit my
stores, and revise. Now I use periods,
quotation mark. Sometimes my stories
are longer I usd to mis·rspell my
~~words~~ and now I look in a
dictionary or ask a friend and now
I write exciting and scary stories
and now I have very good endings
Now I use capitals I usd to leavc out
words and ʌwrote short simple stories.

FIGURE 10.5. Samples of students' reflections on the writing samples they include in their portfolios

SOURCE: Paulson, F. L., Paulson, P. R., & Meyer, C. A. (1991). What makes a portfolio a portfolio? *Educational Leadership, 48* (5), 62–63. Reprinted with permission of the Association for Supervision and Curriculum Development. Copyright © 1991 by ASCD. All rights reserved.

Organizing Students for Instruction

Children are grouped for reading instruction in most elementary school classrooms. Further, in most classrooms a variety of organizational structures are used for reading and writing: pairs, teams, ability groups, or total class. The grouping arrangements you select depend on your instructional goals. The problem for you as a teacher is to think about the composition of your class and your own goals and values. Then you must consider what forms of grouping may work for you.

Historically, most grouping for reading instruction was done on the basis of achievement (Barr & Dreeben, 1991). More recently, teachers have developed repertoires of flexible grouping strategies to meet students' individual needs in reading. Students work in large groups with support strategies in place for less able readers. They are grouped cooperatively for paired and shared learning. Teachers have minilessons for both small and large groups and continue to work with individuals when the larger class is involved in independent work. The type of group that is formed depends on the needs of the students, the goals you have for instruction, the constraints of the classroom, and the stages of reading represented in the classroom (Barr, in press).

Most reading researchers agree that the beginning stages of reading differ in certain fundamental ways from subsequent stages. Most important, beginning readers must learn about the nature of print and how print relates to their spoken language. Chall (1983) describes the initial stages of reading as learning to decode and then learning to read fluently. Typically, this focus on reading occurs in the first two or three grades of elementary school. The developmental nature of learning to read during this period becomes obvious. Children who are able to read beginning first-grade level materials usually have extreme difficulty reading second- or third-grade-level materials because they have not yet acquired the needed sight vocabulary nor the skill to identify unknown words.

As we described in Chapter 3, once children have learned a substantial number of words and can identify them easily, they consolidate this learning to become fluent readers. For most children, this integration occurs sometime during the second or third grade. Learning about print is no longer a major emphasis of instruction; reading instruction focuses even more on the strategies that children must acquire in order to comprehend effectively and critically. The materials that children encounter in the intermediate grades pose many new problems for them: Often the vocabulary is unfamiliar; the structure of reading in science and social studies differs from the narrative forms experienced in the basal series; children are expected to read longer selections silently.

Most important to our discussion here, what children need to learn to become effective readers is no longer developmentally organized. Whereas in the early stages children's skill with print relates directly to the level of the material they will be able to read, in later stages their interest in and prior knowledge about the topic are more important (Anderson & Davison, 1989). Accordingly, in the intermediate grades and above it becomes more difficult to predict whether a child can comprehend a particular story or article. As we discussed in Chapter 4, prereading discussions encourage students to share their knowledge about the topic of a selection and thereby better prepare them to comprehend the selection. Several useful teaching strategies, developed to encourage students to think about what they may learn from the text and what they already know about the topic, were described in Chapters 5 and 6. Remember, however, that word identification and fluency will still have a bearing on the reading of low-achieving students; special instructional provisions may need to be made to accommodate deficiencies in these areas.

Grouping children by their reading proficiency may make it easier for you to match closely the demands of selections with students' developing knowledge. And yet, children grouped together on the basis of achievement, particularly groups composed of those developing their reading skill most slowly, may be deprived of the more stimulating discussions that characterize groups including a cross-section of children.

Children who are less well prepared for a reading or writing task can participate in the activity with their peers who are more proficient readers if you help them with one of several instructional strategies. Even children in the beginning stages of reading are able to read fairly demanding books (for which they know few sight words) when the story is familiar to them. You can make the books familiar by reading them aloud previously in class or by asking parents to read them to their children at home. Reading in pairs or choral reading provides support for children who are experiencing difficulty learning print. Finally, rereading stories helps children develop and consolidate their knowledge of print.

Beyond the beginning stages of reading, all children can be supported through instruction in a way that will enable them to read selections with comprehension. In particular, some of the strategies for sharing prior knowledge discussed in Chapter 4 enable even students with limited experiences to read and comprehend.

When you are thinking about how to organize your students for different aspects of instruction, consider your goals, the characteristics of your students, and the instructional support they require to be active participants. When you choose to form groups that are diverse in reading ability, you will need to provide special support for those children who are developing their reading strategies more slowly than others in your class.

CASE 10.2: ORGANIZING DIANE'S CLASS

Let us return to Diane's class to consider how she will organize her students for instruction. Diane has for many years grouped her students on the basis of their reading achievement. Typically, she forms two groups: one composed of children reading at the fourth-grade level and the other of children reading below grade level who need intensive instructional help to develop their reading strategies. In the past she chose to do this because the fourth-grade basal stories were extremely difficult for some of the students in her class. While she forms groups for basal instruction, every afternoon she provides 30 to 60 minutes of reader's workshop. Children read books they have selected, either alone or with a partner or interest group, and keep a reading log or journal in which they record their reactions and ideas. Diane and her student teacher react to the journals, as do reading partners. Finally, the entire class participates in a Friday session of reader's workshop in which books, ideas, and ongoing activities are shared.

Diane is thinking about using this organizational arrangement again this year. If she does, she will have a large group using the fourth-grade reading series and a smaller group using the third-grade materials. Yet she will have some activities in which she combines the two groups. For example, she may focus one of her thematic units on "challenge" because both levels of materials have selections appropriate for the topic.

PAUSE AND REFLECT. How do you think Diane will initially compose the two groups of students for reading instruction? Consider the information included in Figure 10.2. Which students might be more independent (I) in the large group? Which might need more guidance (G) in the large group? Which might work best in a smaller group with lower level materials (S)? When you have finished, compare your judgments with those of Diane.

Figure 10.6 shows Diane's initial decisions about the reading needs of her students. These will, of course, be modified as she learns more about her class. In considering the test scores, she places more weight on the comprehension score because it involves the reading of textual passages. She decides to form a small group (S) composed of Dottie, Grace, Jean, John, Lottie, Walter, and Wanda. These are the children she had tentatively identified as needing special instructional support in the small group setting. Diane's goal is to have all these children reading with the rest of the class by the end of the year.

Diane selects the remainder of the class to form the large group (L). Within this group, she identifies two children, Dorothy and Jeff, whom she will challenge with some independent book club activities (I). She is also going to find special and more demanding activities for David, who also shows strong comprehension.

This initial grouping will be modified many times during the year. At different times Diane forms focused trade book reading groups. For example, when the holocaust is the topic of social studies, students read from a designated group of related trade books. The groups formed for this purpose are heterogeneous in composition. As needed, she provides any children from the class with special, small group support.

Diane's grouping each Friday for the reading workshop includes all class members. This experience provides her the opportunity to see how well the children in the small group read more challenging materials. In the afternoon period for independent reading and writing, she observes the selections of

Student	Reading Vocabulary	Reading Comprehension	Third-Grade Group	Diane's Hypothetical Group
Ann	3.4	3.7	L	G
Candy	4.1	3.8	M	G
Carol	3.0	4.3	L	G
Connie	4.3	4.0	M	G
Cornelia	4.1	3.9	H	G
Daniel	4.1	3.8	H	G
David	4.0	4.3	M	G
Denise	4.5	4.0	H	G
Donald	4.8	3.7	H	G
Dorothy	4.3	5.1	M	I
Dottie	3.1	3.1	L	S
Gary	3.4	3.9	M	G
Gordon	3.7	3.9	M	G
Grace	3.5	3.0	H	S
Greta	4.4	3.9	H	G
Jean	2.9	2.0	M	S
Jeff	5.7	4.9	H	I
John	3.1	2.8	L	S
Kay	4.3	4.0	H	G
Lois	3.4	3.3	M	G
Lottie	2.7	1.8	L	S
Tia	4.5	3.9	H	G
Walter	1.9	2.2	L	S
Wanda	2.2	2.7	L	S

FIGURE 10.6 Standardized test results: Third-grade grouping and hypothetical groups based on comprehension scores

children and the partners with whom they choose to work. She encourages children to form partnerships on the basis of their interests.

Selecting Appropriate Material

Children read materials they select as well as those selected by teachers. It is your responsibility, as teacher, to make sure that the materials your students read are at the appropriate level—not frustrating and not too easy. It is also your responsibility to see that children read a variety of text: nonfictional materials (science and social studies articles, biography, history) as well as narratives. There is a clear bias by teachers toward the selection of narrative materials. Yet, studies have shown that even young children—particularly boys, but girls as well—prefer nonfiction (Pappas, 1993).

We believe that one useful way to approach the selection of materials is to decide on one or several themes that you and the class will pursue during the year. In her class, Diane has selected the theme of "Challenge." She has already examined the basals in her class and found narratives that fit this theme. Now she needs to locate articles, some of which are nonfiction, that also develop this idea. Typically, teachers over the years develop appropriate collections of trade books or nonfiction materials from which they draw. These collections must be reviewed and supplemented to remain current and interesting to specific classes of students.

The selection of materials occurs on two levels. On one level teachers select what they believe will be interesting and conceptually challenging reading experiences for their students. On another level, teachers attempt to ensure that the assigned materials, the "normal reading task demands," can be read by all children to whom they are assigned. Selection of materials in this second sense involves knowing enough about the reading strengths of students to be able to develop an appropriate match. Reading comprehension or the ability to construct meaning from text is viewed as the central and most important goal. Thus, if children cannot read the assigned materials with comprehension, then either easier materials need to be found or greater instructional support needs to be provided. We believe that children will continue to develop their reading strategies if the normal reading task demands permit reading with comprehension. Text that is too difficult will lead them to develop maladaptive strategies.

At the beginning of the school year, teachers must work from limited information to determine whether the materials they have selected are appropriate. In the earlier section on instructional organization, the decision of how to cluster children for appropriate instruction was based mainly on a decision about materials. That is, the instructional arrangements selected are influenced to a great extent by the diversity of the class in reading skill. If class members are quite similar in reading comprehension, there is no need for special materials and instructional strategies. On the other hand, if a class is highly diverse, the teacher will need to have materials available at several different levels of difficulty so that all children can read with comprehension.

Diane made her decision about the selection of materials on the basis of her past experience with similar children, the standardized test scores of the present class, and information from their third-grade teachers. She decided that children scoring low on the comprehension section of the standardized test would find the fourth-grade basal narrative and nonfiction selections too demanding, and that they would make better progress reading less challenging materials.

A teacher must exercise considerable caution in using standardized test scores in this way. As discussed in earlier sections of this chapter, scores may not be accurate estimates of reading ability for some children for a variety of reasons. Thus, although we believe that scores can be used as one piece of information, we are concerned when instruction is established solely on this basis. Scores can be used as an initial estimate, if, and only if, teachers faithfully examine and reexamine earlier decisions by observing the reading and writing of their students.

Similarly, the level at which children were reading during the prior school year should also be treated in a tentative fashion. The reading progress of children does not occur in a straight line, nor do all children progress through the same stages. Reading development is somewhat like growth in height; at times there can be periods of amazing growth. Further, you don't know that children during the prior year were being instructed at the appropriate level. Glenn and associates (1989) report that

New Zealand children who had participated in Reading Recovery (a first-grade tutorial program) were reading in books more than four levels (about a half year) below where they were capable of reading as indicated by passage tests. Thus, when children have made spurts in their reading development, their earlier basal placement may be inaccurate. The main point is that no single observation or piece of information should underlie a major instructional decision. Rather, decisions, particularly those made at the beginning of the school year, should be viewed as tentative and subject to modification as you gather other information about children's reading and writing.

Once Diane has made her initial decisions, during subsequent months she must study the comprehension of her children in order to identify those who are ready to read with the large group. Her observations during reader's workshop where she has the entire class read the same short stories will be particularly informative. This flexibility will help her to achieve her goal of having all children in her class reading in the large group before the end of the year. Studies of grouping show that effective teachers have a pattern of moving their students into higher-achieving groups during the course of the school year (Barr & Dreeben, 1983).

CASE 10.3: THE CASE OF GRACE

Diane was particularly uncertain about the decision she had made for Grace. In third grade, Grace had been in the high reading group; yet her comprehension score suggested that she was reading as well as students at the beginning of third grade. This conflicting information raised questions in Diane's mind about whether Grace should be reading with the small group. To pursue this question, Diane decided to have Grace read aloud for her the initial portion of a story from the fourth-grade basal. After Grace had finished reading the story silently, Diane asked her to summarize it. She did so fluently and with enthusiasm. Figure 10.7 shows a sample of Grace's oral reading and her retelling.

PAUSE AND REFLECT.   Study the sample of Grace's oral reading shown in Figure 10.7. In terms of her strategies for dealing with print, is this passage at an appropriate level of difficulty? How did you arrive at your decision? Now examine her retelling. Does she represent the most important ideas? On the basis of this information would you have her read from easier material in the small group or the fourth-grade-level material in the large group?

Diane was pleased with Grace's reading. Her print strategies appeared to be well developed, certainly good enough to cope with most of the fourth-grade basal selections. Her retelling was brief, but suggests that she comprehended most of the story. On the basis of this evidence, Diane decided to have Grace read with the large reading group. She asked Grace if she remembered taking the reading

Cheating
by
Susan Shreve

che-ⓒ

I cheated on a unit test in math class this

morning during second period with Mr. Burke.

Afterward, I was too sick to eat lunch just

thinking about it.

    I came straight home from school, went to

my room, and lay on the floor trying to decide

whether it would be better to run away from home

now or after supper. Mostly I wished I was dead.

assident ⓒ

    It wasn't even an accident that I cheated.

an nocked

Yesterday Mr. Burke announced there'd be a

unit test and anyone who didn't pass would have

partic ly

to come to school on Saturday, most particularly

me, since I didn't pass the last unit test. He said

that right out in front of everyone as usual. You

im-ag-in

can imagine how much I like Mr. Burke.

Retelling: This is a story about a kid who wasn't very good in math. Anyway, he didn't study for a test and he decided to cheat. But he came home from school and felt sick . . . didn't eat his dinner. He started feeling awful about himself . . . thinking maybe he was really bad. His dad asked what was wrong, and finally, he told him the truth. His dad made him call his teacher.

FIGURE 10.7 A record of Grace's oral reading and retelling of "Cheating" by Susan Shreve

SOURCE: In *The World is Round Just Like an Orange* (pp. 26–36). Glenview, IL: Scott Foresman, 1993.

test at the end of third grade. Grace told Diane that she always gets extremely nervous when she takes tests and that she had difficulty concentrating. On the basis of Grace's reading, Diane decided that Grace's test scores were invalid.

Developing Appropriate Instructional Support

Just as decisions about the appropriateness of materials and grouping of students have implications for each other, the development of appropriate instructional support is also involved. Through instruction, you can prepare students to read a story or article. Selections that might otherwise be too difficult for them can be made accessible through various prereading activities. Thus, in making selections, you can select more complex materials if you are able to prepare students to read them. On the other hand, if the possibilities for instructional support are limited, children may not be able to bridge the gap between the difficulty of the reading materials and their reading skill.

The size of the group is also an important consideration. If a group is small, you have greater opportunity to listen to and interact with students. You can thereby personalize the support you offer to your students.

In Diane's class, for example, she will have all students in her large fourth-level group take part in the initial background setting and final discussion for each selection. She will individualize instruction by having her more independent learners (I), who tend to finish their reading faster, meet with their cooperative book club teams while others finish their reading. At the same time, Diane will work with those students needing more guidance in this larger group (G), typically by working through some of the guided reading techniques described in Chapter 6.

Diane will introduce a similar set of reading techniques to her smaller group who are reading less demanding text. At the same time, she will also focus on the development of print strategies (see Chapter 3) and vocabulary concepts (see Chapter 4). Her instruction will be responsive to the specific needs of group members.

There will also be discussions of the total class focusing on the theme of challenge in which subgroups of students will describe the new insights they have gained from their reading and writing. Students will draw not only from their reading instruction but also from their independent reading and writing, their content area reading, and the selection read as a part of reader's workshop.

COMMUNICATING INFORMATION

You will gain new insights through conversations with students, their parents, and professional colleagues. Such conversations will help you check the accuracy of what you are learning about your students. In this final section, we discuss ways you can learn and share knowledge with these three important groups.

Talking with Students

Conversations with students are particularly informative. They let you learn how students see themselves as readers and writers; what their immediate and long-term goals are; and how they feel about reading, writing, and the classroom instructional program. It is through such conversations that you will gain your best insights into the feelings of students and their ideas about how you may help them most in developing their reading and writing strategies.

Conversations are usually most informative when they focus on specific activities. An approach we recommend is to meet with each student once every two or three weeks during the independent reading and writing period or a silent sustained reading period. Meetings should be more frequent with younger students.

Use the student's daily portfolio as the focus of your conversations. During this time, students will describe the reading they are doing at home and at school and tell you what they have particularly enjoyed, and why. They will also share drafts of their most recent writing so that you will be able to see the progress they have made. You may wish to have students reflect on their progress, and to identify areas in which they will focus their attention.

On the basis of this conversation, the two of you can make joint decisions about what reports on their reading and samples of their writing should be placed in their permanent portfolios. Since these portfolios will be shared with parents, they should contain the samples that most clearly illustrate the progress students are making.

Meeting with Parents

Parent–teacher conferences typically create some degree of uneasiness, but this discomfort can be alleviated in several ways. First, try to establish relationships with parents from the beginning of the year. Some schools have a tradition of holding open-house during the first month of school, which gives teachers the opportunity to describe their programs and allows parents to ask questions. If this is not the tradition in your school, an alternative is to send brief letters home to parents describing the activities on which you and the students are working. Invite phone calls when parents have questions.

A second way is to plan for conferences with parents by gathering samples of their children's work that provide insight into the children's learning. You may wish to have children identify the work of which they are most proud, the areas in which they feel that they have made most progress, and ways in which they believe their parents could support their reading and writing work at home.

It is important to frame your comments about a child's work in objective terms, beginning with positive statements about the child's strengths, continuing with areas of concern, and ending with a statement about progress that has been made. Having examples of children's work is a powerful tool. For children still developing their skill with print, oral reading tapes may be useful. Written summaries of stories children have read can be used to illustrate their skill in reading comprehension and writing.

These may also indicate the children's attitudes and enjoyment of reading. Children's work communicates much better than letter grades or summary comments since parents can see for themselves their children's strengths and weaknesses in reading and writing.

It is extremely useful to have children attend at least some of the conferences with parents so they can display their own work. When problems exist, it is helpful to have the child as a participant in the conference to consider alternative solutions. Planning for the conference by the child and teacher represents an authentic evaluation activity.

Conferring with Professionals

Teachers interact with specialists in related areas (psychologists, social workers, learning disability personnel, special educational professionasl) in several ways. They frequently receive reports from other specialists concerning the academic achievement and abilities of their students; they attend staff conferences in which the placement of one of their students is being considered; on occasion, specialists observe children in the teachers' classrooms. In this section, we first discuss the unique insights of teachers concerning the learning of their students and how this information contributes to the decision-making process. Then we consider how the reports from specialists may provide further insight into the learning and adjustment of a child.

Participation in Staff Conferences.   As a teacher, you have a unique role to play in staff conferences because you interact with your students on a day-in, day-out basis. That is, you have had the opportunity to observe your students over a long period of time as they interact with other children and engage in school work. In terms of our earlier discussion, your knowledge of children is based on a highly valid set of experiences. How can you share your knowledge at a staff conference?

Like parents, other specialists appreciate judiciously selected samples of a child's work, particularly when these permit assessment of the student's progress over time. Samples of writing, for example, collected at three points during the year may reveal little progress, erratic changes, or considerable development. Similarly, tape recordings of a child's oral reading will enable other participants to appreciate the integration of his or her strategies for dealing with print. Written summaries of stories and answers to comprehension questions will let them judge the child's ability to comprehend and reason. The complexities of these behavioral samples provide a complementary richness to normative scores.

Equally important are your entries into your class portfolio. These are observations you make periodically as significant events occur. Taken together they yield insight into a child's adjustment and progress in the classroom.

To illustrate the contribution you can make at a staff conference, let us consider the comments Diane made at a staffing for her student, Walter, in the middle of October. She brought his portfolio, which contained samples of his writing and a running record of his oral reading. In addition, she shared the entries she had made for Walter during the first months of school. They read as follows:

8/30 Walter: Eager and attentive, but rarely volunteers to answer questions

9/13 Walter: Read aloud from a trade book (second grade); showed good correction strategies

9/23 Walter: A wonderful artist; works with Jason who helps him write his stories in exchange for illustrating Jason's work

10/5 Walter: Took running record on story his small group was reading; recognized most sight words, but had difficulty decoding two three-syllable words

From this variety of evidence, it is clear that Walter is adjusting well to the class and forming good relations with peers. Further, he seems to be responding well to instruction. On the basis of the conference, the team decided not to refer him for further assessment for special education placement.

Reports from Specialists.   A specialist typically sees a student for a limited period of time for the specific purpose of evaluating his or her achievement and abilities. The evaluation is typically based on interviews and/or a variety of standardized and informal tests of adjustment, aptitude, and achievement. This form of assessment views the progress of a child normatively, in terms of what children, on average, typically know or can do. Unlike teachers who consider children's relationships to other children in their class or school, specialists use national samples as their frame of reference.

CASE 10.4: WALTER'S READING PROGRESS

In order to consider the value of reports to teachers, we examine here a report that Diane received from a reading specialist concerning Walter. As you will recall from Figure 10.6, Walter's test scores are fairly low (1.9 in vocabulary and 2.2 in comprehension). Last year he met with the lowest reading group. Diane received the report the first week of September. The report, shown in Figure 10.8, includes diagnostic information on Walter's areas of reading strength and weakness, a description of the tutorial program in which he had participated the prior summer, and recommendations for further instruction.

PAUSE AND REFLECT.   Read the report shown in Figure 10.8. What do you learn about Walter's reading skill from this report? In what areas (skill with print, prior knowledge and vocabulary, and reading comprehension) does he need to receive instruction? As Walter's teacher, would you find this a useful report?

Midwest College of Education
Reading Center

Student's name: Walter Smith

School: Hillside School

Grade: Entering grade 4

Age: 9

Date of testing: 6/12–13

Date of instruction: 6/14–7/7

Reading Specialist: Kathleen Brown

INITIAL DIAGNOSIS

Walter was given the Basic Reading Inventory (Johns), which is a series of graded word lists and passages that are read orally and silently. After reading, he responded to literal and inferential comprehension questions. Parallel forms of these passages are also used to assess listening comprehension. From an analysis of oral reading and comprehension responses, the level at which Walter can read material independently, the level at which he needs instructional support, and the level at which he becomes frustrated by the material were determined. These results are summarized below:

	Independent	Instructional	Frustration
Oral Reading	1st	2nd	3rd
Silent Reading	1st	1st–2nd	2nd
Listening		4th	

On the passages he read orally, Walter experienced considerable difficulty with word recognition at the third-grade level although he was still able to comprehend. On the passages he read silently, he experienced some comprehension difficulty at the second-grade level and considerable difficulty at the third. Walter's strengths include his use of context to self-correct decoding errors as well as to derive meaning of unfamiliar vocabulary. He also refers to the text to find factual information he has forgotten. Yet, his listening comprehension is strong. Moreover, a definite strength is his positive attitude about reading and his willingness to persevere on difficult tasks. Walter's reading weaknesses include his poor sight word vocabulary and very slow rate of reading. His print strategies, particularly his ability to decode vowel sounds, are also weak (e.g., he read *men* as *man* and *tan* as *ten*). His weak comprehension is also of concern, although this may reflect his problems with print.

Walter was also given the Developmental Spelling Test (Morris & Perney, 1984), involving a list of 10 words which he was asked to write. This test was used to assess his awareness of the sound segments in words and his knowledge of the spelling patterns of English. His spellings included correct beginning and ending sounds, as well as the correct long vowels and appropriate short vowel substitutions. The results of this test suggest that he has knowledge of letter–sound associations that he is not yet able to apply during word identification.

TUTORIAL PROGRAM

Based on the results of diagnostic testing, goals were established to help Walter improve his reading in the following areas: sight vocabulary, fluency, decoding, and comprehension strategies. To achieve these goals, several instructional approaches were followed: reading and rereading of easy materials, sorting short words on the basis of spelling patterns, sentence writing, and the K-W-L comprehension strategy.

Reading and rereading of easy materials. During each session Walter read a new predictable book and several previously read patterned books. This intense reading practice on material with which he experienced few word identification problems helped him to increase his sight vocabulary, improve his fluency, and increase his self-confidence and independence in reading.

FIGURE 10.8 Walter's reading diagnostic and instructional report

Sorting words and sentence writing. Through the Word Sort, children become aware of the likeness and differences among words. Walter worked on words that included the following patterns: *ap, at, an, am,* and *ack.* He is now able to say how words are similar and to read words containing these patterns with various beginning consonant sounds, blends, and digraphs. Through composing sentences and writing some of the words involved, Walter became more aware of the sounds in words and their written representation.

Comprehension strategies. In the K-W-L strategy, the student brainstorms all he knows about a particular subject prior to reading a selection. He is then asked to list questions about what he would like to learn about the subject. Walter was able to assume control over these two strategies after about 10 instructional sessions. In working on his literal comprehension, the third step of K-W-L was employed: He was asked to formulate statements about what he had learned from reading the selection. Walter is most successful when he is asked to retell what he learned after each individual page; he is becoming able to generate a retelling that captures the overall idea of a section as well as individual facts.

PROGRESS AND RECOMMENDATIONS

Despite the short length of the program, Walter made definite progress in developing his sight vocabulary and fluency, in becoming more aware of the spelling patterns of words, and in becoming a more strategic comprehender. Walter needs further individual or small group work to continue his progress in these areas.

Diane found this report to be useful in delineating the areas on which she would continue working with Walter. The results from the diagnosis were consistent with the results from his standardized tests. But after the diagnostic testing, he had received daily tutorial instruction for about six weeks. Thus, during the independent reading time, Diane had him read some first-grade-level books. She was amazed at his fluency. He seemed to have a fairly good knowledge of sight words and showed some facility with word identification. Walter's reading of selections from the third-grade basal was more labored and required considerable prior support. Perhaps because of his good listening comprehension, and with highly supportive instruction, he would be able to make progress reading this level of materials.

Diane's experiences are not exceptional. As a teacher, you will be called on to provide information and your thoughts about some of the children in your class who may be experiencing difficulties either at home or at school. Your ability to be a good observer during class instruction will increase the value of your reports.

SUMMARY

In this chapter we have focused on standardized tests, which we believe are a useful supplement to other information available to you about the reading of your students, particularly at the beginning of the year. In order to make good use of standardized test information, you must understand the advantages and problems with such tests and know how to interpret scores based on them.

Class portfolios provide ways to organize your own observations about your students' reading and writing. Records made on single days, when considered together, form patterns that can lead you to further awareness and searching. Such records are useful in tracing the progress of students, and in this capacity they complement other available assessment procedures.

Student portfolios provide ways for you to help your students organize and value their work. These records are particularly useful when you meet individually with your students to discuss their progress. They are also helpful in conferring with parents and other specialists.

The information you collect and organize will help you in making key instructional decisions. This includes the varieties and levels of materials that your students will read, how they will be paired or grouped together to accomplish their work, and the degree of support you will offer.

CONCLUSION

Learning to diagnose the reading problems of students is not a simple process. This is because the process of learning to read is itself extremely complex and there are important differences from one stage of reading development to another. We believe that you must understand the nature of this development in order to be an effective diagnostician. This means having an overview of the reading process and a thorough understanding of its component processes. Instead of providing a simple "cookbook" solution to problems, we have in this book attempted to build, step by step, a conceptual framework for viewing the component process of reading development: (1) print skill, (2) vocabulary and prior knowledge, and (3) reading comprehension. But it is not enough to understand how the three components work as separate entities. You must also understand how they combine to form a balanced and smoothly operating system—and to recognize when imbalances occur that interfere with effective literacy development.

One way we attempted to show the nature of these imbalances was through detailed case studies of students with various reading problems and teacher diagnoses of their problems. We carefully selected the cases to reflect major types of problems that students encounter as they attempt to establish a balance among the component processes of reading.

Just as we believe that students are active problem solvers responding to the demands of their instructional materials, so we believe that you as teachers must become active problem solvers as you learn to diagnose reading problems. To this end, we have focused on developing the observational skills you need for gathering evidence about reading, and the interpretive skills you must have for making sense of the evidence. In presenting the case studies, we encouraged you to assume an active role in assessing the observational evidence, drawing conclusions, and deriving appropriate instructional recommendations. We included specific Pause and Reflect activities to encourage your active involvement and problem solving.

But skill in diagnosis can be acquired only if you go beyond this book, carrying out projects that build on the concepts and skills presented here. To this end, we included Try It Out activities to help you apply your newly acquired concepts to your teaching practice. This book will have been used most effectively if you undertook such projects as you read each chapter of the book. And this is just the beginning. The development of diagnostic skill is in many ways similar to the development of literacy skill. Just as your students need to undertake much contextual reading and writing to become proficient, so must you continue to study the reading and writing problems of your students in order to consolidate your diagnostic strategies.

Finally, we emphasize once again that the purpose of diagnosis is to create instruction that is responsive to the needs of students. If this last step is omitted, the diagnosis is an idle exercise. There are two prerequisites to effective instructional planning. One is to understand the strengths and difficulties of a student well enough that instruction is "on the mark." In this book we have attempted to provide the basis for such an understanding. The second—and more difficult, perhaps—is to create instruction that captures the interest and energy of students and leads them to assume an active role. Accordingly, many of the instructional procedures we have described are designed to create active learners. As in the development of diagnostic skill, you will become more expert in providing high-quality instruction through experimentation with these and other procedures.

TRY IT OUT

1. Collect standardized test and portfolio information from your class and analyze it. How does it match with the grouping and organizational decisions you've made during the year? If you are not in your own classroom, analyze someone else's data and then compare it with the teacher's perceptions.

2. Reflect on your own class or interview a teacher. Choose several children whose standardized test results are a poor match for their portfolio performance. Can you determine why the test results did not reveal true performance?

3. **For Your Teaching Portfolio:** Take the standardized tests administered in your school or district and record your observations. Then examine the manual that describes reliability and validity. Critique content, format, and validity. See if you can locate a review of the measure in *Mental Measurements Yearbook* (Buros, 1938–1985) or in a professional journal review. Retain this to help you interpret standardized test performance for yourself and for parental communication.

4. **Student Portfolio Ideas:** Where appropriate, share your class portfolio results with individual students and use them for planning goals. Include goal plans in their portfolios.

FOR FURTHER READING

Hansen, J. (1992). Student's evaluations bring reading and writing together. *The Reading Teacher, 46*(2), 100–105.
Discusses the impact of student goal setting and self-assessment on students' understanding of literacy.

Paris, S. G., Calfee, R. C., Filby, N., Hiebert, E. H., Pearson, P. D., Valencia, S. W., & Wolf, K. P. (1992). A framework for authentic literacy assessment. *The Reading Teacher, 46*(2), 88–98.
Describes a framework for examining seven critical dimensions of literacy programs in schools and districts.

Winograd, P., Paris, S., & Bridge, C. (1991). Improving the assessment of literacy. *The Reading Teacher, 45*(2), 108–116.
Offers guidelines for improving the assessment of literacy.

Dolch Basic Sight Vocabulary

a _____	big _____	down _____
about _____	black _____	draw _____
after _____	blue _____	drink _____
again _____	both _____	eat _____
all _____	bring _____	eight _____
always _____	brown _____	every _____
am _____	but _____	fall _____
an _____	buy _____	far _____
and _____	by _____	fast _____
any _____	call _____	find _____
are _____	came _____	first _____
around _____	can _____	five _____
as _____	carry _____	fly _____
ask _____	clean _____	for _____
at _____	cold _____	found _____
ate _____	come _____	four _____
away _____	could _____	from _____
be _____	cut _____	full _____
because _____	did _____	funny _____
been _____	do _____	gave _____
before _____	does _____	get _____
best _____	done _____	give _____
better _____	don't _____	go _____
goes _____	never _____	stop _____
going _____	new _____	take _____

SOURCE: E. W. Dolch, Basic Sight Vocabulary, *Elementary School Journal,* 1936, *36,* 456–560.

good _____	no _____	tell _____
got _____	not _____	ten _____
green _____	now _____	thank _____
grow _____	of _____	that _____
had _____	off _____	the _____
has _____	old _____	their _____
have _____	on _____	them _____
he _____	once _____	then _____
help _____	one _____	there _____
her _____	only _____	these _____
here _____	open _____	they _____
him _____	or _____	think _____
his _____	our _____	this _____
hold _____	out _____	those _____
hot _____	over _____	three _____
how _____	own _____	to _____
hurt _____	pick _____	today _____
I _____	play _____	together _____
if _____	please _____	too _____
in _____	pretty _____	try _____
into _____	pull _____	two _____
is _____	put _____	under _____
it _____	ran _____	up _____
its _____	read _____	upon _____
jump _____	red _____	us _____
just _____	ride _____	use _____
keep _____	right _____	very _____
kind _____	round _____	walk _____
know _____	run _____	want _____
laugh _____	said _____	warm _____
let _____	saw _____	was _____
light _____	say _____	wash _____
like _____	see _____	we _____
little _____	seven _____	well _____
live _____	shall _____	went _____
long _____	she _____	were _____
look _____	show _____	what _____
made _____	sing _____	when _____
make _____	sit _____	where _____
many _____	six _____	which _____
may _____	sleep _____	white _____
me _____	small _____	who _____
much _____	so _____	why _____
must _____	some _____	will _____
my _____	soon _____	wish _____
myself _____	start _____	with _____
work _____	yellow _____	your _____
would _____	yes _____	
write _____	you _____	

Blachowicz Informal
Phonics Survey

This informal survey gives subtests for many sound–symbol correspondence patterns. It is rarely useful or advisable to give the *whole* test to any student. It should be used after an oral reading diagnostic test to pinpoint those areas that look like possible weaknesses.

Since the test utilizes nonsense syllables, some mispronunciations will be artifacts of the test. Often a child will try to make a nonsense syllable into a real word. All conclusions from this test should be verified in real reading situations. For example, if you think a student has done badly on *bl-*, you might want him or her to read a paragraph containing words like *blue*, *blend*, *blood*, and so forth. Never lose sight of the fact that phonics used in context is the important tool.

GENERAL GUIDELINES

1. The subtests get harder. For very young children, start at subtest 1. For most students, subtest 3 is a good starting point.
2. For subtests 3 and up, always write down what the student says when he or she mispronouces a stimulus item. This is essential for final analysis.
3. Stop whenever the student shows signs of distress. If you want to give other subtests, do them another day.
4. Always tell the students what you are doing and why. Be sure to tell them that THESE ARE NOT REAL WORDS and that they are not expected to know them all.
5. Give praise and encouragement whenever you can. Start a child on any easy subtest to give success. If a student flounders, you can go back to an easier subtest to end with success.

SOURCE: *Blachowicz Informal Phonics Survey.* C. L. Z. Blachowicz (Unpublished assessment device). Evanston, IL: National College of Education, 1980. Reprinted by permission.

6. Try to modify the materials to make them more usable. You might want to cut and mount the subtests for the student's copy. This makes the order less obvious.

7. A most effective use of the material is to turn it into a board game. Place the stimulus items on index cards and have the student draw cards and move spaces for each one correctly pronounced. You can put different subtests on different colored cards for easy use and sorting.

ANALYSIS

1. Look for patterns.
2. Test your conclusions with real reading materials.
3. Try to break down the task into its parts when conclusions don't add up. For example, if the student could recognize *up*, knows the consonant sound associated with *t*, but could not pronounce *tup*, perhaps he or she cannot blend sounds.
4. Keep a record of your findings to check out in the real-life reading situation. Remember, testing is always artificial.

TEST ITEMS

1. *Naming upper and lower case letters.* Circle those not known when pointed to.

a	S	q	I	R	h	k
s	J	d	A	f	O	U
l	w	z	Q	v	X	B
n	H	T	b	e	G	P
V	N	j	y	K	w	f
F	r	Z	x	L	m	O
E	o	C	D	P	g	A
i	M	t	u	c	Y	d
S	j					

2. *Sound values of isolated consonants.* Point to each letter and ask the child to tell you what sound "this letter makes" or to give you a word that starts with this letter. Circle those not known.

b	c	k	j	g	t	v	d	m	h	r
p	z	l	f	n	s	u	w	y	qu

3. *Short vowel phonograms blended with initial consonants.* Check to see if the student knows the following simple sight word phonograms: *up*, *it*, *am*, and *on*. (If they are not known, try to train the student to recognize them, or choose phonograms the child does know.) Point to each item and have the child pronounce it. If an item is mispronounced, write the mispronunciation above it for later analysis.

mup	zam	yup	sam	con	rit	gam	kno
dup	vit	hon	quam	bup	pon	wup	jam
nit	fup	lam	yup				

4. *Consonant blends plus short vowel phonograms.* This and all subsequent tests follow the same procedure as test 3. Have the child pronounce each item, and write in any mispronounced words.

brup	scon	plit	skam	slup	twit	dron
gram	swis	spup	fron	blit	snam	glup
clam	trit	flon	smam	slup	cron	prit

5. *Consonant digraphs plus short vowel phonograms.*

chup	shon	thup	whit	pham	shup	whon
chon	thon					

6. *VC\# pattern plus initial consonants.*

dake	mime	fole	tule	mede	tate	fope
dute	dite	sede				

7. *Long vowel digraphs.*

leat	mied	boad	tay	ley	moe	teef
buel	moes	lail	bie	toat	meep	tay
lue	bain	leam				

8. *R-controlled vowels.*

mer	tir	hur	dir	fer	dar	mor	tur
sar	dor	bur					

9. *Ending-blend phonograms.*

selt	mext	basp	mick	dunch	mulk	tand
goft	sunch	mimp	kent	munk	jung	dulf
baft	dilk	nolt	satch	fodge	hink	disp
folt	namp	dist	gelf	mond	bant	ting
dast	holf	fask	rept	felp	nold	hent

10. *Ending-digraph phonograms.*

tath fash nich baph dith sosh tach ruph

11. *Alternate sounds of* c *and* g.

gap gity cot came gend cend git cim

12. *Three-letter blends.*

splan	chrin	thrup	schon	strat	scrup
squit	spron	chris	thrat	scris	spron
strup	splup	squis	schan	shrat	

13. *Diphthongs.*

dow doy dound doint doy doud doil down

14. *Silent letters.*

talf tamb demn falm knop wrid gnap
knop ghat wrod gnom phot pnip psin

15. *Multisyllabic words.* Show division points in responses with slash marks.

buffle hotrat rewant sunting fendle
inserg unpottle rembat rebark bullingable
minkfall refizwissing wenkerfil mendle submarkable
raction bunded madsion

appendix C

Complete Records of Performance on an IRI: James

Analytical Reading Inventory, Word Lists

Level 3	Flash	Untimed	Level 4	Flash	Untimed
1. beginning	✓	___	1. worm	✓	___
2. thankful	✓	___	2. afford	afforded	✓
3. written	✓	___	3. player	✓	___
4. reason	✓	___	4. scientific	✓	___
5. bent	✓	___	5. meek	✓	___
6. patient	✓	___	6. rodeo	✓	___
7. manage	✓	___	7. festival	✓	___
8. arithmetic	✓	___	8. hillside	✓	___
9. burst	✓	___	9. coward	✓	___
10. bush	✓	___	10. boom	✓	___
11. gingerbread	✓	___	11. booth	✓	___
12. tremble	treb—	✓	12. freeze	✓	___
13. planet	✓	___	13. protest	✓	___
14. struggle	✓	___	14. nervous	✓	___
15. museum	✓	___	15. sparrow	✓	___
16. grin	✓	___	16. level	✓	___
17. ill	✓	___	17. underground	✓	___

SOURCE: *Analytical Reading Inventory,* 2nd ed., by M. L. Woods & A. J. Moe. Columbus, OH: Charles E. Merrill, 1981. Word Lists and Questions reprinted by permission of Charles E. Merrill Publishing Co. Passages reprinted by permission of original sources.

Analytical Reading Inventory, Word Lists (*Continued*)

	Flash	Untimed		Flash	Untimed
18. alarm	✓		18. oxen	✓	
19. cool	✓		19. eighty	✓	
20. engine	*ing – ✓*		20. shouldn't	✓	

Number correct	95	100	Number correct	95	100

Level 5	Flash	Untimed	Level 6	Flash	Untimed
1. abandon	✓		1. seventeen	✓	
2. zigzag	✓		2. annoy	✓	
3. terrific	✓		3. dwindle	*dind –*	✓
4. terrify	✓		4. rival	✓	
5. plantation	✓		5. hesitation	✓	
6. loaf	✓		6. navigator	✓	
7. hike	✓		7. gorge	✓	
8. relative	✓		8. burglar	✓	
9. available	✓		9. construction	✓	
10. grief	✓		10. exploration	✓	
11. physical	✓		11. technical	✓	
12. commander	*commanded*	✓	12. spice	✓	
13. error	✓		13. spike	✓	
14. woodcutter	✓		14. prevail	*pre ✓*	
15. submarine	✓		15. memorial	✓	
16. ignore	✓		16. initiation	✓	
17. disappointed	✓		17. undergrowth	✓	
18. wrestle	✓		18. ladle	*lădle ✓*	
19. vehicle	*vick*	✓	19. walnut	✓	
20. international	*in-ter*	✓	20. tributary	*tri – ✓*	

Number correct	90	100	Number correct	95	100

ANALYTICAL READING INVENTORY, FORM A, LEVEL 6
(192 WORDS, 12 SENTENCES)

EXAMINER'S INTRODUCTION

Dr. Charles Drew overcame many obstacles to become a remarkable black American surgeon. Dr. Drew, who died in an auto crash at the age of forty-six, lived a life of dedication and kindness. The following information was derived from a book entitled *Black Pioneers of Science and Invention*, by Louis Haber.[1]

"Thousands of people are dying on the battlefields from loss of blood," said Dr. Charles Drew. "I must give my time to solving the problems of blood transfer transfusion."

physics
Physicians had studied blood transfusion for years. However, they had met with many difficulties because the whole blood spoiled within days, and the matching of blood types was time-consuming. Nevertheless, Dr. Drew found there were fewer problems if plasma, instead of whole blood, was used in transfusion. Plasma, the liquid part of the blood without the cells, could be stored much longer and made the matching of blood types unnecessary. Anybody could be given plasma, and this was important on the battlefields of World War II.

In 1940 the Blood Transfusion Association set up a program for war-torn France. Dr. Drew asked them to send plasma rather than whole blood. But, it was started too late since France had fallen into the hands of the enemy.

Later, when Great Britain suffered heavy losses from air raids, Dr. Drew was asked to run a program called "Plasma for Britain." He organized the entire project, and thousands of Americans gave blood to help the British.

* *Miscues occurring more than twice were not counted.*

---

[1]Excerpt from *Black Pioneers of Science and Invention* by Louis Haber, copyright © 1970 by Harcourt Brace Jovanovich, Inc., reprinted by permission of the publisher.

Errors: $^5/_{192}$ = 3%

Comp: $^8/_8$ = 100%

Rate: 96 sec = 1.6 min

192 words / 1.6 min = 120 w/m

COMPREHENSION QUESTIONS AND POSSIBLE ANSWERS

✓ 1. What was the area of Dr. Drew's major work?
(blood transfusion) *blood — transfusions*

✓ 2. What is meant by the word *difficulties*?
(problems) *problems*

✓ 3. Why did Dr. Drew decide to devote his time to solving the problems of blood transfusion?
(Thousands were dying on the battlefields of World War II.)
because of men dying- World War II

✓ 4. What is *plasma*?
(the liquid portion of the blood without cells)
part of blood - not cells

✓ 5. In 1940 what program was organized to aid war-torn France?
(Blood Transfusion Association)
Blood Transfusion Program — No, Association

✓ 6. What is meant by the phrase "fallen into the hands of the enemy"?
(France had lost battles to the enemy.)
You lose a battle to the enemy.

✓ 7. Why did Americans give blood to help their British neighbors?
(Britain had suffered heavy losses from air raids.)
Because air raids killed lots of them

✓ 8. What is said in this story that makes you think more people survived injuries on the battlefield because of Dr. Drew's work in blood transfusion?
(Stated: Plasma could be stored longer; with plasma, blood typing was unnecessary; anybody could be given plasma.)
There were fewer problems with plasma — it didn't spoil as easy as blood.

Retelling: This doctor, Drew was his name, discovered plasma. Because it didn't spoil as easy as blood, it was better for transfusions — and blood types didn't have to match. It was used during World War II, not in France because it was too late, but in Britain for air raid victims

Scoring Guide	
Word Rec.	Comp.
IND 2	IND 0–1
INST 10	INST 2
FRUST 20+	FRUST 4+

ANALYTICAL READING INVENTORY, FORM A, LEVEL 7
(262 WORDS, 14 SENTENCES)

EXAMINER'S INTRODUCTION

S. E. Hinton wrote a very sensitive book called *The Outsiders*,[2] showing the loyalties teenagers in gangs have toward one another. In this passage, Johnny is in serious trouble, and his friends, Ponyboy and Dally, prefer to stick by him until he can decide how best to solve his problem. Please read a retelling of one of the incidents from this memorable book.

While he had been hiding out for the past five days, Johnny had given

serious thought to the whole mess. He had decided to return home, turn

himself in to the police, and take the consequences of his crime. Being only

sixteen, he was too young to have to run away for the rest of his life. He knew

the fight had been in self-defense, but the fact still remained that he had

killed another person, and the thought of that miserable night in the city

park sent Johnny into a terrifying panic.

He told Dally and Ponyboy of his decision, and now Dally reluctantly

began the long drive home. Dally had gone to jail before, and this was one

wretched experience he did not want his friend to have to endure.

As they reached the top of Jay Mountain, Dally slammed on the brakes!

The old church where Johnny and Ponyboy had been hiding was in flames!

Ponyboy and Johnny bolted from the car to question a bystander who ex-

plained that they were having a school picnic when the church began to burn.

Suddenly, the crowd was shocked to hear desperate cries from inside!

Ponyboy and Johnny ran into the burning church, and the boys lifted the

children one by one through a window to safety. Chunks of the old roof were

already beginning to fall as the last child was taken out. Ponyboy leaped

through the window, vaguely hearing the sound of falling timber. Then, as he

lay coughing and exhausted on the ground, he heard Johnny's terrifying

scream!

[2]Hinton, S.E. (1967). *The Outsiders.* New York: Viking.

Errors: $13/262 = 5\%$
Comp: $7/8 = 88\%$
Rate: $150 \text{ sec} = 2.5 \text{ min}$
$262 \text{ words}/2.5 \text{ min} = 105 \text{ w/m}$

COMPREHENSION QUESTIONS AND POSSIBLE ANSWERS

✓ **1.** What difficult conflict did Johnny have to solve?
(He had committed a crime, and he had decided to turn himself in to the police or to run away.) *whether to go home and turn himself in or stay out.*

✓ **2.** What is meant by the phrase, "take the consequences"?
(take the punishment for his crime) *he would take whatever punishment they gave him.*

✓ **3.** Where did the crime take place?
(in the city park) *in New York. (James was familiar with the book.)*

✓ **4.** Why were Dally and the boys returning home?
(Johnny had decided to return home and turn himself in.) *So Johnny could turn himself in.*

✓ **5.** Why did Dally slam on the brakes?
(He saw the burning church.) *because the church was burning.*

✓ **6.** How did the boys get the children out of the burning church?
(lifted them through the window) *They ran in and the roof was caving in — the boy jumped out the window with the children.*

✗ **7.** What is meant by the word *vaguely*?
(not clearly defined, unclear) *D.K.*

✓ **8.** What is said in the story that makes you think Johnny thought he should turn himself in?
(Stated: He said that he was too young to run and hide for the rest of his life; the fact still remained that he had killed another person, and this was apparently something he felt he couldn't live with.)
He was running and hiding and things and he just didn't want to stay away from people and be afraid of everyone.

Scoring Guide	
Word Rec.	Comp.
IND 2-3	(IND 0-1)
(INST 13)	INST 2
FRUST 26+	FRUST 4+

ANALYTICAL READING INVENTORY, FORM A, LEVEL 8
(286 WORDS, 15 SENTENCES)

EXAMINER'S INTRODUCTION
Witch-hunts took place in England back in the 1600s. The following information was derived from an article entitled "East Anglican and Essex Witches," from *Man, Myth, and Magic: An Illustrated Encyclopedia of the Supernatural*.

Witch-hunts were common in seventeenth-century England. The mere presence of a witch-hunter in a village caused such fear among the people that children would even denounce their parents.

Belief in magic was common in those days. Perhaps some of the victims of these hunts did think themselves guilty of witchery, but history has proven that the majority of men and women accused and tortured by witch-hunters were but poor, defenseless victims of the times.

One of the best-known methods for the detection of a witch was the "swimming test." In this ordeal the suspect was dragged into a pool or stream after he was already tired from torture and fear. If the suspect floated to the top he was found guilty, and long pins were plunged into his body in search of the devil's marks. If he sank to the bottom, he was presumed innocent.

In 1645 a man who titled himself, Witchfinder General Matthew Hopkins, led a severe and cruel hunt. Because a civil war was raging in England at the time, tensions and fears were common among the people. The time was ripe for persecution.

In that same year Hopkins imprisoned as many as 200 persons, all charged with witchcraft. Among eighteen of those who died by hanging was one John Lowes, a seventy-year-old clergyman who had been accused of witchcraft by his congregation. After undergoing intolerable torture, the old man admitted ownership of an evil spirit which he allegedly ordered to sink a ship. No one bothered to check out the existence of such a vessel or to ask

ⓒ an
ⓒ over

about ~~any~~ reported sinkings on that day, and he was hanged ~~after~~ reading his   2

own burial service.

Errors: 22/286 = 8%
Comp: 5/8 = 62.5%
Rate: 188 sec = 3.13 min
286 words / 3.13 min = 91 w/m

COMPREHENSION QUESTIONS AND POSSIBLE ANSWERS

✓**1.** What commonly happened in seventeenth-century England?
(witch-hunts) *they had trials of bewitched*

✓**2.** According to this passage, what has history proven about witch-hunts?
(Most of the men and women accused and tortured for being witches
were but poor and defenseless people.) *that there really is no such
thing as witchcraft.*

✗**3.** Why would children even denounce their parents as witches?
(The mere presence of a witch-finder caused such fear among the people
and children.) *if their parents got mad at them and accused
them and told.*

✓**4.** What is meant by the phrase, "method of detection"?
(way of finding something out) *it's a test to see if a person's
a witch or evil*

✓**5.** In seventeenth-century England, why was the time ripe for persecution?
(A civil war was raging, causing tension and fear.) *a civil war*

✗**6.** What is meant by the word *allegedly*? *he said he would sink a ship*
(asserted to be true or exist but not proven) *and the people thought
he was a witch because they got no report.*

✗**7.** What did John Lowes allegedly do?
(owned an evil spirit which sank a ship) *he was the guy who committed
people to death was in the with hunts.*

✓**8.** What is said in the story that makes you think the swimming test was
unjust?
(Stated: If the accused person sank, thus being proven innocent, he or
she was probably dead from drowning.) *If they weren't a witch, they
would die anyway. If they were innocent, they would die anyway.*

Scoring Guide	
Word Rec.	Comp.
IND 3	IND 0–1
INST 15	INST 2
FRUST 30+	FRUST 4+

ANALYTICAL READING INVENTORY, FORM A, LEVEL 9
(339 WORDS, 18 SENTENCES)

EXAMINER'S INTRODUCTION

This selection, based upon information from two articles appearing in a 1973 issue of *Plain Truth*, entitled "Who's That Polluting My World?" and "How One Town Solves Pollution and Saves Water," describes some interesting facts concerning pollution and its control.

"This lake is all treated sewer water," the old gentleman murmured in admiration. The old man sat on a bench as close to the bank as possible with his elbows resting on his knees while gazing at the rippling water. The breeze sweeping across the lake caused the sailboats to glide about with amazing ease.

"We are making great ecological strides," he thought to himself. He knew well the story of this remarkable lake nestled in the foothills of southern California. He swelled with pride to recall the wise choice the Santee citizens had made when they elected not to join the metropolitan sewage system where the waste would have been discharged into the Pacific with only inadequate primary treatment. Rather, the residents constructed their own sewage facility, reclaiming the sewer water, thus extending their own supply to provide basic needs and clean recreational extras.

"This is probably the only city park in the world which is built just yards downstream from a sewer plant," the gentleman thought. He leaned forward scooping up a handful of water. "This lake is more sanitary than most natural streams."

It has taken ingenious foresight to make this unprecedented plan viable. Its resourcefulness lay in the fact that clean water provided not only lucrative recreational facilities, but the sewage waste solids furnished marketable soil conditioners and plant fertilizers.

As the old gentleman arose he caught sight of paper trash carelessly
←
                    content   © charged
tossed beside the shore. His ~~contented~~ expression ~~changed~~ to one of concern. 2
                            ←
                        discharged
He already knew that twenty million tons of paper are ~~discarded~~ each year in 1
                    © thirty
the United States representing a net loss of ~~340~~ million trees to the envi- 1
                            ←
                        © needle
ronment. The gentleman shook his head to think of this ~~needless~~ waste. He 1
                                ←
knew the United States comprises only 6 percent of the world's population,
    the
    ←
yet ~~its~~ citizens consume 30 percent of the world's total energy output, only to 1
            ←
waste half of it. The old gentleman shuddered at these thoughts as he picked

up the discarded paper and placed it into the trash container.

Errors: 24/339 = 7%

Comp: 2/8 = 25%

Rate: 234 sec = 3.90 min

339 words / 3.9 min = 87 w/m

COMPREHENSION QUESTIONS AND POSSIBLE ANSWERS

X **1.** What is the main idea of this passage?
       (We are making progress in pollution control, but still there is needless
       waste.) *how many people think bad thoughts about pollution.*

X **2.** What is meant by the phrase *inadequate primary treatment?*
       (insufficient water treatment) *does not give good treatment to the water*

✓ **3.** Where is this remarkable lake?
       (in Santee in southern California) *in a city park — in California*

X **4.** What happened when the Santee citizens constructed their own sewage
       facility?
       (It provided basic needs and clean recreational extras.)
       to stop pollution and sewage from going into the lake

X **5.** What is meant by the phrase *an unprecedented plan?*
       (one not done before)
       it wasn't given to them — it wasn't stated to them

X **6.** How much of the world's total energy does the United States use?
       (30 percent) *350%*

✓ 7. Why did the old gentleman's expression change when he got up from the bench?

(He caught sight of paper trash carelessly tossed beside the shore.)

He saw a piece of paper and it kills the beauty and the trees around the lake

X 8. What is said in the story that makes you think the Santee plan to reclaim sewage water was an ingenious and well thought-out ecological one?

(Stated: The clean water provided not only lucrative recreational facilities, but the waste solids furnished marketable soil conditioners and plant fertilizers.)

He would stop pollution going into the lake.

Scoring Guide			
Word Rec.		Comp.	
IND	3–4	IND	0–1
INST	18	INST	2
FRUST	36+	FRUST	4+

ANALYTICAL READING INVENTORY, FORM B, LEVEL 7
(234 WORDS, 15 SENTENCES)

EXAMINER'S INTRODUCTION

Dave's Song, a book by Robert McKay, is a very sensitive story about a young girl who finds out that she can learn to appreciate and care for someone quite different from other young adults in her class. Please read a retelling of some of the information from this memorable book.

Kate sat in her senior biology class, but she wasn't hearing a single word the teacher was saying since her mind was thoroughly preoccupied. She could only think about Dave and her date with him last Friday night.

The entire thing was so confusing and distracting that she kept glancing sideways to where he was sitting near the windows. He was by far the most handsome boy at Tylerton High. He was tall, strong, with shaggy hair, and brilliant blue eyes, but there was something very different about Dave Burdick which she found difficult to accept. She knew that he was independent, and at times he seemed actually defiant. She found this disturbing. He always neglected his appearance as if he didn't care what others thought. He was an excellent football player, probably the best in the entire school, but he quit the team. He was stubborn and belligerent, and he would argue with anyone over anything. He never hung around the other kids, so it seemed to her that he was a loner. He drove an old Ford pickup, which had chicken feathers and farm tools scattered all over the floor. Kate felt that he was more interested in raising chickens than in having friends. Yet, even knowing all of these things, there was something crazy going on in her mind. To her surprise she found Dave Burdick fascinating and quite to her liking.

Comp: 4 1/2 /8 = 56%
Rate: 126 sec = 2.1 min
  234 words/2.1 min = 111 w/m

COMPREHENSION QUESTIONS AND POSSIBLE ANSWERS

✓**1.** Why was Kate confused and distracted?
(Dave was very different from her other friends but she still found that she liked him.) *cause she kept thinking about the last date she had with Dave*

✓**2.** Why didn't Kate hear anything the biology teacher was saying?
(She was preoccupied.) *cause she was too interested in dreaming about Dave*

✗ **3.** What is meant by the word *independent*?
(not dependent upon others) *he's dedicated to work*

✓ **4.** What did Kate find disturbing about Dave?
(his defiant attitude) *he didn't care for other people.*

✗ **5.** What is meant by the word *belligerent*?
(hostile, waging war) *D.K.*

✓ **6.** What did Dave's truck have in it?
(chicken feathers and old farm tools) *chicken feathers and farm equipment*

✗ **7.** Why did Kate think Dave was a loner?
(because he never hung around other kids) *because he wouldn't talk at all – just sit around and think to himself.*

½ **8.** What is said in the story that makes you think Dave had a negative attitude?
(Stated: He seemed defiant, stubborn, belligerent.) *The one date he had with the girl – she said he was too much to himself. If anyone said something about him, he didn't care what they said about him.*

Retelling : *It's about this one girl saying about she was in class– she was sitting there dreaming about that one last dream that she had with Dave and she felt that he was the cutest boy in school – she saw how strong he was and she said he has furry hair and he was skinny and had shaggy hair and all – he was on the football team – he was the best one on the football team and he quit the team and he drove a pick-up truck that had feathers in the back of it. She knew that he was more interested in farming than he was in school.*

Scoring Guide		
Word Rec.		Comp.
IND	2–3	IND	0–1
INST	13	INST	2
FRUST	26+	FRUST 4+

ANALYTICAL READING INVENTORY, FORM B, LEVEL 6
(186 WORDS, 12 SENTENCES)

EXAMINER'S INTRODUCTION

Garrett A. Morgan, a black American inventor, was born in 1877. He not only invented the first electric traffic signal but also other important inventions. The following information was derived from a book entitled *Black Pioneers of Science and Invention*, by Louis Haber.[3]

The explosion was horrible that tragic day in Cleveland, Ohio, in 1916. Thirty-two men were trapped in a tunnel 250 feet below Lake Erie. No one could enter the smoke-filled tunnel to rescue the survivors.

"Someone get Garrett Morgan to help those men down there," shouted a man from the crowd. "Morgan and his breathing device are the only chance those men have!"

Garrett Morgan and his brother quickly came to the aid of the men trapped in the tunnel. Morgan had invented what he called a "Breathing Device," later to be known as the *gas mask*. Two years before, Morgan's invention had been tested by filling an enclosed tent with the foulest, thickest smoke possible. Placing the device over his head, a man entered this suffocating atmosphere, stayed twenty minutes, and emerged unharmed! Later, using a poisonous gas in a closed room, another test also provided the same successful results.

Although not all lived, every man was brought to the surface by the brothers. It was Morgan's concern for safer working conditions that saved lives that day and in the years to come.

Comp: 6½/8 = 81 %

Rate: 115 sec = 1.92 min

186 words/1.92 min = 97 w/m

COMPREHENSION QUESTIONS AND POSSIBLE ANSWERS

✓ 1. What did Garrett Morgan invent?
(gas mask — breathing device) *a gas mask*

✓ 2. Where was the tunnel located in which the men were trapped?
(250 feet below Lake Erie) *Cleveland, Ohio - 250 feet down*

½ 3. What happened as a result of the terrible explosion in Cleveland?
(thirty-two men were trapped) *gas filled the tunnel*

✓ 4. What is meant by the phrase, "this suffocating atmosphere"?
(the air in the tent was without oxygen)
run out of air - can't breathe - you'll die

✓ 5. What is meant by the word *device*?
(something intricate in design; a machine)
Something used to help someone — like a camera is a device.

✓ 6. What happened to the man who stayed in the tent for twenty minutes?
(He emerged unharmed.) *he survived — he got out of it*
— he could breathe

X 7. What was used to test the gas mask the second time?
(a poisonous gas) *smoke — I don't know*

✓ 8. What is said in the story that makes you think Morgan cared for the safety of others?
(Stated: It was Morgan's concern for safer working conditions which saved lives that day.)

He came as fast as he could with the breathing thing —
and he invented it to save lives.

Scoring Guide	
Word Rec.	Comp.
IND 2	IND 0–1
INST 10	INST 2
FRUST 20+	FRUST 4+

ANALYTICAL READING INVENTORY, FORM B, LEVEL 5 (197 WORDS, 12 SENTENCES)

EXAMINER'S INTRODUCTION

This is a story about Robyn Smith, who left a career as a movie star to become one of the first female jockeys. The following information was derived from an article appearing in *The Lincoln Library of Sports Champions*.

"I know that I was last in the race," announced Robyn Smith, "but I am determined to be the best woman jockey! I want to ride race horses!"

It was a rainy morning in 1969, and as Robyn stood outside talking to the trainer, Frank Wright, she was so dripping wet that water came running out of the top of her boots. Many people had doubts about Robyn's riding ability, but Wright was sure she could be a successful rider. He decided to give her a first big chance.

By December of that same year she had proven herself by placing fourth in a race. Robyn not only had skill as a jockey, but she also had a way with horses which made them run fast for her.

Soon, she became accepted by others as an excellent rider. She went on to highlight her career with a surprising victory riding a horse named North Star. This horse was known for being wild on the track, but Robyn was able to handle him. Together they outran a horse named Onion. This was a special victory for Robyn because later, in another race, Onion defeated the famous horse, Secretariat!

Comp: 8/8 = 100%

Rate: 108 sec = 1.8 min

197 words / 1.8 min = 109 w/m

COMPREHENSION QUESTIONS AND POSSIBLE ANSWERS

✓ 1. What was Robyn Smith determined to be?
(the best woman jockey) *the best woman jockey*

✓ 2. Why did water run out of the top of Robyn's boots?
(because she was standing outside in the rain)
She was in the rain

✓ 3. What did Frank Wright do for Robyn?
(gave her a first big chance) *gave her a chance to ride*

✓ 4. What is meant by the phrase, "proven herself"?
(She showed that she could ride well.) *to show she could do it*

✓ 5. What did others think of Robyn when she proved her riding skill?
(She was accepted as a good jockey.)
thought she was a good jockey

✓ 6. What was North Star known for?
(being wild on the track) *being wild and hard to handle*

✓ 7. Why was this a special victory for Robyn?
(North Star defeated Onion; Onion defeated the famous horse Secretariat.) *because she beat the horse who later beat Secretariat*

✓ 8. What is said in the story that makes you think Robyn's trainer had
confidence in her riding?
(Stated: Wright was sure she could be a successful rider; she had a way
with horses which made them run fast for her; she had skill as a rider.)
Because he gave her a chance

Scoring Guide	
Word Rec.	Comp.
IND 2	IND 0–1
INST 9	INST 2
FRUST 18+	FRUST 4+

ANALYTICAL READING INVENTORY, FORM C, LEVEL 8
(257 WORDS, 15 SENTENCES)

EXAMINER'S INTRODUCTION
The next selection you are to read is about vampires. At one time in our history vampires and other supernatural beings were believed to exist. The following information was derived from an article entitled "Vampires," from *Man, Myth, and Magic: An Illustrated Encyclopedia of the Supernatural*

"I am . . . Dracula," murmured a black-caped, fanged-toothed, pointed-eared monster. "I never drink . . . wine," he declared as moviegoers sat petrified in their seats.

In 1931, a novel by Irish author Bram Stoker became vividly alive on the movie screen as thousands flocked to see this re-creation of the vampire superstition which dates back to the sixteenth century.

According to the novel, a vampire looks pale, lean, and has a death-like icy touch. His eyes gleam or flash red, his ears are pointed like those of a werewolf, and his fingernails are curled and sharp. Some tales describe him as skeletal and often dressed in a black costume. His limited diet of blood gives him a foul-smelling breath. Old legends depict him with only one nostril and a barbed tongue. These creatures have the power to change their form into a cloud of mist or a bizarre nocturnal animal.

Despite modern disbelief in vampires, during the seventeenth century many thought they existed. It was believed that once a person died he could possibly return as a vampire. A corpse was often fastened in its grave with pegs or iron skewers to prevent a potential vampire from escaping.

Since the vampire was dormant during the day, graves were examined for small holes through which the monster could escape. If a grave was discovered with such holes, vampire hunters would remove the body and destroy it. This procedure took place during the daytime hours and all the

hunters returned to their homes before sunset.

Comp: 7/8 = 88%

COMPREHENSION QUESTIONS AND POSSIBLE ANSWERS

✓ 1. What is the main idea of this article?
      (Belief in vampires existed in the 16th and 17th centuries.)
      they used to believe in vampires

✓ 2. What are a vampire's eyes supposed to look like?
      (gleaming or flashing red) flash red

✓ 3. What is meant by the phrase, "bizarre animal"?
      (unique or strange) strange

✓ 4. How did old legends describe a vampire?
      (one nostril and a barbed tongue) one nostril [Anything else?]
      a funny tongue - a barb tongue

X 5. What is meant by the phrase, "barbed tongue"?
      (a forked or pointed tongue) D.K.

✓ 6. Why were iron skewers used to fasten a corpse to its grave?
      (to prevent it from escaping) to stop it from getting away

✓ 7. Why were the graves examined during the day?
      (There was less danger as vampires slept during the day.)
      the vampires slept then

✓ 8. What is said in this story that makes you think people in the 16th and
      17th centuries believed in and feared vampires?
      (Stated: They fastened corpses in their graves with iron skewers; they
      searched graves for perforations and if holes were found they destroyed
      the corpse.) they went hunting for them

Scoring Guide	
Word Rec.	Comp.
IND 3	IND 0-1
INST 15	INST 2
FRUST 30+	FRUST 4+

ANALYTICAL READING INVENTORY, FORM C, LEVEL 9
(315 WORDS, 17 SENTENCES)

EXAMINER'S INTRODUCTION

Jean-Pierre Haller, a Belgian explorer and author, was born and raised in the Belgian Congo. Since his childhood playmates had been members of the Efé Pygmy society, he returned in 1957 to become an adopted member and assist them in their dramatic struggle for survival. The following information was derived from an article entitled "To Save a People," appearing in a 1975 issue of *The Plain Truth.*

A young Pygmy stood in the parching equatorial African sun. He stood but five feet tall and his stature was bent from hard labor. His skin was golden brown and his hair was short and curled tightly to his head. His feet were bare and his clothes tattered. His eyes had the dull stare of a man once proud and free, but now deprived of the will to maintain his own gentle life-style.

The Pygmies are central Africa's oldest known surviving people and in the 1930's about 35,000 proudly lived in the Itiru Forest of the eastern Congo, now called Zaire. By 1957 their population had fallen to 25,000.

During the fifties, the Pygmies' ancestral forest was wastefully chopped down by lumber industrialists, robbing them of the vegetation and game they depended upon for survival. Consequently, the people were forced into the blistering sun to which they were unaccustomed. Large plantations closed in on their environment. National parks and game reserves were established, but no land was set aside to aid the Pygmy societies in their struggle for survival. Tourists brought contagious diseases to which the Pygmies had no immunity, and as a result their population continued to decline.

In 1960 the Belgian Congo received political independence, becoming the nation of Zaire. This political change brought civil war for which the nonaggressive Pygmies were the first to suffer and their number rapidly dwindled to 15,000. They became victims of new burdens such as paying income taxes, being drafted into the Zaire army, further loss of cultural identity, and by 1975 their size numbered some 3,800.

The Pygmies have a warm and gentle life-style with a dignified moral code which forbids killing, lying, theft, devil worship, sorcery, disrespect for elders, and blasphemy. They do not engage in cannibalism, mutilation, ritual murder, intertribal war, initiation ordeals, or other cruel customs sometimes associated with equatorial Africa.

Comp: 6½/8 = 81%

COMPREHENSION QUESTIONS AND POSSIBLE ANSWERS

✓ 1. What is the main idea of this passage?
      (This Pygmy tribe is facing near extinction.) *about how Pygmies were forced to become like our society*

✓ 2. Where is the Itiru Forest?
      (eastern Congo, now called Zaire) *in Africa*

½ 3. What happened to the Pygmy society when their forests were chopped down?
      (They were robbed of the vegetation and game they depended upon for survival.) *they weren't used to the sun beating down on them*

✓ 4. What is meant by the word *immunity*?
      (condition of being able to resist a particular disease) *if a person isn't immune to a sickness, they'll probably get it*

✓ 5. What did tourists bring to the Pygmies?
      (contagious diseases) *diseases*

✗ 6. What is meant by the phrase, "nonaggressive Pygmies"?
      (nonhostile, nonwarlike) *you're not selfish, like someone who is crazy and always wanting something, they're nonaggressive*

✓ 7. In 1960, what happened when the Belgian Congo received political independence?
      (civil war and new suffering for the Pygmies) *they had to pay taxes and were drafted into the army.*

✓ 8. What is said in this story that makes you think no one cared enough to
       protect the Pygmies' rights?
       (Stated: Lumber industrialists wastefully chopped down the Pygmies'
       forests; parks and game reserves were set aside but no land was saved for
       the Pygmies.)
       they had to move to the cities and countryside
       with people

Scoring Guide	
Word Rec.	**Comp.**
IND 3-4	IND 0-1
INST 18	(INST 2)
FRUST 36+	FRUST 4+

References

Adams, M. J. (1990). *Beginning to read: Thinking and learning about print*. Cambridge, MA: MIT Press.

Allington, R. L. (1983). Fluency: The neglected reading goal. *The Reading Teacher, 36,* 556–561.

Anderson, R. C. (1972). How to construct achievement tests to assess comprehension. *Review of Educational Research, 42,* 145–170.

Anderson, R. C., & Davison, A. (1989). Conceptual and empirical bases of readability formulas. In G. Green & A. Davison (Eds.), *Linguistic complexity and text comprehension*. Hillsdale, NJ: Erlbaum.

Anderson, R. C. & Freebody, P. (1981). Vocabulary knowledge. In J. Guthrie (Ed.), *Comprehension and teaching: Research reviews*. Newark, DE: International Reading Association.

Anderson, T. H., & Armbruster, B. B. (1984). Studying. In P. D. Pearson, R. Barr, M. Kamil, & P. Mosenthal (Eds.), *Handbook of reading research* (pp. 657–679). White Plains, NY: Longman.

Anglin, J. M. (1977). *Word, object, and conceptual development*. New York: Norton.

Asch, S. E., & Nerlove, H. (1960). The development of double-function terms in children: An exploratory investigation. In B. Kaplan & S. Wapner (Eds.), *Perspectives in psychological theory: Essays in honor of Heinz Werner*. New York: International Universities Press. Cited in Gardner, H., Winner, E., Bechhofer, R., & Wolf, D. (1978). The development of figurative language. In K. E. Nelson (Ed.), *Children's language* (Vol. 1). New York: Gardner.

Baghban, M. (1984). *Our daughter learns to read and write: A case study from birth to three*. Newark, DE: International Reading Association.

Bakhtin, M. M. (1981). *The dialogic imagination*. Austin: University of Texas Press.

Baldwin, R. S., Luce, T. S., & Readence, J. E. (1982). The impact of subschemata on metaphorical processing. *Reading Research Quarterly, 17,* 528–543.

Ball, E. W., & Blachman, B. A. (1991). Does phoneme segmentation training in kindergarten make a difference in early word recognition and developmental spelling? *Reading Research Quarterly, 26*(1), 49–66.

Bannon, E., Fisher, P. J. L., Pozzi, L., & Wessel, D. (1990). Effective definitions for word learning. *Journal of Reading, 34,* 301–302.

Barr, R. (1974). Influence of instruction on early reading. *Interchange, 5,* 13–22.

Barr, R. (in press). What research says about grouping in the past and present and what it suggests about the future. In M. Radencich & L. McKay (Eds.), *Flexible grouping in the elementary grades*. Needham Heights, MA: Allyn & Bacon.

Barr, R., & Dreeben, R. (1983). *How schools work*. Chicago: University of Chicago Press.

Barr, R., & Dreeben, R. (1991). Grouping students for reading instruction. In R. Barr, M. Kamil, P. Mosenthal, & P. D. Pearson (Eds.), *Handbook of reading research* (Vol. 2, pp. 885–910). White Plains, NY: Longman.

Barron, R. (1969). The use of vocabulary as an advance organizer. In H. L. Herber & P. L. Sanders (Eds.), *Research in reading in the content areas: First year report*. Syracuse, NY: Syracuse University Reading and Language Arts Center.

Bartlett, B. J. (1978). *Top-level structure as an organizational strategy for recall of classroom text.* Unpublished doctoral dissertation, Arizona State University. Cited in Meyer, B. J. F., Brandt, D. M., & Bluth, G. J. (1980). Use of top-level structure in text: Key for reading comprehension of ninth-grade students. *Reading Research Quarterly, 16,* 72–103.

Bartoli, J., & Botel, M. (1989). Reading/learning disability: An ecological systems view. *Reading Instruction Journal, 32*(3), 13–19.

Bean, T. W., Singer, H., & Cowan, S. (1985). Acquisition of a topic schema in high school biology through an analogical study guide. In J. A. Niles & R. V. Lalik (Eds.), *Issues in literacy: A research perspective* (Thirty-fourth yearbook of the National Reading Conference). Rochester, NY: National Reading Conference.

Beck, I. L., & McKeown, M. G. (1981). Developing questions that promote comprehension: The story map. *Language Arts, 58,* 913–918.

Beck, I. L., McKeown, M. G., McCaslin, E. S., & Burkes, A. M. (1979). *Instructional dimensions that may affect reading comprehension: Examples from two commercial reading programs.* (LRDC Publication 1979/20). Pittsburgh: University of Pittsburgh, Learning Research and Development Center.

Beck, I. L., Omanson, R. C., & McKeown, M. G. (1982). An instructional redesign of reading lessons: Effects on comprehension. *Reading Research Quarterly 17,* 462–481.

Beck, I. L., Perfetti, C. A., & McKeown, M. G. (1982). The effects of long-term vocabulary instruction on lexical access and reading comprehension. *Journal of Educational Psychology, 74,* 506–521.

Becker, W., Dixon, R. C., & Inman-Anderson, L. (1980). *Morphographic and root word analysis of 26,000 high-frequency words.* Eugene, OR: College of Education, University of Oregon.

Betts, E. A. (1946). *Foundations of reading instruction.* New York: American Books.

Betts, E. A. (1954). *Foundations of reading instruction* (rev. ed.). New York: American Book Company.

Biemiller, A. (1970). The development of the use of graphic and contextual information as children learn to read. *Reading Research Quarterly, 6,* 75–96.

Biemiller, A. (1979). Changes in the use of graphic and contextual information as functions of passage difficulty and reading achievement level. *Journal of Reading Behavior, 11,* 307–318.

Bissex, G. L. (1980). *GNYS AT WRK: A child learns to write and read.* Cambridge, MA: Harvard University Press.

Blachowicz, C. L. Z. (1977). Cloze activities for primary readers. *The Reading Teacher, 31,* 300–302.

Blachowicz, C. L. Z. (1984). Reading and remembering: A constructivist perspective on comprehension and its disorders. *Visible Language, 18,* 391–403.

Blachowicz, C. L. Z. (1985). Vocabulary development and reading: From research to instruction. *The Reading Teacher, 38,* 876–881.

Blachowicz, C. L. Z. (1986). Making connection: Alternatives to the vocabulary notebook. *Journal of Reading, 29,* 643–649.

Blachowicz, C. L. Z. (1993). C2QU: A metacognitive model for context instruction. *The Reading Teacher, 47*(3), 268–269.

Blachowicz, C. L. Z., & Fisher, P. J. L. (1989). Defining is an unnatural act: A study of written definitions. In S. McCormick & J. Zutell (Eds.), *Cognitive and social perspectives for literary research and instruction* (Thirty-eighth yearbook of the National Reading Conference) Chicago: National Reading Conference.

Blachowicz, C. L. Z., Fisher, P. J. L., Costa, M., & Pozzi, M. (1993). *Researching vocabulary learning in middle school cooperative reading groups: A teacher-researcher collaboration.* Paper presented at the Tenth Great Lakes Regional Reading Conference, Chicago.

Blachowicz, C. L. Z., & Zabroske, B. (1990). Context instruction: A metacognitive approach for at-risk readers. *Journal of Reading, 33,* 504–508.

Bortnick, R., & Lopardo, G. (1973). An instructional application of the cloze procedure. *Journal of Reading, 16,* 296–300.

Bradley, L., & Bryant, P. E., (1983). Categorizing sounds and learning to read: A causal connection. *Nature, 301,* 419–421.

Bridge, C. A., & Tierney, R. J. (1981). The inferential operations of children across text with narrative and expository tendencies. *Journal of Reading Behavior, 13,* 201–214.

Brown, C. (1986). A tutorial procedure for enhancing the reading comprehension of college students (Doctoral dissertation, University of Pennsylvania). *Dissertation Abstracts International, 47,* 3719A.

Bruce, D. 1964. Analysis of word sounds by young children. *British Journal of Educational Psychology, 34,* 148–169.

Buikema, J. L., & Graves, M. F. (1993). Teaching students to use context clues to infer word meanings. *Journal of Reading, 36*(6), 450–457.

Buros, O. K. (Ed.). (1938–1985). *Mental measurements yearbook* (Vols. 1–8). Highland Park, NJ: Gryphon Press.

Buros, O. K. (Ed.). (1961). *Tests in print I.* Highland Park, NJ: Gryphon Press.

Buros, O. K. (Ed.). (1968). *Reading tests and reviews I.* Highland Park, NJ: Gryphon Press.

Buros, O. K. (Ed.). (1974). *Tests in print II.* Highland Park, NJ: Gryphon Press.

Buros, O. K. (Ed.). (1975). *Reading tests and reviews II.* Highland Park, NJ: Gryphon Press.

Buros, O. K. (Ed.). (1978). *Eighth mental measurement yearbook.* Highland Park, NJ: Gryphon Press.

Bussis, A. M., Chittenden, E. A., Amarel, M., & Klausner, E. (1985). *Inquiry into meaning: An investigation of learning to read.* Hillsdale, NJ: Erlbaum.

Calkins, L. (1986). *The art of teaching writing.* Portsmouth, NH: Heinemann Educational Books.

Carpenter, P. A., & Just, M. A. (1977). Reading comprehension as eyes see it. In M. A. Just & P. A. Carpenter (Eds.), *Cognitive processes in comprehension.* Hillsdale, NJ: Erlbaum.

Carr, E., & Wixson, K. K. (1986). Guidelines for evaluating vocabulary instruction. *Journal of Reading, 29,* 588–595.

Carver, R. P. (1983). Is reading rate constant or flexible? *Reading Research Quarterly, 18,* 190–215.

Chall, J. S. (1983). *Stages of reading development.* New York: McGraw-Hill.

Chall, J. S., & Squire, J. R. (1991). The publishing industry and textbooks. In R. Barr, M. Kamil, P. Mosenthal, & P. D. Pearson (Eds.), *Handbook of reading research* (Vol. 2, pp. 120–146). White Plains, NY: Longman.

Chomsky, C. (1976). After decoding: What? *Language Arts, 53,* 288–296, 314.

Clark, E. V. (1973). What's in a word? On the child's acquisition of semantics in his first language. In T. E. Moore (Ed.), *Cognitive development and the acquisition of language.* New York: Academic Press.

Clay, M. M. (1967). The reading behavior of five year old children: A research project. *New Zealand Journal of Educational Studies, 2,* 11–31.

Clay, M. M. (1975). *What did I write?* Portsmouth, NH: Heinemann Educational Books.

Clay, M. M. (1979). *Reading: The patterning of complex behavior.* Auckland, N.Z.: Heinemann.

Clay M. M. (1985). *The early detection of reading difficulties* (3rd ed.). Portsmouth, NH: Heinemann.

Clay, M. M. (1991). Introducing a new storybook to young readers. *The Reading Teacher, 45*(4), 264–273.

Clarke, L. K. (1989). Encouraging invented spelling in first graders' writing: Effects on learning to spell and read. *Research in the Teaching of English, 22,* 281–309.

Cochran-Smith, M. (1984). *The making of a reader.* Norwood, NJ: Ablex.

Cohen, A. S. (1974–1975). Oral reading errors of first grade children taught by a code emphasis approach. *Reading Research Quarterly, 10,* 616–650.

Cramer, R. L. (1989). *Scott, Foresman language.* Glenview, IL: Scott, Foresman.

Crothers, E. J. (1978). Inference and coherence. *Discourse Processes, 1,* 51–71.

Cunningham, P. M. (1975–1976). Investigating a synthesized theory of mediated word identification. *Reading Research Quarterly, 11,* 127–143.

Cunningham, P. M. (1978). Decoding polysyllabic words: An alternative strategy. *Journal of Reading, 21,* 608–614.

Cunningham, P. M. (1979). A compare/contrast theory of mediated word identification. *The Reading Teacher, 32,* 774–778.

Dahl, K. L., & Freppon, P. A. (1991). Literacy learning in whole-language classrooms: An analysis of low socioeconomic urban children learning to read and write in kindergarten. In J. Zutel & S. McCormick (Eds.), *Learner factors/teacher factors: Issues in literacy research and instruction* (pp. 149–158) (Fortieth yearbook of the National Reading Conference). Chicago: National Reading Conference.

Daskal, J. (1983). *Basic strategies for improving comprehension of written materials.* Unpublished manuscript, Chicago.

Davidson, J. L., & Wilkerson, B. C. (1988). *Directed reading-thinking activities.* Monroe, NY: Trillium Press.

Davis, F. B. (1944). Fundamental factors of comprehension in reading. *Psychometrika, 9,* 185–197.

Davis, F. B. (1968). Research in comprehension in reading. *Reading Research Quarterly, 3,* 499–544.

Dearborn, W. F. (1906). The psychology of reading. *Archives of Philosophy, Psychology and Scientific Methods, 1,* 71–132.

Diederich, P. B. (1974). *Measuring growth in English.* Urbana, IL: National Council of Teachers of English.

Dodge, R. (1905). The illusion of clear vision during eye-movement. *Psychological Bulletin, 12,* 193–199.

Dodge, R. (1907). An experimental study of visual fixation. *Psychological Review Monograph Supplements, 8,* 1–96.

Dolch, E. W. (1936). Basic sight vocabulary. *Elementary School Journal, 36,* 456–460.

Draper, A. G., & Moeller, G. H. (1971). We think with words (therefore, to improve thinking, teach vocabulary). *Phi Delta Kappan, 52,* 482–484.

Drum, P. A. (1983). Vocabulary knowledge. In J. A. Niles & L. A. Harris (Eds.), *Searches for meaning in reading/language processing and instruction* (Thirty-second yearbook of the National Reading Conference). Rochester, NY: National Reading Conference.

Duffelmeyer, F. A. (1980). The influence of experience-based vocabulary instruction on learning word meanings. *Journal of Reading, 24,* 35–40.

Duffy, G., Roehler, L., & Herrmann, B. (1988). Modeling mental processes helps poor readers become strategic readers. *The Reading Teacher, 41*(8), 762–767.

Durkin, D. (1978–1979). What classroom observations reveal about reading comprehension instruction. *Reading Research Quarterly, 14,* 481–533.

Ehri, L. C. (1979). Linguistic insight: Threshold of reading acquisition. In T. G. Waller & G. E. MacKinnon (Eds.), *Reading research: Advances in theory and practice* (Vol. 1., pp. 63–114). New York: Harcourt Brace Jovanovich.

Ehri, L. C. (1980). The development of orthographic images. In U. Frith (Ed.), *Cognitive processes in spelling.* London: Academic Press.

Ehri, L. C. (1983). How orthography alters spoken language competencies in children learning to read and spell. In J. Downing & R. Valtin (Eds.), *Language awareness and learning to read.* New York: Springer Verlag.

Ehri, L. C. (1991). Development of the ability to read words. In R. Barr, M. Kamil, P. Mosenthal, & P. D. Pearson (Eds.), *Handbook of reading research,* (Vol. 2, pp. 383–417). White Plains, NY: Longman.

Ekwall, E. E. (1976). *Diagnosis and remediation of the disabled reader.* Boston: Allyn & Bacon.

Elbow, P. (1986). Portfolio assessment as an alternative in proficiency testing. Notes from the National Testing Network on Writing, 6, 3, and 12.

Elkonin, D. B. (1963). The psychology of mastering elements of reading. In B. Simon (Ed.), *Educational psychology in the U.S.S.R.* London: Routledge & Kegan Paul.

Eller, R. G., Pappas, C. C., & Brown, E. (1988). The lexical development of kindergartners: Learning from written context. *Journal of Reading Behavior, 20,* 5–24.

Farr, R., & Carey, R. F. (1986). *Reading: What can be measured?* Newark, DE: International Reading Association.

Feifel, H., & Lorge, I. (1950). Qualitative differences in the vocabulary responses of children. *Journal of Educational Psychology, 41,* 1–18.

Fernald, G. M., & Keller, H. (1926). The effect of kinesthetic factors in the development of word recognition in nonreaders. *Journal of Educational Research, 4,* 355–377.

Ferreiro, E. (1984). The underlying logic of literacy development. In H. Goelman, A. Oberg, & F. Smith (Eds.), *Awakening to literacy.* Portsmouth, NH: Heinemann Educational Books.

Ferreiro, E., & Teberosky, A. (1982). *Literacy before schooling.* Portsmouth, NH: Heinemann Educational Books.

Ferroli, L., & Shanahan, T. (1987). Kindergarten spelling: Explaining its relation to first-grade reading. In J. E. Readence & R. S. Baldwin (Eds.), *Research in literacy: Merging perspectives* (Thirty-sixth yearbook of the National Reading Conference). Rochester, NY: National Reading Conference.

Fisher, P. J. L., Blachowicz, C. L. Z., & Smith, J. C. (1991). Vocabulary learning in literature discussion groups. In J. Zutell & S. McCormick (Eds.), *Learner factors/teacher factors: Issues in literacy research and instruction* (pp. 201–209) (Fortieth yearbook of the National Reading Conference). Chicago: National Reading Conference.

Fitzgerald, J. (1989). Enhancing two related thought processes: Revision in writing and critical reading. *The Reading Teacher, 43*(1), 42–48.

Freebody, P., & Anderson, R. C. (1983a). Effects of differing proportions and locations of difficult vocabulary on text comprehension. *Journal of Reading Behavior, 15,* 19–39.

Freebody, P., & Anderson, R. C. (1983b). Effects of vocabulary difficulty, text cohesion, and schema availability on reading comprehension. *Reading Research Quarterly, 18,* 277–294.

Froese, V., & Kurushima, S. (1979). The effects of sentence expansion practice on the reading comprehension and writing ability of third graders. In M. L. Kamil & A. J. Moe (Eds.), *Reading research: Studies and applications* (Twenty-eighth yearbook of the National Reading Conference). Clemson, SC: National Reading Conference.

Galda, L. (1990). A longitudinal study of the spectator stance as a function of age and genre. *Research in the Teaching of English, 24*(3), 261–278.

Gambrell, L., Pfeiffer, W., & Wilson, R. (1985). The effects of retelling upon reading comprehension and recall of text information. *Journal of Educational Research, 7,* 216–220.

Gardner, H., Winner, E., Bechhofer, R., & Wolf, D. (1978). The development of figurative language. In K. E. Nelson (Ed.), *Children's language* (Vol. 1). New York: Gardner.

Garner, R. (1987). *Metacognition and reading comprehension.* Norwood, NJ: Ablex.

Garner, R., & Reis, R. (1981). Monitoring and resolving comprehension obstacles: An investigation of spontaneous lookbacks among upper-grade good and poor comprehenders. *Reading Research Quarterly, 16,* 569–582.

Geva, E. (1983). Facilitating reading comprehension through flowcharting. *Reading Research Quarterly, 18,* 384–405.

Gilbert, D. W. (1959). *Breaking the reading barrier.* Englewood Cliffs, NJ: Prentice-Hall.

Gillet, J. W., & Temple, C. (1982). *Understanding reading problems: Assessment and instruction.* Boston: Little, Brown.

Glynn, T., Crooks, T., Bethune, N., Ballard, K., & Smith, J. (1989). *Reading Recovery in context.* Wellington, NZ: New Zealand Department of Education.

Golden, J. M., & Pappas, C. C. (1987). *A critical review of retelling procedures in research on children's cognitive processing of written text.* Paper presented at the annual meeting of the National Reading Conference, St. Petersburg, FL.

Goodman, K. S. (1965). A linguistic study of cues and miscues in reading. *Elementary English, 42,* 639–643.

Goodman, K. S. (1967). Reading: A psycholinguistic guessing game. *Journal of the Reading Specialist, 6,* 126–135.

Goodman, K. S. (1969). Analysis of reading miscues: Applied psycholinguistics. *Reading Research Quarterly, 5,* 9–30.

Goodman, K. S. (1976). Reading: A psycholinguistic guessing game. In H. Singer & R. Ruddell (Eds.), *Theoretical models and processes of reading.* Newark, DE: International Reading Association.

Goodman, Y. M., Watson, D. J., & Burke, C. L. (1987). *Reading miscue inventory: Alternative procedures.* New York: Richard C. Owen.

Goswami, U., & Bryant, P. E. (1990). *Phonological skills and learning to read.* Hillsdale, NJ: Erlbaum.

Goswami, U., & Mead, F. (1992). Onset and rime awareness and analogies in reading. *Reading Research Quarterly, 237,* 152–162.

Gourley, J. W. (1978). This basal is easy to read—or is it? *The Reading Teacher, 32,* 174–182.

Graves, D. H., & Sunstein, B. S. (1992). *Portfolio portraits.* Portsmouth, NH: Heinemann.

Graves, M., & Prenn, M. (1986). Costs and benefits of various methods of teaching vocabulary. *Journal of Reading, 29,* 596–602.

Gray, C. T. (1922). *Deficiencies in reading ability: Their diagnosis and remedies.* Boston: D. C. Heath.

Gray, W. S., & Holmes, E. (1938). *The development of meaning vocabularies in reading* (Publications of the Laboratory Schools, No. 6). Chicago: University of Chicago.

Gray, W. S., with Kibbe, D., Lucas, L., & Miller, L. W. (1922). *Remedial cases in reading: Their diagnosis and treatment* (Supplemental Educational Monograph). Chicago: University of Chicago Press.

Griffith, P. L., & Olson, M. W. (1992). Phonemic awareness helps beginning readers break the code. *The Reading Teacher, 45,* 516–523.

Guszak, F. J. (1967). Teacher questioning and reading. *The Reading Teacher, 21,* 227–234.

Hafner, L. E. (1977). *Developmental reading in middle and secondary schools: Foundations, strategies, and skills for teaching.* New York: Macmillan.

Hammill, D. D., & Larsen, S. C. (1988). *Test of Written Language*-2. Austin, TX: Pro-Ed.

Hannan, E. (1984). Writing: What to look for, what to do. *Language Arts, 61,* 364–366.

Hansen, J. (1987). *When writers read.* Portsmouth, NH: Heinemann.

Harris, A. J., & Jacobson, M. D. (1982). *Basic reading vocabularies.* New York: Macmillan.

Harris, A. J., & Sipay, E. R. (1980). *How to increase reading ability: A guide to developmental and remedial methods* (7th ed.). White Plains, NY: Longman.

Harris, A. J., & Sipay, E. R. (1985). *How to increase reading ability: A guide to developmental and remedial methods* (8th ed.). White Plains, NY: Longman.

Harris, L. A., & Lalik, R. M. (1987). Teacher's use of informal reading inventories: An example of school constraints. *The Reading Teacher, 40,* 624–630.

Harris, T. L., & Hodges, R. E. (1981). *A dictionary of reading and related terms.* Newark, DE: International Reading Association.

Harste, J., Woodward, V., & Burke, C. (1984). *Language stories and literacy lessons.* Portsmouth, NH: Heinemann Educational Books.

Heller, M. F. (1991). *Reading-writing connections: From theory to practice.* White Plains, NY: Longman.

Henderson, E. H. (1981). *Learning to read and spell.* DeKalb, IL: Northern Illinois University Press.

Henderson, E. H. (1985). *Teaching spelling.* Boston: Houghton Mifflin.

Henderson, E. H., & Beers, J. W. (Eds.). (1980). *Developmental and cognitive aspects of learning to spell: A reflection of word knowledge.* Newark, DE: International Reading Association.

Hiebert, E. H. (1981). Developmental patterns and interrelationships of preschool children's print awareness. *Reading Research Quarterly, 16,* 236–260.

Holdaway, D. (1979). *The foundations of literacy.* Sydney: Aston Scholastic.

Huey, E. B. (1898). Preliminary experiments in the physiology and psychology of reading. *American Journal of Psychology, 9,* 575–586.

Huey, E. B. (1990). On the psychology and physiology of reading. I. *American Journal of Psychology, 11,* 283–342.

Huey, E. B. (1968). *The psychology and pedagogy of reading.* Cambridge, MA: MIT Press. (Originally published, 1908).

Hughes, A., Bernier, S. A., & Gurren, L. (Eds.). (1979). The eagle and the baker. In *The Gold Book, The Headway Program.* LaSalle, IL: Open Court Publishing.

Irwin, P. I., & Mitchell, J. N. (1983). A procedure for assessing the richness of retellings. *Journal of Reading, 2,* 391–396.

Jenkins, J. R., Pany, D., & Schreck, J. (1978). *Vocabulary and reading comprehension: Instructional effects* (Technical Report No. 100). Urbana: University of Illinois, Center for the Study of Reading. (ERIC Document Reproduction Service No. ED 160 999).

Johns, J. J. (1993). *Basic reading inventory* (5th ed.). Dubuque, IA: Kendall/Hunt.

Johnson, D. D., & Pearson, P. D. (1984). *Teaching reading vocabulary* (2nd ed.). New York: Holt, Rinehart & Winston.

Juel, C., & Roper/Schneider, D. (1985). The influence of basal readers on first grade reading. *Reading Research Quarterly, 20,* 134–152.

Kameenui, E. J., & Carnine, D. W. (1982). An investigation of fourth-graders' comprehension of pronoun constructions in ecologically valid texts. *Reading Research Quarterly, 17,* 556–580.

Kameenui, E. J., Carnine, D. W., & Freschi (1982). Effects of text construction and instructional procedures for teaching word meanings on comprehension and recall. *Reading Research Quarterly, 17,* 367–388.

Karpova, S. N. (1955). Osoznanie slovesnogo sostava rechi rebenkom doshkol'nogo vozrasta (The preschooler's realization of the lexical structure of speech). *Voprosy Psikhol,* No. 4, 43–55.

Kibby, M. W. (1979). Passage readability affects the oral reading strategies of disabled readers. *The Reading Teacher, 32,* 390–396.

Kimmell, S., & MacGinitie, W. H. (1985). Helping students revise hypotheses while reading. *The Reading Teacher, 37,* 768–771.

Kucer, S. (1985). The making of meaning: Reading and writing as parallel processes. *Written Communication, 2,* 317–336.

LaBerge, D., & Samuels, S. J. (1974). Toward a theory of automatic information processing in reading. *Cognitive Psychology, 6,* 293–323.

Lake, M. L. (1971). Improve the dictionary's image. *Elementary English, 48,* 363–365.

Langacker, P. W. (1973). *Language and its structure: Some fundamental linguistic concepts* (2nd ed.). New York: Harcourt Brace Jovanovich.

Leslie, L., & Caldwell, J. (1990). *Qualitative reading inventory.* Glenview, IL: Scott, Foresman.

Liberman, I., Shankweiler, D., Fischer, F., & Carter, B. (1974). Explicit syllable and phoneme segmentation in the young child. *Journal of Experimental Child Psychology, 18,* 201–212.

Lipson, M. Y., Cox, C., Iwanowski, S., & Simon, M. (1984). Explorations of the interactive nature of reading: Using commercial IRIs to gain insights. *Reading Psychology, 5,* 209–218.

Lopardo, G., & Sadow, M. W. (1982). Criteria and procedures for the method of repeated readings. *Journal of Reading, 26,* 156–160.

Lundberg, I., Frost, J., & Petersen, O. (1988). Effects of an extensive program for stimulating phonological awareness in preschool children. *Reading Research Quarterly, 23,* 263–284.

Lytle, S. L. (1982). Exploring comprehension style: A study of twelfth grade readers' transactions with text. Unpublished dissertation, University of Pennsylvania, Philadelphia, 317 pp.

Manzo, A. V. (1969). The ReQuest procedure. *Journal of Reading, 11,* 123–126.

Manzo, A. V. (1975). Guided reading procedure. *Journal of Reading, 18,* 287–291.

Marshall, N., & Glock, M. (1978–1979). Comprehension of connected discourse: A study into the relationships between the structure of text and information recalled. *Reading Research Quarterly, 16,* 10–56.

Martinez, M. G., & Roser, N. L. (1991). Children's responses to literature. In J. Flood, J. M. Jensen, D. Lapp, & J. R. Squire (Eds.), *Handbook of research on teaching the English language arts* (pp. 643–654). New York: Macmillan.

Mason, J. (1980). When *do* children begin to read: An exploration of four-year-old children's letter and word reading competencies. *Reading Research Quarterly, 15,* 203–227.

Mason, J. M., & the Staff of the Center for the Study of Reading, University of Illinois. (1984). A schema-theoretic view of the reading process as a basis for comprehension instruction. In G. G. Duffy, L. R. Roehler, & J. Mason (Eds.), *Comprehension instruction: Perspectives and suggestions.* White Plains, NY: Longman.

Masonheimer, P. E., Drum, P. A., & Ehri, L. C. (1984). Does environmental print identification lead children into word reading? *Journal of Reading Behavior, 16,* 257–271.

Masztal, N. B., & Smith, L. L. (1984). Do teachers really administer IRI's? *Reading World, 24*(1), 80–83.

Mayers, P. (1993). *Experiencing a novel: The thoughts, feelings, and motivation of adolescent readers.* Unpublished doctoral dissertation, National-Louis University, Evanston, IL.

McDonald, G. E. (1978). *The effects of instruction in the use of an abstract structural schema as an aid to comprehension and recall of written discourse.* Unpublished doctoral dissertation, Virginia Polytechnic Institute and State University. Cited in Meyer, B. J. F., Brandt, D. M., & Bluth, G. J. (1980). Use of top-level structure in text: Key for reading comprehension of ninth-grade students. *Reading Research Quarterly, 16,* 72–103.

McGee, L. M. (1992). Exploring the literature-based reading revolution (Focus on Research). *Language Arts, 69*(7), 529–537.

McGee, L. M., & Richgels, D. J. (1985). Teaching expository text structure to elementary students. *The Reading Teacher, 38,* 739–748.

McKeown, M. G. (1985). The acquisition of word meaning from context by children of high and low ability. *Reading Research Quarterly, 20,* 482–496.

Meyer, B. J. (1975). *The organization of prose and its effect on memory.* Amsterdam: North Holland.

Meyer, B. J. F., Brandt, D. M., & Bluth, G. J. (1980). Use of top-level structure in text: Key for reading comprehension of ninth-grade students. *Reading Research Quarterly, 16,* 72–103.

Meyers, J., & Lytle, S. (1986). Assessment of the learning process. *Exceptional Children, 53*(2), 138–144.

Mezynski, K. (1983). Issues concerning the acquisition of knowledge: Effects of vocabulary training on reading comprehension. *Review of Educational Research, 53,* 253–279.

Miller, G. A. (1977). *Spontaneous apprentices.* New York: Seabury Press.

Morgan, W. P. (1896). A case of congenital word blindness. *British Medical Journal, 2,* 1378.

Morris, D. (1980). Beginning readers' concept of word. In E. H. Henderson & J. W. Beers, *Developmental and cognitive aspects of learning to spell: A reflection of word knowledge.* Newark, DE: International Reading Association.

Morris, D. (1986). *Teaching reading in kindergarten: A language-experience approach.* Occasional Paper No. 13. Evanston, IL: The Reading Center, National College of Education.

Morris, D. (1988). *The relationship between word awareness and phoneme awareness in learning to read.* A longitudinal study in kindergarten. Occasional Paper No. 17. Evanston, IL: The Reading Center, National College of Education.

Morris, D., & Perney, J. (1984). Developmental spelling as a predictor of first-grade reading achievement. *Elementary School Journal, 84,* 441–457.

Morrow, L. (1988). Retelling stories as a diagnostic tool. In S. M. Glazer, L. W. Searfoss, & L. M. Gentile (Eds.), *Reexamining reading diagnosis: New trends and procedures* (pp. 128–149). Newark, DE: International Reading Association.

Morrow, L. (1992). The impact of a literature-based program on literacy achievement, use of literature, and attitudes of children from minority backgrounds. *Reading Research Quarterly, 27,* 250–275.

Morrow, L., Gambrell, L., Kapinus, B., Koskinen, P. S., Marshal, N., & Mitchell, J. (1986). Retelling: A strategy for reading assessment and instruction. In Niles, J. A., & Lalik, R. (Eds.), *Solving problems in literacy: Learners, teachers, and researchers.* (Thirty-fifth yearbook of the National Reading Conference), San Diego, CA, December 3–7, 1985.

Morrow, L. M., & Weinstein, C. S. (1986). Encouraging voluntary reading: The impact of a literature program on children's use of library centers. *Reading Research Quarterly, 21*(3), 330–346.

Nagy, W. E. (1988). *Teaching vocabulary to improve reading comprehension.* Newark, DE: International Reading Association.

Nagy, W. E., & Herman, P. A. (1987). Depth and breadth of vocabulary knowledge: Implications for acquisition and instruction. In M. G. McKeown & M. E. Curtis (Eds.), *The nature of vocabulary acquisition.* Hillsdale, NJ: Erlbaum.

Nelson, K. (1974). Concept, word, and sentence: Interrelations in acquisition and development. *Psychological Review, 81,* 267–285.

Nelson, L. J., & Morris, D. (1988). Echo reading with taped books. *Illinois Reading Council Journal, 16,* 39–42.

Ogle, D. M. (1986). K-W-L: A teaching model that develops active reading of expository text. *The Reading Teacher, 39,* 564–570.

Otto, W. S., & Askov, E. (1972). *The Wisconson design for reading skill development.* Minneapolis: National Computer Systems.

Page, W. D., & Barr, R. C. (1975). Use of informal reading inventories. In W. D. Page (Ed.), *Help for the reading teacher: New directions in research.* Urbana, IL: National Conference on Research in English, ERIC Clearinghouse on Reading and Communication Skills, National Institute of Education.

Palincsar, A. S., & Brown, A. L. (1983). *Reciprocal teaching of comprehension-monitoring activities* (Technical Report No. 269). Champaign: University of Illinois, Center for the Study of Reading.

Pappas, C. (1993). Is narrative "primary?" Some insights from kindergartners' pretend readings of stories and information books. *Journal of Reading Behavior, 25,* 97–129.

Pappas, C., Kiefer, B. Z., & Levstik, L. S. (1990). *An integrated language perspective in the elementary school: Theory into action.* White Plains, NY: Longman.

Parker, S. L. (1984). *A comparison of four types of initial vocabulary instruction.* Unpublished master's thesis, University of Minnesota, Minneapolis.

Paulson, F. L., Paulson, P. R., & Meyer, C. A. (1991). What makes a portfolio a portfolio? *Educational Leadership, 48*(5), 60–63.

Pearson, P. D., & Johnson, D. D. (1978). *Teaching reading comprehension.* New York: Holt, Rinehart & Winston.

Pelosi, P. L. (1977). *The origin and development of reading diagnosis in the United States: 1896–1946.* Unpublished doctoral dissertation, State University of New York at Buffalo.

Perfetti, C. A. (1985). *Reading ability.* New York: Oxford University Press.

Pikulski, J. A. (1974). A critical review: Informal reading inventories. *The Reading Teacher, 28,* 141–153.

Pils, L. L. (1991). Soon anofe you tout me: Evaluation in a first-grade whole language classroom. *The Reading Teacher, 45,* 46–50.

Powell, W. R. (1970). Reappraising the criteria for interpreting informal reading inventories. In D. L. Deboer (Ed.), *Reading diagnosis and evaluation.* Newark, DE: International Reading Association.

Powell, W. R. (1984). Mediated (emergent) reading levels: A construct. In J. Niles (Ed.), *Changing perspectives on research in reading language processing and instruction* (pp. 247–251). Rochester, NY: National Reading Conference.

Powell, W. R., & Dunkeld, C. G. (1971). Validity of the IRI reading levels. *Elementary English, 48,* 637–642.

Pressley, M., Levin, J. R., & Miller, G. E. (1981). How does the keyword method affect vocabulary comprehension and usage? *Reading Research Quarterly, 16,* 213–226.

Raphael, T. (1986). Teaching question–answer relationships, revisited. *The Reading Teacher, 39,* 516–522.

Read, C. (1971). Preschool children's knowledge of English phonology. *Harvard Educational Review, 41,* 1–34.

Readence, J. E., Baldwin, R. S., & Rickelman, R. J. (1983). Instructional insights into metaphor and similes. *Journal of Reading, 27,* 109–112.

Rhodes, L. K., & Nathenson-Mejia, S. (1992). Anecdotal records: A powerful tool for ongoing literacy assessment. *The Reading Teacher, 45,* 502–509.

Robinson, H. M. (1937). The study of disabilities in reading. *Elementary School Journal, 38,* 15–38.

Rogoff, B. (1990). *Apprenticeship in thinking.* New York: Oxford University Press.

Rosch, E. H. (1973). On the internal structure of perceptual and semantic categories. In T. E. Moore (Ed.), *Cognitive development and the acquisition of language.* New York: Academic Press.

Rosenblatt, L. M. (1985). Viewpoints: Transaction versus interaction—A terminological rescue operation. *Research in the Teaching of English, 19,* 96–107.

Roser, N., & Juel, C. (1982). Effects of vocabulary instruction on reading comprehension. In J. A. Niles & L. A. Harris (Eds.), *New inquiries in reading research and instruction* (Thirty-first yearbook of the National Reading Conference). Rochester, NY: National Reading Conference.

Rosner, J., & Simon, D. (1971). The auditory analysis test: An initial report. *Journal of Learning Disabilities, 4,* 384–392.

Sadow, M. W. (1982). The use of story grammar in the design of questions. *The Reading Teacher, 35,* 518–522.

Samuels, S. J. (1979). The method of repeated readings. *The Reading Teacher, 32*(4), 403–408.

Sanders, N. M. (1966). *Classroom questions: What kinds?* New York: Harper & Row.

Schlein, M. (1966). The big cheese. In B. Martin, Jr. (Ed.), *Sounds of the storyteller.* New York: Holt, Rinehart & Winston.

Schwartz, R., & Raphael, T. (1985). Concept of definition: A key to improving students' vocabulary. *The Reading Teacher, 30,* 198–205.

Sentell, C., & Blachowicz, C. L. Z. (1989). Comprehension court: A process approach to inference instruction. *The Reading Teacher, 42,* 347–348.

Shanahan, T. (1984). The reading-writing relation: An exploratory multivariate analysis. *Journal of Educational Psychology, 76,* 466–477.

Simmons, J. (1992). Portfolios for large scale assessment. In D. Graves & B. Sunstein (Eds.), *Portfolio portrait.* Portsmouth, NH: Heinemann.

Sloan, C., Trathen, W., & Dole, J. A. (1992). *Teaching vocabulary within the context of literature: An instructional study.* Paper presented at the 42nd annual meeting of the National Reading Conference, San Antonio, Texas, session #64.

Slobin, D. (1966). English abstract of Soviet studies of child language. In F. Smith & G. Miller (Eds.), *The genesis of language.* Cambridge, MA: MIT Press.

Smith, F. (1971). *Understanding reading.* New York: Holt, Rinehart & Winston.

Spache, G. D. (1972). *Diagnostic reading scales.* Monterey, CA: CTB/McGraw-Hill.

Spache, G. D. (1976). *Diagnosing and correcting reading disabilities.* Boston: Allyn & Bacon.

Spiro, R. (1980). Constructive processes in prose comprehension and recall. In R. Spiro, B. Bruce, & W. Brewer (Eds.), *Theoretical issues in reading comprehension.* Hillsdale, NJ: Erlbaum.

Stahl, S. (1983). Differential word knowledge and reading comprehension. *Journal of Reading Behavior, 15,* 33–50.

Stahl, S. A. (1992). Saying the "p" word: Nine guidelines for exemplary phonics instruction. *The Reading Teacher, 45,* 618–625.

Stahl, S., & Fairbanks, M. (1986). The effects of vocabulary instruction: A model-based meta-analysis. *Review of Educational Research, 56,* 72—110.

Stahl, S., & Vancil, S. (1986). Discussion is what makes semantic maps work in vocabulary instruction. *The Reading Teacher, 40,* 62–69.

Stanovich, K. E. (1980). Toward an interactive-compensatory model of individual differences in the development of reading fluency. *Reading Research Quarterly, 16,* 32–71.

Stanovich, K. E. (1986). Matthew effects in reading: Some consequences of individual differences in the acquisition of literacy. *Reading Research Quarterly, 21,* 360–407.

Stauffer, R. G. (1969). *Directing reading maturity as a cognitive process.* New York: Harper & Row.

Stauffer, R. G. (1970). *The language experience approach to the teaching of reading.* New York: Harper & Row.

Stein, N. L., & Glenn, C. G. (1979). An analysis of story comprehension in elementary school children. In R. O. Freedle (Ed.), *Advances in discourse processes, Vol. 2: New directions in discourse processing.* Norwood, NJ: Ablex.

Sternberg, R. (1987). Most vocabulary is learned from context. In M. G. McKeown & M. E. Curtis (Eds.), *The nature of vocabulary acquisition.* Hillsdale, NJ: Erlbaum.

Straw, S. B., & Schreiner, R. (1982). The effect of sentence manipulation on subsequent measures of reading and listening comprehension. *Reading Research Quarterly, 17,* 339–352.

Stotsky, S. (1984). Research on reading/writing relationships: A synthesis and suggested directions. In J. Jensen (Ed.), *Composing and comprehending* (ED 243 139, pp. 7–22). Urbana, IL: ERIC Clearinghouse on Reading and Communication Skills and the National Conference on Research in English.

Sulzby, E. (1985). Children's emergent reading of favorite storybooks: A developmental study. *Reading Research Quarterly, 20,* 458–481.

Sulzby, E., & Teale, W. H. (1987). *Emergent literacy: Writing and reading.* Norwood, NJ: Ablex.

Taylor, D. (1983). *Family literacy: The social context of learning to read and write.* Portsmouth, NH: Heinemann Educational Books.

Taylor, S. E. (1965). Eye movements in reading: Facts and fallacies. *American Educational Research Journal, 2,* 187–202.

Temple, C., Nathan, R., Burris, H., & Temple, F. (1988). *The beginnings of writing* (2nd ed.), Newton, MA: Allyn & Bacon.

Thorndike, E. L. (1917). Reading as reasoning: A study of mistakes in paragraph reading. *Journal of Educational Psychology, 8,* 323–332.

Thorndike, R. L. (1973). *Reading comprehension education in fifteen countries.* New York: Wiley.

Thorndike, R. L. (1973–1974). Reading as reasoning. *Reading Research Quarterly, 9,* 135–147.

Thorndike, R. L., & Hagen, E. P. (1977). *Measurement and evaluation in psychology and education* (4th ed.). New York: John Wiley.

Thurstone, L. L. (1946). Note on a reanalysis of Davis's reading tests. *Psychometrika, 11,* 185–188.

Tierney, R., & Pearson, P. D. (1983). Toward a composing model of reading. *Language Arts, 60,* 568–580.

Treiman, R. (1985). Onsets and rimes as units of spoken syllables: Evidence from children. *Journal of Experimental Child Psychology, 39,* 161–181.

Tuinman, J. J. (1974). Determining the passage-dependency of comprehension questions in five major tests. *Reading Research Quarterly, 9,* 207–223.

Tuinman, J. J., & Brady, M. E. (1974). How does vocabulary account for variance on reading comprehension tests? A preliminary instructional analysis. In P. L. Nacke (Ed.), *Interaction:*

Research and practice in college-adult reading (Twenty-third yearbook of the National Reading Conference). Clemson, SC: National Reading Conference.

Tunmer, W. E., Herriman, M. L., & Nesdale, A. R. (1988). Metalinguistic abilities and beginning reading. *Reading Research Quarterly, 23,* 134–158.

Uhl, W. L. (1916). The use of the results of reading tests as a basis for planning remedial work. *Elementary School Journal, 17,* 266–275.

Vacca, R. T. (1981). *Content area reading.* Boston: Little, Brown.

Valencia, S. (1990). A portfolio approach to classroom assessment: The whys, whats, and hows. *The Reading Teacher, 43,* 338–340.

Valencia, S. W., & Pearson, P. D. (1986). Reading assessment: Time for a change. *The Reading Teacher, 40,* 726–732.

Vaughan, J. L., Castle, G., Gilbert, K., & Love, M. (1982). Varied approaches to preteaching vocabulary. In J. A. Niles & L. A. Harris (Eds.), *New inquiries in reading research and instruction.* (Thirty-first yearbook of the National Reading Conference). Rochester, NY: National Reading Conference.

Venezky, R. (1970). *The structure of English orthography.* The Hague: Mouton.

Vygotsky, L. S. (1978). *Mind and society.* Cambridge, MA: Harvard University Press.

Walker, B. J. (1988). *Diagnostic teaching of reading.* Columbus, OH: Merrill.

Weaver, C. A., & Kintsch, W. (1991). Expository text. In R. Barr, M. Kamil, P. Mosenthal, & P. D. Pearson (Eds.), *Handbook of reading research* (Vol. 2, pp. 230–245). White Plains, NY: Longman.

Weaver, P. A. (1979). Improving reading comprehension: Effects of sentence organization instruction. *Reading Research Quarterly, 15,* 129–146.

Weber, R. (1968). The study of oral reading errors: A review of the literature. *Reading Research Quarterly, 4,* 96–119.

Whaley, J., & Kibby, M. W. (1981). The relative importance of reliance on intraword characteristics and interword constraints for beginning reading achievement. *Journal of Educational Research, 74,* 315–320.

White, E. B. (1952). *Charlotte's web.* New York: Harper & Brothers.

Wittrock, M. C., Marks, C. B., & Doctorow, M. J. (1975). Reading as a generative process. *Journal of Educational Psychology, 67,* 484–489.

Wixson, K. K., Peters, C. W., Weber, E. M., & Roeber, E. D. (1987). New directions in statewide reading assessment. *The Reading Teacher, 40,* 749–754.

Wolman, R. N., & Barker, E. N. (1965). A developmental study of word definitions. *Journal of Genetic Psychology, 107,* 159–166.

Woods, M. L., & Moe, A. (1989). *Analytical Reading Inventory.* Columbus, OH: Charles E. Merrill.

Yopp, H. K. (1992). Developing phonemic awareness in young children. *The Reading Teacher, 45*(9), 696–703.

Zirbes, L. (1918). Diagnostic measurement as a basis for procedure. *Elementary School Journal, 18,* 507–523.

Index